In the Heart of the Sierras

From Painting by C. D. Robinson.   Photo-Typo By Britton & Rey, S. F.

" In the Heart of the Sierras."

Edition number four was the only one to have this reproduction
of a Robinson painting, opposite the title page.

In the Heart
of the
Sierras
Yo Semite Valley
and the
Big Tree Groves

James M. Hutchings
Edited by Peter Browning

GREAT WEST BOOKS　　LAFAYETTE, CALIFORNIA

Cover design by Larry Van Dyke
Front cover photograph: El Capitan ånd Half Dome from
    the Old Big Oak Flat Road, by Peter Browning
Back cover engraving: Grizzly Bear, designed by Charles C. Nahl,
    and engraved by Durbin Van Vleck, circa 1858

Printed in the United States of America

Great West Books
PO Box 1028
Lafayette, CA 94549

Library of Congress Cataloging-in-Publication Data

Hutchings, J. M. (James Mason), 1820–1902.
    In the heart of the Sierras : Yo Semite Valley and the big tree
groves / by James M. Hutchings ; edited with an introduction by
Peter Browning. — New ed.
        p.   cm.
    Originally published: Yo Semite Valley : Published at the
Old Cabin ; Oakland, Calif. : Pacific Press Pub. House, 1886.
    Includes bibliographical references.
    Summary: Describes the history and scenic wonders of
California's Yosemite Valley.
    ISBN 0–944220–10–X (alk. paper).
    ISBN 0–944220–04–5 (pbk. : alk. paper).
    1. Yosemite Valley (Calif.)—History. 2. Indians of North
America—California—Yosemite Valley—Wars. 3. Sierra Nevada
Mountains (Calif. and Nev.)—History. 4. Yosemite Valley (Calif.)—
Description and travel. 5. Indians of North America—California—
Yosemite Valley—Social life and customs. 6. Hutchings, J. M.
(James Mason), 1820–1902. [1. Yosemite Valley (Calif.)—History.
2. Sierra Nevada Mountains (Calif. and Nev.)—History.
3. Yosemite Valley (Calif.)—Description and travel. 4. Indians of
North America—California—Yosemite Valley.]
    I. Browning, Peter, 1928–.
    II. Title.
F868.Y6H92 1990
979.4'4—dc20   90–35773
                                                                    CIP
                                                                    AC

CONTENTS OF NEW EDITION

EDITOR'S PREFACE

My interest in republishing James M. Hutchings' *In the Heart of the Sierras* arose from doing research on another book, *Yosemite Place Names*, which I published in 1988. When I came to realize how much there was of general interest in Hutchings' book—quite aside from my quest for information on the origin of place names—I read it through from cover to cover. Once I had paid thorough attention to the depth of the historical detail, the delightful character of Hutchings' use of nineteenth-century American and English language, and the range and quality of the engravings and photographs in the book, I was certain that this classic of California history should be resurrected. When I learned that the book had never been reprinted, I modestly— and secretly—appointed myself the one to do it.

Since I did not want to do a facsimile reprint, I had perforce to type the entire text of the book into my computer. You can imagine how long it took to type in approximately 147,000 words by the two-finger method. Yet although this was a time-consuming task, it was actually enjoyable: I could see the line of characters inching its way across the screen, and felt encouraged and enthused by my visible progress. Once the words were secured, I embarked on the quest for modern-day prints of the old photographs, a task that consumed much more time than the typing and provided a much greater measure of gratification.

It was in the hunt for photographs that I required—and received—the assistance of other people. First among these are people whom I shall not name . . . because there are too many of them: all those at the Bancroft Library in Berkeley. Without fail, everyone at the Bancroft helped me in whatever way possible, always with good will, always with my interests in mind, and always seeming to ignore the fact that I was requesting materials by the armload and perhaps—due to my own ineptitude—not progressing as fast as I ought to.

I wish to thank Peter E. Palmquist for his generous advice, for quickly produced prints of several photos in his collection, and for exposing me to his vast knowledge of early California photographers.

The staff at the California State Library in Sacramento brought out hundreds of reference prints for my perusal, dealt with my every request, and—as though by a miracle—turned up several items that I did not think existed.

Jim Snyder and Linda Eade at the Yosemite Research Library and Dave Forgang at the Yosemite Museum gave me their time, energies, and knowledge, and enabled me to acquire half a dozen choice photographs.

My friend Shirley Sargent was the best source of information on James Mason Hutchings, and has essentially let me borrow the numerous details of his life from her books *Yosemite & Its Innkeepers; Seeking the Elephant, 1849;* and *Pioneers in Petticoats.*

Another friend, Malcolm E. Barker (Londonborn Publications), author and publisher of *Book Design & Production for the small publisher,* was a sounding board, a sympathetic ear, and invariably the one who could provide reasonable answers for my often unreasonable questions.

I also wish to thank Keith Schreiber at the Center for Creative Photography in Tucson who churned through the George Fiske collection on my behalf, and provided me with an excellent print of an obscure photograph.

EDITOR'S INTRODUCTION

About the Author

James Mason Hutchings was born February 10, 1820 in Towcester, Northamptonshire, England. He came to America in 1848, arriving in New York on June 22. In late August he took ship to New Orleans, where he was apparently employed as a newspaper correspondent until May of 1849. He was restless, and eager for travel and adventure, and the discovery of gold in California moved him to cross the continent to seek out his home and fortune—as so many others were doing. He went by steamboat up the Mississippi and Missouri rivers to St. Joseph, Missouri, and from there took the overland route to California. His diary of that journey was published in 1980 as *Seeking the Elephant, 1849. James Mason Hutchings' Journal of his Overland Trek to California*, edited by Shirley Sargent.

Hutchings had better than average success at gold mining, and in his first few months in California managed to acquire several thousand dollars—which he lost in a bank failure in March 1850. He continued mining, and built up his capital again. Some aspects of life in the mines repelled him, especially the habit of many miners of profaning the Sabbath by gambling and drinking. In what Hutchings later described as "an accidental circumstance [that] led to an entire change in occupation," he wrote a strongly-worded parody of the Fourth Commandment. It found such a sympathetic audience that he expanded it into a tract called "The Miner's Ten Commandments," which was printed in the *Placerville Herald* on July 2, 1853. This in turn was enthusiastically received. The demand was so great that

Hutchings reprinted it a number of times in letter-sheet form, with illustrations, and in little over a year sold 97,000 of them.

That was the end of his mining days. Literary endeavor became his new occupation, with the aim of publishing a monthly illustrated magazine dedicated to travel and to describing the scenic glories of California. This goal fit well with his penchant for exploration and adventure. For the next two years Hutchings traveled throughout northern and central California, from the cities to the Big Trees to the quicksilver mine at New Almaden, to the Geysers and the mining country and the Farallon Islands, gathering material for his magazine. His most momentous trip of all was in late July of 1855, when he led the first tourist party to visit Yosemite Valley—just four years after the valley had first been entered by anyone other than Indians, during the Mariposa Indian War. He wrote an account of the trip for the *Mariposa Gazette,* and when he began publication of *Hutchings' California Magazine* in July 1856 the feature article was about Yosemite Valley. From that time until his death in 1902, Hutchings was the foremost publicizer and promoter of Yosemite. He was also an early hotelkeeper in Yosemite, and for many years was its most prominent citizen.

Hutchings remained single until February 2, 1860, when—eight days before his fortieth birthday—he married Elvira Sproat, the seventeen-year-old daughter of his San Francisco landlady. They had three children; their daughter Florence was the first white child born in Yosemite Valley. The marriage ended in divorce about 1875. About 1879 Hutchings was remarried to a San Francisco woman who had recently been widowed. She died in 1881, and sometime later in that decade Hutchings married a third time. Late in his life he took up hotelkeeping again, this time at the Calaveras Grove of Big Trees. He visited Yosemite often, and it was while entering the valley with his wife for a camping trip on October 31, 1902 that he was thrown from the buggy when his horse reared, and was killed almost instantly.

About the book

Everything that Hutchings published was well illustrated. Obviously he was acquainted with many of the prominent (and some of the obscure) photographers, artists, engravers, and illustrators in northern California over a period of several decades. A significant number of the engravings that appeared in his magazine during its five years of existence—July 1856 through June 1861—were used again in later publications. Although Hutchings refers in his preface to *In the Heart of the Sierras* to the "many finely executed wood engravings that were expressly prepared for this book," he is being more than a little disingenuous. Eighty-three of the engravings in the book appeared originally in his magazine between 1856 and 1861. Many of those engravings were also used in Hutchings' book *Scenes of Wonder and Curiosity in California*, which was published in eight editions from 1860 to 1876.

Hutchings put everything he knew about Yosemite into *In the Heart of the Sierras*. The book is a wonderful mélange of autobiography, history, geography, geology, botany, anthropology, and travel guide. He reworked the basic material from his earlier writings, added a great deal to it, and was also enabled— by the new techniques of the day—to include actual photographs in a book rather than simply printing engravings based on the photographs. These early photographic reproductions, called "Photo-Typo" in the original book, are "collotypes"—a method for printing a photo by a 'continuous tone' process that shows a range of gray shades between white and black. The book also had a few 'halftone' reproductions of photographs, which is the method that has been used almost exclusively for the past century to print photographs in books, magazines, and newspapers. Hutchings had the eye of a photographer, of an artist. It was through his instigation that the first drawings and the first photographs of Yosemite Valley were created. When he led that first small group of adventurous tourists into the valley in July of 1855, one of the members was the artist Thomas Ayres, whose task it was to make drawings for Hutchings' magazine-to-be. Ayres' "General View of Yosemite Valley" is reproduced on page 88. (The drawing is dated June 20, 1855. On page 80, Hutchings gives June 20 as the approximate date when he began to organize this tourist party. But his diary for 1855, which is now in the Library of Congress, has the party in Yosemite Valley in late July, and returning to Mariposa on August 1. I am indebted to Hank Johnston, the writer and publisher, for the information about the diary.)

In 1859 Hutchings invited the photographer Charles L. Weed to join a small party on an excursion to Yosemite Valley. Weed took the first photographs ever made in Yosemite, several of which are reproduced in this book.

There were at least four distinct printings—or editions—of *In the Heart of the Sierras.* There are three dated 1886, and one in 1888. All the editions have the same wording on every page, and also the same engravings, on the same pages. The sole exception, in a way, is that on page 123 the engraving was round in editions one, two, and three, and staggered down the page in an oblique fashion in edition four. But the text on those pages is the same. Every edition had the same typographic errors—fifty-eight of them, by my count—all of which means, of course, that only one set of printing plates was made.

It is the photographic content of the various editions that differentiates them. The four editions have most of their photographs in common, but these didn't always appear opposite the same pages in the text. Not only did the photos move around, or come and go, but their quality also changed. It seems plain that if Hutchings, or his printer, was dissatisfied with the results obtained with photo-typos of particular photographs, then for the next printing they would try working with a different photo—often a variation of the first one. In the captions to many photographs I state where the photo appeared in which editions. What I refer to as edition one is the only edition to have a photo-typo in it that was made by a Philadelphia firm. Thereafter all the photo-typos were prepared by Britton & Rey of San Francisco. The designation of editions two and three was dictated by which photos were new, which were replaced, and which had most in common with either edition one or edition four—the latter being the one published in 1888. There was also a 'Tourists Edition,' which had no photos. On the other hand it had seven engravings (including one of Mt. Shasta) that were not in the other editions. It also had a different title page, on which were small engravings of four of Yosemite's waterfalls; a street map of San Francisco tipped in between pages 170 and 171; and at the back of the book a map of summer and winter resorts near the Central Pacific and Southern Pacific railroads in California. There was also a full-page advertisement for the better editions, which had to do not with my numbering system of one through four but rather with the kind of binding.

Fine English Cloth, Embossed in Jet and Gold	$3.25
Same as above, but with Gilt Edges	$3.75
Full Sheep, Library Style, Marbled Edges	$4.25
Half Morocco, Gilt Edges	$5.00
Full Morocco, Gilt Edges	$6.00

This book is not a facsimile reprint. It has been completely reset, in a typeface—Century Expanded—that is almost identical to the one used in the original book, which was Century Roman. The pagination is the same as the original, so that all the engravings appear on the same pages and in relation to the same text. The typographical errors I found have been corrected. I have added an index, which the original editions did not have. Because of the cost, and because I do not believe that anything will be lost by the omission, I have not included the single color illustration to appear in the original editions. This was a full-page picture of a bright red snow plant, which faced page 466 in all editions except the Tourists Edition. In the back of the book is a full-size copy of the Wheeler Survey's "Topographical Map of the Yosemite Valley and Vicinity," published in 1883. Although the map is called a "Preliminary Edition," it's the only edition that was ever published. In all the original editions except the Tourists Edition a copy of this map was tipped in near the front of the book. These were printed on flimsy paper, and were reduced in size by about ten per cent. The one in this book is printed on acid-free paper—as is the book itself—and will last several lifetimes.

There is one significant omission by Hutchings that is worth mentioning. In a book of some 147,000 words, in which he mentions the names of dozens of people connected with Yosemite between 1851 and 1886, one quite famous name does not appear: John Muir. It is more than a little odd, since Hutchings actually refers to Muir on one occasion but fails to give his name. The "good practical sawyer" he hired (page 129) is Muir. There is speculation that Hutchings resented Muir who, beginning in 1871, became prominent and much sought after through his many newspaper and magazine articles on Yosemite and the High Sierra. Or that Hutchings resented Muir because the latter was attracted to Hutchings' young wife—or that she was attracted to him. No proof has been adduced to prove either suspicion.

The sole thing that I regret about this book is the use of the word *Sierras* in the title. It is, quite simply, an incorrect plural. *Sierra* means 'mountain range,' and that's what Hutchings meant—in the heart of that particular mountain range. In the book he is inconsistent, seeming to use "Sierras," "Sierra," and "High Sierra" interchangeably.

I hope and trust that those who read or scan this book, or perhaps only look at the illustrations, will get at least a tenth of the pleasure that I derived from hunting out the old photographs, typing in the old text, and publishing a new book. If you do, you will be well rewarded.

PETER BROWNING

Photo by Houseworth

Edition one of *In the Heart of the Sierras* had this portrait of
Hutchings facing the dedication page. All subsequent editions
had the engraving shown on the following page.

Ever faithfully yours,
J. M. Hutchings.

IN THE

OF THE

THE

YO SEMITE VALLEY,

BOTH HISTORICAL AND DESCRIPTIVE:

AND SCENES BY THE WAY.

BIG TREE GROVES.

THE HIGH SIERRA, WITH ITS MAGNIFICENT SCENERY, ANCIENT AND
MODERN GLACIERS, AND OTHER OBJECTS OF INTEREST;

WITH

TABLES OF DISTANCES AND ALTITUDES, MAPS, ETC.

PROFUSELY ILLUSTRATED.

———

By J. M. HUTCHINGS,

OF YO SEMITE.

———

PUBLISHED AT THE OLD CABIN, YO SEMITE VALLEY,
AND AT
PACIFIC PRESS PUBLISHING HOUSE, OAKLAND, CAL.
1886.

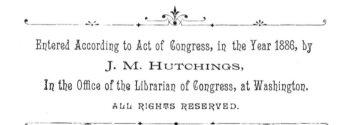
PACIFIC PRESS PUBLISHING HOUSE,

PRINTERS, ELECTROTYPERS,
AND BINDERS,

OAKLAND AND SAN FRANCISCO, CAL.

DEDICATION.

To the many pleasant friends I have met, and
others whom I hope to meet at Yo Semite,
in the Heart of the Sierras, this volume is most gratefully and
feelingly dedicated, by
THE AUTHOR.

FISKE.

#301.

Photo by Geo. Fiske

YO SEMITE VALLEY, CAL.
General View from Artist Point, and Wawona Road.
Fiske #301. Facing the title page in edition one.

PREFACE.

——:o:——

THE inquiries made by appreciative and intelligent visitors to the Yo Semite Valley, have suggestively prompted the themes that should be descanted upon in this volume. The information desired I have endeavored to embody and present. In this labor of love my long residence, and many attendant circumstances, have been supplemented by valuable historic and scientific details, obtained from various sources. For early records of the Valley I am mainly indebted to Dr. L. H. Bunnell, who was not only one of its first visitors, and discoverers, but its earliest and principal historian;* and through the kindness of Hon. W. J. Howard, of Mariposa, and Major James Burney, of Modesto, California, and others, I have been able to supply the missing links needed for the completion of the historical chain of events, so much desired, and so unavailingly sought after, by Dr. Bunnell, concerning some of the Valley's earlier history.†

The designs for the embossed covers, in black and gold, are by Mr. Thomas Hill, the eminent and well-known California artist; who has also generously furnished other sketches for this work. To Mr. George Fiske, the resident photographic artist of Yo Semite, Mr. S. C. Walker, Taber, and other photographers, I desire to acknowledge my obligation for many of the representative subjects here presented. And to those who by their financial aid have made the publication of this work possible, I gratefully tender my sincere thanks.

Nor would I forget the faithful Indian "Tom," who, no matter how biting cold the weather, or deep the snow in winter, not only brought us our letters and papers, but supplied us with much interesting data of his race in connection with the Valley and its primitive inhabitants, and I thank him.

* See "Discovery of the Yo Semite," an invaluable and deeply interesting narrative of personal observation and adventure.

† Ibid, page 30.

PREFACE.

By the courteous permission of the Chief of Engineers of the U. S. A., Washington, D. C., I am enabled to publish their official map of the Valley and its surroundings.

To the Pacific Press Publishing House, Oakland, California, I desire to acknowledge my many obligations for the uniform and untiring urbanity and kindly services of every officer and employé. The workmanship of its multifarious departments will speak for itself in this volume.

It will readily be seen that in addition to the many finely executed wood engravings that were expressly prepared for this book, I have pressed into service the new and beautiful process of photo-lithography for its more complete embellishment.

For the convenience of those who may be desirous of making hurried consultations of portions of this work, sub-headings will be found running through its various chapters.

Having done the very best that I could, I now leave the success of my endeavor in the hands of my friends and the public.

J. M. H.

TABLE OF CONTENTS.

————:0:————

Pom-pom-pa-sa!

ILLUSTRATIONS.

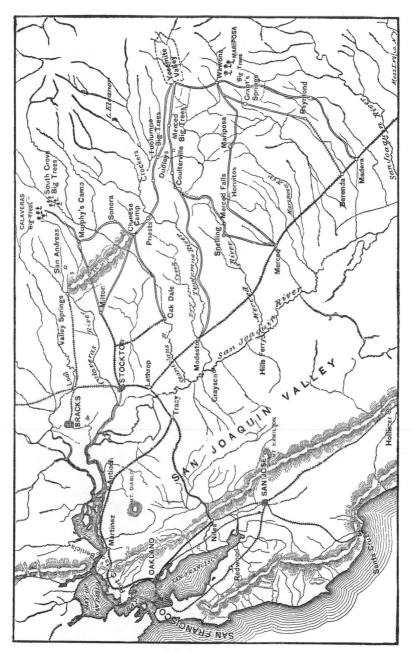

MAP OF ROUTES TO THE YO SEMITE VALLEY

Photo. by Geo. Fiske.

Photo-Typo by Britton & Rey, S. F.

Yo Semite Valley, Cal.
General View from Artist Point, and Wawona Road.

A later version of the photograph facing page 1. Note that it is taken from a lower vantage point, that there is a young woman in the buggy, and that there is now a lean-to attached to the cabin. In an effort to make the nearby trees stand out better, a retoucher has outlined them in white. This version faced the title page in edition three, and faced page 13 in editions two and four.

THE

THE

YO SEMITE VALLEY.

CHAPTER I.

AS OTHERS SEE IT.

Like thoughts whose very sweetness yieldeth proof
That they were born for immortality.
—WORDSWORTH'S *Sonnet.*

To him who in the love of nature holds
Communion with her visible forms, she speaks
A various language.
—BRYANT'S *Thanatopsis.*

The roaring cataract, the snow topt hill,
Inspiring awe, till breath itself stands still.
—BLOOMFIELD'S *Farmer's Boy.*

Voiced impressions of Horace Greeley, Rev. Thomas Starr King, Prof. J. D. Whitney, Samuel B. Bowles, John S. Hittell, Prof. O. S. Fowler, Hon. Robt. Marsham, Prof. Wm. H. Brewer, James Vick, Rev. W. P. Abbott, Benjamin F. Taylor, James A. Garfield (President of the U. S.), Mrs. C. A. Chamberlain, Hon. Thomas Scott, Hon. Therese Yelverton, Helen Hunt Jackson, His Grace the Duke of Sutherland, Albert D. Richardson, Sidney Andrews, Mrs. Jean Bruce Washburn, Charles L. Brace, Mary E. Blake, and others. It is with reluctance and sincere regret that the recorded sentiments of many other distinguished visitors to Yo Semite are necessarily omitted from this representative galaxy.

Of the grandest sights I have enjoyed—Rome from the dome of St. Peter's, the Alps from the valley of Lake Como, Mount

Blanc and her glaciers from Chamouni, Niagara, and the Yo Semi-te,—I judge the last named the most unique and stupendous. It is a partially wooded gorge, 100 to 300 rods wide, and 3,000 to 4,000 feet deep, between almost perpendicular walls of gray granite, and here and there a dark yellow pine, rooted in a crevice of either wall, and clinging with desperate tenacity to its dizzy elevation. The isolation of the Yo Semite, the absolute wilderness of its sylvan solitudes, many miles from human settlement or cultivation, its cascade 2,000 feet high, though the stream which makes this leap has worn a channel in the hard bed-rock to a depth of 1,000 feet, renders it the grandest marvel that ever met my gaze.—HORACE GREELEY, *N. Y. Independent of March, 1860.*

Nowhere among the Alps, in no pass of the Andes, and in no cañon of the mighty Oregon Range, is there such stupendous rock scenery as the traveler here lifts his eyes to.—REV. THOMAS STARR KING, *San Francisco.*

The peculiar features of the Yosemite are: First, the near approach to verticality of its walls; next, their great height, not only absolutely, but as compared to the width of the valley itself; and finally, the very small amount of *debris* or *talus*, at the bottom of these gigantic cliffs. These are the great characteristics of the valley throughout its whole length; but besides these, there are many other striking peculiarities and features, both of sublimity and beauty, which can hardly be surpassed, if equaled, by those of any other mountain scenery in the world.—PROF. J. D. WHITNEY, *State Geologist of California.*

The overpowering sense of the sublime, of awful desolation, of transcendent marvelousness and unexpectedness, that swept over us, as we reined our horses sharply out of green forests, and stood upon a high jutting rock that over-looked this rolling, upheaving sea of granite mountains, holding, far down in its rough lap, the vale of meadow and grove and river—such a tide of feeling, such stoppage of ordinary emotions, comes at rare intervals in any life. It was the confrontal of God face to face, as in great danger, or sudden death. It was Niagara magnified. All that was mortal shrank back; all that was immortal swept to the front, and bowed down in awe.—Samuel D. Bowles, *Springfield Republican.*

Yo Semite is the crowding of a multitude of romantic, peculiar, and grand scenes within a very small space.—John S. Hittell's *Guide Book.*

The longer we look the greater the scenes appear.—Prof. O. S. Fowler, *Boston, Mass.*

I wish to keep the view in my mind forever.—J. A. Brillinger, *Ewingsville, Pa.*

I was never so near Heaven in my life.—H. Windel, *San Francisco.*

I have spent seventeen days in Yo Semite, and I never left a place with so much regret in my life. I have several times visited all the noted places of Europe, and many that are out of the regular tourist's round; I have crossed the Andes in three different places, and been conducted to the sights deemed most remarkable: I have been among the charming scenery of the Sandwich Islands, the Himalayas of India, and the mountain districts of Australia, but never have I seen so much of sublime grandeur, relieved by so much beauty, as that I have witnessed in Yo Semite.—Hon. Robt. Marsham, *Maidstone, Kent, England.*

As a member of the State Geological Survey I have visited the Yosemite Valley four times—June, 1863, August, 1864, September, 1864, and April, 1875—and the valley seems grander on this fourth visit than it did on the first.—Prof. Wm. H. Brewer, Yale College, *New Haven, Conn.*

The road to Yo Semite, like the way of life, is narrow and difficult, but the end, like the end of a well-spent life, is glorious beyond the highest anticipation.—James Vick, *Rochester, N. Y.*

Here speaks the voice of God, and here his power is seen. Let man be dumb.—Rev. W. P. Abbott, *New York City.*

Yo Semite awaited us without warning, met us without coming. Spectral white in the glancing of the sun, the first thought was that the granite ledges of all the mountains had come to resurrection, and were standing pale and dumb before the Lord. I turned to it again, and began to see the towers, the domes, the spires, the battlements, the arches, and the white clouds of solid granite, surging up into the air and come to everlasting anchor till "the mountains shall be moved." You hasten on; you hear the winds intoning in the choral galleries a mile above your head; you hear the crash of waters as of cataracts in the sky; you trample upon broad shadows that have fallen thousands of feet down, like the cast-off garments of descending Night.—BENJ. F. TAYLOR'S *Between the Gates.*

This is the crowning glory of all views on this continent. —CHAS. CASPAR, *Meridian, Conn.*

If my business interests lay upon this coast, I would build a railroad to this truly marvelous valley, within one year from this date.—HON. THOMAS SCOTT, *Pennsylvania Central R. R.*

I have spent the four happiest months of my life in this glorious valley.—HON. THERESE YELVERTON *(Lady Avonmore).*

An indescribable delight took possession of me; the silence seemed more than silence; it seemed to quiver without sound, just as the warm air shimmered without stir, all along the outlines of the rocky walls. On my left hand rose the granite watch-tower Loya (Sentinel Rock) on my right the colossal buttress Tu-tock-ah-nu-la (El Capitan). The Cathedral Spires, the Three Brothers, all were in full sight. Wherever I stood, the mountain walls seemed to shut close around me in a circle. I said to myself, again and again: "Only between 3,000 and 4,000 feet high!" But the figures had lost their meaning. All sense of estimated distance was swallowed up, obliterated, by the feeling of what seemed to be immeasurable height.—H. H.'s *Bits of Travel.*

One might stay here for months and see new beauties every day.—MRS. A. W. GILLETTE, *Grass Lake, Mich.*

No one can study this valley and its surroundings without being broader-minded thereafter.—JAMES A. GARFIELD, *President of the United States.*

I linger'd till a shaft of fire
Shot o'er the mountains—spire by spire,
Burned in the swift and broadening flame
That onward swelled, till it became
A wide and mellow amber flood,
That poured o'er mountain, stream, and wood,
And lit the blue, deep dome above
With Deity's warm smile of love;
How fair that place—how radiant all
The scene beneath that mountain wall!

Then suddenly awoke to me
The pine wood's varied melody;—
The murmurous music of the river,
The aspen's low, light, dreamy quiver,
The jay-bird's quick, discordant cry,
The robin's tender minstrelsy
I heard—and full, and deep, and strong—
(Would I could ever keep that song!)
The pean of the water-fall
Came to me 'neath that mountain wall.

And flowers were there—the old dear flowers—
The first I loved in childhood's hours;
There glowed the wildling rose, that grew
Beside my home when life was new;—
O golden heart—O lips so red,
Naught from thy precious smile had fled
Through the long years;—thy odorous breath
Yet told of love that knows no death!
O life, thy stern, thy gentle call
Came to me, 'neath that mountain wall!

—MRS. C. A. CHAMBERLAIN, *Sacramento.*

Real estate is very high hereabouts!—DERRICK DODD, *S. F. Evening Post.*

This spoils one for any other scenery upon earth.—HIS GRACE, THE DUKE OF SUTHERLAND, *England.*

Nature has here lifted her curtain to reveal the vast and the infinite. It elicited no adjectives, no exclamations. With a bewildering sense of divine power and human littleness, I could only gaze in silence till the view strained my brain and pained my eyes, compelling me to turn away and rest from its oppressive magnitude.—ALBERT D. RICHARDSON'S *Beyond the Mississippi.*

Speech may be silver, but in this marvelous vale, where grandeur and majesty have met, "Silence is golden."—E. EDMONSTON, *Santa Barbara, Cal.*

Suddenly, as I rode along, I heard a shout. I knew the valley had revealed itself to those who were at the front of the line. I turned my head away. I couldn't look until I had tied my horse. Then I walked down to the ledge and crawled out upon the overhanging rocks. I believe some men walk out there—it's a dull sort of soul who can do that. In all my life, let it lead me where it may, I think I shall see nothing else so grand, so awful, so sublime, so beautiful—beautiful with a beauty not of this earth—as that vision of the Valley. How long I sat there I shall never know. I brought the picture away with me; I have only to shut my eyes, and I see it as I saw it in that hour of hours. I think I shall see nothing else so sublime and beautiful, till, happily, I stand within the gates of the Heavenly City.—SIDNEY ANDREWS' *Letter to the Boston Advertiser.*

I may as well try to measure a rainbow with a two-foot rule as to take this in.—WM. DARRACK, *New York City.*

> My soul bowed down in wondering, humble awe,
> When first thy peaks and water-falls I saw;
> And every hour but shows how vain 'twould be
> For my frail mind to hope to picture thee.
> Thy spell shall live when those who view thee now,
> Have passed with ages 'neath thy mighty brow,
> And like thy mists, in gorgeous gleamings curled,
> Our names have melted from this changing world.
> —MRS. JEAN BRUCE WASHBURN, *San Francisco.*

From the hotel there are excursions enough to occupy one for weeks among the beautiful scenes of the valley. One of the most enjoyable features of these excursions is simply riding up and down it, getting the new aspects which open freshly every half mile, and are different every hour of the day. The wonderful thing about the cañon, and which will hereafter draw many an invalid here from distant lands, is its divine atmosphere. To me, just recovering from a tedious fever, it seemed the very elixir of life—cool, clear, stimulating, and filled with light and glory from the sun of the south, which here never seems in summer to have a cloud. The nights are cool, but midday would be too warm were it not for the delicious sea-breeze which every day at eleven blows in from the Golden Gate, 150 miles away. The gorge is fortunately east and west, just opposite San Francisco, and about midway between the two flanks of the Sierras—here some seventy miles in width. Were it a north and south valley, even at its altitude (4,000 feet above sea level), it would be almost intolerable. Now, nothing can surpass its mild, invigorating climate, and harmonious atmosphere. The charm of the wonderful valley is its cheerfulness and joy. Even the awe-inspiring grandeur and majesty of its features does not overwhelm the sense of its exquisite beauty, its wonderful delicacy, and color, and life, and joy.

As I recall those rides in the fresh morning, or the dreamy noon, that scene of unequaled grandeur and beauty is forever stamped on my memory, to remain when all other scenes of earth have passed from remembrance—the pearly gray and purple precipices, awful in mass, far above one, with deep shadows on their rugged surfaces, dark lines of gigantic archways or fantastic images drawn clearly upon them, the bright white water dashing over the distant gray tops seen against the dark blue of the unfathomable sky, the heavy shadows over the valley from the mighty peaks, the winding stream and peaceful green sward with gay wild flowers below, the snowy summits of the Sierras far away, the atmosphere of glory illuminating all, and the eternal voice of many waters wherever you walk or rest! This is the Yo Semite in memory.—CHARLES L. BRACE'S *The New West.*

Dropped at our very feet, and clothed in such fair proportions of majesty and beauty as made it more a spiritual joy than an earthly loveliness. The valley rested, silent and set apart, as if human eyes for the first time beheld it, wrapped in a veil of soft, purple mist, that made it seem, in spite of its nearness, like a vision that would fade while we gazed. In front, El Capitan, erect and fearless, as became the warden of the magic world beyond, lifting its bare white front 3,300 feet in one superb perpendicular line from base to summit; opposite, the soft-falling, swaying foam of the falls bounding nearly 1,000 feet through the air before it struck the broken rocks below; beyond, the rounding curves of the Three Graces, the sweeping line of the South Dome, and far away the veiled summit of Cloud's Rest, piled with soft, gray shadows. A broken line of shining water came like a silver thread, showing here and there in the depths of the lovely valley, and broadened into a small mirrored lake almost at our feet below. It was beyond conception and utterance. The sense of solitude, of peace, and of an inspiration which sprang from both was so profound as to be oppressive. Even the most frivolous spirits among us were struck with sudden calm, as if they stood at the portals of some divine mystery, and it was with a feeling almost of relief that we turned away at last, and went down the slope of the dizzy mountain to enter in at the gates below.—MARY E. BLAKE'S *On the Wing.*

The only spot that I have ever found that came up to the brag.—RALPH WALDO EMERSON.

After such strikingly graphic, word-clothed impressions and confessions as those above presented, a more detailed descriptive picture of this marvelous locality, and its matchless surroundings, would seem to be suggestive of an attempt to compass the impossible. Even a residence within its sublime environments of nearly a quarter of a century, in winter as well as in summer, while making me lovingly familiar with its many æsthetic charms, and amazing natural phenomena, only convinces that approximate justice in delineation is simply unattainable. One may tell of its vertical or tree-studded walls, and their relative heights; of the hoary-headed and dome-crowned summits around it; of its lofty and picturesque waterfalls, feathered, it may be, with vapory rockets; of its deep and bowlder-strewn tributary cañons; of its defiant and cloud-draped crags and peaks; of its beautiful and tree-margined river; of its flower-carpeted and shrub-framed meadows; or press into valuable service the figures and comparisons of experienced scientists, and determine the diameter, and angle, and altitude of every cliff, or rock, and forest tree; but these are only facts. And one may explain the interesting incidents of its discovery; the geological theories of its formation; its many explicit lessons in botanical science; the habits, customs, life and legends of its Indians; and present the many characteristic phases of tourist experiences; but these, with hundreds of other kindred themes, are, after all, nothing but hard and unfeeling facts; whereas Yo Semite, to the poet, is the grandest of lyrics; to the artist, Nature's ever-captivating picture gallery; to the preacher, the most suggestively eloquent of sermons; and to the worshiper, the sublimest of temples—where God is always within. Who, then, can enter into the holy of holies of all of these? He who might attempt it should not be unmindful of the divine command to Moses: "Draw not nigh hither: put off thy shoes from off thy feet, for the place whereon thou standest is holy ground."

Then who may fully apprehend the law by which the many-voiced choral symphonies of the wind-swept trees, or leaping water-falls, or bounding cataracts, or "babbling brooks," may be set to music? Or conceive how the blessed sunlight, as it plays hide and seek among the shadows, or maps surrounding forms upon our path, or gilds the mossy trunks of stately trees, can be painted? And supposing it more than possible that the height, and depth, and breadth of the many time-cut furrows upon and in the grand old face of one of these mountain walls were accurately determined, could the exact shade of purple. or gray, or golden, or roseate haze, that is ever sleeping among its wrinkles, or burnishing up its ridges, be faithfully portrayed? No, Mr. Gradgrind, you are, at best, compelled to "stick to facts," and leave individual apprehension, good taste, and imagination to supply the rest. To present such facts concerning Yo Semite, and other sublime fastnesses of the High Sierra, as it is hoped will be welcome to the reader, will be the devoted purpose of each subsequent chapter of this book.

CHAPTER II.

CAUSES LEADING TO ITS DISCOVERY.

> I am not covetous for gold;
> Nor care I who doth feed upon my cost;
> It yearns me not if men my garments wear;
> Such outward things dwell not in my desires;
> But if it be a sin to covet honor
> I am the most offending soul alive.
> —SHAKESPEAR'S *Henry V., Act IV.*

> Tender-handed stroke a nettle,
>   And it stings you for your pains;
> Grasp it like a man of mettle,
>   And it soft as silk remains.
> —AARON HILL, *written upon a window in Scotland.*

After the discovery of gold at Sutter's saw-mill, Coloma, California, January 19, 1848, by James W. Marshall—who died, poor, August 10th, 1885, at the age of 73 years—and the news of that auspicious event had winged its electrifying flight to the farthest corner of the civilized world, men, filled with ambitious hopes and yearnings, began to flock towards the new El Dorado from every clime and country. The beautiful and land-locked Bay of San Francisco was soon plowed by the prows of vessels of every class and tonnage, and its recently uneventful calm broken by the health-giving breezes of a new and vigorous commercial activity.

> "Awake but one, and lo! what myriads rise!
> Each stamps its image as the other flies!"

The streets of the sleeping pueblo of San Francisco, filled by the in-flowing tide of humanity thus attracted, awoke it at once to a business energy that eventually grew into a habit, and laid the foundation of its present commercial prosperity.

(22)

Feverish with enlarged expectations, and eager to realize the day-dreams of their susceptible imaginations, any and every kind of conveyance, by water or by land, was pressed into immediate service, for speeding them to the gold mines. Discomfort, exposure, pleasure postponed, disappointment, suffering, danger, and possible sickness or prospective death, held them in no restraint; like the proverbial youth who had heard in his native village that the streets of a certain city were paved with gold, would give himself no rest, either day or night, until it could be reached, and "a hat full of it" obtained.

Beguiled by this fascination, that became almost an infatuation, side-hills and flats, ravines and gulches, cañons and rivers, threading far among the spurs of the Sierras, became familiar to the footsteps of the dauntless prospector. Unbroken solitudes, untrodden fastnesses, far from civilized habitation or human succor, created in him no sense of fear, or thought of peril. The occasional sight of Indians, whether singly or in groups, evoked no surprise, invited no uneasiness, and elicited no suspicion. A casual, perhaps an inquisitive glance, might occasionally be thrown over the shoulder of the one to the other in indifferent recognition as they passed; but that was in no way to be interpreted as unfriendly. In time, presents of food and cast-off garments apparently became

CONNECTING LINKS OF KINDNESS

Between civilized and savage, and seemingly bound their common interests closer together. The absence even of grunted gratitude for favors received, excited no comment, and quickened no resentment. Civilities and gratuities imperceptibly indicated the opening of a broader pathway to mutual confidences and concessions between whites and Indians, that left no doubt of ultimate harmonious concert of action. Meanwhile,

"The greatest of the angels of men—Success"—

Had crowned the gold miner's efforts in unearthing the precious metal. This attracted a rapidly increasing multitude of devotees

to its captivating standard; and men poured in from every
quarter, to enlist under its enchanting banner, and in full chorus
to sing around their camp-fires:—

> " 'Tis time the pick-axe and the spade,
>   Against the rocks were ringing,
> And with ourselves the golden stream
>   A song of labor singing;
> The mountain sod our couch at night;
>   The stars keep watch above us;
> We think of home, and fall asleep—
>   To dream of those who love us."

The good fortune and wants of the miner developed the necessity for the packer and trader, with their assistants; and, as a
sequence, kept constantly swelling the army of occupation in the
very haunts and homes of the Indian; and without invitation
divided with him his hunting and fishing grounds. Tents pitched
and cabins erected, became sufficient foundation for the impression that the new-comers were intending permanently to stay.
There seems to have been no expressed or implied objections to
this. The Indian men, moreover, had been pressed into willing
service as miners and laborers, and the women to laundry work—
for which, in many instances, they were liberally paid. All of these
very naturally gave color to the assurance that a mutually advantageous community of interests had spring up that was as
gratifying as it was profitable. But these eventually proved to be

THE LULL BEFORE THE STORM

The rapid increase of horses, mules, and cattle—as well as
men—presented visible evidences of accumulating prosperity
and wealth among the whites, that were unshared by the Indian.
This soon bore the poisonous fruit of jealousy. Germs of unrest
and discontent quickly ripened into resentment; and, with stealthy growth, hatred for the whites and cupidity for their possessions began, irrepressibly, to extend to every mountain tribe
throughout the State, and prepare the way for openly hostile
demonstrations. It is however but

AN ACT OF SIMPLE JUSTICE

To the Indian, here to record—without in any measure attempting to apologize for, or condone, his misdeeds—that the spirit of reciprocal fairness was not an invariable characteristic of the whites, in their dealings and conduct with the inferior race. Every old Californian can bear blushing testimony to the truthfulness of this too self-evident admission. This will be more than manifest from the official report of Maj. Gen. Thomas J. Green, to Gov. Peter H. Burnett, dated May 25, 1850,* as follows: "Heretofore a few persons have monopolized much of their labor, by giving them a calico shirt per week, and the most indifferent of food." Brig. Gen. Thomas B. Eastland, in his report to his excellency Governor Burnett, dated June 15, 1850,† thus continues: "It is a well-known fact that among our white population there are men who boast of the number of the Indians they have killed, and that not one shall escape." If, therefore,

> "In men we various Ruling Passions find,
> And Ruling Passion conquers Reason still."

No spirit of prophetic divination need be evoked, to foretell the ultimate results of such aggressive wrong-doing. Before pouring unmixed anathemas, therefore, upon the Indian's head, will not an intuitive sense of right first prompt us to

> "Find out the cause of this effect;
> Or, rather, say, the cause of this defect;
> For this effect defective comes by cause."

TELEGRAPHING BY FIRE AND SMOKE.

In the days of their numerical prosperity, moreover, it should be remembered that the Indians thoroughly understood and practiced a primitive method of telegraphing by fire and smoke, by which the fitful flashes of the one, and the gusty clouds of the other,‡ according to the number or the intensity of the signals

---

* See page 769 of Journals of the Legislature of California, for 1851.

† Page 770, *Ibid.*

‡ This was done by covering a large fire with a wet hide, and lifting it at intervals.

Photo. by Geo. Fiske.   Photo-Typo by Britton & Rey, S. F.

EL CAPITAN, HALF DOME, AND VALLEY.
From Big Oak Flat Road.
Facing page 26 in editions two, three, and four.

Glimpse of El Capitan—3300ft.

From Big Oak Flat Road

Fiske #412. Edition one, facing page 32.

given, would readily communicate the kind of trouble they were in, and the nature of the assistance they required. All prominent peaks, and favorable points of bluffs on the margin of valleys, were signal stations; and there was always a signal watcher on duty, both by day and by night. To this was supplemented a very

EFFICIENT SYSTEM OF RUNNERS,

Composed of their best-trained, swiftest-footed, and strongest-lunged young men, who would run at the height of their speed from one village to the other. These advantages naturally and effectively supplied speedy tribal communication, and enabled them not only to discuss with each other the social or political significance of such an unparalleled influx of strangers amongst them, but to report every overt act or aggressive movement of the whites, from San Diego to Siskiyou.

ISOLATED INSTANCES OF INDIAN VIOLENCE

Had been early reported from central portions of the State, but as these had been visited by swift retaliation, the impetuously turbulent were, for the time being at least, checked in their marauding and murderous career. Meanwhile the forces of their enmity were silently cumulating, like a storm over an almost cloudless sky, in the more southerly sections of California; eventually to culminate and break among the gold mines of Mariposa County—then very large, and embracing the counties now known as Mariposa, Merced, Fresno, Tulare, Mono, and Inyo.

THE FIRST OPENLY HOSTILE DEMONSTRATION

Was led by the Yo Semites, in May, 1850, when an attack was made upon the trading-post of Mr. James D. Savage, located on the Merced River, about twenty-five miles below the Yo Semite Valley, under the pretense of claiming all the country in that vicinity; but in reality in the expectation and hope of plunder. By the personal pluck and energy of Savage, assisted by his Indian miners, the attack was successfully repulsed.

The isolation of that station, and the known murderous

tendencies of the Yo Semites, induced Savage to remove his store to Mariposa Creek, near Agua Fria, some six miles westerly of the village, now the prosperous town and county seat, of Mariposa. His unexampled success in this new location tempted him to establish a branch post on the Fresno River, which also gave abundant promise of similar results. "In the midst of renewed prosperity"—says Dr. L. H. Bunnell, in his interesting narrative of "The Discovery of the Yosemite," from which I shall frequently quote in introductory chapters, and to which I heartily refer the reader—"he learned that

ANOTHER CLOUD WAS GATHERING.

"To strengthen his influence over the principal tribes, Savage had, according to the custom of many mountain men at that time, taken wives from among the Indians, supposing that his personal safety would be somewhat improved by so doing. This is the old story of the prosperous Indian trader. One of his squaws assured him that a combination was maturing among the mountain Indians to kill or drive all the white men from the country, and plunder them of their property." These unmistakable evidences of threatened hostilities suggested the adoption of precautionary measures, and preparation for warlike surprises, without exciting suspicion or alarm. In the hope of averting impending danger,

SAVAGE QUIETLY PLANNED A COUP D'ETAT.

Having to visit San Francisco early in the ensuing September (1850) for the purpose of securing a safe place of deposit for his rapidly accumulating quantities of gold-dust, extracted from the mines by himself and his Indian assistants, and received through his stores,* and also to purchase goods, he concluded to

---

* The amount, as given by reliable authority, was about six hundred pounds, Troy. As an illustrative example of one of Savage's habits, and an additional proof of the old adage, "Easily earned—carelessly spent." after his safe arrival in San Francisco with his treasure, he sought the gaming-table, where he became a heavy loser; as though reckless of consequences, he jumped upon the card table, and, standing upon a particular card, wagered his own weight in gold-dust on that card—and lost!

take with him two of his Indian wives, and an influential Indian
chief named Jose Jaurez,* that by showing them the overwhelming numbers and resources of the whites, he could impress upon
them, and through them all the unfriendly disposed, the utter
hopelessness of any bellicose movements on their part. This
skillfully-planned stratagem, although substantially carried out
by Savage, was

NOT FRUITFUL IN RESULTS,

Inasmuch as Jose, having been liberally supplied with money by
his generous patron, invested it as liberally in "fire water;" and,
under its influence, became either stupidly unconscious or insult-
ingly abusive. Remonstrance only stimulated a more emphatic
indulgence in that graceless vice. When forbearance had ceased
to be a virtue, and the wanton gratification of insulting epithets
had reached their climax, in an unguarded moment, Savage felled
him with a blow. This invited, and probably deserved punishment,
was a source of constant subsequent regret; but, as the journey
homeward developed no signs of any vengeful remembrances, it
was hoped that the unpleasant incident had been either overlooked or excused. Therefore, nothing doubting in that, or in the
happy results of Jose's visit to the larger cities, as numerous
Indians had collected around his Fresno store, seemingly to welcome them on their arrival, and to compare notes, and learn or
tell the news, Savage concluded this to be

A FITTING OPPORTUNITY FOR A TALK

About the sights they had seen, with a view of conciliating their
prejudices—if any still existed—and convincing their judgments
of the relative advantages that would naturally arise from a
good understanding between the whites and the Indians. After
presenting the case in a strikingly terse and forcible manner,
Savage called upon Jose to bear testimony to the truthfulness of
his explanations, and the undoubted strength of his arguments.
To his surprise, however, "The cunning chief, with much

*A name probably given him at one of the old missions.

dignity"—I again quote from Doctor Bunnell—"deliberatively stepped forward, with more assurance than he had shown since the belligerent occurrence at San Francisco, and spoke with more energy than Savage had anticipated, as follows:—

JOSE JUAREZ, THE INDIAN CHIEF, MAKES A SPEECH.

" 'Our brother has told his Indian relatives much that is true; we have seen many people; the white men are very numerous; but the white men we saw are of many tribes; they are not like the tribe that digs gold in the mountains. They will not help the gold-diggers, if the Indians make war against them. If the gold-diggers go to the white tribes in the big village they give their gold for strong water, and games; when they have no more gold the white tribes drive the gold-diggers back to the mountains with clubs. They strike them down' (referring to the police) 'as your white relative struck me when I was with him.' (His vindictive glance assured Savage that the blow was not forgotten or forgiven.) ' The white tribes will not go to war with the Indians in the mountains. They cannot bring their big ships and big guns to us; we have no cause to fear them. They will not injure us.' "

This was followed by a glowingly humorous and sarcastic picture of the pale faces, their tall hats, walking canes, eyeglasses, fancy clothes, and other supposed frivolous articles of the toilet; and the manners and customs of white people in large cities were so grotesquely mimicked that he frequently convulsed his Indian auditors with laughter, broken occasionally with guttural utterances of contempt.

No replying arguments of Savage, filled to overflowing as they were with kindness and common sense, could counteract the magical effects of such a speech. But, fearing that they might, Jose again stepped forward, and

BREATHING DEFIANCE, EXCITEDLY INTERRUPTED SAVAGE

By exclaiming,* "He is telling you words that are not true. His

* Dr. L. H. Bunnell.

tongue is forked and crooked. He is telling lies to his Indian relatives. This trader is not a friend to the Indians. He is not our
brother. He will help the white gold-diggers to drive the Indians
from their country. We can now drive them from among us; and if
the other white tribes should come to their help, we will go to the
mountains; if they follow us they cannot find us; none of them will
come back; we will kill them with arrows and with rocks.' " These
war-like utterances of Jose Juarez were warmly seconded by

JOSE REY, THE LEADING CHIEF OF THE CHOW-CHILLAS,

In the following speech, also reported by Dr. Bunnell: "My people
are now ready to begin a war against the white gold-diggers. If all
the tribes will be as one tribe, and join with us, we will drive all the
white men from our mountains. If all the tribes will go together,
the white men will run from us, and leave their property behind
them. The tribes who join in with my people will be the first to
secure the property of the gold-diggers."

"The dignified and eloquent style of Jose Rey," continues Dr.
Bunnell, "controlled the attention of the Indians. This appeal to
their cupidity interested them; a common desire for plunder
would be the strongest inducement to unite against the whites.
Savage was now fully aware that he had been defeated at the
impromptu council he had himself organized, and at once
withdrew to prepare for the hostilities he was sure would follow.
As soon as the Indians dispersed, he started with his squaws for
home, and again gave the settlers warning of what was
threatened, and would soon be attempted.

"These occurrences were narrated to me by Savage. The incidents of the council at the Fresno Station were given during the
familiar conversations of our intimate acquaintance. The Indian
speeches here quoted are, like all others of their kind, really but
poor imitations. The Indian is very figurative in his language. If a
literal translation were attempted, his speeches would seem so
disjointed and inverted in their methods of expression that their
signification could scarcely be understood; hence only the substance is here given."

UNHEEDED WARNINGS.

It would seem that, notwithstanding the warnings given, the miners and settlers were unwilling to concede that an Indian war was possible, even with such conclusive evidence

"To mark the signs of coming mischief,"

As they were deemed as absurd as they were improbable. Even Cassady, a rival trader to Savage, "especially scoffed at the idea of danger, and took no precautions to guard himself or his establishment"—and was afterwards among the first murdered.

In their minds there evidently lingered a doubt, and perhaps with it a mental questioning whether or not

"The chance of war
Is equal, and the slayer oft is slain,"

As active hostilities did not actually commence until the middle of December following. This will be apparent from an official letter by Col. Adam Johnston, sub. Indian Agent of the United States, under Gen. John Wilson, and addressed to His Excellency, Peter H. Burnett, then Governor of California; and as it is not only an interesting narrative, but lucidly explanatory, it is here transcribed.

COL. ADAM JOHNSTON'S LETTER.

San Jose, January 2, 1851.*

Sir: I have the honor to submit to you, as the Executive of the State of California, some facts connected with the recent depredations committed by the Indians, within the bounds of the State, upon the persons and property of her citizens. The immediate scenes of their hostile movements are at and in the vicinity of the Mariposa and Fresno. The Indians in that portion of your State have, for some time past, exhibited disaffection and a restless feeling toward the whites. Thefts were continually being perpetrated by them, but no act of hostility had been committed by them on the person of any individual, which indicated general enmity on the part of the Indians, until the night of the 17 December last. I was then at the camp of Mr. James D. Savage, on the Mariposa, where I had gone for the purpose of reconciling any difficulty that might exist between the

* See Journals of the Legislature of California for 1851, page 563.

Indians and the whites in that vicinity. From various conversations which I had held with different chiefs, I concluded there was no immediate danger to be apprehended. On the evening of the 17th of December, we were, however, surprised by the sudden disappearance of the Indians. They left in a body, but no one knew why, or where they had gone. From the fact that Mr. Savage's domestic Indians had forsaken him and gone with those of the rancheria, or village, he immediately suspected that something of a serious nature was in contemplation, or had already been committed by them.

The manner of their leaving, in the night, and by stealth, induced Mr. Savage to believe that whatever act they had committed or intended to commit, might be connected with himself. Believing that he could over-haul his Indians before others could join them, and defeat any con-templated depredation on their part, he, with sixteen men, started in pursuit. He continued upon their traces for about thirty miles, when he came upon their encampment. The Indians had discovered his approach and fled to an adjacent mountain, leaving behind them two small boys asleep, and the remains of an aged female, who had died, no doubt from fatigue. Near to the encampment Mr. Savage ascended a mountain in pursuit of the Indians, from which he discovered them upon another mountain at some distance. From these two mountain tops, conversation was commenced and kept up for some time between Mr. Savage and the chief, who told him they had murdered the men on the Fresno, and robbed the camp. The chief had formerly been on the most friendly terms with Savage, but would not now permit him to approach him. Savage said to them that it would be better for them to return to their villages—that with very little labor daily they could procure sufficient gold to purchase them clothing and food. To this the chief replied it was a hard way to get a living, and that they could more easily supply their wants by stealing from the whites. He also said to Savage he must not deceive the whites by telling them lies, he must not tell them that the Indians were friendly, they were not, but on the contrary were their deadly enemies, and that they intended killing and plundering them so long as a white face was seen in the country. Finding all efforts to induce them to return, or to otherwise reach them, had failed, Mr. Savage and his company concluded to return. When about leaving, they discovered a body of Indians, num-bering about two hundred, on a distant mountain, who seemed to be approaching those with whom he had been talking.

Mr. Savage and company arrived at his camp in the night of Thurs-day, in safety. In the meantime as news had reached us of murders committed on the Fresno, we had determined to proceed to the Fresno, where the men had been murdered. Accordingly, on the day following,

Friday, the 20th, I left the Mariposa camp, with thirty-five men, for the camp on the Fresno, to see the situation of things there, and to bury the dead. I also dispatched couriers to Agua Fria, Mariposa, and several other mining sections, hoping to concentrate a sufficient force on the Fresno to pursue the Indians into the mountains. Several small companies of men left their respective places of residence to join us, but being unacquainted with the country, they were unable to meet us. We reached the camp on the Fresno a short time after daylight. It presented a horrid scene of savage cruelty. The Indians had destroyed everything they could not use, or carry with them. The store was stripped of blankets, clothing, flour, and everything of value; the safe was broken open and rifled of its contents; the cattle, horses, and mules had been run into the mountains; the murdered men had been stripped of their clothing, and lay before us filled with arrows; one of them had yet twenty perfect arrows sticking in him. A grave was prepared, and the unfortunate persons interred. Our force being small, we thought it not prudent to pursue the Indians further into the mountains, and determined to return. The Indians in that part of the country are quite numerous, and have been uniting other tribes with them for some time. On reaching our camp on the Mariposa, we learned that most of the Indians in the valley had left their villages and taken their women and children to the mountains. This is generally looked upon as a sure indication of their hostile intentions. It is feared that many of the miners in the more remote regions have already been cut off, and Agua Fria and Mariposa are hourly threatened.

Under this state of things, I come here at the earnest solicitations of the people of that region, to ask such aid from the State Government as will enable them to protect their persons and property.

I submit these facts for your consideration, and have the honor to remain.　　　　Yours very respectfully,

To His Excellency,　　　　　　　　ADAM JOHNSTON.
　　PETER H. BURNETT.

SAD EXPERIENCES AT SAVAGE'S FRESNO STORE.

Upon the morning above mentioned in Colonel Johnston's letter, according to the testimony of Mr. Brown, the only survivor of the massacre, straggling groups of Indians, unattended by women and children, contrary to usual custom when on a peaceful mission, commenced wending their way, saunteringly, from different directions, towards Savage's store upon the Fresno. They entered it in their ordinary listless manner, as though for purposes of trade; but, when within it, by some evidently preconcerted plan of attack, they sprang simultaneously forward, and with hatchets, axes, crow-bars, and bows and arrows, first murdered Mr. Greeley, who was in charge of the store; then, turning upon the three other white men there present, named Canada, Stiffner, and Brown, killed all except the latter, whose life was saved by an Indian named Polonio,* to whom Brown had shown favors, jumping in between him and the attacking party, at the risk of his own personal safety, thus affording Brown the chance of escape, of which he confesses to have made the best use, by running all the way to Quartzburg at the top of his speed. Thereafter horses, mules, and cattle belonging to the whites, began to disappear, cabins were broken open and despoiled in the absence of their owners; solitary prospectors were waylaid, robbed, and murdered; isolated settlers, and secluded miners delving in some far off and shadowy cañon, unsuspicious of active race antagonisms, were sought out, overpowered, and slaughtered in cold blood. The perpetrators of these satanic crimes, going undetected and unpunished, for a time reveled in a frenzy of diabolical excesses.

SAVAGE'S OTHER STORE PILLAGED AND DESTROYED.

Simultaneously with these outrages, Savage's other store and residence on the Mariposa, after the sudden disappearance of the resident Indians, as given in Colonel Johnston's letter, were attacked, during the absence of the proprietor, and everything stolen. Similar onslaughts having been made at various points on the Merced, San Joaquin, Fresno, and Chow-chilla Rivers, it became too painfully evident that a general Indian war was being forced upon the whites.

MAJOR BURNEY AND JAMES D. SAVAGE RAISE A COMPANY.

In this emergency Maj. James Burney, Sheriff of Mariposa County, and Mr. James D. Savage, the trader, with other prominent citizens, immediately commenced to raise a company of volunteers, and at once led it into active and efficient service.

* So christened by the whites probably from some peculiar characteristic of his.

As experiences of this courageous little band are graphically told by Major Burney, in a letter to His Excellency, John McDougal, Governor of the State, and emphatically certified to and indorsed by Hon. J. M. Bondurant, County Judge, and Richard H. Daly, County Attorney, no apology will be necessary for introducing it entire, from the Legislative Journals of California for 1851.

MAJOR BURNEY'S LETTER TO GOVERNOR MCDOUGAL.

AGUA FRIA, January 13, 1851.

SIR: Your Excellency has doubtlessly been informed by Mr. Johnston,* and others, of repeated and aggravated depredations of the Indians in this part of the State. Their more recent outrages you are probably not aware of. Since the departure of Mr. Johnston, the Indian Agent, they have killed a portion of the citizens on the head of the San Joaquin River, driven the balance off, taken away all the movable property, and destroyed all they could not take away. They have invariably murdered and robbed all the small parties they fell in with between here and the San Joaquin. News came here last night that seventy-two men were killed on Rattlesnake Creek; several men have been killed in Bear Valley. The Fine Gold Gulch has been deserted, and the men came in here yesterday. Nearly all the mules and horses in this part of the State have been stolen, both from the mines and the ranches. And I now in the name of the people of this part of the State, and for the good of our country, appeal to Your Excellency for assistance.

In order to show Your Excellency that the people have done all that they can do to suppress these things, to secure quiet and safety in the possession of our property and lives, I will make a brief statement of what has been done here:—

After the massacres on the Fresno, San Joaquin, etc., we endeavored to raise a volunteer company to drive the Indians back, if not to take them or force them into measures. The different squads from the various places rendezvoused not far from this place on Monday, 6th [December, 1850], and numbered but seventy-four men. A company was formed, and I was elected Captain; J. W. Riley, First Lieutenant; E. Skeane, Second Lieutenant. We had but eight days' provisions, and not enough animals to pack our provisions and blankets, as it should have been done. We, however, marched, and on the following day struck a large trail of horses that had been stolen by the Indians.† I sent forward James D. Savage,

* Col. Adam Johnston.

† In a subsequent letter of Major Burney, addressed to the Hon. W. J. Howard, occurs the following passage:—

with a small spy force, and I followed the trail with my company. About two o'clock in the morning, Savage came in and reported the village near, as he had heard the Indians singing. Here I halted, left a small guard with my animals, and went forward with the balance of my men. We reached the village just before day, and at dawn, but before there was light enough to see how to fire our rifles with accuracy, we were discovered by their sentinel. When I saw that he had seen us, I ordered a charge on the village (this had been reconnoitered by Savage and myself). The Indian sentinel and my company got to the village at the same time, he yelling to give the alarm. I ordered them to surrender; some of them ran off, some seemed disposed to surrender, but others fired on us; we fired, and charged into the village. Their ground had been selected on account of the advantages it possessed in their mode of warfare. They numbered about 400, and fought us three hours and a half. We killed from 40 to 50, but cannot tell exactly how many, as they took off all they could get to. Twenty-six were killed in and around the village, and a number of others in the chaparral. We burned the village and provisions, and took four horses. Our loss was six wounded, two mortally; one of the latter was Lieutenant Skeane, the other a Mr. Little, whose bravery and conduct through the battle cannot be spoken of too highly.

We made litters, on which we conveyed our wounded, and had to march four miles down the mountain, to a suitable place to camp, the Indians firing at us all the way, from the peaks on either side, but so far off as to do little damage. My men had been marching or fighting from the morning of the day before, without sleep, and with but little to eat. On the plain, at the foot of the mountain, we made a rude, but substantial fortification; and at a late hour those who were not on guard were permitted to sleep. Our sentinels were (as I anticipated they would be) firing at the Indians occasionally all night, but I had ordered them not to come in until they were driven in.

I left my wounded men there, with enough of my company to defend the little fort, and returned to this place for provisions and recruits. I send them to-day reinforcements and provisions, and in two days more I march by another route, with another reinforcement, and intend to attack another village before going to the fort. The Indians are watching the

"The first night out you came into my camp and reported that the Indians had stolen all your horses and mules—a very large number—that you had followed their trail into the hill country, but, deeming it imprudent to go there alone, had turned northward, hoping to strike my trail, having heard that I had gone out after Indians. I immediately, at sunset, sent ten men (yourself among the number) under Lieutenant Skeane—who was killed in the fight next day—to look out for the trail, and report, which was very promptly carried out."

movements at the fort, and I can come up in the rear of them unsuspectedly, and we can keep them back until I can hear from Your Excellency.

If Your Excellency thinks proper to authorize me or any other person to keep this company together, we can force them into measures in a short time. But if not authorized and commissioned to do so, and furnished with some arms and provisions, or the means to buy them, and pay for the services of the men, my company must be disbanded, as they are not able to lose so much time without any compensation.

Very respectfully, your obedient servant,

JAMES BURNEY.

THE FIRST CONFLICT ALMOST A DEFEAT.

This battle took place upon the upper waters of the Fresno; and notwithstanding the measurable success of this hastily planned and impetuous attack, there is no reason to fear that, owing to the absence of efficient discipline and drill, in so rapidly mustered a company of volunteers, but for the dauntless pluck and daring of this heroic band, it would have been a defeat. Nothing but reckless personal exposure, and hand-to-hand conflict, eventually brought a partial victory. After the conflict they were abundantly willing to retire to camp for rest, council, reorganization, and future discipline; and the experience gained proved to be of inestimable value in the future conduct of the war.

GOVERNOR McDOUGAL'S PROMPT RESPONSE

From apparently sympathetic anticipation of the sentiments and wants expressed in Major Burney's manly letter, His Excellency, Governor McDougal (having through Col. Adam Johnston's official communication, and other sources, already received information of the struggle progressing in Mariposa County), had issued an order—by a singular coincidence bearing exactly the same date, January 13, 1851,* as Major Burney's letter—authorizing the Sheriff of Mariposa County to call out one hundred able-bodied militia, with which to meet the pressing exigencies of the times, and teach the Indians that, while the whites could be considerate of their interests in times of peace,

* See Journals of the Legislature of California for 1851, page 600.

they were prepared at all hazards to assert and maintain their rights the moment that war was forced upon them.

To this prompt and considerate action was supplemented an appealing message from Governor McDougal to the State Legislature, then in session, calling upon it for means to meet such pressing emergencies; a communication addressed to the Indian Commissioners, appointed by the General Government for co-operation; and to General Persifer S. Smith, commanding Pacific Division of the United States Army, informing him of the Indian disturbances, of his official orders calling out two hundred able-bodied militia, and asking him what aid might be expected from his department, the number of effective troops to be relied on, whether there could be furnished arms and ammunition to volunteers, and if so the character and number of arms and ammunition, and concluding with the question, "Will you deem it advisable to co-operate in the present emergency?"*

Without awaiting a reply from Gen. P. F. Smith, such was the anxiety of the Governor lest any omission on his part should cause an unnecessary sacrifice of human life and property, he dispatched Col. J. Neely Johnson, an officer of his staff, to the United States Indian Commissioners, Messrs. Wozencraft, McKee, and Barbour, with offers of safe-conduct to the scene of the disturbances, accompanied with the assurance that "Colonel Johnson will afford you with every facility in his power to co-operate with you in all measures necessary to insure a return of those friendly feelings which are so desirable to us, and so essential to the happiness of both whites and Indians." Too much commendation of Governor McDougal's praiseworthy and intelligent assiduity cannot well be accorded him, not only for his unwearying watchfulness, but for providing the "sinews of war," as well as for his continuous efforts to establish an early and enduring peace.

The Governor's offer was cordially accepted by the United

---

* To this inquiry there seems to have been no response published—at least none can be found by the writer. It is however matter of record that the State assumed the responsibility for the disbursements of this war, but the expenses were afterwards allowed by the United States Government.

States Indian Commissioners, who, under the escort of Col. J. Neely Johnson and a small body of State troops, as related elsewhere, set out on their peaceful mission as soon as possible, after securing the services of some friendly mission Indians, as interpreters and messengers, and the providing of suitable presents and supplies. While they are repairing thither, let us return, at least in imagination, to the camp of the volunteers.

In the interim of Major Burney's absence at the settlements, for munitions and reënforcements, no time was lost by the little corps remaining at their post among the Indians, in drilling, reörganizing, and otherwise preparing for future contact with the foe. Growing tired, however, of the commonplace inactivities of camp life, and longing for the excitements attendant on an encounter with the enemy, but a few restful days were allowed to pass before they were again upon the march.

The Indian trail was soon struck, and upon the top of a rugged knoll, near the north fork of the San Joaquin River, surrounded by a dense undergrowth of shrubbery, among rocks and trees, they found the adversary in force, apparently numbering about five hundred. Defiant taunts of their late defeat, intermixed with sneering accusations of cowardice, were menacingly hurled at the whites; and the Indians even boasted of their robberies and murders, and challenged Savage, who was then in command, to come up and fight them. But as it was late in the day when the Indians were discovered, and feeling, with Shakespeare, that

"The better part of valor is discretion,"

Instead of commencing an immediate attack, a careful reconnoissance was made before nightfall, and the assault postponed.

Almost before morning light revealed the position of their antagonists, thirty-six men were detached for preliminary operations, under Captain Kuykendall, to be followed by the reserves, under Major Savage and Captain Boling—and fortunately the Indian camp was reached by Kuykendall's command without discovery. Dashing into their midst, and seizing lighted brands from their own camp-fires, the wigwams were set on fire, and, by their light, they attacked the now alarmed camp. So rapidly and so bravely were the charges made that the panic-stricken warriors fled precipitately from their stronghold. "Jose Rey was among the first shot down," says Dr. Bunnell. "The Indians made a rally to recover their leader; Lieutenant Chandler, observing them, shouted, 'Charge, boys! Charge!!' when the men rushed forward, and the savages turned and fled down the mountain, answering back the shout of Chandler by replying, 'Chargee! Chargee!' as they disappeared. The whole camp was routed, and sought safety among the rocks and brush, and by flight. This was an unexpected result. The whole transaction had been so quickly and recklessly done that the reserves under Boling and Savage had no opportunity of participating in the assault, and but imperfectly witnessed the scattering of the terrified warriors. Kuykendall, especially, displayed a coolness and valor entitling him to command—though outrun by Chandler in the assault. The fire from the burning village spread so rapidly down the mountain side towards our camp as to endanger its safety. While the whites were saving their camp supplies, the Indians, under cover of the smoke, escaped. No prisoners were taken; twenty-three were killed; the number wounded was never known. Of the settlers but one was really wounded, though several were scorched and bruised in the fight. None were killed. The scattering flight of the Indians made further pursuit uncertain. Supplies being too limited for an extended chase, as none had reached the little army from those who had returned, and time would be lost in waiting, it was decided to go back to the settlements before taking further active measures. The return was accomplished without interruption."

Their safe arrival home again was the spontaneous signal for a general jubilee, intensified by the cheering intelligence of the complete victory won over the savages; and augmented, on the following day, by the welcome tidings that the Governor's authority had arrived to organize and equip a volunteer force against the enemy.

CHAPTER III

HOW AND WHEN DISCOVERED

Ill news is winged with fate, and flies apace.

—Dryden

Over all things brooding slept
The quiet sense of something lost.

—Tennyson's *In Memoriam.*

Peace hath higher tests of manhood
Than battle ever knew.

—Whittier's *The Hero.*

Intelligence of the utter discomfiture of so large a force of their best warriors and ablest chiefs, by "a mere handful" of white men, flew with inexpressible rapidity to all the disaffected Indians; and, with the news, carried dismay and sadness to many hearts; not, however, to accelerate their conversion to honest traits, or peaceful paths. Memories of the rich harvests of booty and of pillage, so recently gathered through spoilation and carnage, still held them in irresistible bondage. Wrong-doing, therefore, to them was only a question of convenience and opportunity. It is true their recent and terrible disasters became forcibly suggestive of others still in reserve, should they defiantly persist in repeating their marauding and murderous exploits. The temporary withdrawal of the whites from further present pursuit, while it gave the Indians favorable opportunity for binding up their wounds, and for recuperating their wasted energies and lost courage, also supplied them with leisure to brood over their losses, and to weigh the contingent results, to themselves, of their flagitious courses. Leaving them, therefore, to their self-criminating reflections, it may not be inopportune, at this juncture, to recur to the protective measures in active preparation at the settlements.

While the volunteers were enjoying the sweet repose that

(41)

generally follows successful physical and mental labor, and in their case its attendant convivialities, a new excitement made its advent among them, and came almost like an inspiration or revelation; it was an order from His Excellency, Gov. John Mc-Dougal, bearing date January 13, 1851, to Maj. James Burney, Sheriff of Mariposa County, to enlist one hundred men, which, by a subsequent order of January 24, 1851, was increased to

A CALL FOR TWO HUNDRED ABLE-BODIED MILITIA,

"And to organize them at the earliest practicable moment into independent companies, not to exceed four; and, under officers of their own selection, to proceed at once to punish the offending tribes."* This inspiriting mandate was not only a recognition and indorsement of the past, but an encouraging augury for the future, to those who had so recently borne the brunt of victorious battle with the foe; and became a strong incentive for their immediate re-enlistment. And it is but an act of well-merited honor to those brave men here to make emphatic declaration, that much of the success attending the rapid mustering into service of the required quota, was largely attributable to the chivalric zeal and energy, of both officers and men, forming the pioneer company of Mariposa volunteers.

FORMATION OF THE MARIPOSA BATTALION.

The full complement of volunteers authorized, numbering two hundred and four, rank and file, reported to Maj. James Burney, at Savage's old store—then in partial ruins—near Agua Fria, February 10, 1851, equipped, mounted, and ready for service. Here the Mariposa Battalion was organized. It was formed into three companies: A, with seventy men; B, with seventy-two; and C, with fifty-five, exclusive of surgeons, quartermaster, etc.

When the time arrived for the election of officers Major Burney, to whom the honor of commanding the battalion naturally belonged, magnanimously declined to be a candidate,

---

* See Journals of the California Legislature for 1851, page 670.

partially owing to the pressing duties of his office as Sheriff of so large a county, but mainly for the purpose of insuring harmony, by avoiding all jealous and ambitious rivalries.

OFFICERS ELECTED TO COMMAND THE BATTALION.

In this emergency James D. Savage was elected Commander, not only on account of his soldierly qualities, but for his knowledge of the habits, customs, haunts, and language of the Indians, as well as of the country to be traversed. The following is the muster-roll of the battalion:* Major, James D. Savage; Adjutant, M. B. Lewis; Surgeon, Dr. A. Bronson, who afterwards resigned and was succeeded by Dr. Lewis Leach; Assistant Surgeons, Drs. Pfifer and Black; Sergeant-Major, Robt. E. Russell. Captains—Co. A, seventy men, John I. Kuykendall; Co. B, seventy-two men, John Bowling; Co. C, fifty-five men, William Dill; First Lieutenants, John I. Scott, Co. A; Reuben T. Chandler, Co. B; Hugh W. Ferrell, Co. C. Thus officered,

THE MARIPOSA BATTALION TOOK UP ITS LINE OF MARCH.

The troops supplied their own horses and equipments, and the State the provisions and baggage wagons. Owing to the uncertainty of payment at that early day, and other untoward circumstances, almost fabulous prices were charged for articles purchased in the mining districts.

A large grassy meadow, located on Mariposa Creek, some fifteen miles below the village of Mariposa, was made the first head-quarters of the battalion, where drilling, manœuvering, and other preparatory exercises necessary for efficient military service, were duly put into practice. Occasional scouting parties would sally out for short distances in search of the enemy, known to be amazingly near, from the numerous thefts committed in cattle and horses; but these seemed to have had no more decisive result than the cultivation of watchfulness, and exercise, and the retirement of the Indians farther into the mountains. Meanwhile,

* "Elliott's History of Fresno County," pages 177, 178.

THE DAWN OF A NEW ERA WAS BREAKING.

While all these warlike tactics were progressing, potential humanitarian influences were giving birth to a nobler policy than a mere conflict of races, and more in consonance with the enlightened spirit of the age. Communications, glistening with enlarged views and generous impulses on this question, began to flow in a steady stream to the Executive, and from persons of high official position, such as, for instance, that indicated in the following extract from the

LETTER OF GEN. THOMAS B. EASTLAND.*

The Indians have been more "sinned against than sinning" since the settling of California by the whites, is the opinion of many old inhabitants, as well as miners, who have lived in their midst, and watched the rise and progress of the many disturbances that have occurred; they are naturally inoffensive, and perhaps less warlike than any other tribes on the continent; indeed, they have not even the resources necessary for defense; the bow and arrow are their only arm; they are destitute of animals even for transportation purposes; they have no means of support within themselves, save the transitory fruits of the seasons, some few esculent plants and acorns, the latter being garnered up for their winter supplies, by which they must stay or starve; they are to a man, almost in a state of nature, without a single comfort in the way of clothing, and during the cold months huddle together in their *holes*, as their only protection against the inclemency of the weather; in fact, all their habits are peaceful, and in their whole character it is not discoverable that *naturally* they possess the first element of a warlike people; but the germ of a hostile spirit has been *created* in them, that, without some prompt and decisive action on the part of the General Government, will grow and spread among them a deadly hate towards the whites, which erelong may cause our frontier to be marked with lines of blood. If they are apt scholars they will not only be taught how to fight, but in time will muster many warriors, each with his firelock and butcher-knife, taken from the bodies of murdered white men.

I have the honor to be Your Excellency's obedient servant,

THOMAS B. EASTLAND
Brig. Gen. 1st. Division, Cal. Ma. comm'g.

Such well-timed and considerate sentiments carried with

* See Journals of the Legislature of California for 1851, page 770.

them the force of conclusive argument, and gave full strength to the moulding of a more generous future for the campaign. At this important juncture, such was Governor McDougal's anxiety lest every possible contingency should not be anticipated and provided for, that he invited earnest conferences with other State officers, and with all the most influential members of both Senate and Assembly, upon this all-absorbing question, regardless of any political differences whatsoever. Moreover, upon the eve of Colonel Johnson's departure, His Excellency issued the following

INSTRUCTIONS TO COL. J. NEELY JOHNSON

SAN JOSE,* January 25, 1851.

The force provided may or not be sufficient; the difficulties of communication with the scene of the disturbances are so great as to render it almost if not quite impracticable to be perfectly advised of the exact state of affairs. I am left, therefore, to act as the emergency seems to require, and without that degree of particular and minute information so important to the prompt and efficient suppression of Indian hostilities. Such being the case, and being desirous to do all in my power to afford our citizens protection in life and property, I have deemed it advisable to dispatch an officer of the staff to the scene of the disturbances, with the view to ascertain, collect, and report all facts respecting them, which are or may be required to direct intelligently the further operations of the State authorities. You have been selected for this purpose.

You will proceed at once, and by the most expeditious route, to the county of Mariposa, where you will communicate with the officer in command of the forces which have been recently ordered out. If possible, let the Indians be conciliated. Indian war is at all times to be deprecated, but especially so by us now, in the infancy of our career as a State, and before the General Government has provided us with the necessary means of protection and defense. We are in no condition to be harassed by expensive and protracted disturbances, which, when the best provision has been made for them, prove seriously detrimental to the best interests of the people among whom they exist. I cannot, therefore, too strongly impress upon you, and through you upon our citizens, to avoid studiously the commission of any act calculated to excite and exasperate unnecessarily the Indian tribes.

While the measures it may become necessary to adopt shall be firm,

* Then the seat of State Government.

let them be tempered with kindness and forbearance, manifesting at all times a disposition to restore relations of friendship, and perpetuate a mutual good understanding. The great object is to effect *a peace* with the least bloodshed, and at the least expense, and no means should be left untried to bring it about. In this connection I would suggest that, before leaving San Francisco, an interview be had by you with the United States Commissioners on this subject, who will, no doubt, cordially cooperate with you in whatever shall serve to effect an object so desirable. You will also assure them that every facility within your power will be extended to them, in the execution of their mission; and for this purpose, if they deem it necessary, you will order out such force as will securely protect their persons and property. If the Indians are still found to be obstinate and intractable after your endeavors, as well as the endeavors and means used by the Commissioners, to bring about an amicable adjustment of the existing difficulties, it will then become your duty to decide upon the line of offensive policy to be pursued. Where pacific measures fail, a vigorous prosecution of the war is our most efficient remedy. As before remarked, the force already ordered out may be sufficient for all purposes, but this is a matter which I have not the means of determining; it must be left to your discretion and better judgment after you shall have clearly ascertained, by personal observation, the actual exigency. Should an emergency exist now, or arise hereafter, requiring an additional number of troops, which will not admit of the delay necessary to communicate with me, you are authorized to call out such additional numbers as may be necessary. But it is to be hoped this will not be required; and unless absolutely demanded by circumstances, of which you must be the judge, the call will not of course be made. We have every reason to believe that as soon as at all practicable, the General Government will take steps to afford us adequate protection; at present, however, efficient aid need not be expected. There are but few United States troops in the State, and those few are stationed at points distant from each other, and remote from the scene of disturbances, requiring time to collect and fit them for actual service; time, too, which may be all-important in speedily terminating our difficulties with the Indians, and thus saving many valuable lives, as well as preserving much valuable property. . . . Further advice, if it is deemed necessary, will be sent to you by express.

I have the honor to be, &c.,

JOHN McDOUGAL.

The tendency of these well-timed and comprehensive instructions to Colonel Johnson gave assurance of a two-fold advantage: *first*, in giving him the power to augment the State forces com-

mensurately with the strength developed by the enemy; and
second, in securing to the Indian Commissioners the ability to
compel obedience, should their pacific labors become ineffectual.

Conferences between the Governor of the State and the Indian Commissioners sent out by the General Government became
both frequent and effectual, and superinduced the adoption of a
more just and more benignant policy toward the Indians. Finally,
an agreement was made between the Executive of California,
Governor McDougal, and the U. S. Indian Commissioners,
Messrs. Wozencraft, McKee, and Barbour, that the latter, in the
interests of humanity, should take full command of the State
troops, then in the field near Mariposa. Accordingly, instructions
were dispatched immediately to Major Savage, informing him of
this arrangement, and ordering him to suspend all active hostile
demonstrations against the enemy, until further directed.

Thus provided, therefore, against all possible contingencies,
the Commissioners lost no unnecessary time in making

SUITABLE PREPARATIONS FOR THE COMING CAMPAIGN.

Stores of many kinds, adapted to Indian tastes and wants, as
well as to their own, had to be selected and dispatched. And, for
conferring more readily with the mountain tribes, the services of
a few peaceful mission Indians were secured, as messengers and
interpreters, so that through these they could the more readily
find access to the hearts and prejudices of the hostile Indians.
Much anxious care and intelligent inquiry were needed in this, to
insure such material as was best adapted to the work; because
success or failure might largely depend upon their efficiency and
adaptability to the important task. All things being in readiness,
the U. S. Indian Commissioners, under the escort of Colonel
Johnson, and a small detachment of State troops, repaired as
rapidly as possible to the camp of the Mariposa Battalion.

After a cordial though informal welcome, Colonel Johnson
introduced himself, the Commissioners, and the subject in the
following explanatory

SOLDIERS AND GENTLEMEN: Your operations as a military organization will henceforth be under the direction of the United States Commissioners. Under their orders you are now assigned to the duty of subduing such Indian tribes as could not otherwise be induced to make treaties with them, and at once cease hostilities and depredations. Your officers will make all reports to the Commissioners. Your orders and instructions will hereafter be issued by them. Your soldierly and manly appearance is a sufficient guarantee that their orders will be conscientiously carried out. While I do not hesitate to denounce the Indians for the murders and robberies committed by them, we should not forget that there may perhaps be circumstances which, if taken into consideration, might to some extent excuse their hostility to the whites. They probably feel that they themselves are the aggrieved party, looking upon us as trespassers upon their territory, invaders of their country, and seeking to dispossess them of their homes. It may be that they class us with the Spanish invaders of Mexico and California, whose cruelties in civilizing and Christianizing them are still traditionally fresh in their memories. As I am soon to leave you I will now bid you "good-bye," with the hope that your actions will be in harmony with the wishes of the Commissioners, and that in the performance of your duties, you will in all cases observe mercy where severity is not justly demanded.

PEACE MESSENGERS SENT TO THE INDIAN VILLAGES.

The mission Indians, so called, who acted so important a part at this crisis in preliminary peace negotiations, were those who had been gathered into the fold of the Catholic Church, established by the Spanish missionaries between the years 1768 and 1780, under the able leadership of Junipero Serra—who also discovered and named the bay of San Francisco, in October, 1769. These Indians, under a rude kind of both religious and secular civilization, having shared its advantages, had taken no part whatsoever in the hostilities of the times. Many had formerly belonged to the mountain tribes, and could speak their language, yet had no sympathy with the hostiles. Among these there seems to have been one named Russio, who was pre-eminently qualified for the service of messenger and interpreter; and who, owing to

* Reported by Dr. L. H. Bunnell.

his discriminating apprehension of the good intentions and mo-
tives of the Commissioners, his superior intelligence, and convinc-
ingly persuasive manners, became an invaluable auxiliary in the
establishment of peace relations.

With a less intelligent Indian named Sandino, and other assistants, Russio set out for the nearest Indian villages, where,
by his graphic pictures of the invincible power of the whites, and
the utter folly of resisting and fighting them; the liberal supplies
of blankets, provisions, and ornaments for their women and children, to be most generously distributed among them; with assurances of kindly treatment and protection, he induced many to
visit the Commissioners, converse with them (through Russio),
and finally to accept the proffered conditions. It is true some
were very shy, and, being conscience-smitten for the culpable
part they had previously taken, were suspiciously doubtful of
results; but the lavish distribution of presents, and the uniform
good treatment received by those who had submitted, eventually charmed others into satisfied acquiescence.

At this time the California Indians numbered, according to
Major Savage's representation,* as follows: San Joaquin River,
and its tributaries, 6,500; Tuolumne, 2,100; Merced, 4,800; King's
River, 2,000; Kern, 1,700; Tulare, 1,000; Umas, 5,000; on the east
side of the Sierra Nevada—embracing Owen's Lake and River,
Walker, Carson, and Truckee—31,000; Klamath, Trinidad,
Sacramento, and branches, 30,000; Clear Lake, Trinidad Bay,
and Russian River, 6,000;making a total of 90,100. Of these the
San Joaquin, Tuolumne, Merced, King's, Kern, Tulare, and Umas
of Tulare Lake, numbering some 23,000, not only sympathized
with the hostile Indians, but, for the most part, took active
measures against the miners and settlers of Mariposa County.

Among the earliest arrivals was Kee-chee, whom Dr.
Bunnell calls Vow-ches-ter, but whose Christian name, given
him at the missions probably, was Baptista, according to Dr.

* "Elliott's History of Fresno County," page 181.

Wozencraft, one of the Indian Commissioners, and was pronounced Beauteesta, who was the recognized leader of all the Mariposa bands. Kee-chee had been generally friendly to the whites, but, through the influence of Jose Rey, he had united his fortunes with the unfriendly Indians. It is reasonably presumable, however, to suppose, that the havoc made among his people, at almost their first encounter, had not been without its impressive lesson; inasmuch as, when assured of forgiveness, safety, and beneficent treatment, he not only submitted willingly to the policy of the Commissioners but promised to bring in as many of his people as he possibly could. But, according to Dr. Bunnell, when questioned about the mountain Indians, he made answer: "The mountain tribes would not listen to any terms of peace involving the abandonment of their territory; that in the fight near the north fork of the San Joaquin, Jose Rey had been badly wounded and would probably die; that his tribe was very angry, and would not make peace."

FIRST INTIMATIONS GIVEN OF THE EXISTENCE OF YO SEMITE.

Russio said:* "The Indians in the deep rocky valley on the Merced River do not wish for peace, and will not come in to see the chiefs sent by the great father to make treaties. They think the white man cannot find their hiding-places, and that therefore they cannot be driven out!" The other Indians of the party confirmed Russio's statements. Vowchester [Kee-chee] was the principal spokesman, and he said: "In this deep valley spoken of by Russio, one Indian is more than ten white men. The hiding-places are many. They will throw rocks down on the white men, if any should come near them. The other tribes dare not make war upon them, for they are lawless like the grizzlies, and as strong. We are afraid to go to this valley, for there are many witches there!"

In the earnest and hopeful expectation of peacefully gathering in the disaffected tribes and permanently providing for their comfort and safety, the Indian Commissioners established

* Dr. Bunnell.

RESERVATION GROUNDS AND QUARTERS

On the Fresno River—a few miles easterly of where the present town of Madera is situated, and now known as the Adobe Ranch, owned by Mr. J. G. Stitt—to which all pacifically disposed Indians could resort, and find shelter and protection. This became the place of general rendezvous for both soldiers and Indians. Yet, notwithstanding these timely and humane preparations, and their acceptance by some, the many still hesitated, doubtingly, of the ultimate intentions of the whites, and kept themselves hidden in their silent retreats. The positive statements of Russio and Kee-chee placed it beyond peradventure that the Yo Semites had not abated their hostile feelings and determinations one iota; to which their failure in response to the many invitations sent, became additional proof.

Therefore, being weary with waiting, and annoyed constantly with depredations committed upon the cattle and horses of the miners and settlers, as well as those belonging to the command, the Commissioners resolved upon aggressive movements, and ordered

THE BATTALION TO FORM INTO LINE.

This was delightful music to the ears, and great joy to the hearts of the volunteers, who had been impatiently chafing at their prolonged inactivity, so that when the injunction was given to "mount," every saddle was filled, with alacrity.

The entire absence of roads in those days compelled them to march in Indian, or single, file, and over the most indifferent of trails. Notwithstanding this, and the evidence of a gathering storm, the order, "Forward, march," was cheerfully obeyed. Under the directions of Major Savage, the advance was made in silence; "For," said he, "we must all learn to be still as Indians, or we shall never find them." Braving with becoming unanimity the heavy rain, that was now coming down in torrents, their fearlessness was rewarded by the welcome discovery of "Indian signs." They were then on the south fork of the Merced River, about two miles below where Wawona Station (Clark's) now is. As night was advancing, and the rain was turning into snow, they went quietly

RIBBON FALLS—LUNG-OO-TOO-KOO-YAH.

(See page 398.)

Facing page 48 in edition one. Facing page 42 in all other editions.

Tᴜ-ᴛᴏᴄᴋ-ᴀʜ-ɴᴜ-ʟᴀʜ, ᴏʀ Eʟ Cᴀᴘɪᴛᴀɴ.

3,300 Feet above the Valley, Looking West.
Facing page 54 in edition one. Facing page 58 in all other editions.
Fiske #311.

into camp. At daylight the following morning, after leaving their animals and encampment in charge of a strong guard, two of the companies under Captains Boling and Dill, with one of Savage's Indians named "Bob" as guide, advanced without any hesitation, or effort at concealment, to the Indian village.

"On discovering us," Dr. Bunnell remarks, "the Indians hurriedly ran to and fro, as if uncertain what course to pursue. Seeing an unknown force approaching, they threw up their hands in token of submission, crying out at the same time in Spanish, '*Pace! pace!*' (peace! peace!). We were at once ordered to halt, while Major Savage went forward to arrange for the surrender. The Major was at once recognized, and cordially received by such of the band as he desired to confer with officially. We found the village to be that of Pon-wat-chee, a chief of the Noot-chü tribe, whose people had formerly worked for Savage under direction of Cow-chit-ty, his brother, and from whose tribe Savage had taken Ee-e-ke-no, one of his former wives. The chief professed still to entertain feelings of friendship for Savage, and expressed himself as now willing to obey his counsels.

"Savage at once told the chief the object of the expedition, and his requirements. His terms were promptly agreed to, and before we had time to examine the captives or their wigwams, they had commenced packing their supplies, and removing their property from their bark huts. This done, the torch was applied by the Indians themselves, in token of their sincerity in removing to the reservation on the Fresno."

After this bloodless victory, the captured chief, Pon-wat-chee, volunteered the information to Savage of a camp of the Po-ho-no-chees on the opposite side of the river, not far below his old village. Messengers were immediately dispatched there; and as the Po-ho-no-chees, through their runners, had already learned of the surprise, and peaceful abduction of the Noot-chiis, and of their kindly treatment by the whites, they timidly, yet unhesitatingly, gave themselves up.

Messengers and runners were now sent out in all directions

to discover the hiding-places of other Indian bands, with instructions to promise safety, protection, food, and clothing, if they surrendered, and extermination if they refused. This significant mandate had its desired effect; and although their movements were characterized by timidity and fear, all found in this immediate vicinity quietly surrendered.

These encouraging auguries gave measurable promise of like successes with the defiant Yo Semites, and other Indians, still hidden in their mountain fastnesses. Similar messages to the above had been conveyed to the Yo Semites; but, as yet, not a single Indian had consented to present himself, and accept the proffered conditions. To avoid compulsory measures and possible slaughter, it was deemed desirable to send a special courier to Ten-ie-ya, the chief of the Yo Semites, bearing a kindly, yet decided, ultimatum. To this the old chief concluded it best to respond at once, and in person, on the following day.

INTERVIEW BETWEEN TEN-IE-YA AND MAJOR SAVAGE.

From Dr. Bunnell's graphic picture of the conference, as an eye-witness, the chief of the Yo Semites had the courage to go alone, and to present himself in dignified silence to the guard, there to remain standing until motioned to enter Savage's tent. He was immediately recognized and respectfully greeted by Pon-wat-chee as the chief of the Yo Semites. Both officers and men received him kindly, and most cordially tendered him the hospitalities of their camp:—

"After which, with the aid of the Indians, the Major informed him of the wishes of the Commissioners. The old sachem was very suspicious of Savage, and feared he was taking this method of getting the Yo Semites into his power, for the purpose of revenging his personal wrongs. Savage told him that if he would go to the Commissioners and make a treaty of peace with them, as the other Indians were doing, there would be no more war. Ten-ie-ya cautiously inquired the object of taking all the Indians to the plains of the San Joaquin, and said: 'My people do not want anything from the Great Father you tell me about. The Great Spirit is our father, and he has always supplied us with all that we need. We do not want anything from white men. Our women are able to do our work. Go, then; let us remain in the mountains where we were born; where the ashes of our fathers have been given to the winds. I have said enough!'

"This was abruptly answered by Savage in Indian dialect and gestures. 'If you and your people have all you desire, why do you steal our horses and mules? Why do you rob the miners' camps? Why do you murder the white men, and plunder and burn their houses?'

"Ten-ie-ya sat silent for some time; it was evident he understood what Savage had said, for he replied: 'My young men have sometimes taken horses and mules from the whites. It was wrong for them to do so. It is not wrong to take the property of enemies who have wronged my people. My young men believed the white gold-diggers were our enemies; we now know that they are not, and we will be glad to live in peace with them. We will stay here and be friends. My people do not want to go to the plains. The tribes who go there are some of them very bad. They will make war upon my people. We cannot live on the plains with them. Here we can defend ourselves against them.'

"In reply to this, Savage very deliberately and firmly said: 'Your people must go to the Commissioners and make terms with them. If they do not, the young men will again steal our horses; your people will again kill and plunder the whites. It was your people who robbed my stores, burned my houses, and murdered my men. If they do not make a treaty, your whole tribe will be destroyed, not one of them will be left alive.' At this vigorous ending of the Major's speech, the old chief replied: 'It is useless to talk to you about who destroyed your property and killed your people. If the Chow-chillas do not boast of it, they are cowards, for they led us on. I am old, and you can kill me if you will, but what use to lie to you who know more than all the Indians, and can beat them in their big hunts of deer and bear. Therefore I will not lie to you, but promise that if allowed to return to my people I will bring them in.' He was allowed to go. The next day he came back, and said his people would soon come to our camp; that when he had told them they could come with safety, they were willing to go and make a treaty with the men sent by the Great Father who was so good and rich. Another day passed, but no Indians made their appearance from the 'deep valley,' spoken of so frequently by those at our camp. The old chief said the snow was so deep that they could not travel fast; that his village was so far down (gesticulating, by way of illustration, with his hands) that when the snow was deep on the mountains they would be a long time climbing out of it. As we were at the time having another storm, Ten-ie-ya's explanation was accepted, but he was closely watched."

As each returning day brought with it no tangible evidence of the arrival of the Yo Semites, it was resolved that they should be sought after in their boasted stronghold; and, notwithstanding the discouraging pictures so graphically painted, in both language and gesture, by Ten-ie-ya, of the difficulties and dangers to be encountered on the way, coupled with assurances of the early arrival of his people,

AN EXPEDITION TO THE MYSTIC VALLEY WAS RESOLVED UPON.

When volunteers were called for, according to the usual custom of the battalion, the entire command stepped to the front. Here a new dilemma became strikingly apparent. As the Indian captives, as well as baggage, had to be protected, a camp-guard was as essential as an advancing cohort. A call for this duty was then made, but as very few responded, the officers decided to provide for it by a good-natured piece of strategy—a foot race—the fleetest to be the favored ones for the expedition, and the slowest to form the camp-guard. This novel method of selection was greeted with hilarious applause, as it made provisions for both emergencies, without hurtful discrimination.

Amid many jocular allusions at the possible value of their fleet-footedness (on a retreat?) when they met the enemy, the troops on the following morning made an early start, with Major Savage in the advance, accompanied by Ten-ie-ya as guide. Deep snow, attended with the usual difficulties of making a trail through it, was soon encountered and overcome, by the rider in advance frequently falling out of line, and the next taking his place. By this old-fashioned method a passably good horse-trail was made over it, especially considering the rough and rocky country being traveled over.

YO SEMITES MET UPON THE TRAIL.

About midway between camp and the valley seventy-two of the Yo Semites were met, forcing their way flounderingly through the snow, loaded down with children and wares, yet, on their route to the place of general rendezvous, at the south fork of the Merced. This was at least partial proof that Ten-ie-ya was acting in good faith, by carrying out his promises. But, as his band was estimated to number over two hundred, the question very naturally arose, where could be the remainder? Ten-ie-ya, by way of apology for his limited following, contended that many of his people had intermarried with distant tribes, and gone away; that these were all that were willing to leave their mountain homes and move to the plains; that some few were sick and unable to come now, but would join them in the future, and other similar excuses. Such unsatisfactory statements, implying as they did at best, that only a portion of the Yo Semites was here represented, the troops determined upon advancing. As Ten-ie-ya was a reluctant, if not an unwilling guide, one of his young "braves" was selected in his place, and the old chief allowed to accompany his people to the camp.

THE YO SEMITE VALLEY FIRST SEEN BY WHITE MEN.

After separating from the Indians, and before advancing many miles, the great valley opened before them like a sublime revelation.*[1] But here Dr. Bunnell, an eye-witness and participant in the honor, must be allowed to express his own sensations, and to paint the graphic picture.†

It has been said that "it is not easy to describe in words the precise impressions which great objects make upon us." I cannot describe how completely I realized this truth. None but those who have visited this most wonderful valley, can even imagine the feelings with which I looked upon the view that was there presented. The grandeur of the scene was but softened by the haze that hung over the valley—light as gossamer— and by the clouds which partially dimmed the higher cliffs and mountains. This obscurity of vision but increased the awe with which I beheld it, and, as I looked, a peculiarly exalted sensation seemed to fill my whole being, and I found my eyes in tears with emotion.

To obtain a more distinct and *quiet* view, I had left the trail and my

* This was on May 5 or 6, 1851, although Dr. Bunnell incorrectly gives the latter part of March as the date. See dispatches of Maj. James D. Savage, in "Elliott's History of Fresno County," pages 179, 180.

† "Discovery of the Yosemite," page 54.

1. The correct date is March 27, 1851. (*The Mariposa Indian War, 1850–1851. Diaries of Robert Eccleston.* Ed. by C. Gregory Crampton. Salt Lake City: University of Utah Press, 1957.) The dates in early May actually refer to the second expedition to Yosemite Valley, by one company of the Mariposa Battalion.

horse, and wallowed through the snow alone to a projecting granite rock. So interested was I in the scene before me, that I did not observe that my comrades had all moved on, and that I would soon be left indeed alone. My situation attracted the attention of Major Savage—who was riding in the rear of the column—who hailed me from the trail below with, "You had better wake up from that dream up there, or you may lose your hair; I have no faith in Ten-ie-ya's statement that there are no Indians about here. We had better be moving; some of the murdering devils may be lurking along this trail to pick up stragglers." I hurriedly joined the Major on the descent, and as other views presented themselves, I said with some enthusiasm: "If my hair is now required, I can depart in peace, for I have seen the power and glory of a Supreme Being; the majesty of His handy-work is in that ' Testimony of the Rocks.' "

To the Mariposa Battalion, then, commanded by Major Savage, is to be accorded the honor of first entering the Yo Semite Valley, May 5th or 6th, 1851. It is true the writer has heard of various persons having visited it, when prospecting for gold, as early as 1849, but no responsible data to establish the fact has yet come to his knowledge. Still, if this were proven beyond peradventure, their neglect to publish so marvelous a discovery to the world, is presumable evidence of a lack of appreciation, or of an absorbed attention to other pursuits that utterly diverted it from this sublime theme. And while discussing this question I hope to be forgiven for expressing surprise that so little was said or written upon it by its discoverers at the time. Even Dr. L. H. Bunnell, to whom the public is so largely indebted for his interesting narrative, "The Discovery of the Yosemite," only published his description of it in 1880. Extenuating mention should, however, be made of the fact that, at that time, nearly everyone's thoughts and energies were mainly centralized upon the acquisition of wealth, or in combatting the too frequent disappointments that followed in its train, for a moment to permit such a divertisement as an intellectual banquet on scenery, or in the preparation and serving up of one for others.

CHAPTER IV.

THE NAME—"YO SEMITE"—ITS ORIGIN AND MEANING.

On the choice of friends
Our good or evil name depends.

—GAY.

I do beseech you
(Chiefly that I might set it in my prayers),
What is your name?

—SHAKSPEAR'S *Tempest, Act III.*

Time is lord of thee:
Thy wealth, thy glory, and thy name are his.

—THOMAS LOVE PEACOCK'S *Time.*

After the safe arrival of the command on the floor of the cliff-encompassed home of the "Grizzlies," as the Yo Semites were invariably termed by the troops, it would seem that although supposed to be surrounded by hostile Indians, and that, too, in their much-vaunted stronghold, there evidently existed an utter absence of precaution, as of fear, inasmuch as all kinds of rollicking mirth and jollity held unchecked court in the lair of the enemy, and around a huge camp-fire, on the very evening of their arrival. It was here, and under these circumstances, and on this occasion, that the now famous valley received

THE MUSICAL NAME—YO SEMITE.

Its meaning is, according to the very best authorities, *a large, or full-grown, grizzly bear;* and is pronounced *Yo Sem-i-tee.* The old Indian name was Ah-wah-nee, and the tribe which inhabited it—the remote ancestors of Ten-ie-ya—were Ah-wah-nee-chees, the origination or signification of which is still veiled in mystery. All these considerations, and other proposed names meriting attention, were fully discussed at this opportune juncture; but

(58)

"Yo Semite," the one suggested by Dr. L. H. Bunnell, was finally adopted by an almost unanimous vote.

From an intelligent Indian, whose life the writer was once instrumental in saving, and from whom many interesting facts concerning his race have been obtained, and will be given in due season, he received the following

LEGENDARY TRADITION CONCERNING "YO SEMITE."

A band of the Ah-wah-nee-chees, then a tribe numbering over one thousand, was encamped among the oaks near the foot of Indian Cañon; when, early one morning, an athletic chief determined upon going to Mirror Lake (called by them "Ke-ko-too-yem," or Sleeping Water, and "Ah-wi-yah") for the purpose of spearing a number of its delicious trout. On threading his way among the bowlders that strewed the ground, and when passing one of the largest, he was suddenly met by an enormous grizzly bear. The abruptness of this unexpected meeting must have been interpreted by the grizzly as an unjustifiable intrusion upon his ursine privileges and domain, as he immediately declared it a *casus belli*, by an instantaneous and ferocious attack upon the Indian. Unprepared as the young chief was for such an unequal encounter, he resolved upon standing his ground, and doing his best, as nobly as he could, so that the children of Ah-wah-nee might see that the valorous blood of their ancestors was still flowing in the veins of their descendants. The dead limb of a tree, lying near, provided him with a weapon of defense, and with it he dealt out heavy and lusty blows upon the head of his antagonist; and, although badly lacerated and torn by the teeth and claws of the infuriated brute, the Indian courageously held to the uneven contest, until the eyes of bruin began to glaze in the cold glare of death; and "victory had perched upon the banners" of the chief. The astonished Indians, in admiring acknowledgment of the unexampled prowess of the dauntless Ah-wah-nee-chee, thenceforth called him "Yo Semite" in honor of his successful and great achievement. This well-won cognomen was eventually transmitted to his children; and, finally, to the whole tribe; so that the

"Yo Semites" were known, and feared, by all the Indians around their wildly defensive habitation.

It is apparent from Dr. Bunnell's statement* that the signification of "Yo Semite" was not generally known to the battalion; nor was there any uniformity in its general pronunciation, even among the Indians themselves, some calling it Oo-soom-i-tee, others Oo-hum-i-tee, Yo-hum-i-tee, Yo-hem-i-tee, and still others Yo-ham-i-tee, while Bullack, the oldest of the Yo Semites now living, calls it Ah Hum-a-tee—all, however, having the same meaning. Nor is this much to be wondered at, from a people entirely without a written language. Even in England—intelligent and progressive England—(as well as some portions of the United States) there is an anomaly existing in pronunciation. In London, for instance, the word "corn" is enunciated *cawn;* in Hampshire, it is *carn;* while on the borders of Scotland it is *coorn,* and all intending to speak it corn. In Herefordshire, beef is spoken *bif;* and feet, *fit.* Who, then, can wonder at the unlettered savage varying in his pronunciation.

In the summer of 1855, Thomas Ayres, Alexander Stair, Walter Millard, and the writer, made *the first tourist trip to Yo Semite ever attempted*—about which something more will be presented hereafter. We engaged two Yo Semite Indians as guides. Towards night of the first day out, we inquired of the principal guide, Kossum, how far it might possibly be to Yo Semite—for then we knew it by no other name. He looked at us earnestly, and replied: "No *Yo Semitee! Yo Hamitee; sabe, Yo-ham-i-tee.*" In this way we were corrected not less than thirty-five or forty times. After returning to San Francisco, having arranged for the publication of a large lithograph of the Yo Semite Falls, before attaching the name to it, I wrote to Mr. John Hunt, who was keeping a store on the Fresno River, and from whom we had obtained our Indian guides, requesting him to go to the most intelligent among them, and ascertain the exact way of pronouncing the name given to the valley. His

* "Discovery of the Yo Semite," page 62.

answer was, "The correct pronunciation is *Yo-ham-i-te* or *Yo-hem-i-te.*" This, then, was the name placed on the lithograph.

After the first attempted portrayal of the valley in *Hutching's California Magazine,* July, 1856, wherein Yo-ham-i-tee* was still used, there ensued a spirited though good-natured newspaper contest between Dr. Bunnell and the writer, upon its orthography; the former contending for *Yo Semite,* and the latter for *Yo Hamitee,* on account of the reasons above given. This discussion disclosed information, generally unknown before, of the naming of the valley, as proposed by Dr. Bunnell, on the night of its first entrance by white people, May 5th or 6th, 1851, and naturally invited acquiescence in the privilege and right of its first visitors to give it a nomenclature most in accordance with their own expressed selection; hence, unquestioned concurrence in perpetuating the now well-established name, "Yo Semite."

Before fully closing these inquiries, it may not be inappropriate to consider why preference is given here to the construction of the word *Yo Semite* with a capital *S* on its second syllable. It is this: Dr. Bunnell, to whom the world is indebted for the choice and adoption of this euphonious name, so gave it to the writer, some thirty years ago, and before the present slovenly way of spelling it came into practice. It is true, Dr. Bunnell, in his valuable work, "The Discovery of the Yosemite," has fallen into that habit; but, when asked his reasons for making the change, replied, "I allowed the printer to follow his own way of spelling it. Yours, however, is the correct one, and I must give you credit for keeping up its pure orthography, that being the construction given to it, and agreed upon, at our first camp-fire in Yo Semite in 1851." The Act of Congress making the donation of the valley to the State, so gives it.

---

* Dr. Wozencraft, chairman of the United States Indian Commission, still gives this as the only name known in 1851, and the correct one.

CHAPTER V.

CLOSE OF THE INDIAN CAMPAIGN.

Not in the clamor of the crowded street,
Not in the shouts and plaudits of the throng,
But in ourselves, are triumph and defeat.
—LONGFELLOW'S *The Poets.*

The arms are fair
When the intent for bearing them is just.
—SHAKESPEAR'S *Henry IV., Part I., Act V.*

How calm, how beautiful comes on
The stilly hour, when storms are gone.
—MOORE'S *Lalla Rookh, The Fire Worshippers, Part III.*

On the early morning following the day of their arrival in the much-vaunted fastness of the "Grizzlies," when the order was given to "fall in," every saddle was instantly occupied, and the advance commenced. The immense piles of talus lying beneath the granite walls of the Po-ho-no* Fall, intercepted their progress on the south side of the Merced, and compelled the fording of its ice-cold waters. The irregular depth of the river, with its obstructive bowlders, gave involuntary invitation to several for an unintentional bath; and which, but for the danger of being swept down by the current into the cañon below, and to certain death, was only the signal for additional hilarity.

SMOKE FROM A SLUMBERING PICKET FIRE

Near El Capitan* unmistakably revealed the presence of Indians, and that they knew of the advent of the whites, and were evidently watching their movements. The near vicinage of a large collection of Indian huts that had been but recently inhabited, and now gave evidence of hasty desertion, was proof positive that the

---

* All local objects of interest were without known names at this time.

(62)

game sought was near at hand, but had been driven away by lack of circumspection. A short distance from camp was an abundant supply of acorns, their article of bread-stuff. It would seem, however, by the tracks made, that their pretentious valor was, like their footsteps, rapidly taking departure. Far up the valley other manifest signs gave hopeful promise of nearness to the foe; but again "delusive hope" was to experience another dash of disappointment, as nothing but evidences in abundance of hasty departure were discoverable—except a very old woman "that could only be likened to

A VIVIFIED EGYPTIAN MUMMY,"

And who, when questioned of the whereabouts of her companions, curtly replied (in Indian), "You can hunt for them, if you want to see them!" Hunt they did for several days, but none were found, as the rocky talus over which the hostiles had made their escape, left no tracks of their course.

On all hands, and at every deserted camp, were found large stores of Indian food, such as acorns, pine and chincapin nuts, grass seeds, wild oats scorched, dried caterpillars, roasted grasshoppers, sun-dried larvæ and pupæ of flies, obtained mostly from Mono Lake; home-made baskets, of many sizes and patterns, and for different uses; a few rabbit or squirrel-skin robes, for bed coverings,* obsidian (for arrow heads), pumice-stone, salt, relics of clothing and trinkets, the picked bones of horses and mules, and other property stolen from the whites, were found in liberal abundance—but not a single Indian was seen other than the old woman, and the "brave," brought with them as guide.

Provisions becoming exhausted in the camp at Yo Semite, and the outlook for collecting the scattered Yo Semites very discouraging, without a prolonged search among the mountains around, after burning up the Indian food supplies, camp furniture, and huts, as the only available means now at command for compelling a surrender, this unsuccessful campaign was closed by a return of the battalion to camp at the South Fork.

* For full description of all such articles, with the fabrics and methods of manufacture, see Bunnell's "Discovery of the Yo Semite," pages 78–80.

CAPTIVES LEAVE SOUTH FORK FOR THE RESERVATION.

As the capture of any additional Indians, for the present at least, was strongly problematical, and supplies were running short, upon the arrival of the Yo Semite expedition, it was determined to break up camp, and convey such Indians as had been secured, to the reservation on the Fresno. On their way thither the complement of "captives" was increased by about one hundred by the voluntary surrender of that number to Captain Dill's command.

An appetizing march of several days brought the entire cavalcade to within a few miles of their intended destination. The general deportment of the Indians had been such as to successfully win the confidence of both officers and men, so that a strict guard over them was considered as altogether unnecessary. Under these conditions, permission was asked for a large portion of the command to accompany Major Savage to the reservation. "The Major finally assented to the proposition, saying, 'I do not suppose the Indians can be driven off, or be induced to leave, until they have had the feast I have promised; besides, they will want to see some of the commissioners' finery. I have been delighting their imaginations with descriptions of the presents in store for them.' " Therefore Captain Boling, with nine men as camp guard, was the only force left. All apprehensions allayed, the kindly-hearted Captain told his men to take their sleep, and that he would watch, as he was not sleepy. "Towards morning I took another round," relates Captain Boling, "and finding the Indian camp wrapped in slumber, I concluded to take a little sleep myself, until daylight. This now seems unaccountable to me, for I am extremely cautious in my habits. I confess myself guilty of neglect of duty; I should have taken nothing for granted. No one can imagine my surprise and mortification when I was told that

THE INDIAN CAMP WAS ENTIRELY DESERTED,

And that none were to be seen except the one asleep by our camp-fire. Consternation was in every face, as not one of the three hundred and fifty captives, seen in such apparently peaceful slumber that night, was now left to explain the cause of their hasty departure. Effort in pursuit only disclosed their successful exodus, and the utter hopelessness of one officer and nine men attempting to recapture them. No choice was left, therefore, other than for those to report themselves at head-quarters, and tell their own sad story. The long-delayed arrival of the expected caravan at the reservation, gave some cause for uneasiness there; but not one was prepared to realize the full force of such an appalling disclosure, as, that every one of the Indians, whom they had been months in collecting, were, in a single night, and when within a few miles of the anticipated goal, all scattered abroad. Still, however reluctant the admission, the startling fact stood boldly out, that

" "Tis revelation satisfies all doubts."

With this came also the dawning consciousness of some unexplainable cause for their sudden departure. As Kee-chee had invariably proven himself to be unswervingly loyal to the interests of peace, he was immediately summoned, for both conference and service, and dispatched among the affrighted fugitives. Then developed the certainty that on the preceding eventful night several Chow-chilla runners had visited the camp, and enjoled the unsuspecting captives into the belief that they were being decoyed into a trap, and would all be murdered. They also assured them that Dr. Wozencraft, one of the Commissioners, had already killed Kee-chee, the principal chief of their united tribes, and that there was a plot on foot to slaughter every one, the moment they had them in their power. These grossly infamous representations, then, very naturally caused the totality of the stampede. Kee-chee's appearance among them, alive, was not only conclusive proof of his safety, but of the fraudulently deceptive stories of the Chow-chillas. His personal explanations and assurances soon restored their confidence, and the major portion cheerfully consented to seek the comforts and protection of the reservation, where they expressed sincere regret for allowing themselves to be so readily imposed upon. One desire now was manifestly uppermost, the speedy punishment of the Chow-chillas, as being the cause of all their trouble.

As the Yo Semites had again returned to the valley, and with the Chow-chillas had refused to respond to the messages sent,

A NEW CAMPAIGN WAS RESOLVED UPON.

Accordingly about one hundred men, led by Captains Boling and Dill, and under the command of Major Savage (who was shortly afterwards summoned to return), commenced scouring the country in all directions for Indians—all now found being considered "hostiles." A large band of Chow-chillas, having a war dance, was discovered upon the south bank of the main San Joaquin River, arranged to give battle; but, after crossing the stream, in full expectation of meeting them, the enemy had fled. Examination of a smouldering fire gave evidence that the body of Jose Rey, with his articles of value, had just been consumed.

All the lodges and stores were destroyed, and the trail of the retreating Indians taken; but after exploring this entire section, crossing and recrossing the swollen streams, and enduring many hardships, not a single Indian was either killed or captured. The destruction of supplies, and starving them out, was now considered about the only way of reaching and successfully conquering them, and the troops marched back to the Fresno. This view was proven to be correct, for not many days had elapsed after their return, when Tom-kit and Frederico, successors to Jose Rey, as chief of the Chow-chillas, with much bombastic gasconading, finally made a treaty, and accepted terms. This ended the war with this defiant and once powerful tribe, leaving only the "Grizzlies" to grapple with.

THE SECOND EXPEDITION TO THE YO SEMITES.

Suitable preparations completed, the advance was commenced under Captain Boling—"the services of Major Savage being indispensable to the Commissioners"—the main column following under Lieutenant Chandler. In the hope of surprising the

Indians, if possible, or "cut off the escape of the women and children, and thus bring the warriors to terms," a rapid and stealthy march was made, and the valley quietly entered, but no Indians were discovered. A few newly built but now deserted huts, with heaps of hulled acorns, some of which had been set on fire, and were still burning, that had evidently been prepared for human transportation across the Sierras, were the only visible signs of Indian life. The entrance of the pursuers to the valley had evidently been anticipated and closely watched.

THREE OF TEN-IE-YA'S SONS TAKEN PRISONERS.

Their advance, however, was soon to be rewarded by the sight of living forms flitting from tree to tree, and from rock to rock; these proving to be a portion of the enemy of which they were in search, a lively chase commenced that resulted in the capture of five Indians, probably scouts, three of whom were sons of Ten-ie-ya, and as they had been caught near three singularly uniform mountain peaks, these peaks were called, and are still known, as "The Three Brothers." Hence the derivation of that appellation.

An excited search in different directions speedily disclosed unmistakable indications of the near proximity of Indians, in considerable numbers, and who were manifestly secreting themselves among the rocky talus bordering the open meadows, or on the adjacent cliffs, and were then probably espying all their movements. Countless tracks, baskets, scattered acorns, and other "signs," apparently indicated the way to their hiding-place, or trail of exit. These were at first eagerly followed, but gradually the conviction forced itself upon some that they had been intentionally placed there by the Indians to

LURE THEIR PURSUERS INTO A TRAP;

While others, more valorous than prudent, hurried for the foe, to "beard the lion in his den." This incautious temerity was at the risk of their lives, for huge masses of rock came thundering down; fortunately, however, some projecting cliffs, under which they were enabled to speedily find shelter, saved them

from extermination. One man, named Spencer, was struck by a
fragment and hurled over fifty feet; yet he, although badly cut
and bruised, eventually recovered. This was carrying out the
threatened method of warfare indicated by Kee-chee.

Ten-ie-ya's sons made no secret of the certainty that the old
chief was near, and intimated that he would in nowise be averse
to coming in, if sent for, to "have a talk with the white chief."
One son, and the son-in-law of Ten-ie-ya, were accordingly dispatched for him, in charge of Dr. Bunnell, the other prisoners
being kept as hostages. Meeting the sorrowful and angry cavalcade with the wounded man, upon the way, it required all the
doctor's firmness to prevent their shooting the messenger prisoners under his charge upon the spot.* After safely escorting
them to the foot of the mountain, where the trail leaves the
cañon,† he allowed the Indians to proceed upon their mission,
and returned to camp; calling, however, on the way to dress the
wounds of the suffering soldier.

ESCAPE OF A PRISONER.

While awaiting the arrival of tidings of, or from, Ten-ie-ya,
and indulging in the restful recreation of witnessing the expert
use of the bow and arrow by the Indians, the target having been
set at long range; while pretending to examine the closeness of
the shots, one of the hostages made his successful escape up the
North Cañon—naturally to the indescribable mortification of
those ostensibly in charge. To avoid a repetition of so undesirable
a circumstance, the remaining two were tied together, and, for
still greater security, had been fastened to a tree; but later, when
supposing that their movements had been unnoticed, they succeeded in releasing themselves, and immediately started upon
the run for the same cañon that had afforded escape for their
companion. It is more than presumable that these proceedings

* For full and graphic recitals of these adventures, read "Discovery of the
Yosemite."

† This is the old and long-used Indian trail by Mt. Watkins to Lake Ten-ie-ya and
Mono.

had been approvingly watched by the guard, who, it is supposed, was longingly anxious for an excusable opportunity for killing them and effectually ridding both the camp and the country of their presence, although contrary to the orders and policy of those in command. Be that as it may,

TEN-IE-YA'S YOUNGEST SON WAS SHOT DEAD,

When scarcely twenty yards from the tree to which he had been bound; the other would have shared the same fate but for "a bullet-pouch that had been hung upon the muzzle of one of the guard's rifles;" owing to this circumstance he escaped unharmed. The act was uniformly deplored and condemned by nearly the whole command, and its perpetrators deservedly shunned and despised by all, from that time thenceforward.

MESSENGERS SENT TO TEN IE YA.

The morning passed* and the hour of ten arrived, without Ten-ie-ya. Captain Boling then sent out Sandino and the scouts to hunt for him, and, if found, to notify him that he was expected. Sandino soon came back, and reported that he had seen Ten-ie-ya and talked with him; but that he was unable to reach him from below, on account of the steepness of the ledge. Sandino reported that Ten-ie-ya was unwilling to come in; that he expressed a determination not to go to the Fresno. He would make peace with the white chief, if he would be allowed to remain in his own territory. Neither he nor his people would go to the valley while the white men were there. They would stay upon the mountains, or go to the Monos.

CAPTURE OF TEN-IE-YA.

This positive, though somewhat unexpected answer from the old chief, could not well be misunderstood, and Captain Boling promptly resolved upon the execution of such measures as would compel acquiescence in his wishes. Having ascertained from Sandino the probable locality occupied by Ten-ie-ya upon the cliff, he dispatched Lieutenant Chandler and a necessary force, accompanied by a few Noot-chü and Po-ho-no-chee scouts, for the purpose of surrounding and bringing him into camp, according to

* "Discovery of the Yosemite."

orders, *alive if possible*. He was found near the expected place, eagerly scanning every movement passing below, and, to appearance, utterly unconscious of the approach of the platoon.

The unwelcome discovery made, and seeing that his retreat above had been cut off, Ten-ie-ya at first ran along westerly, on the slope of the mountain towards Indian Cañon;* but finding that he was cut off in that direction also, by the Noot-chü and Po-ho-no-chee scouts, he turned and came down a trail, through an oak tree top to the valley, which Sandino had by this time reached, and where he had been attracted by the noise made in pursuit. Lieutenant Chandler had not climbed up the trail, and hearing Sandino's cry for help, and the noise above him, he was able to reach the place where Ten-ie-ya descended, in time to secure him. Ten-ie-ya said the men above him were rolling down stones, and he did not like to go up, as they broke and flew everywhere; for that reason he came down. Ten-ie-ya accompanied his captors without making any resistance, although he strongly censured the Indians for being instrumental in his capture.†

With the proud bearing of a chief who represented a long line of ancestors, and a tribe that commanded the respectful fear of surrounding bands, although a prisoner, he walked almost defiantly erect into camp. The first object that met his gaze upon arrival was the dead body of his favorite son. Here let us silently drop the mantle of sympathetic sorrow over the feelings of a bereaved father, while we make sad confession that

"When all is past, it is humbling to tread
O'er the weltering field of the tombless dead."

The most benignant condolence, followed by the fullest regretful explanations, could not restore his latest-born son. Not a word escaped his quivering lips for many days. The most persistent of questionings elicited no articulate response.

As Ten-ie-ya would give no clew to the whereabouts of his people, even if he knew (and which was very doubtful) a well-organized and scrutinizing search was instituted in many directions, and mostly on foot. While these were being systematically

* This was the name given to the "North Cañon" after the escape of the Indian fugitives up it; and by which it has ever since been known.

† Bunnell's "Discovery of the Yosemite."

conducted among the mountainous surroundings of the valley, there arose considerable excitement within it, from

TEN-IE-YA ATTEMPTING HIS ESCAPE.

But "as he rushed from his keeper, Cameron dashed after and caught him before he was able to plunge into and swim the river." Supposing that he was to be condemned and shot for this, when led to Captain Boling, whom he considered responsible for the loss of his son, his feelings at last found utterance in the following characteristic speech, as presented by Dr. Bunnell:—

> *Kill me*, sir, Captain! Yes, *kill me*, as you killed my son; as you would kill my people if they were to come to you! You would kill all my race if you had the power. Yes, sir, American, you can now tell your warriors to kill the old chief; you have made me sorrowful, my life dark; you killed the child of my heart, why not kill the father? But wait a little; when I am dead, I will call to my people to come to you; I will call louder than you have had me call [referring to the expressed wishes of the officers that he should call in his people]; that they shall hear me in their sleep, and come to avenge the death of their chief and his son. Yes, sir, American, my spirit will make trouble for you and your people, as you have caused trouble to me and my people. With the wizards I will follow the white men and make them fear me. You may kill me, sir, Captain, but you shall not live in peace. I will follow in your footsteps, I will not leave my home, but be with the spirits among the rocks, the water-falls, in the rivers and the winds; wheresoever you go, I will be with you. You will not see me, but you will fear the spirit of the old chief, and grow cold.* The great spirits have spoken! I have done.

Instead of killing him, however, they regaled him with a good supper, their sorrow changing into admiring veneration for his fearless bravery.

As sundry explorations in the immediate vicinity of the valley had brought no hoped-for results, an expedition was resolved upon to the High Sierra, and, if necessary, across them. Ten-ie-ya was taken with them.

---

* It is claimed by all Indian "Medicine Men" that the presence of a spirit is announced by a *cool* breeze, and that sometimes they turn cold and shake as with an ague.—*Dr. Bunnell.*

SURPRISE OF THE INDIAN VILLAGE.

Before advancing over twenty miles above the valley, the blue ascending smoke of some camp fires indicated the near vicinity of an Indian village. Cautiously approaching it, and after capturing their outlying pickets, they found the Yo Semites in force by a beautiful lake. Judiciously moving upon it, before they were discovered they succeeded in surrounding and surprising the whole, so that not one of them had time or opportunity for escaping. This was a master-stroke of good fortune. Finding themselves utterly powerless, they piteously cried out for peace. There was not even the semblance of resistance or of apparent objection. Here Ten-ie-ya rejoined his four squaws, and their re-union once more was a joy-giving event. As all seemed worn out with watching, and they were in a starving condition, they gave abundant proof of abject willingness to accept almost any terms.

THE NAMING OF LAKE TEN-IE-YA.

"Looking back to the lovely little lake," writes Dr. Bunnell, "where we had been encamped during the night, and watching Ten-ie-ya as he ascended to our group, I suggested to Captain Boling that we name the lake after the old chief, and call it 'Lake Ten-ie-ya.'" In concurrent response to this, the Captain, addressing those assembled, replied: "Gentlemen, I think the name an appropriate one, and shall use it in my report of the expedition. Besides this, it is rendering a kind of justice to perpetuate the name of the old chief." This, therefore, was the origin and time of naming one of the most charmingly picturesque lakes of any country, concerning which more will be said in a future chapter.

THEY MARCH FOR YO SEMITE.

The total number of Indians found here was thirty-five, "nearly all of whom were in some way a part of the family of the old patriarch, Ten-ie-ya." All of the remainder of those that had escaped were supposed to have joined the Tuolumne and Mono Indians, among whom they had intermarried. Deeming it better to proceed with, and care for, those already in safe-keeping, than to pursue others at the neglect of these, and against orders, the men were placed under guard, and the women and children allowed to go free, and in this manner the motley cavalcade took up its line of march.

According to Indian custom, the women performed all the manual labor, including the carrying of all their heavy packs; and the men the eating, the grumbling, and the sleeping. This arrangement, to the officers in charge, was demurred to as an unequal division, and in the hope of adjusting it, and facilitating a more rapid advance of the entire party, the men were ordered to bear a fair share of the burdens. Against this, however, to the amusing surprise of all, the squaws themselves were the most violently opposed. Ten-ie-ya, it is said, waxed eloquent against such an unheard-of innovation of their customs. As all parties in interest were averse to any such change, it was accordingly abandoned.

ON THE MARCH.

END OF THE MARIPOSA INDIAN WAR.

Diversified by numerous scenes and experiences by the way, every captive with which they had started was eventually delivered safely over to the Indian Commissioners at the Fresno, and the expedition formally commended for its success. This virtually terminated the Mariposa Indian War. That accomplished, the Mariposa Battalion was mustered out of service, July 1, 1851.*

* See Elliott's "History of Fresno County," page 181.

CHAPTER VI.

EARLY HISTORICAL INCIDENTS.

Ill habits gather by unseen degrees.
As brooks make rivers, rivers run to seas.
—Dryden's *Ovid, Metamorphoses, Bk. XV.*

Guilt's a terrible thing.
—Ben Jonson's *Bartholomew Fair.*

Angels for the good man's sin
Weep to record, and blush to give it in.
—Campbell's *Pleasures of Hope.*

Chafing under the restraint attending his residence at the reservation, in addition to many tribal squabbles, and the ostensible lack of dignity showed him by his fellow-captives, Ten-ie-ya implored permission to return to his home in the mountains, promising faithfully to conform to every requirement asked of him by the Commissioners. This permission was eventually conceded, under certain conditions, and the old chief, with his family, was once more allowed to return to the Yo Semite. Other members of his tribe, shortly after Ten-ie-ya's departure, silently stole away from the reservation and joined him; "but as no complaints were made by their chiefs, it was understood that they were glad to get rid of them; therefore no effort was made to bring them back."

After the severe lessons already taught these renegades, it was reasonable to suppose that they would have accepted the situation, and kept upon their best behavior, but with the return of winter came also the Indians, and with them their old bad habits. Numerous animals being missed from their pasture-grounds, it was presumed that the Yo Semites had stolen them; "but as some of them were found in the possession of Mexicans, who were promptly executed for the theft, no charge was preferred against the Yo Semites."

(74)

N or about May 28th, 1852,* a party of five prospectors for gold, consisting of Messrs. Tudor, Grover, Sherman—or Sherbon—Babcock, and Rose, left Coarse Gold Gulch, Fresno County (now used as one of the stage routes between Madera and Wawona), for the Yo Semite Valley. They had scarcely entered it before they were attacked by Indians, that lay in ambush among the rocks, at the foot of the old Indian trail. Rose and Sherman—or Sherbon, as Dr. Bunnell gives it—were instantly killed. Tudor was seriously wounded; but he and the others secreted themselves among the rocks, and fought the Indians, until darkness enabled them to make good their escape.

THE ATTACK.

* Elliott's "History of Fresno County."

The arrival of the survivors in Mariposa with the exciting news of these murders, and the renewal of Indian hostilities, very naturally stirred up the old defiant hate, and the Indian Commissioners were blamed for permitting Ten-ie-ya's return. It was, moreover, feared that this would be a signal for the wholesale desertion of Indians from the reservation. Instead of this, however, those living on the outside fled within for protection, fearing that the guilt of others would be visited upon their own heads.

UNITED STATES EXPEDITION SENT AGAINST THE YO SEMITES.

The officer in command at Fort Miller, on the San Joaquin River, was informed, by special courier, of these murders; when a detachment of regular soldiers, under Lieutenant Moore, U.S.A., was immediately sent out against the enemy, accompanied by scouts and guides that had formed portions of the first and second expeditions, and a few friends of the murdered men. They surprised and captured five of the Indians; the others, led by Ten-ie-ya, fled and escaped. The naked bodies of the murdered men were found, and buried, near the Pohono, or Bridal Veil Fall. Satisfied of the proof being conclusive that the Indians caught were the blood-stained murderers of the whites, the clothing of the murdered men being found upon their persons, Lieutenant Moore ordered them to be shot upon the spot.

These effectually disposed of, Moore and his forces, after searching for the remaining Yo Semites in their hiding-places about the valley, pursued them into, and even across the mountains to, the Mono country; but as the Indians had every advantage, both in the start, and in their knowledge of the ways and by-ways of escape, they were never overtaken, and the command reluctantly returned to Fort Miller, without a single prisoner as a trophy.

THE YO SEMITES NEARLY EXTERMINATED BY THE MONOS.

Nothing more was heard of the Yo Semites, after their successful flight to, and hiding among, the Monos, with whom they found shelter and protection, until the early summer of 1853, when, being dissatisfied with their dependent position, and more so with the locality assigned them, they returned once more to the Yo Semite Valley. Fearing the just retaliation of the whites, however, they made their abiding places among the talus, whence they could notice every movement of the enemy, without themselves being seen. There are several of these places of shelter still to be found among the rocks near Indian Cañon, and elsewhere.

Life, in their old home, unspiced with mischief, became unbearably monotonous to them after the habit had been acquired, and learning through their runners that the Monos had stolen a large band of fine horses from the vicinity of Los Angeles, the Yo Semites became jealously uneasy, and planned a foraging excursion, to obtain some of this living plunder for their own use; indulging the impression that it would be safer, under present circumstances, to steal from the Monos than from the whites. The raid was accordingly executed with masterly cunning, and their arrival with the stolen horses successfully accomplished. By this time they had mustered sufficient courage to form an encampment down in the valley, near the mouth of Indian Cañon, where, according to Dr. Bunnell, who is probably the best informed of any man living, on such topics:—

After a few days' delay, and thinking themselves secure, they killed one or more of the horses, and were in the enjoyment of a grand feast in honor of their return, when the Monos pounced down upon them. Their gluttony seemed to have rendered them oblivious to all danger to themselves, and of the ingratitude by which the feast had been supplied. Like sloths, they appear to have been asleep after having surfeited their appetites. They were surprised in their wigwams by the wronged and vengeful Monos, and before they could rally for the fight, the treacherous old chief was struck down by the hand of a powerful young Mono chief.

DEATH OF TEN-IE-YA, THE LAST CHIEF OF THE YO SEMITES.

Ten-ie-ya had been the principal object of attack at the commencement of the assault, but he had held the others at bay until discovered by the young chief, who, having exhausted his supply of arrows, seized a fragment of rock and hurled it with such force as to crush the skull of "the old Grizzly." As Ten-ie-ya fell, other stones were cast upon him by the attacking party, after Pai-ute custom, until he was literally stoned to death. All but eight of Ten-ie-ya's young braves were killed; these escaped down the valley, and through the cañon below. The old men and women who survived the first assault were permitted to escape from the valley. The young women and children were made captives, and taken across the mountains to be held as slaves or drudges to their captors.

Thus substantially ended the once famous tribe of the Yo Semites. The few that escaped eventually found their way to "Hunt's Store" on the Fresno. It was from these that we obtained our Indian guides in 1855, as related in the ensuing chapter.

DEATH OF MAJOR SAVAGE.

Before closing this recital, it may not be deemed irrelevant to state that Major Savage, the chosen officer of command for the Mariposa Battalion, fearing that the best interests of the Indians were being jeoparded by the course of speculative and unscrupulous men, denounced some of the leaders in unmeasured terms. This brought on a personal altercation, and re-encounter, between Savage and a man named Harvey, which ended in the death of Savage, August, 1852.

The Indian tribes represented in the Peace Treaty were as follows: The Howechais, Chookchancies, Chowchillas, Pohonoches, Nootchoos, Pitcaches, Capoos, Toomanehs, Tallinchees, Poskesas, Wachahets, Itaches, Choenemnes, Chokimenas, Notohotos, and Narmelches—16.*

As Dr. Bunnell most graphically states: "It was a well-known fact that these people [the Indians] preferred horse-flesh and their acorn jelly to the rations of beef that were supposed to have been issued by the Government;" and, moreover, as an ultimate sequence, the reservation on the Fresno gradually became unpopular on this account, but mainly, from bad management; was afterwards abolished by the Government; and, finally, its lands and buildings were gobbled up by sharp-sighted, if not unprincipled men who, like many others of that class, became rich out of the acquisition.

CHAPTER VII.

FIRST TOURIST VISITORS TO YO SEMITE.

God is the author, men are only the players.
—Balzac.

There are two worlds; the world that we can measure with line and rule, and the world that we feel with our hearts and imaginations.
—Leigh Hunt's *Men, Women, and Books.*

And this our life, exempt from public haunt,
Finds tongues in trees, books in the running brooks,
Sermons in stones and good in everything.
—Shakespeare's *As You Like It.*

Upon the return of the Mariposa Battalion to the settlements—the exploits of which are briefly outlined in chapters two and three—and when, like

"The broken soldier, kindly bade to stay,
Sat by his fire, and talked the night away."

They recounted their

"Moving accidents by flood and field,"

But little seems to have been said, and that little very casually, about *the marvelous grandeur* of the Yo Semite, at least but little found its way, impressibly, to the public through the press of that day. It was therefore only a historical verity to confess that, but for the contemplated publication of an illustrated California monthly—afterwards issued for a number of years in San Francisco—its merely fortuitous mention would probably have escaped the attention of the writer altogether as it seemed to have done that of the public. As the account given, however, mentioned the existence of "a water-fall nearly a thousand feet high," it was sufficient to suggest a series of ruminating queries. A water-fall a thousand feet in height, and that is in California? A thousand feet? Why, Niagara is only one hundred and sixty-

(79)

Photo. by Geo. Fiske.

Photo-Typo by Britton & Rey, S. F.

ENCHANTMENT POINT—TOO-UN-YAH
(See page 400.)
Facing page 82 in editions two, three, and four.

Photo by Geo. Fiske

Courtesy, The Bancroft Library

ENCHANTMENT POINT—TOO-UN-YAH
(See page 400.)

Opposite page 80 in edition one. Note that this was taken from about 50 yards back
from the one opposite, and at a different season of the year, or a different year
—judging from the flow of water over Bridalveil Fall.

four feet high! *A thousand feet!!* The scrap containing this valuable and startling statement, meager though it was, was carefully treasured.

THE FIRST TOURIST PARTY.

About the twentieth of June, 1855—some four years after Yo Semite had been first seen by white men, and when entirely unaware of the sublime mountain scenery afterwards found there—the "water-fall a thousand feet high" induced the writer to form a party to visit it. That party—whose names are also given in a previous chapter—consisted of the then well-known artist, Thomas Ayres (who had been specially engaged by the writer to portray the majesty and beauty of the lofty water-fall expected to be found there), Walter Millard, and J. M. Hutchings. Mr. Alexander Stair afterwards joined us at Mariposa.

Upon our arrival at Mariposa, whence the principal members of the battalion had started out against the Indians, in 1851, to our surprise, the very existence of such a place as the Yo Semite Valley, was almost unknown to a very large proportion of its residents. Numerous and persistent inquiries, however, eventually revealed the fact that a man named—say—Carter, was one of those who had gone out against the Indians, in 1851. Accordingly, Mr. Carter's residence was anxiously inquired for, and finally found about two miles below town. Mr. Carter was at home.

"Is this Mr. Carter?"

"Yes, sir; it is."

"You were a member of Company B, Captain Boling's, I believe, during the Indian campaign of 1851?"

"Yes, sir; I was."

"Did you go to the Yo Semite Valley with that company?"

"I did, sir."

"Then you are the very man that we wanted to find. We have just arrived here from San Francisco, and want to learn our way to that valley. Will you, therefore, please to give us such plain directions, that we cannot possibly misunderstand them, so that we can get there?" He looked at us in bewildered and nervous astonishment, and replied:—

"Me, sir? I couldn't do it. I am not worth a worn-out old pick at that business. Why, bless your life, I only live about two miles from town, and if I don't notice particularly what I am about, I am sure to take the wrong trail, and get lost. The fact is, sir, I am about the poorest man you could have come to, on that business. Now if you had only gone to John Fowler's, John could have told you all about it. John Fowler is the man that you want."

"Where does he live?"

"Only about a mile and a quarter from here. You couldn't very well miss the trail, if you were to turn to the left at the bottom of this ravine; about two hundred yards from there, by bearing a little to the right, you will cross Blanket Ridge into Shay's Gulch; well, you follow that down nearly to the mouth, where you go over a rocky point to Slum-gullion Creek; here, let me caution you to keep a sharp lookout for miner's prospecting holes, that are full of soft mud, although apparently dry and hard on the top; for, if you ever walk into one of those, the chances are against your ever getting out, to say nothing about the bright red color you would be painted, if you could come out at all. Well, John Fowler's cabin is on the west side of Slum-gullion Creek, about three-quarters of a mile above where you first strike it. If John hasn't gone to town—and I don't think this is his day for going—he can give you all the directions."

So we thanked Mr. Carter for his information, wished him good-day, and set out in search of "John Fowler's." Many were the

INTERESTING OLD-TIME MINING SCENES

That we witnessed by the way, and which, of themselves, would have been sufficient, under ordinary circumstances, to fully compensate us for our jaunt, and even now they beguiled and rewarded our every footstep. Perseverance is generally crowned

with success, and although the day was sultry, and the trail sometimes doubtful as well as rough, we finally found ourselves at the
door of Mr. Fowler's cabin. According to the most invariable custom among gold miners, no matter how rough their exteriors, we
were most courteously re-
ceived. His answers to our
questions soon disclosed
the fact that although a
member of the expedition
of 1851, and had entered
the valley with the others,
having stood guard a good
deal at night, he generally
felt too sleepy in the day-
time to take particular
notice of the country over
which they were traveling.
He could probably give us
some general directions,
yet they would not be sufficiently consecutive to
enable us to follow them.
But there was a member of

SEE! I'VE STRUCK IT.

Company C, named Lovejoy, who could accompany us with the
very knowledge we were seeking.

Accordingly, Mr. Lovejoy was sought after, and found. From
him we ascertained, not the route to the Yo Semite Valley, but
that he had been the undisputed owner of a bad sick-head-ache,
which he had kept in unquestioned possession for several successive days, when on the march; and that, as a consequence, he
had noticed nothing outside, or apart from that. He could not tell
us anything. Finally, a number of regretful shadows began to file
into the furrows of his sun-burned face, and to gather among the
wrinkles at the corners of his eyes, possibly at the thought of the
distance we had journeyed to find him, and the little satisfaction

MINER'S CABIN.

he had given to pay us for our time and trouble. Looking steadfastly and musingly into our faces, the shadows began to lift, and the wrinkles to smooth away, as though a dawning intelligence was breaking slowly through him to our relief, as he exclaimed: "Gentlemen! I have it at last! There is Thomas Osborne, who lives down at Bogus Thunder Bar, not over a mile from here, who can," etc. etc. So we called on Mr. Osborne, and Mr. Osborne sent us to Mr. Giles, and Mr. Giles referred us to Mr. Harris, and Mr. Harris directed us to someone else, and thus we continued until, at last, night overtook us when questioning the eleventh fraction of the two hundred and four, forming the Mariposa Battalion. The outlook for the information needed was not the most inspiriting.

In this dilemma we met Captain Boling, the gentleman in charge of Company B, of the Mariposa volunteers, and who, being really very desirous of assisting us in every possible manner, confessed that although he considered himself about as good as an expert in wood-craft, could not now find the way to Yo Semite; as the trails were all overgrown with grass and weeds; and, as a matter of course, if he could not find the way there himself, it would be simply impossible for him to describe it so that we could find it. "No," said he, "if I were in your place, gentlemen, and wanted to go to the Yo Semite, I should first make a trip to John

Hunt's store on the Fresno—it is thirty miles directly out of your way—but there you will find the few Yo Semite Indians living of the entire tribe; tell Mr. Hunt your wants and wishes, also say to him that I sent you, and I am satisfied that he will provide you with a couple of good Indian guides who can take you straight to the spot." We considered this most excellent advice, and, so expressing it, carried out his recommendations.

WE EMPLOY YO SEMITE INDIANS TO GUIDE US TO THE VALLEY.

Mr. Hunt received us very kindly, and, acceding to our request, procured us two of the most intelligent and trustworthy Indians that he had, whose names were Kos-sum and So-pin; and on the following day we set out upon our enigmatical course for the valley.

HO! FOR THE MOUNTAINS.

Believe me there is an indescribable charm steals over the heart when wandering among the untrodden fastnesses of the mountains for the first time, especially under circumstances similar to ours. We were entering a mysterious country—to us unknown. The journey before us was full of uncertain lights and shadows—so might its ending possibly be. Our guides were Indians, and from a tribe that bore no enviable reputation; and were, moreover, strangers to us. They were conducting us among the unbroken solitudes of the forest, and away from civilization.

The roads near the settlements left behind, there was scarcely the outline of an Indian trail visible; unused as they had been, all were now overgrown, or covered up with leaves, as dead as the hopes of the Indians that once trod them. The boughs of seemingly impenetrable thickets were parted asunder, and our way forced through them in silence. Not a sound relieved the unbroken stillness of our discursive progress. Even the woods were voiceless with the songs of birds. A band of deer might occasionally shoot across an opening, or a covey of grouse beat the air heavily with their wings in clumsy flight; but these were all that could be seen or heard of life, except our own desultory or nonsensical converse.

Stolidly our Indian guides advanced; unquestioningly we followed. Not a thought of inquietude, or of distrust, or of misgiving

WE TAKE A "CUT-OFF."

intruded itself. As a natural sequence to a mountain jaunt like
ours, and over a supposed Indian trail—when there was one, the
best of which was never one of the smoothest—our experiences
were not only diversified but numerous. Now the ridge up which
we were ascending was at an angle so steep that, when on foot,
the tails of our horses would be used as hands to assist us in
climbing it. At times there was a fear lest our animals should fall
over backwards, or break their limbs between bowlders. Then
the descent would become so rapid, and the pine-needles so slippery, that riding was impossible, and pedestrianism brought us
into all sorts of (un) artistic positions. (See illustration on preceding page as well as on this.) Sometimes the Indians would cross a
ravine in one place and ourselves in another.

AND WE FIND A "CUT-OFF."

Of course we knew more about the way to go than they did—and proved it! There was one comforting solace to all our mishaps—they brought an enjoyable laugh to the Indian guides. These, and their meals, were always in order, and ever pleasantly taken. Successively and successfully, we passed through dark and apparently interminable forests, penetrated brushy thickets, ascended rocky ridges, and descended talus-covered slopes, until, on the afternoon of the third day of our deeply interesting expedition, we suddenly came in full view of

THE MARVELOUS VALLEY.

The inapprehensible, the uninterpretable profound, was at last opened up before us. That first vision into its wonderful depths was to me the birth of an indescribable "first love" for scenic grandeur that has continued, unchangeable, to this hour, and I gratefully treasure the priceless gift. I trust, moreover, to be forgiven for now expressing the hope that my long afterlife among the angel-winged shadows of her glorious cliffs, has given heart-felt proof of the abiding purity, and strength of that "first love" for Yo Semite.

This mere glimpse of the enchanting prospect seemed to fill our souls to overflowing with gratified delight, that was only manifest in unbidden tears. Our lips were speechless from thanksgiving awe. Neither the language of tongue nor pen, nor the most perfect successes of art, can approximately present that picture. It was sublimity materialized in granite, and beauty crystallized into object forms, and both drawing us nearer to the Infinite One.

It would be difficult to tell how long we looked lingeringly at this unexpected revelation; for,

"With thee conversing, I forget all time."

Our sketches finished—the first probably ever taken—the fast-lengthening shadows admonished a postponement of that intensely pleasurable experience, and in response we hastened our descent to the camp-ground on the floor of the valley.

GENERAL VIEW OF THE YO SEMITE VALLEY.

Sketched by Thos. Ayres, June 20, 1855—first ever taken.

[From Open-eta-noo-ah, on the old Indian trail.]

OUR FIRST SLEEP IN YO SEMITE.

It was late in the night before the nervous excitement, created by our imposing surroundings, permitted "sleep to come to our eyes, or slumber to our eyelids;" and, even then, from our dreams arose the shadowy forms of a new species of genii! After a substantial breakfast, made palatable by that best of all sauces, a good appetite, and the sun had begun to wink at us from between the pine trees on the mountain tops, or to throw shimmering lances down among the peaks and crags, we commenced our entrancing pilgrimage up the valley.

A few advancing footsteps brought us to the foot of a fall, whose charming presence had long challenged our admiration; and, as we stood watching the changing drapery of its watery folds, the silence was eventually broken by my remark, "Is it not as graceful, and as beautiful, as the veil of a bride?" to which Mr. Ayres rejoined, "That is suggestive of a very pretty and most apposite name. I propose that we now baptize it, and call it, 'The Bridal Veil Fall,' as one that is both characteristic and euphonious." This was instantly concurred in by each of our party, and has since been so known, and called, by the general public. This, then, was the time, and these the circumstances, attending

THE ORIGIN OF THE NAME "BRIDAL VEIL FALL."

About its Indian appellation and signification, with its legends and associations, more will be said in a future chapter.

Our progress upon the south side of the valley—the one on which we had entered it—was soon estopped by an immense deposit of rocky talus, that compelled us to ford the Merced River. Advancing upward upon its northern bank, after threading our way among trees, or around huge blocks of granite that were indiscriminately scattered about, passing scene after scene of unutterable sublimity, and sketching those deemed most noteworthy; again crossing and recrossing the river, we found ourselves in immediate proximity to the "water-fall a thousand feet high," and which had been the magnetic incentive to our visit to Yo Semite. This, from our measurements of prostrate pine-trees, by which was estimated the height of those standing (as we had no instruments with us adapted to such purposes), we deduced its altitude to be from fifteen to eighteen hundred feet! By subsequent actual measurements of the State Geological survey, its absolute height is given at 2,634 feet; with which those made by the Wheeler survey, under Lieutenant M. M. Macomb, U. S. A., very closely approximate. This inadequate realization of heights at Yo Semite is often strikingly manifest in visitors, on their first advent, even at the present day.

"TO-COY-AE" AND "TIS-SA-ACK." (North, and South, or, Half Dome.)
[From a sketch taken in 1855.]

It will be both unnecessary and inexpedient to detain the reader, now, with detailed recitals of the many objects of interest witnessed on this ramble, inasmuch as they are to be more fully presented with illustrations, in succeeding chapters. It may, however, be desirable here to mention that our explorations were limited to the valley, terminating at Mirror Lake—so named by our party. We did not see the "Vernal" or "Nevada" Falls, and only the Too-lool-we-ack, or Glacier Cañon Fall, from the Mirror Lake Trail. But we had seen sufficient to fill our hearts with gratitude that the All Father had created so many majestic and beautiful objects for human eyes to feast upon, that thereby humanity might grow nearer to Him, and thenceforth be nobler, higher, purer, and better for the sight.

We spent five glorious days in luxurious scenic banqueting here, the memory of which is, like the mercies of the Almighty, "new every morning, and fresh every evening." We left it reluctantly, even when our sketch and note-books were as full to repletion with elevating treasures, as our souls were with loving veneration for their wonderful Author. I believe that each one of us was responsively in sympathy with Byron, as expressed in the following lines from "Childe Harold:"—

> "I love not man the less, but Nature more,
> From these our interviews, in which I steal
> From all I may be, or have been before,
> To mingle with the Universe, and feel
> What I can ne'er express, yet cannot all conceal."

THE STORY HERALDED.

Our return to the settlements was the signal for the curious and inquisitive to besiege and interview us with eager questionings, to ascertain what we had seen and experienced; for there was a vague novelty in such a trip in those days. Among these came the editor of the Mariposa *Gazette*, Mr. L. A. Holmes (the memory of whom is still lovingly enshrined in the hearts of all who intimately knew him), and requested a full rehearsal of all the sights we had seen. Compliance with so reasonable a request was attended with a modest exposition of our sketches, accompanied with explanatory remarks to elucidate them. These ended, Mr. Holmes thus addressed the writer:—

"Mr. H., I have been quite ill all this week. My paper has to make an appearance day after to-morrow or—, and I have not been able to write a line for it, yet. You can therefore see that you can infinitely oblige me, if you were to sit down at that table there and throw me off an article upon what you have seen in this county, to help me out."

The response promptly came, "All right. I will do so. I take real pleasure in helping a man out of a corner, if I can, when he finds himself in one." Accordingly, a descriptive sketch of what had been seen was written for Mr. Holmes, and was published in the Mariposa *Gazette* of about July 12, 1855.

GENERAL ATTENTION FIRST ATTRACTED TO YO SEMITE.

This sketch happened to enlist the attention of journalists, was copied into most of the leading newspapers of the day, and for the first time the attention of the public, *generally*, was awakened towards the marvelous scenery of the Yo Semite Valley. In this connection it should be remembered that it is not by any means claimed that ours was the first party making the trip there, nor *that* the first article written concerning it; but, inasmuch as the sentiment accredited to Cicero,

"Justice renders to every man his due,"

Will, in the interests of historical accuracy, permit the statement that, whether from preoccupied attention, or other causes, the fact remains the same that the Yo Semite Valley, at that time, was *as a sealed book to the general public*, and that it was our good fortune to be instrumental in opening its sublime pages to the public eye, that it might be "known and read of all men." *Fiat justitia, ruat cœlum.*[1]

PARTIES FORMED TO VISIT THE NEW WONDER.

In and around Mariposa the new revelation seems to have become the theme of many tongues, as plans were discussed and parties organized for visiting it. Early the ensuing August two companies of kindred spirits, one of seventeen from Mariposa, and another of ten from Sherlock's Creek, an adjacent mining

1. Let there be justice, though the heavens fall.

camp, started in search of the new scenic El Dorado; the former party engaged the same Indians as guides who had conducted us there so successfully, and the latter was led by Mr. E. W. Haughton, who had accompanied the Savage expedition, under Captain Boling, in 1851. The members of the last-mentioned company were

THE DISCOVERERS OF THE VERNAL AND NEVADA FALLS.

And as this was an event of untold importance in the development of the stupendous scenery of Yo Semite, great pleasure is taken in transcribing portions of Mr. James H. Lawrence's deeply interesting and graphic account of it—he being one of the party—given in the *Overland Monthly* for October, 1884:—

As I must trust to memory alone for the names of my companions,

STEADY, THERE! STEADY!

not even knowing whether any of them are still alive, the list is necessarily incomplete. There were two of the Mann brothers, Milton and Houston, abbreviated to "Milt" and "Hugh," E. W. Haughton, J. E. Connor, Geo. C. Dickerman, a man by the name of Priest, the long-legged boy [?], and one other, whose name is forgotten. "The party was composed of ten as fearless spirits and noble-hearted fellows as ever shouldered a rifle or gathered around a camp-fire."

E. W. Haughton, who was with the Boling expedition in 1851, was our guide. Two pack-mules loaded with blankets, a few cooking utensils, and some provisions, constituted our camp outfit; while a half-breed blood-hound, whose owner claimed that he was "the best dog on the Pacific Coast," and who answered to the name of "Ship," trotted along with the pack-mules. There was some talk about going mounted, but the proposition was voted down by a handsome majority, on the ground that superfluous animals were "too much bother."

In fancy, I see them yet, and hear the ringing chorus, the exultant whoop, and the genuine, unrestrained laughter at the camp-fire. It would be worth a year of humdrum civilized society life to recall the reality of one week of the old time.

One evening, after a series of dare-devil escapades for no other purpose except to demonstrate how near a man can come to breaking his neck and miss it, some one suggested an expedition up the main river, above the valley. Haughton was appealed to for information. He favored the proposition, and said he would cheerfully make one of the party. As for information, he had none to give; neither he nor any of the Boling expedition ever dreamed of attempting it. They came on business—not to see sights or explore for new fields of wonder. Their mission was hunting Indians. There was no sign of a trail. It was a deep, rough cañon, filled with immense bowlders, through which the river seethed and roared with a deafening sound, and there had never been seen a foot-print of white man or Indian in that direction. The cañon was considered *impassable*.

There was a chorus of voices in response.

"That's the word."

"Say it again."

"Just what we are hunting."

"We want something rough."

"We'll tackle that cañon in the morning."

"An early start, now."

It was so ordered. "With the first streak of daylight you'll hear me crow," was Connor's little speech as he rolled himself in his blankets. Next morning we were up and alive, pursuant to programme. Everybody seemed anxious to get ahead.

Three of us—Milton J. Mann, G. C. Pearson, and the writer of this sketch—lingered to arrange the camp-fixtures, for everybody was going up the cañon. When we came to the Glacier Cañon, or Tuloolweack, our friends were far in advance of us. We could hear them up the cañon shouting, their voices mingling with the roar of the waters. A brief consultation, and we came to the resolve to diverge from the main river and try to effect an ascent between that stream and the cañon. It looked like a perilous undertaking, and there were some doubts as to the result; nevertheless, the conclusion was to see how far we could go. Away up, up, far above us, skirting the base of what seemed to be a perpendicular cliff, there was a narrow belt of timber. That meant a plateau or strip of land comparatively level. If we could only reach that, it was reasonable to suppose that we could get around the face of the cliff. "Then we will see sights," was the expression of one of the trio. What we expected to discover somewhere up the main stream was a lake or perhaps a succession of lakes—such having been the result of the explorations up the Pyweah Cañon, and mountain lakes being not unfrequently noted as a feature of the sources of mountain streams.

But to reach the plateau—that was the problem. It was a fearful climb. Over and under and around masses of immense rocks, jumping across chasms at imminent risk of life and limb, keeping a bright lookout for soft places to fall, as well as the best way to circumvent the next obstacle, after about three hours' wrestling, "catch as catch can," with that grim old mountain-side, we reached the timber. Here, as we had surmised, was enough of level ground for a foothold, and here we took a rest, little dreaming of the magnificent scene in store for us when we rounded the base of the cliff.

The oft-quoted phrase, "A thing of beauty is a joy forever," was never more fully realized. The picture is photographed on the tablets of my memory in indelible colors, and is as fresh and bright to-day as was the first impression twenty-nine years ago. To the tourist who beholds it for the first time, the Nevada Fall, with its weird surroundings, is a view of rare and picturesque beauty and grandeur. The rugged cliffs, the summits fringed with stunted pine and juniper bounding the cañon on the southern side, the "Cap of Liberty" standing like a huge sentinel overlooking the scene at the north, the foaming caldron at the foot of the fall, the rapids below, the flume where the stream glides noiselessly but with lightning speed over its polished granite bed, making the preparatory run for its plunge over the Vernal Fall, form a combination of rare effects, leaving upon the mind an impression that years cannot efface. But the tourist is in a measure prepared. He has seen the engravings and photographic views, and read descriptions written by visitors who have preceded him. To us it was the opening of a sealed volume. Long we lingered and admiringly gazed upon the grand panorama, till the descending sun admonished us that we had no time to lose in making our way campward.

Our companions arrived long ahead of us. "Supper is waiting," announced the chief cook; "ten minutes later and you would have fared badly; for we are hungry as wolves."

"Reckon you've been loafing," chimed in another. "You should have been with us. We struck a fall away up at the head of the cañon, about four hundred feet high."

"Have you? We saw your little old four hundred-foot fall and go you four hundred better"—and then we proceeded to describe our trip, and the discovery which was its result.

The boys wouldn't have it. None of them were professional sports, but they would hazard a little on a horse-race, a turkey-shooting, or a friendly game of "draw"—filling the elegant definition of the term "gambler" as given by one of the fraternity, viz.: "A gentleman who backs opinion with coin." Connor was the most voluble. He got excited over it, and made several rash propositions.

"Tell me," said he, "that you went further up the cañon than we did? We went till we butted up against a perpendicular wall which a wild cat couldn't scale. The whole Merced River falls over it. Why, a bird couldn't fly beyond where we went. Of course, you think you have been further up the river, but you are just a little bit dizzy. I'll go you a small wad of gold-dust that the fall you have found is the same as ours."

Connor was gently admonished to keep his money—to win it was like finding it in the road—nay, worse; it would be downright robbery—but to make the thing interesting we would wager a good supper—best we could get in camp, with the "trimmings"—upon our return home, that we had been higher up the cañon, and that our fall beat theirs in altitude. It was further agreed that one of us should accompany the party as guide.

"Better take along a rope—it might help you over the steep places," was a portion of our advice, adding by way of caution to "hide it away from Connor" when they returned, for "he would feel so mean that he would want to hang himself."

To Pearson, who was ambitious to show off his qualities as a mountain guide, was delegated the leadership—an arrangement which was mutually satisfactory—"Milt" agreeing with me that a day's rest would be soothing and helpful. Besides, we had laid a plan involving a deep strategy to capture some of those immense trout, of which we had occasional glimpses, lying under the bank, but which were too old and cunning to be beguiled with the devices of hook and line.

The plan was carried out, on both sides, to a successful issue. On our part, we secured two of the largest trout ever caught in the valley, and had them nicely dressed, ready for the fry-pan, when our companions returned, which was about sunset. Soon as they came within hailing distance, their cheerful voices rang out (Connor's above all the rest), "We give it up!" They were in ecstasies, and grew eloquent in praise of the falls and scenery, at the same time paying us many compliments.

A courier was dispatched to notify the Mariposa party of our discovery. It was a surprise to them, but they had made their arrangements to leave for home early the next morning. They regretted the necessity, but business arrangements compelled their departure.

Upon the return of our party to San Francisco, the writer, being in pleasant intimacy with the late Rev. W. A. Scott, D.D., and family, paid them a visit, when the subject of the scenery of the Yo Semite was discussed, and sketches shown. The doctor manifested remarkable interest in the theme, and added: "Mr. H., I am badly in need of a vacation, and if I can induce a number of my friends to join me, I should like very much to visit such a marvelous locality. I shall esteem it a personal favor to myself if you will dine with us at an early day, on which occasion I will invite a few intimate friends to join us, and discuss the subject of visiting that astonishingly magnificent creation." This invitation was cordially accepted, and in due time and order the proposed dinner party assembled, when the matter was thoroughly canvassed, and a company formed for making the journey. On the evening of their arrival in Mariposa, on the way up, it was their good fortune to meet some of the members of the Mariposa party, just returned from Yo Semite; from these additional information was received, and timely suggestions made, born of recent experiences. The Indian guides, Kos-sum and So-pin, having satisfactorily conducted themselves on each former occasion, and being now at liberty, were reëngaged by the Scott party. After a very satisfactory and soul-satisfying jaunt, Dr. Scott, upon his return to San Francisco, gave several eloquent discourses, and published some tersely written articles upon it. His magnetic enthusiasm largely contributed to the development of an interest in the minds of the public, to witness such sublime scenes as those he had so graphically portrayed. From that day to this the great valley has been visited—and by tens of thousands; but *this was the inauguration of tourist travel to Yo Semite.*

In October, 1855, was published a lithographic view of the Yo Semite Fall (then called *Yo-Ham-i-te*), from the sketch taken for the writer by Mr. Thomas Ayres, in the preceding June, and which was the first ever pictorial representation of any scene in the great valley ever given to the public.

CHAPTER VIII.

ITS EARLY DEVELOPMENT AND PROGRESS.

Though varying wishes, hopes, and fears,
Fevered the progress of those years,
Yet now, days, weeks, and months, but seem
The recollection of a dream.
—SCOTT'S *Marmion, Canto IV.*

There is no life of a man, faithfully recorded, but is a heroic poem of its sort.
—CARLYLE'S *Essays.*

The west yet glimmers with some streaks of day;
Now spurs the lated traveler apace,
To gain the timely inn.
—SHAKESPEAR'S *Macbeth, Act III.*

As time rolled on, delighted visitors kept flocking to Yo Semite. The dangerous roughness, and uncertainty of the old Indian trails (where there were any), or the inconveniences and discomforts of open-air life, in no way deterred or discouraged them. This induced two enterprising brothers, Milton and Houston Mann, in 1856—who had formed a portion of the Sherlock's Creek party the preceding year—to survey and construct a new horse path from "Clark's," on the south fork of the Merced, to the valley. This was completed in August, 1856, and opened as a toll trail. Proving unremunerative as such, it was subsequently sold to the county of Mariposa, at about one-third of its cost, and made free. Every visitor that has passed over this trail in early days will call to pleasant memory the unpretentious hospitality and comfort of the wayside inn known as "Peregoy's;" and never forget the emotions evoked by the magnificent view of the distant Sierras from "the meadows," or the inexpressively impressive scenes from "Inspiration Point," and "Mt. Beatitude." Now, these are seldom seen except by sheep and cattle herders, who

(98)

make the succulent pastures of these mountain steppes a place of temporary refuge for themselves and flocks, during the summer months.

CONSTRUCTION OF OTHER TRAILS.

The liberal patronage coming from the public to hotel keepers, livery men, and others upon the line of travel from Mariposa to Yo Semite, became a strong incentive to the businessmen of Coulterville and Big Oak Flat to seek similar advantages for themselves. Accordingly, mountaineers were sent among the forest solitudes beyond those settlements, trails surveyed, built, and soon thronged with expectant pilgrims on their way to the new Mecca of scenic devotion. About this time, moreover, the newly discovered "diggings" of Mono (now included in the Bodie Mining District) were attracting great attention from miners and traders, and very naturally intensified the interest in all such enterprises, and stimulated their rapid completion. Scarcely a turn could be made upon either of these routes without revealing some wonderful picture of majesty or beauty.

In the earliest infancy of trail travel to Yo Semite,

ALL HAD TO CAMP OUT.

And to many there was, and still is, a peculiar charm about camp-life in the country that is unknown and unexperienced in the world's crowded thoroughfares. The absence of certain civilized formulas and restraints; its freedom from ordinary cares; its opportunities for buoyant dilatation and cheerfulness; its constantly recurring changes; its tendencies to develop the best (and, sometimes, the worst) of human qualities; its resultant trending to fearlessness; its uniform healthiness, in a climate like that of California, and especially in the mountains; and, certainly not among the smallest of these considerations, is its uniform economy (and which, in these latter days, is by no means the least), unite to make "camping out" one of the most invigorating and enjoyable of divertisements. But successful camping out is "a fine art," and it is not every one that can efficiently manage, or successfully conduct it. A few hints upon this will be found in a future chapter.

An "overwhelming majority" of tourists, however, do not like to camp out. Some there are who could not if they would; and there are others who would not if they could. For these, therefore, hotel accommodations became desirable.

PIONEER HOTEL BUILDING AT YO SEMITE.

To meet such emergencies, a very primitive kind of a house, the frame of which consisted of pine poles—some of them set in the ground to form posts—and the covering of "shakes," or "boards," riven from logs of pine, its gable, or triangular end, forming the front, was commenced in the fall of 1856, near the location known as "Black's," by Messrs. Anderson, Ramsdell, Coward, and Walsworth; but which was not finished that year.

Almost simultaneously with these movements, Mr. S. M. Cunningham and Mr. Buck Beardsley formed a co-partnership for hotel and trading purposes at Yo Semite, and started for the valley; but a heavy snow-storm compelling a retreat, they cached their tools and supplies, and returned to their old residence on Bull Creek, to spend the winter. Early the following March, they again set their faces for Yo Semite, where they arrived March 17, 1857. As Beardsley had to return with the pack-mules, Cunningham was left entirely alone. This latter remark may need a little qualification, inasmuch as he was surrounded by a large band of Indians, who, on account of a bounteous acorn crop the preceding fall (acorns forming the Indian staple of bread-stuff), had made an unusually early visit this year. But these gave him no trouble.

Cunningham and Beardsley erected a "shake" cabin* just above the other location, and at once commenced business. These, eventually, buying out the interests of the others above named, finished the building commenced by them, and occupied it. During the winter of 1857–58 the heavy snows broke down the new building, and constrained the erection of another more substantial, in

* Afterwards temporarily occupied by Mr. T. Hill, Mr. W. Keith, Mr. Virgil Williams, and other artists.

1858. This was opened and kept, for S. M. Cunningham (who had separated his business connection with Mr Beardsley in the fall of 1857), by Mr. and Mrs. John H. Neal, who thus became

THE FIRST HOTEL KEEPERS AT YO SEMITE.

The following seasons of 1859–60 it was kept by its owner, Mr. Cunningham. In 1861, these premises were sold to Mrs. A. G. Black—then living at Bull Creek—who rented it to Mr. P. Long-hurst, and others; and, in after years, to Mr. G. F. Leidig, until occupied by her husband and herself, in 1869, by whom it was taken down to make way for other much-needed improvements. Not a vestige now remains of this pioneer structure to mark the spot where it stood. Unassuming and simple as it was, many eminent persons, known to fame, once found shelter beneath its humble roof.

After Beardsley's co-partnership with Cunningham had ceased, he united with Mr. G. Hite—brother to the successful miner and millionaire, Mr. John Hite, of "Hite's Cove"—when, in the fall of 1857, they commenced the business of hotel keeping and trading, in a blue tent, while preparing the timbers for the building now known as

THE OLD HUTCHINGS HOUSE.

As this was much more commodious than the other, its construction was necessarily attended with more difficulties and expense; especially where everything had to be "created"—so to speak—upon the spot, or brought fifty miles on pack-mules. As there was no saw-mill for their needed supply of lumber, every board or plank, rafter or joist, had to be hewed, or cut out by whip-saw. These primitive contrivances took time as well as money, so that the new structure could not be utilized for visitors until May, 1859. Soon after its formal opening, Mr. C. L. Weed, the pioneer photographer of Yo Semite, Rev. F. C. Ewer and family, Miss M. Neill, and the writer, were among its first guests. The accompanying illustration is from the first photograph ever taken in Yo Semite, and by C. L. Weed, in June, 1859.

Owing to a heavy indebtedness incurred in building the hotel, and the lack of success in attending the first "Fourth of July Party" given, for which extensive preparations had been made, and from which much had been expected, its projectors and builders, unable to meet their obligations, assigned it to creditors for their protection. The following two years it was leased to Mr. Charles Peck, then to Mr. P. Longhurst, after which it was either let temporarily, or remained closed, until purchased by the writer in 1864.

In this connection it may be remarked that at that time the land here was a part of the public domain of the United States, and as such was considered to be open to preemption and settle-ment under the Pre-emption Laws of the United States. Being unsurveyed, however, as no regular plot could be filed of any given portion of it in the United States Land Office, its loca-tion, giving metes and bounds, was entered upon the records of the county, and such

THE OLD HUTCHINGS HOUSE.

entry was interpreted as a legal guarantee of title, until surveyed by the United States, and in the market. Under this impression settlements were made, titles respected, and frequent transfers of such title given from one to the other, without their validity being questioned. And it is a matter of historical interest to state that, at one time (about 1860), an enterprising citizen secured nearly the whole of such titles, and put them all into a "Grand Lottery Scheme," for the purpose of raffling off the entire valley to the "lucky winner." But a "justifiable" number of tickets not having been sold, most of the money (as his enemies assert) was (un)returned, and the speculation abandoned.

The Old Hutchings House (the Upper Hotel). This was the second photograph
made in Yosemite Valley—in June 1859—and the first to show a building and
people. The engraving on the opposite page was made from this photograph.

The Lamon Cabin, built in 1859 and still standing when Fiske was photographing
in Yosemite in the 1870s and 1880s. The engraving on page 136 was made from this
photograph. No doubt the decision to use this illustration as an engraving rather
than a photograph was dictated by the fact that the cabin is quite dark and the
foreground and background are very light—and the photo-typo process would
not produce a good result. Fiske #509.

Photo. by S. C. Walker.   Photo-Typo by Britton & Rey, S. F.

THE YO SEMITE FALL—CHO-LOCK—DURING HIGH WATER.
With "reflections."
Facing page 176 in edition one. Facing page 178 in all other editions.

CHAPTER IX.

ITS FIRST WINTER VISITOR.

The blood more stirs
To rouse a lion than to start a hare.
—Shakespear's *Henry IV., Part I., Act I.*

I argue not
Against Heaven's hand or will, nor bate a jot
Of heart or hope; but I still bear up and steer
Right onward.
—Milton's *Sonnet.*

God tempers the wind to the shorn lamb.
Sterne's *Sentimental Journey.*

That inestimable of earthly blessings called "health," having given unerrable premonitions of early departure, from more than one member of our little home circle, the family physician was duly consulted, who gave emphatic enunciation to the opinion that unless we left the city at an early day, we should soon do so from the world; we concluded the former journey—being the shortest, best known, and upon the whole pleasantest to take, for the present—would be the most desirable. This point satisfactorily determined, without a single "if" or "but," the question naturally presented itself, "Where can we go?" Resolving ourselves into a "Committee of Consultation," the "pros" and "cons" of different localities were considered, when its feminine members unequivocally expressed their decided preferences for Yo Semite. Now, is it not a reasonable question to ask any man "not set in his ways," if there would be more than one course left him, under the circumstances, and that one "immediate and unconditional surrender"—especially when in perfect concert with his own predilections and convictions? So, Yo Semite was chosen. Another and equally pertinent inquiry now interposed, "What

(103)

can we do after our arrival there?" We could not support physical life on scenery, sublimely beautiful as it unquestionably was! What then? It was true we had some means, but to live upon and absorb them, in comparative indolence, or unproductive personal occupation, was as repellent to every ennobling intuition as it was adverse to provident business foresight. This momentous conundrum, therefore, was propounded to the ladies, and was instantly met with another, "Why cannot we keep hotel?" Why, indeed! There was at least one condition in our favor, not knowing anything about such a business we possessed the usual qualifications for conducting it. This was something! Learn it? Certainly. Of course we could; but what were the much-tried public to do in the unpleasant interim? Yes, it is very easy to answer, "Do as we would do, and as they have always done. Try your best; take the best that you can find; and make the best of what you get." But good meals, well cooked, and pleasantly served, with clean-bed accompaniments, are always preferred by the public to either philosophy or argument.

All objections being gracefully overruled, it was decided that in the early spring we should move all our earthly goods, ourselves, and household gods, to Yo Semite, and there enter into the mysterious and unthankful calling of "hotel keepers." Accordingly, our books, chinaware, and other dispensable articles, were carefully packed, at leisurable intervals, so as to anticipate possible hurry at the start. The sky of our future was not only filled with beatified castles, but was brilliant with the prismatic colors of Hope; and, although

> "Hope, like the gleaming taper's light,
> Adorns and cheers our way;
> And still, as darker grows the night,
> Emits a brighter ray."[1]

At this particular season of day-dreaming expectancy

A CLOUD SWEPT ACROSS OUR HORIZON,

Brought by that ill-omened and unprincipled old storm-fiend known as Dame Rumor, who asseverated, with untold assurance,

1. Oliver Goldsmith, *The Captivity, An Oratorio.*

that "no one could ever make a permanent winter home in Yo Semite, inasmuch as snow from the surrounding mountains drifted into it, as into a deep railroad-cut, and filled it half full," and as its granite walls were from three thousand three hundred to six thousand feet in height, the half of that amount, in snow banks, under the most liberal provision—even including a generous supply for fashionable drinks—might well be deemed excessive for the ordinary purpose of residence there in winter, notwithstanding its admitted value, in reasonable quantities, for snow-shoe evolutions. There could be no doubt of the tenability of these deductions from such premises. No one could be found who had ever been there in winter, therefore no one could be appealed to for the affirmation or contradiction of these stories from Madam Rumor. Therefore before accepting the responsibility of removing the family to such a spot, proof must be positive this way or the other. But one path seemed open for making it so, and duty impelled me to take it, and it was this,—

AN EXPLORATORY WINTER JAUNT TO YO SEMITE.

On the afternoon of the first day of January, 1862, therefore, although vast banks of clouds had, for several days, been drifting up from the south and indicated an approaching rain, the home valedictory was spoken, and departure made by steamboat for Stockton. There were no railroads here in those days. On the following morning, January 2, a seat was secured upon the out-going stage, to a ranch some few miles out, where my horse was kept, and whence I soon started on my mystery-resolving expedition.

Before many miles had been traversed, the threatened rain began to fall, heavily, and to compel a shelter in the nearest wayside house. This was continued for the whole of that day, and the next, and the two days following. A few hours' suspension of hostilities on the fifth day enabled me to again renew the journey. But this time, however, all the shallow hollows across the road had been converted into deep streams, and the ravines into rushing torrents. The difficulty, if not danger of fording these swollen

NOW, FOR ANOTHER START.

streams suggested necessary delay for their subsidence; and the expense of horse-keeping, the desirability of returning him to the ranch, and continuing the trip afoot. Carrying out these presumptive conjectures and chafing at the long prolonged freaks of the warring elements, frequent efforts at progress were attempted, during every cessation of the down-pour. Passing on from one way-side inn to another, during brief intermissions of the storm, and by frequent wadings of water-courses up to the chin, Coulterville, seventy-one miles from Stockton, was finally reached on the evening of the seventeenth day from the latter city! This, verily, was the "pursuit of knowledge under difficulties."

STORM BOUND.

Nor was this other than the beginning of the end, inasmuch as the inundating rain kept pouring down for five successive addi-

tional days; and news arrived of the sweeping away of bridges
and ferry-boats; the tearing up of roads, and the discontinuation
of stage and mail communication; the floating off of houses, and
the general flooding of the valleys. By natural reasoning, therefore, the inquiry enforced consideration, "If these are the doings
of the storm within the boundaries of civilized settlements, what
must they not have been beyond their confines in the mountains?"
Ought a reluctance to acknowledge defeat be allowed to resist the
teachings of common prudence? Who could accomplish impossibilities? Why not return, and await a brightening prospect, for
its accomplishment?

> "When valor preys on reason,
> It eats the sword it fights with."

These considerations admonished postponement and regres-
sion. But how accomplish the latter, with all the ordinary avenues
of return closed up? Conferences with other storm-bound
travelers provided a way. We would accomplish it by water. There
could be no question about this method from quantitative
reasons. Four of us, therefore, united our energies and resources,
and dispatched one of our number to Merced Falls, on the Merced
River, to have a suitable boat constructed for

A VOYAGE DOWN THE MERCED.

Hearing of this, Mr. McKean Buchanan, well known to
histrionic fame in those days, who had, with his troupe, been
performing at "Snellings," upon the eve of this unusual effluence,
and been confined there ever since, desired to join us in our novel
method of exit. This was cheerily conceded, and the uncertain
cruise commenced. Nearly every man, woman, and child residing
near Snellings was present at our departure.

At this time the river upon which we were to venture had
largely overflowed its banks, was over a quarter of a mile in
width, and its waters had become a rushing, foaming torrent. But
out upon its angry bosom we pushed our little craft, and were
instantly hurried down it at the rate of about fifteen miles an
hour. Just before dusk, an immense gathering of drift had given a

sudden sweep to the surging stream, and forced us to a choice between two alternatives—either to jeopard the capsizing of our boat upon the drift, or risk its being swamped by shooting through a narrow opening in it, with an abrupt descent of nearly three feet, through which the water was precipitately plunging. We chose the latter, our steersman shouting, "Pull hard on the oars—pull with all your might;" and, fortunately, the passage was safely accomplished without shipping a quart.

A SHIPWRECK.

Not so, with our fellow-voyagers, however, who, fearing to follow us, had chosen the alternative we had declined, and their boat was overturned upon the drift. This happening far from the shore, and among numerous cross-currents, with darkness closing in, made deliverance impossible before morning. Here, then, they had to remain through the long night, in their wet clothing, without creature comforts, encompassed by surging rapids that might at any moment tear away their insecure foothold, and without knowledge of probable extrication, their boat having floated away.

As illustrative of the devastation caused by the present storm, it should here be mentioned, that on the very spot where we had moored our wherry, there formerly stood a handsome dwelling, surrounded by fertile gardens, and fruitful orchards; but now, the very soil, upon which they were so recently standing had been washed away, leaving a sad scene of sorrow-stirring desolation on every hand. The house furniture had been hastily removed, only in time to prevent its floating off with the house, and now lay scattered high upon the river's bank, exposed to the elements.

Our breakfast fire was kindled long before day-dawn, so as to be in readiness to render assistance at the earliest possible moment; and as its first gleams shot up into the darkness, cries for help that had died away with the fire on the previous night, were again most eagerly renewed. To us those cries were rejoicing music, as they assured us of the continued safety of those to whom we hoped soon to bear deliverance.

Climbing up the bluff bank that here bounded the river, so that we could overlook the watery waste below, and definitely ascertain the exact position of our imprisoned companions, and the best way of reaching them, we saw in the shadowy distance the forms of five men approaching, followed by troops of hogs! The foremost of the men proved to be the owner of the house and lands, once his possessions here, and who, with his assistants, had come to obtain some wet grain that was stored in the only building left, standing on an island of the river, from which to feed his hogs. When made aware of the circumstances of the case, he kindly tendered us assistance. Selecting two of his most trusty hands, after declining our proffered help, and preferring his own boat to ours, he launched out upon the rushing current, and was soon lost amid underbrush and whirling eddies.

ANOTHER SHIPWRECK.

But a few minutes had elapsed before there arose new cries for help, as this boat also had capsized, when its occupants narrowly escaped drowning. Now there were six to be rescued instead of three. Reinforcements for their succor must be obtained, and immediately. Dispatching two men in each direction, up and down the river, for this purpose, the two remaining prepared the boat for service, and investigated the water-swept country, so as to render efficient assistance when other help arrived. Appeal was not in vain; and, by three o'clock, all were at last delivered from their perilous position.

HOTEL ON A CRUISE.

As Buchanan's boat had been found upon a drift, we proposed to share our provisions and continue the voyage. To this, however, he would not listen. "No," said he, "I will return to my wife at Snellings. I would not, for the world, have any other lips than my own tell her the story of this great misfortune. Her nerves are so utterly unstrung by recent experiences that the shock would prove fatal to her. Why, sir, we were in the Snellings Hotel when the flood entirely surrounded us, and it. We felt the building moving, when my wife and daughter, with myself, took the precaution to climb an oak tree that stood by the porch; and just as we had reached it, the entire edifice, with all its contents, floated off, sir! In less than three-quarters of an hour after our deliverance, sir, from the tree, the tree itself was washed away. Then to add this to that sorrow, indiscreetly, would be altogether too much—too much—for her, I assure you, sir."

But, when returning, another mishap overtook him—he lost his way, and spent this night also a shelterless wanderer! Just before morning he saw an empty wagon, stalled in a muddy cross-road, and lay down in it to rest and sleep, but the cold awoke him as day was breaking, when he discovered this to be his own vehicle!—and only half a mile from town! Mr. Buchanan's first voyage down the Merced, therefore, would not be cherished as an altogether pleasant memory.

THE VOYAGE CONTINUED.

On the following day we continued our boating excursion down the Merced to its confluence with the San Joaquin River, spending the night in the second story of Hill's Ferry House, the first story being under water. But even here we were compelled to utilize the table tops for both cook-stove and chairs, and only the upper berths could be used for sleeping. A string north wind, blowing squarely in our faces, so much retarded our progress on the San Joaquin (then several miles wide in places) that six days of hard rowing were required to reach the city of Stockton, although only sixty miles distant. Here we gratefully left our boat for use among the streets of that city—then in a flooded condition—and secured passage on the outgoing steamboat for San Francisco; and which, owing to the very high stage of water, shot straight across the overflowed tule lands, instead of following the usual course of the river. Thus ended the first effort to explore the Yo Semite Valley in winter, and proved the aptness of Burns' sentiment (addressed to a mouse),

> "The best-laid schemes o' mice an' men,
>   Gang aft a-gley."

THE SECOND AND SUCCESSFUL ATTEMPT TO VISIT YO SEMITE IN
WINTER.

In the ensuing March, as the problem whether or not the
great Valley could be safely occupied as a place of residence in
winter, remained unsolved; and the same cloud of uncertainty still
hovered over our movements, and would so continue to do, unless
that theorem was resolved by actual demonstration, another
jaunt was accordingly planned, and this time *via* Mariposa. Here
two others volunteered to accompany me, as they also were
anxious to see the Yo Semite in her winter robes. Three of us,
therefore, set out on this pilgrimage. Colonel Fine, of Mormon
Bar, kindly loaned us a donkey to pack our necessary stores to the
snow-line, beyond which each man had to be his own pack animal.
At Clark's—now called "Wawona"—we were hospitably entertained by its owner, who was one of our party. Here the unsettled
weather detained us for three days. On the fourth we shouldered
our loads and set out. A brighter morning never dawned. That
evening we camped in about ten inches of snow; but this was soon
cleared away; and, around a large camp-fire, many stories were
told to beguile away the hours.

Early on the morrow we were again upon our course—the
trail being covered up. About nine o'clock, snow had deepened to
the knees, and every step was one requiring effort. A fatiguing
climb of one snow-covered mountain spur but revealed another,
and, still beyond, another; the silvery covering increasing in
depth as we advanced. At length one of our companions dropped
his pack, and himself upon it, at the same instant, exclaiming, "I'll
be danged [he never swore] if I go any further. I know we can
never get through. Besides, this is too much like work for me [but
few more industrious men ever lived]. I propose that we all go
back, and wait until some of this snow melts off." To this my other
companion gave reluctant concurrence.

At this crisis of affairs another consideration enforced itself
upon our attention: How could the *winter* status of the Valley be
ascertained if we waited until spring or summer came? This was

intended as a convincing argument to induce a forward movement; but, to make a long story as short as possible, my two
companions could not be persuaded to go on, nor the writer to
turn back—his mission still unaccomplished. This left but one
alternative—

HE MUST ATTEMPT THE PERILOUS JOURNEY ALONE.

The increasing depth of snow, the solitude of its forest
wastes, the absence of all traces of a trail, utter helplessness in
case of accident, its unavoidable fatigue and exposure, danger
from wild animals, and possible sickness,—all of these, while
meriting due solicitude, ought not to deter or hinder him from
treading the path of duty. Certainly no man, worthy of so honored an appellation, would for a moment hesitate at such a crisis,
where the safety of an entire family depended upon his present
movements. No. He must do the best that became his manhood,
and leave its results to the one higher Power. While he could not
blame the others, who were without the pale of such respon-
sibilities, for returning, he must press on to the goal desired.

Packs were therefore readjusted; about fifteen days' rations
secured; blankets, overcoat, ax, and other sundries tied snugly
up; and, after a cheery good-bye to my companions, I started
out—alone. There is still a pleasant memory treasured of their
kindly and long-lingering farewell look, when passing out of
sight—and, as they thought, forever. For several hours after
departure from my companions, a feeling of extreme loneliness
and isolation crept over me, so that the sight and voice of a
chattering tree-squirrel was a real relief; but this soon passed
away. The most trying test of endurance was from the constantly breaking crust of frozen snow, that grew deeper at almost
every step, and dropped me suddenly down among bushes from
which I had again to climb with fatiguing effort, while realizing
the uncertain tenure of my foothold after the surface had been
gained; thus demoralizing one's clothing and incising his flesh,
while taxing both strength and patience to get out again.

SIX DAYS, ALONE, IN THE SNOW.

In this manner six wearying days were passed, not walking merely in or over snow, but wallowing through it, and only averaging about one mile of actual distance per day. At night I slept where any friendly rock or tree offered its reviving shelter. Just as darkness was about to lower down its sable curtain, there being no place of rest or refuge visible in all that snowy waste, and excessive fatigue had seemingly made further progress impossible, I dropped my pack (now grown very heavy) and sat upon it, to write a few loving words to the dear ones at home— possibly the last—before the fast deepening twilight, and increasing chilliness, had forever banished the opportunity; thinking, also, that when the melting snows of spring had fed the rills, some kindly feet would perhaps wander in search of or for whatever remained of the lonely traveler, and thus find the memoranda. The entry finished, upon looking up I saw that the clouds which had previously draped the forest and the mountain, so that the limit of vision was only a few yards off, had lifted and drifted among the tree-tops, so that from my resting place I could look down some three thousand feet upon the river, where to my ineffable joy I could see green grasses growing, and flowers blooming—and no more snow! It was

A LOOK INTO PARADISE.

Tired? Oh! dear no! Before this strength-giving sight, it seemed utterly impossible to advance another quarter of a mile, even to save one's life. But, now, the pack was again shouldered, and, "like a giant refreshed with wine," long and rapid strides were made down the mountain ridge, to the promised land, which was reached about an hour after dark. Out of the snow, the muscle-testing, patience-trying snow! I thanked God with a grateful heart. I have often thought since, that the most gifted of singers could never make the song of "The Beautiful, Beautiful Snow" attractive to me. Even when sweetly sleeping that night, beneath the protecting arms of an out-spreading live-oak tree I forgot all my troubles, but one—the snow, the snow, the unfeeling, the never-yielding, the ever-bullying snow. For months afterwards, in my dreams, it was a ghost-shadow, in white—a ghost that would not be "laid"—and was always present.

Awaking on the morrow my gladdened eyes at first looked, doubtingly, on these new surroundings; but, when thoroughly satisfied they were not the creations of an exuberant fancy, a spring of unalloyed, full-hearted, grateful joy began to well up within me, and one that has ever since kept flowing, whenever memory has brought those circumstances back again into review.

AN OBSTACLE AHEAD.

The frowning face of a lofty bluff, not far above my encampment, became suggestive of possible trouble in ascending the river, without crossing to the opposite side. This must be ascertained. Taking precautionary measures for insuring the safety of my limited supply of provisions, by tying them to the limb of a tree and allowing it to revert upwards, with ax in hand I started. Fears were soon verified by facts. There were but two alternatives left me: the northern bank of the foaming and angry river must be reached, or the snowy wastes above again sought. I had surely seen enough of the latter, and would therefore choose the former. A tall tree was selected for felling, and the ax applied; but such was the exacting tax upon physical strength for the last six days, that but a very small chip was returned for each stroke. Still, it was a chip; and, if I did not succumb to discouragement, every blow must ultimately tell, and compel the tree to fall, and form a bridge for my deliverance. About noon exhaustion compelled a short respite from labor, the soothing and renewing influences of refreshing sleep, and the replenishment of the inner man. On my way to my supplies, to my astonishment and momentary discomfiture, in the distance I saw a large animal of some kind, and that, too, beneath the very tree in which my limited stock of provisions was stored. A nearer approach disclosed the unwelcome presence of

A FULL GROWN GRIZZLY BEAR.

Candid confession must be made that this discovery was not a little startling at first, especially as my only weapons were an ax, and two limber limbs with which to run away, had I been in condition. What should I do? What could I do, but stand in safety behind a rock, and watch his movements? My usual self-possession soon returning, this could have been done with considerable interest and amusement, but for an anxious consideration for the safety of my supplies, to me invaluable under present circumstances. Bruin's grotesque and ludicrous antics, in his efforts to clutch them, for the moment absorbed all sense of danger, to either myself or my food, by their diverting clumsiness.

Now he would sit upon his haunches, apparently ruminating upon some plan that should successfully put him in possession of that which his keen sense of hunger scented from afar. Then he would rise upon his feet, and, by a side lunge, attempt to catch hold of a bough with his fore paw; simultaneously throwing the weight of his huge body upon the opposite hind foot, as though by this he hoped to stretch himself to the required length, to secure the much-coveted prize—but missed it every time. Unlike a passenger once seated at the dinner-table of a Mississippi steamboat, who, being curtly and surlily asked, by his fellow-passenger, "Can you reach that butter?" immediately stretched out his arm, as though about to comply, when he withdrew it, without passing the article in question, and answered, stutteringly, "Ye-ye-yes, I c-c-can j-j-just r-r-reach it!" There was this difference, then, between the gentleman and the butter, and the grizzly with the pack—one *could* reach it, and the other *could not.*

Finding his efforts still unrewarded, and the smell alone possibly being altogether too unsatisfying, he began to cast wistful glances at the trunk of the tree, and along its branches, as though cogitating upon the possibility of securing the coveted treasure by climbing the tree. Doubt evidently had changed to hope, for, dropping to his feet, he ran with a bound to the tree, and began to scramble up it. But, either his body was too heavy

CATHEDRAL SPIRES—POO-SEE-NA CHUCK-KA.

Lowest Spire, 2,579 Feet; Highest Spire, 2,678 Feet above Valley.

(See page 409.)

Fiske #416. Facing page 112 in edition one. A slightly different version
—probably Fiske #415 or #418—faced page 106 in editions two, three, and four.

Photo by Taber   Courtesy, The Bancroft Library

Cascade Falls.

(See page 401.)

Taber number B964. Facing page 96 in edition one. Facing page 98 in all other editions.

for its strength, or, there was an uncommendable lack of will-power—an occasional experience in similar forms of the *genus homo*—inasmuch as less than half of the height had been overcome, when he began to hesitate, then to back down. Fearing, however, that the pangs of hunger might provide bruin with sufficient intelligence to encompass their capture, and my dismay, I struck a rattling blow upon a large hollow log, accompanied with a loud shout; when, looking around towards the spot whence the noise proceeded, he started upon an ambling run in the opposite direction, and was soon lost in the distance. It may not be necessary here to aver that not a single arrow of sorrow pierced my heart at his abrupt departure.

After rest and refreshment, the attack was renewed upon the tree; and, about three o'clock that afternoon, it began to give premonitions of a downfall. As Mungo Park once said, when suffering with thirst upon the deserts of Africa, and heard the croaking of frogs, knowing that the sound was indicative of water being near, with gladness exclaimed, "It was heavenly music to my ears;" so was the cracking of that tree to me. Luckily it fell just right, and reached the other side. Creeping across it—I was too weak to walk it—I discovered signs of a dim and almost unused trail, passing up the northern bank of the river. This augured successful progress in the right direction.

Returning to camp, a fresh supply of bread was made up, and baked upon hot rocks in front of the fire, or upon dried sticks; and on the following day my journey was renewed. For three days I threaded my way among bowlders, creeping under or over, or lowering myself between them, or worked it through underbrush; but as there was no snow to encounter, and the close of each day showed encouraging progress, every indication was in favor of a hopeful *finale*. On the night of the third day in the river cañon, and the tenth of my lonely pilgrimage, I successfully gained the object of my earnest yearnings, and undiscouraged efforts. I had reached the Valley, and, with sympathetic Cowper, felt:—

"O scenes surpassing fable, and yet true
  Scenes of accomplished bliss; which who can see,
  Though but in distant prospect, and not feel
  His soul refresh'd with foretaste of the joy."

Especially after such experiences. Once here, and out of the unknown region wherein I had been a wanderer, every water-fall and mountain peak were dearly "familiar to me as household words." My heart seemed to leap with very joy. In spirit I metaphorically embraced them as well-known friends. Believe me, there was real felicity enjoyed at such a moment, for I was truly happy. And

"When the shore is won at last,
  Who will count the billows past?"

A grateful addition to my gladness of heart at reaching the desired goal was the discovery that snow did not interpose any insuperable obstacles to a safe residence in the grand old valley during winter—and that Dame Rumor, as usual, was in error. It is true there were numerous patches of snow, several feet in depth, hidden away in shady places; but nearly the entire surface of the valley was found to be free from it. This, the sole object of my eventful journey, being demonstrated beyond peradventure, after a brief rest, I left the valley on the eleventh day, and, about noon of the day following, arrived at a little quartz-mill, far down in the cañon of the Merced, where I once more looked upon a human face. I will leave others to guess, for they cannot fully realize, how delightfully welcome was that sight to me. If any one entertains a doubt of this, let him pass eleven days, alone, without it.

Upon the return of my companions to the settlements without me, and the story being told of my having started on through the deep snow, alone, there were gloomy forebodings expressed of my never again being seen, alive. Colonel Fine carefully treasured the note of thanks I had sent him for the use of his donkey, thinking to forward it to my friends, as possibly the last souvenir from me! In this they were fortunately disappointed.

CHAPTER X.

EARLY-DAY REVIEWALS.

Variety's the very spice of life,
That gives it all its flavor.
—Cowper's *Task, Book II.*

To-day is not yesterday; we ourselves change; how can our works and
thoughts, if they are always to be fittest, continue always the same?
—Carlyle's *Essays.*

There comes to me out of the Past
A voice, whose tones are sweet and wild,
Singing a song almost divine,
And with a tear in every line.
—Longfellow.

After the experiences narrated in the preceding chapter, a second visit was paid Yo Semite in the ensuing summer, for the purpose of a thorough examination of the valley, with reference to a suitable location for our proposed new home. The choice fell upon the site since generally known as "Hutchings';" and negotiations were commenced for purchasing the possessory right of two preëmption claims, of 160 acres each, out of which to establish one deemed the most desirable. Owing to sundry delays, from various causes, these were not consummated, and the improvements thereon acquired, until the spring of 1864, when terms were satisfactorily agreed upon; and we set out, with all our household and other wares, arriving, and taking possession, April 20th of that year—1864.

PRIMITIVE METHOD OF TRANSPORTING SUPPLIES.

At that time all our furniture, stores, tools, and other articles, had to be carried fifty miles on the backs of mules and horses. The pack-train was not only the connecting link between comfort and privation, but the interposing medium between plenty and star-

(118)

vation; consequently packing, from its necessities, was elevated into a science, the professors and experts of which were Mexican muleteers. The equal balancing of the pack, and the skillful fastening of it upon the animal, required knowledge, as well as practice and care. It was a serious matter to have a pack become loose, or one-sided, as this called not only

FASTENING ON THE PACKS.

for its re-adjustment, but, frequently, for re-packing. Then the delay thus caused brought other trouble, inasmuch

IN TROUBLE FROM A LOOSE PACK.

as while this was being cared for, the remaining animals of the train were loitering; when others would lie down to rest; and, either by an attempt to roll over, or in the effort to get up, so disarrange their load as to necessitate a repetition of

MEXICAN PERSUASION.

the service. This often became quite a severe tax upon the

packer's patience (time was seldom an object of consideration with representatives of this race in California), seldom an over-abundant article in the possession of a Mexican—and, it might be

PACK-TRAIN WHEN IN MOTION.

added, with people of other nationalities besides. Its lack too frequently developed excesses in temper, attended frequently with much brutality; and this very natural-ly reacted upon the animal's resentment of a wrong; and, possibly, gave rise to the ex-pression, "stubborn as a mule."

INTELLIGENCE OF MULES.

There is something very pleasing and picturesque in the sight of a large pack-train quietly ascending or descending a hill, as each animal care-fully examines the trail, and moves cautiously, step by step, espe-cially on a steep and dangerous declivity, as though he suspected danger to himself, or injury to his pack. This ia particularly noticeable on passing down a steep snow bank, when heavily packed; for, as they cannot step forward safely, they so dispose their feet, and brace their limbs, that they can, and do, unhesitatingly slide down it with their load, in perfect safety. I have seen a train of fifty do this. In some of the more remote settlements, the arrival of the pack-train was an event of importance only secondary to that of the expressman, or the mail-carrier; and its unpacking watched with as much eager interest as though it was expected that some old-time friend would emerge from between the packs.

ENORMOUS WEIGHTS PACKED BY MULES.

The average weights carried would generally range within two hundred and three hundred pounds; although, in some instances, they have been far in excess of this. When the *Yreka Herald* was about to commence publication, in 1852, a press was purchased in San Francisco at a cost of $600, upon which the freight alone amounted to $900. The "bed-piece" weighed three hundred and ninety-seven pounds, and, with the *aparajoes*, ropes, etc., exceeded four hundred and thirty pounds, which was the actual weight of the load. On descending Scott Mountain, the splendid animal carrying this load slipped a little, when the pack, overbalancing, threw the mule down a steep bank, and killed it instantly. In the fall of 1853 an iron safe, nearly three feet square, and weighing three hundred and fifty-two pounds, was conveyed on a very large mule, from Shasta to Weaverville, a distance of thirty-eight miles, and over a rough and mountainous trail, without an accident; but, after the load was taken off, the mule lay down, and died in a few hours. A reliable gentleman informed me that in 1855 two sets of millstones were packed from Shasta to Weaverville, the largest weighing six hundred pounds. Deeming it an impossibility for one mule to carry either, it was tried to "sling" one mill-stone between two animals; but that, proving impracticable, the plan was abandoned, and it was afterwards packed, safely, upon one!

KIND OF MULES PREFERRED.

Mexican mules were considered the most desirable, from their being accustomed to that work; and, having been less tenderly reared than the American, were less liable to disease. The Mexican mules, moreover, are credited with being tougher and stronger than the American; and can travel farther without food than any other quadruped. It is assumed also that this class of animals can carry a person forty miles per day, for ten or twelve consecutive days, and over a mountainous country; while it is difficult for an American mule to accomplish over twenty-five or thirty miles per day. Be this as it may, the Mexican prefers the mule of his own country to that of ours, because he considers the latter altogether too delicate for *his* use. There is another reason—and a very effective one with a Mexican—they can always be kept fat with little care, and less to eat, and that at irregular intervals; while the American mule, to do about half the amount of work, requires good food, regularly given, and to be otherwise well cared for. They seldom drink more than once on the warmest of days, unless their efforts are very exacting and prolonged. The average life of a mule is given at sixteen years; although California muleteers used to assert that "a mule never dies, but simply dries up."

A PROCESSION OF ODDITIES.

One used to be astonished at the singular variety of articles moving along on the backs of animals, such as buggies, windows, cart-wheels, wagon-sides, boxes, barrels, bars of iron, tables, chairs, bedsteads, plows, and mining tools; and not always with the greatest of safety. Once a rocking-chair and large looking-glass were sent us, but, when they reached their destination, the chair was broken into pieces, and the looking-glass resembled a crate of smashed crockery. On the second trip of our packer to Yo Semite, the entire train, frightened at some sight on the way, "stampeded;" when books and jellies, pictures and pickles, and other sundries, were all indiscriminately mixed together, or scattered in all sorts of places, by the roadside.

PRECAUTIONS ADOPTED BY PACKERS.

The Mexicans almost invariably blindfold each mule before attempting to pack it; after which he stands perfectly quiet, until the bandage is removed, no matter how unruly his behavior was before. A *mulatero* generally rides in front of the train for the purpose of stopping it, when anything goes wrong, and becomes a guide to the others; although in every band of horses or mules, there is always a leader, generally known as the "bell

THE PACK-TRAIN AT NIGHT.

mule," or horse—and it is not a little singular that nearly all mules prefer a white horse for that purpose—which they unhesitatingly follow the moment he starts, or wherever he goes, by day or by night.

When about to camp, the almost invariable custom of packers, after removing the goods (by which they always sleep in all kinds of weather), is for the mules to stand side by side, in a line or hollow square, with their heads in one direction, and each one in his customary place, before taking off the *aparajoes;** and, in the morning, when the train of loose mules is driven up from pasture, to receive their packs, every one walks up to his own *aparajoe* and blanket, with the precision of well-drilled soldiers, and rarely makes a mistake.

Notwithstanding the Mexican packer's seeming nonchalance, it is almost incredible the amount of danger and privation they uncomplainingly undergo, when exposed to the elements. This can be more clearly apprehended when the fact is presented that, during one severe winter, there was

A PACK-TRAIN SNOWED IN

Between Grass Valley, Nevada County, and Onion Valley, Sierra County, when, out of forty-eight animals, only three were taken out alive. The packers, unable to get firewood, narrowly escaped perishing, from being frozen to death. Their sufferings were indescribable; yet, when safely out of it, they only laughed at their experiences. On one occasion our pack-train was several hours belated; and, as snow had been falling in heavy flakes all the afternoon, every passing minute only increased our weight of anxiety for its safety. There was no use in further delay; for it must be sought after, and helped, if help was needed. Throwing the saddle across my horse, and taking some well-lined saddle-bags, I sallied out upon the storm. The animal's spirited movements proved her to be in perfect sympathy with the occasion, as

---

* An *aparajoe* is a kind of pack-saddle, or flattish pad, the covering of which is generally made of leather, and stuffed with hair. As they are considered safer and easier for the animal than the ordinary pack-saddle, they are always preferred by Mexicans, although their weight is from twenty-five to forty pounds.

though it was intuitively understood and appreciated. As deeper grew the snow, the stronger came the effort to overcome and conquer it, and that too with a conscious pride which seemed to rise in proportion to the difficulties to be surmounted. Those who

CARRYING DELIVERANCE.

could abuse such invaluable and noble servants ought never to have the privilege of owning or of using one.

On, on, we dashed, through the almost blinding snow, and, just before dusk, in the near distance, broke the welcome sight of the heavily-laden pack-train. With it was the anxious Mexican, earnestly engaged in the attempt to release a load from a fallen mule, whose foot had found a hole in the trail. When he saw me, his somber face became aglow with pleasure, and his tongue spontaneously found musical utterances of joy. As soon as the mule was set free, we both tried the possible good that might come from a good drink of *aguardiente;* and then, although the Mexican's hands were numb, and his limbs nearly stiff with cold, the pack was cheerily replaced, and we started for our home and shelter. Human help and brandy arrived just in time to save both man and beast. The most rabid advocate of "total abstinence," whose reason had not been dethroned, would, I think, concede the advantageous use of stimulants, at such a time, if only as a medicine. At least let us hope so, if only to accord to him the credit of possessing ordinary common sense.

CAUGHT IN A SNOW-STORM.

Upon relating the incident to the late Mr. Charles Nahl, who was unquestionably the best draftsman of animals upon the Pacific Coast, he made the accompanying sketch to illustrate it. At a glance it will be seen that the skill of the artist not only portrays the limbs of the mules in snow, but the determined efforts being made to get them out, in order to secure deliverance and safety for themselves, and riddance for their packs.

"IMPROVEMENTS" IN THE VALLEY.

These were found to be very limited, as they consisted of a two-story frame building, sixty by twenty feet, having two rooms, an upper and a lower. Its doors and windows were made of cotton cloth. Verily, a primitive beginning for novices in hotel keeping. When our first guests arrived (and their arrival caused quite a flutter in the household), the ladies were domiciled upstairs, and the gentlemen down. This arrangement we felt not only had its inconveniences, but was contrary to law, inasmuch as it sometimes separated man and wife. So novel a disposition of visitors, whose names, many of them at least, were already inscribed on the temple of fame, only became a subject for mirthfulness, never of censure. They saw that we were attempting our best—and the very best among us could do no more—and accepted it accordingly.

This, however solacing to our sensibilities, was not satisfying to our convictions. We determined upon changing it. But how? The nearest saw-mill was some fifty miles distant, and over a mountainous country, that was only accessible over steep and zigzagging trails. We knew that almost everything could be packed upon mules; we had even seen our donkey trotting along with two wagon-sides upon him, when only the tips of his ears and the lower part of his limbs were visible; but how could lumber be packed fifty miles? This, therefore, was given up as Quixotic. Bolts of muslin could be packed, and were; and rooms were accordingly made out of that. Guests, in this way, were thus provided with apartments, it is true; but, unless their lights were carefully disposed, there were also added unintentional shadow-pictures, which, if contributory of mirthfulness in a maximum degree, gave only a minimum degree of privacy in return. Better accommodations must be provided, no matter at what cost the lumber might be procured. Two men were accordingly engaged to run *a human saw-mill.*

This method of producing lumber is generally called "pit-sawing." Owing to the severity of the winter, the long absence of sunshine, and the difficulty of obtaining logs, less than fifteen hundred feet were cut that entire season. This set us to considering how many thousand years, more or less, would roll into the past, before an adequate stock of timber could be sawed for making the improvements absolutely necessary. Questioning the probability of so long an extension of life's lease, the irons for a young

SAW-MILL, TO RUN BY WATER,

Were procured from San Francisco, and a man employed to construct it, who professed thoroughly to understand just how to do it; but, when the finishing touches were about to be added, it was discovered that the thing wouldn't run at all; and, before the needful changes could be made, the water decreased so rapidly that even the testing of its capabilities were on the outside of the question. Unlike a prosy politician who, while making his speech, paused to take a drink of water, when his opponent started to his feet, and thus addressed the presiding officer: "Mr. Speaker, I rise to a point of order." "The member from —— will please to state his point of order." "My point of order is this, Mr. Speaker: Is it in order for the member from —— to attempt to run his *wind-mill* by *water?*" Whether that point of order was sustained or not (the fact being unrecorded), we knew that we had made a double discovery for ours; for it would not run either with or without water, and, although in possession of a saw-mill, we were as far off as ever from a supply of lumber.

When the richly colored leaves of autumn were being picked off rapidly by the nightly freezing fingers of the frosty air, and the wind in frolicsome gustiness had begun to drop them sportively on shady pools, or in running streams, or to pile them playfully in eddies, and hide them cautiously in sequestered corners, business in Yo Semite had become as quiet and subdued as nature is after a storm—

> "And only soft airs and sweet odors arise,
> Like the evening incense that soars to the skies"—

And this suggested the present as a propitious season for renewing our attempts at improvements. In this mood the saw-mill was revisited, and its possibilities reconsidered. An inexperienced examination revealed a serious error in its construction, inasmuch as the water, when the gate was lifted, rushed to the axle, instead of to the outer edge of the buckets in the driving wheel, and inundated it. No wheel could work under such conditions. It must be changed; but how? when? and by whom? My knowledge of mechanics was about as limited as that on hotel keeping. There was one comforting reflection stepped in to my assistance,—it was of no earthly use as it stood, therefore, its loss, should it be utterly spoiled, would only be nominal. I would try to correct the error so strikingly manifest. Tools were therefore brought, and the apparently desirable change made.

"EUREKA."

Fortunately a heavy rain came, opportunely, to enable me to make a testing experiment. Timidly and cautiously lifting the gate, a little water was admitted to the wheel. It turned briskly round. An additional quantity promptly increased its speed. With joy, although alone, I shouted, "Eureka!" Lumber might yet be obtained from it. Carefully setting and filing the mill-saw—my first attempt—a small log was fastened in its place, and the mill started. To my joyful surprise the cut was completed to the end without stopping. Again the word "Eureka" was on my lips, but was arrested by the thought—"Is it straight and true?" It was. At this twofold success a boisterous shout of exultation at once relieved my joyous feelings. One cut continued to be successfully made after another; so that when the day closed, there was one-fourth as much lumber sawed, single-handed, as the two men had made in a whole winter! Day by day the quantity produced increased so encouragingly that we felt justified in employing a good practical sawyer, and with him a couple of carpenters, so that the much-needed improvements could be commenced with satisfactory earnestness, and presumptive hope of ultimate and early realization. It was a "one-horse" saw-mill that opened to us the gold discovery.

PROGRESS TOWARD COMFORT.

The ring of the hammer and soft rasping sound of the saw now added their music to that of the water-fall and singing pines, and cloth partitions soon became numbered among the make-shifts of the past. The old house was rejuvenated by porches, and made convenient by lean-to's, in which were kitchen, store, and sitting-room—now known as "The Big Tree Room;" about which, and its associations and stories, more will be said hereafter. Buildings, made necessary by the rapidly increasing throng of tourists, began to spring up as though by magic, and no sooner was one completed and occupied than another was required. The return home of one party of visitors, mentally full to overflowing with praises concerning the wonderful sights they had seen, super-induced others to seek similar delights. As illustrative and demonstrative of this, the following carefully prepared table is herewith submitted, of

TOURIST TRAVEL TO YO SEMITE.

From 1855 to 1864, a period of nine years, the aggregate number of visitors to the valley was 653.

In 1864 147
In 1865 it increased to 369
In 1866 it increased to 438
In 1867 it increased to 502
In 1868 it increased to 623
In 1869 (the year the overland railroad was completed) it increased to 1,122
In 1870 it increased to 1,735
In 1871 it increased to 2,137
In 1872 it increased to 2,354
In 1873 it increased to 2,530
In 1874 it increased to 2,711
In 1875 it decreased to 2,423
In 1876 it decreased to 1,917
In 1877 it decreased to 1,392
In 1878 it decreased to 1,183
In 1879 it increased to 1,385
In 1880 it increased to 1,897
In 1881 it increased to 2,173
In 1882 it increased to 2,525
In 1883 it increased to 2,831
In 1884 it decreased to 2,408
In 1885 it increased to 2,590
In 1886 it increased to . . . . over 4,000.

By this it will be seen that previous to our advent there, for permanent residence, in 1864, the full complement of visitors, as compiled from the registers of that period, was 653. Those unregistered would probably swell the number to about seven hundred—in nine years. It is also interesting to note that the total number for 1864 was 147; and this included every man, woman, and child that entered it, of whatsoever color or condition.

INFLUENTIAL HELPERS.

The table here presented will also show the steady increase in numbers from year to year, as a knowledge of its marvelous grandeur was disseminated by returning visitors, by newspaper and book eulogiums, by photographs and paintings, and by lectures. Nor will justice to the earnest first workers in this deeply interesting field, both in literature and art, permit me to omit such names as Horace Greeley, Samuel B. Bowles, Albert D. Richardson, Charles L. Brace, Prof. J. D. Whitney, Dr. W. A. Scott, Rev. Thos. Starr King, and a host of others, whose books, newspaper articles, and lectures, contributed so largely to extend the fame of the great Valley: Or of C. L. Weed, its pioneer photographer, and C. E. Watkins, who had no superior in photographic art, and whose excellent prints have found their way to every corner of civilization. And, though last, by no means least, must be mentioned such eminent artists as A. Bierstadt, Thos. Hill, William Keith, Thos. Moran, P. Munger, A. Hertzog, and many more whose paintings have so much contributed to the public appreciation of its sublime scenic wonders. In subsequent times, and additional to the above, should be included the successful labors of Benj. F. Taylor, Helen Hunt (Jackson), Mary E. Blake, and a multitude of other writers: Thos. Houseworth, Geo. Fiske, Taber, J. J. Reilly, S. C. Walker, G. Fagersteen, and other photographers: C. D. Robinson, R. D. Yelland, Holdridge, and other artists—and all worthy helpers in advancing its renown.

NEED FOR INDIA-RUBBER ADAPTABILITY.

At the commencement of this encouraging influx of tourists, our utmost accommodations, primitive as they were, were limited to enough for twenty-eight. On one occasion, when every room was occupied, and just as all were about retiring for the night, the muffled tread of horses, mingled with the sound of human voices, was heard upon the outside. To our dismay we learned that a party of eleven had just arrived! What could be done, when every sleeping-place already had its occupant? Dumbfounded with surprised regret, the situation was explained to the new arrivals.

"Cannot take care of us, did you say?"

"That is really the case, as every bed we have has now a tenant."

"But, what *can* we do, Mr. H.? We are all tired out—especially the ladies—and there is no other place where we can go?" (at that time ours was the only inn at Yo Semite.)

"Such an inquiry I know is very pertinent at such a time. Well, come in, and we will do the best we can to make you comfortable. Impossibilities must be made possible under such circumstances."

"Thank you—and God bless you."

These glad tidings were soon communicated with an exultant shout to those outside, and "three cheers" from the tired travelers rung out upon the silent midnight air, sufficiently loud to awaken the now surprised sleepers. Fortunately a bale of new California blankets had been received but a few days before, and with these we improvised both beds and covering. Provisions were abundant.

While supper was progressing with commendable zeal, and apparent satisfaction, new sounds seemed to be floating on the darkness, and the astounding revelation came with them of the arrival of eight others! Good heavens! why India-rubber contrivances would be inadequate for such emergencies. Any number of queries at best, however, would prove but indifferent substitutes for bedding and food. These, too, must be cared for, in some way. And they were. The antiquated proverb, "It never rains but it pours," now became strikingly illustrated; for, before morning dawned, other arrivals had increased the number of guests to fifty-seven! twenty-eight, be it remembered, being the maximum limit in accommodation. The most remarkable feature of this then unparalleled advent of visitors remains to be told: Twenty-seven departures occurred one morning, nineteen the following, the next day every one of the remainder left us, and but five persons, altogether, arrived at Yo Semite in thirty-one days thereafter! Such experiences are by no means proportionally infrequent in hotel life here, even at this present day.

As time gently lifted its misty veil new revelations of majesty and beauty were almost constantly being added to the already comprehensive galaxy of wonderful sights, and the necessities of the hour called for the surveying and constructing of horse-paths to these newly discovered scenic standpoints. Bridges were built, and wagon roads made passable on the floor of the valley, to subserve the convenience of those who were unable to enjoy the exhilarating exercise of horse-back riding. This progressive development, moreover, was, at that day, accomplished entirely by private enterprise.

In due season new hotels sprung up into existence; and, in addition to "the butcher and baker, and the candlestick maker," came the store, the blacksmith's shop, laundry, bath and billiard rooms, cabinet shop for Yo Semite-grown woods, and other con veniences needed by the incoming visitor.

As the history of Yo Semite, for nearly a quarter of a century, has been so closely interwoven with the filaments and threads of one's own life, it makes it difficult to draw the line of demarkation between that which should be introduced, and such as ought to be omitted. In this, as in several other matters, I hope to bespeak the reader's discriminating sympathy and kindly forbearance should any desirable facts be unrecorded, or undesirable ones find a place.

CHAPTER XI.

CABIN HOMES AT YO SEMITE.

You must come home with me and be my guest;
You wilt give joy to me, and I will do
All that is in my power to honor you.
                    —SHELLEY'S *Hymn to Mercury.*

No little room so warm and bright,
Wherein to read, wherein to write.

                                        —TENNYSON.

The glorious Angel, who was keeping
The gates of light, beheld her weeping;
And, as he nearer drew and listen'd
To her sad song, a tear-drop glisten'd
Within his eyelids, like the spray
From Eden's fountain, where it lies
On the blue flow'r, which—Bramins say—
Blooms nowhere but in Paradise.
            —MOORE'S LALLA ROOKH—*Paradise and the Peri.*

There are probably not many persons, even when philosophically predisposed, who can fully comprehend the possibility of comfort and contentment in such an isolated locality as Yo Semite, for a home in winter as well as in summer, unless in unison with the sentiments of Euripides, that,

> "Not mine
> This saying, but the sentence of the sage
> 'Nothing is stronger than necessity.'"

But if to this be added a suggestive stanza from Mary Howitt:

> "In the poor man's garden grow,
>   Far more than herbs and flowers,
>   Kind thoughts, contentment, peace of mind,
>   And joy for weary hours,"

There may be disclosed the soothing sedative of resignation to tolerate and endure it. Still, to the many, every moment of such a life would bring its burden of irksomeness, and perhaps of

(134)

absolute repugnance, if only from its apparently unrelieved monotonousness. So much, however, are we dependent, not only upon ourselves, but upon each other, for mutual assistance and happiness at such a time, that we can either make or mar its pleasures, as we may elect. Isolation does not necessarily foster loneliness or inquietude, only as our own waywardness or neglect may lead to these. The principal objection to such a life is in its utter helplessness in times of sickness and danger, or of death, especially when—as in our experience—our nearest neighbor was thirty miles away, and beyond mountains that were impassable.

JAMES C. LAMON.

After satisfactory demonstration that a residence at Yo Semite in winter was possible, as narrated in a preceding chapter, Mr. Jas. C. Lamon, who formed one of our setting-out party on that occasion, was the first to try the experiment, and spent the winters of 1862–63 and 1863–64 there *entirely alone.* As Mr. Lamon was long and favorably known by visitors, not only for his uniform kindness and many manly virtues, but as one of the early settlers in Yo Semite, I feel that this work would be incomplete without his portrait and a brief biographical outline.

Mr. James C. Lamon was born in the State of Virginia in 1817. In 1835 he emigrated to Illinois; and from there to Texas, in 1839. In 1851 he arrived in California, and located in Mariposa County, where, in connection with David Clark, he engaged in the saw-mill and lumber business, until 1858. In June, 1859, he arrived in Yo Semite, and assisted in building the upper hotel, since known as the Hutchings House. In the fall of that year he located a pre-emption claim at the upper end of the valley; cultivated it for garden purposes, planted a fine orchard, and built

THE LAMON CABIN.

THE FIRST LOG-CABIN IN YO SEMITE.

By his indomitable will, assisted by his general intelligence and unflagging industry, to which were united habits of temperance and frugality, and the denial to himself of many comforts, he caused the spot known as Lamon's Garden, once a wilderness, "to blossom as the rose," and "Lamon's Berry Patch" and orchard, to become synonymous with enjoyment; the memory of a visit to which was pleasurably treasured by tourists, throughout the civilized world.

As the lofty mountains surrounding his cabin and garden threw long and chilling shadow-frowns upon him during winter, he erected a small house on the sunny side of the valley; and, as a precaution against Indian treachery, lived in its basement. This, however, being flooded during a heavy and continuous rain, he afterwards built a commodious log-cabin, that, upon emergency, might be to him both a fortress and a home. The land around it he fenced and cultivated; and it now—under the vigilant care of Mr. A. Harris—presents a picture of pastoral loveliness which is in striking contrast to that outside of it.

COMMISSIONERS AND STATE ACTION.

Notwithstanding these valuable and attractive additions to the enjoyments of the valley, the Board of Yo Semite Commissioners declined in every way to recognize his rights as a *bonâ fide* settler, and he—with the writer—was notified that he must take a lease of all his premises from them, on or before a given time, or leave. As neither of us would accept either of these alternatives, there ensued the conflict briefly outlined in the succeeding chapter, which resulted, finally, in the State's recognizing at least the equities of our claims, and the payment to Mr. Lamon, in 1874, of $12,000 as compensation therefor.

HIS DEATH.

This modest sum, the fruits of fifteen years' laborious toil, although so much calculated to smooth the pathway of his declining years, by lifting him above financial care, was, in its enjoyment, of very brief duration; for, just as he had begun to realize the full fruition of its blessedness, death came with

> "That golden key
> That opes the palace of eternity,"[1]

May 22, 1875, at the age of 58 years. His remains are interred in the Yo Semite Cemetery, near Yo Semite Falls, amid the scenes of grandeur he loved so well; and here a monolith of Yo Semite granite marks the spot where he rests.

1. Milton, *Comus.*

HIS SUPPOSED MURDER.

Incidental mention is above made of Mr. Lamon's residence in the Yo Semite Valley *two winters alone*, without a neighbor, or even a friendly dog, to keep him company.* Supplemental to this there is a sequel that deserves a kindly record: While thus passing his lonely existence there, an Indian had been seen in the settlements with a fine gold watch, that, it was surmised, belonged to Mr. Lamon. Fearing that its supposed owner had been murdered, as well as robbed, three friends left Mariposa— one of whom was Mr. Galen Clark, for many years the guardian of the valley, and still a much respected resident there—for the purpose of ascertaining the facts of the case. Upon arrival, to their great joy, they found the man, presumably murdered, busily engaged in preparing his evening meal. Both Mr. Lamon and his watch were proven to be safe. It can readily be conjectured that their congratulations and rejoicings must have been mutual, although viewed from widely different standpoints.

THE HUTCHINGS CABIN.

"Of all the homes that I have seen, in all my travels, this is the most delectable."
—CANON KINGSLEY.

As the sun did not rise upon the hotel until half past one in the afternoon, and set again, there, at half past three; so small a modicum of sunlight caused us to look out from the depressing and frosty shadows of our mountainous surroundings, to the brightness of the opposite side; and created within us a longing for the sunlight that was there bathing every tree and mountain with cheerfulness and joy. "Ah!" we would all spontaneously ejaculate, "that is the place to live, in winter." Even the poultry, that huddled together in a corner shiveringly, would look at us with seeming remonstrance, as though they would admonish us to remove them over there.

"Besides," the ladies would exclaim, "how beautifully pictur- esque a log-cabin would look over yonder in the sunlight, with a

* He was never married.

Heliotype Printing Co., Boston.

HUTCHINGS' OLD LOG CABIN, YO SEMITE

Facing page 138 in all editions.

Photo. by Geo. Fiske.

EAGLE PEAK, 3,818 FEET ABOVE THE VALLEY

From Upper Iron Bridge, near Barnard's
Fiske #329. A slightly different version of this photograph
faced page 170 in editions two, three, and four.

dark rich setting of oaks around it; to say nothing of the pleasure of listening to the grandest of perpetual anthems from the Yo Semite Fall, just at its back; or of the homelike comfort there would be within and around it."

A site possessing the qualities deemed most desirable was accordingly selected, and a "log-cabin," in all its symmetrical proportions and artistical surroundings, began to stand out upon the landscape. How cheerily anxious did the gentler sex watch the placing of each and every log, and sometimes assisted in putting them in position. By degrees, and with the assistance of our neighbor, Mr. Lamon, and his cattle, it was finished. One rock formed the mantel, and another the hearth-stone, of our broad and cheery open fire-place. Our greatest trouble was with the chimney—it would smoke. Everybody, "including his wife," is familiar with the adage that "a smoking chimney, and scolding ——, etc. [we had not the latter], are among the greatest trials of life." Finally, by means of books (for we had no practical knowledge) we learned that "a chimney, to draw well, should never be less than twice the size of the throat, from the latter to the top, which should always be above the house." This principle, when applied to ours, made it an eminent success. And this item is here introduced for the benefit of those having that dire infliction—a smoky chimney.

The cabin, therefore, with all its comfort-aiding appointments, became a delightful reality, and soon sheltered a happy and contented family, though entirely isolated from the great throbbing heart of the world outside. On bright days we enjoyed the blessed sunshine from nine in the morning until half-past three in the afternoon—a gratifying contrast to the other side—and, when the storm swooped down upon us, we listened thankfully to the music of the rain upon the roof, and to the wind among the tree-tops, or the rushing avalanches down the mountainsides; or watched the crystal forms of the fast-falling snow upon, or from, our windows; or our busy little snow-bird guests eating their daily meal of crumbs from off the window-sill.

THE TRUE SECRET OF HUMAN HAPPINESS.

It must not, however, be supposed that our daily life here was like that pictured by some dreamy Christians of the life hereafter—"sitting, placidly, on a cloud, and blowing a silver trumpet." Far from it. Every day brought its duties, in fair weather or in foul. Here, too, we learned a secret, and one worth revealing, as it is one in which the daily happiness of all largely consists—it is that of *having constant and pleasant occupation, for both body and mind.* This will count better in results, and go farther, than any number of gilded theories, for this life or the next. There are always to be found some kindly services to be rendered, or duties to be performed, not only in the family circle, but in the teeming world around us, if we do not allow ourselves to shirk them. And, believe me, the noble and conscientious performance of a generous act, brings with it a full and generous reward, without waiting for that expected in the hereafter. To those who have both leisure and means—and they must be poor indeed who have not some—I would say, "Know you not some poor child, or woman, or man, to whom you can carry some blessing, if only that of help and sympathy?" By so doing, you not only assist to make up their heaven, and an earthly one for yourselves, but, in my judgment, much better please the loving God, whom you profess to serve. If there should ever come a new religion, it will be founded upon humanity, as being more nearly akin to the beneficent and ennobling plan of the Infinite One. Think of this.

Returning from this diversion, if you could have taken a glimpse on the inside of our cabin on a winter's night, you would have seen not only a bright log fire, and clean hearth-stone, but a little circle of bright faces; almost aglow with watching the phantom forms that might come and go among the scintillations of the blazing heat; or, with busy thoughts were weaving gossamer plans of future happiness; while nimble fingers were plying the needle, or knitting yarn that had been carded and spun from Yo Semite-grown wool, with their own hands.

We professed to take turns at reading, aloud, from some mutually interesting book; but the writer discovered that the recurrence came most frequently to the occupant of the large home-made manzanita chair. Remonstrance even only brought back the rejoinder that, as he had no sewing or knitting to do, and was such an excel—etc., etc., reader, it would seem most eminently proper that he should favor the company with another chapter! Sometimes a song, at others a game of whist, or euchre, would add a pleasing variety to the entertainment. Saturday evenings were especially devoted to cards and song, as then our only neighbor, Mr. Lamon, would come out from his hermit-like solitude and grace the circle with his presence, and cheer it with his converse; occasionally dining with us on Sunday afternoons. It may appear almost incredible to confess that, notwithstanding this constant round of seeming sameness and isolation, there was an utter absence of the feeling of loneliness. Many times the query has been put, questioningly, "Do you not feel such entire seclusion from the world oppressive?" and the response was promptly and conscientiously returned, "No. We should, perhaps, if we had time to think about it!"

Thus our long winter evenings and stormy days, while putting us into enjoyable social communion with each other, supplied also the opportunity of conversing with great authors, through their works, of which, fortunately, we had nearly eight hundred volumes, collected, mainly, while publishing the old-time *California Magazine.* Our summers were made delightful by pleasant converse with the kindliest and most intelligent people upon earth, many of whom were eminent in letters, in science, and in art. Who, then, with this elevating companionship, and its many advantages, united with such sublime surroundings, could help loving the Yo Semite Valley, and being contented with it as a home, even though isolated from the great world outside?

In after years, as residents in the valley became more numerous—and some winters since then we have had over forty, including children—the circle of neighbors proportionately extended, and our divertissements would include parties, sleigh-rides, and snow-shoe excursions.

THE ORCHARD AND STRAWBERRY PATCH.

The spring succeeding the completion of the cabin, called for the cultivation and fencing of a garden-ground, and the planting of an orchard. Many of the trees for the latter were grown from seeds of choice apples that had been sent us, the plants from which were afterwards budded or grafted. In this way a thrifty orchard, of about one hundred and fifty trees, came into being, and now bears many tons, annually, of assorted fruit.

To this, in due time, was added a large strawberry patch, that afterwards became famous from its productiveness and the quality of its fruit. Here perhaps may be given a single illustration of the difficulties to be overcome in such a far-off corner of the earth. The pomological works of the day were full to overflowing with praises of a certain variety of this valuable berry. Specimens were sent for, the price asked accompanying the order. When the plants arrived, owing to the mails of that day coming by Panama, and the necessary delays attending their delivery in the Valley, they were all dried up and dead. Others were ordered, which, upon arrival, were falling to pieces from excessive moisture. The mail-bag containing the next parcel, owing to its too close contact with the steamship's funnel, was nearly burnt up, and with it the new invoice of strawberry plants. As it is never wise to become discouraged, or to give up until you win, in some form, or prove such a feat to be impossible, still others were sent for; and this time with success, as thirteen living plants rewarded our perseverance. These thirteen small rootlets cost us exactly $45.00. Still, what was that sum in comparison with their future value? With careful culture, these increased to thousands; and many of the largest bunches produced nearly two hundred berries each! In after-times, delicious strawberries could be gathered *ad libitum;* what, then, was $45.00 for such a luxury? especially when to this is added that of success.

PLANTING AN AVENUE.

To connect the high ground near the hotel on the south side of the valley with that at the cabin on the north side, and at the same time make the Yo Semite Fall and other attractions accessible to visitors, a causeway was thrown up across the intervening meadow, and an avenue of elms planted on either side, that were grown from seed sent us by the Rev. Joseph Worcester of Waltham, Massachusetts. But few of these now survive, as, during my absence in the mountains on one occasion, some thoughtless young men cut them down for walking-canes, and carried them off. I hope when they see this, they will feel their cheeks warm with shame; but I would not go so far as Young, in his "Night Thoughts," and say,

"Shame burn thy cheeks to cinders,"

As that would be rather too severe and heavy a penalty.

BRIEF ABSENCE FROM THE VALLEY.

Owing to the current of events briefly chronicled in the ensuing chapter, necessity, not choice, impelled my absence from the valley for a season; inasmuch as the Board of Commissioners, of that time, became so much angered at my unfaltering persistency in resenting their claims, that they would not even lease to me the old premises, after all other matters had been adjusted, and the title to both land and improvements had legally passed into their hands. They evidently overlooked the fact that I was contending for a home for my family and self, and to which we believed ourselves honorably entitled under a United States general law— a home made sacred, too, by many memories, and where each of our three children were born—and my convictions then, as now, were that any man who would not defend his hearth-stone and his home, to the last drop of his life-blood, when he felt that right was on his side—even when against "forty millions of people,"* and a half dozen Boards of Commissioners thrown in—belittled his manhood, and proved himself unworthy of the respect accorded

* See chapter XII.

to his race. Those very Commissioners, if standing in my place, would (I hope) have acted as I did. It is much to be regretted, however, that some of those men still live, demonstratively, for no other purpose than to perpetuate their old antagonisms. I am their superior in one thing—I have learned to *forgive.* Life is too short, and too uncertain, to fritter it away in unprofitable and ignoble frictions, and has a holier mission.

By an Act of the State Legislature, at its session of 1880, and a subsequent decision of the Supreme Court, the old Board of Commissioners was retired, and a new one appointed by the Executive in its place, April 19, 1880. The Board elected the writer "Guardian of the Valley;" and, upon my return, Mr. John K. Barnard, the lessee of my old premises, with considerate and large-hearted kindness, again placed the dear old cabin indefinitely at my disposal; and through his continued courtesy, it has been my fondly cherished residence ever since.

But it is not to be supposed that so rare and supernal a flower as unalloyed happiness could ever germinate and bloom in earthly dwellings. This would be to convert terrestrial habitations into celestial. Hence the angel of sorrow, and, alas! of death, with drooping or baneful wings, is frequently, though uninvitedly, permitted to enter human homes and hearts. It was thus with us. Our gifted daughter Florence—given to us during the eventful first year of our residence here, and whose birth was noteworthy from the fact that she was *the first white child born at Yo Semite*—was called away from us in her eighteenth year, just as she was blooming into womanhood and great prospective usefulness. With agonized hearts, and, seemingly, helpless hands,

"We watched her breathing through the night,
  Her breathing soft and low,
 As in her breast the wave of life
  Kept heaving to and fro

"Our very hopes belied our fears,
  Our fears our hopes belied;
 We thought her dying when she slept,
  And sleeping when she died."

Nor was ours the only Yo Semite home thus visited at this season; as Effie, the beautiful step-daughter of Mr. J. K. Barnard,

> "Passed through glory's morning gate,
> And walked in Paradise."[1]

Only about thirty days before. The portrayal of this dual loss and affliction, so feelingly presented by my late beloved and gifted wife, Augusta L., is gratefully transcribed from the San Francisco *Evening Post,* for which she was special correspondent:—

BIG TREE ROOM, BARNARD'S HOTEL,
YO SEMITE VALLEY, Sept. 28, 1881.

It has seemed that the Angel of Death had overlooked this "gorge in the mountains," but at length he has learned how sweet were the flowers that bloom in our beautiful valley. First, he came for our lily—sweet, gentle, spiritual Effie, beloved daughter of this house. For a long time he stood afar off, and sent only withering glances and baleful breath, under which she slowly drooped and faded from our sight, till her life passed away with the summer, for on its last day she left us for a home among the angels. Gifted with rare esthetic tastes and talents, which these grand scenes were developing and cultivating, she would doubtless have been prominent among those who shall interpret and perpetuate by their sketches, the poetic beauties of Yosemite. We chose her a final resting-place in a grove of noble oaks, where Tissaac, goddess of the valley, keeps constant watch; and the sun's last rays, reflected from her brow, give each evening their parting benison upon her slumbers, while the singing waters of Cholock* murmur an eternal lullaby.

As we were around her grave, rendering the last services, prominent over all, in a band of young friends singing "Safe in the Arms of Jesus," stood the glorious rose of this wild nature—Florence ("our Floy"), eldest daughter of Mr. Hutchings, guardian of the valley. Full of exuberant, gushing life, she has shed far and wide its fragrance. The child of the valley, for she was the first white child born within these inclosing walls, and the greater part of her life spent here, her whole being was permeated with its influences. Nothing daunted her, nothing gave her so much pleasure as the occasion to help others. Generous, unselfish, her deeds of kindly courtesy will long be remembered by a vast number of visitors, who have enjoyed their benefit and been interested in her bright, original thoughts; for her mind, though unsystematic in its training, was

* The Yo Semite Fall.

1. James Aldrich, *A Death Bed.*

well stocked with good material, and she was rapidly developing into a grand woman.

But again the dread angel looked down, and without waiting to give warning to those who held her close to their hearts, with one fell swoop caught her to his breast, and bore her away; that the Lily and Rose might bloom side by side, in a garden where no frost can blight, no tempest uproot, and the ever-outgoing perfume of their blossoms shall enter our lives to purify and bless them. So we have laid her, who, only a week before she was called away, was climbing heights and scrambling through ravines where only eagles might be looked for, under the same oaks with Effie; and the dearly loved friends in life, who there seemed to us to be so quietly resting together, are doubtlessly wandering hand in hand through fairer scenes than even these they loved and enjoyed so much.

Oh! the questionings that come up as to the why and the wherefore. As an Indian woman, with a puny, sickly infant, bound in its basket, that has been wailing and whining all its little life of two years, unable even to sit or crawl, came to take a last look at the plucked Rose, I could not but ask myself why such an apparently useless and burdensome existence was allowed to go on, while the helpful, earnest, energetic life had been quenched. But "God knows."

Mr. Robinson, the artist, from San Francisco, who, in the absence of a clergyman, read the solemn burial service of the Episcopal Church, as Mr. Hutchings had done upon the former sad occasion, read also the following beautiful

IN MEMORIAM.

Florence Hutchings, born August 23, 1864. Died, September 26, 1881. Of a bold, fearless disposition, warm and generous temperament, far advanced and original in thought beyond her years, with a kind word and pleasant greeting for every one. Always ready to do a self-denying action, or an act of kindness; such was she who now lies cold and pallid before us. She was the first white child ever born in the Yosemite Valley, and the same giant walls that witnessed her birth shall keep watch and ward over her grave through all time. The music of the great Cholock that sang in cheerfulness through her infancy and childhood, shall chant an eternal requiem over her early grave. Here, in her grand and lonely home, where almost every rock, tree, and blade of grass were known to her, and were her playthings and playfellows in childhood, and the objects of her contemplation and veneration in youth, shall she lay down to her calm and peaceful rest. Eternal music shall be hers—the winds sighing through the tall pine trees, the murmur of the great water-falls, and the twilight calls of the turtle doves to each other from their far-off homes, the heights Tocoyæ* and Law-oo-Too. All nature unites to lull to rest and peace and

* North, and South Domes.

quiet the gentle dead. So, friends, temper your griefs to calmness, with the consolation that if the loss is yours, the gain is God's.

Ahwahnee,* who could protect its first born in youth and life, will guard her with a loving mother's embrace in death. Let us leave her in resignation and cheerfulness, knowing that it is but a span between the hour that has called her from us, and the one which is to summon us also to the unknown, whence no one returns. And as she calmly lies, with all nature whispering love and protection over her last resting-place, let us in reverence depart, and leave her soul in joy and peace, safe in the arms of the good and great God who gave it, for so brief a season, to gladden her parents' hearts, and bloom within the world.

Mr. B. F. Taylor, in his charmingly sunny book, "Between the Gates," page 238, makes the following suggestion: "Let us give the girl, for her own and her father's sake, some graceful mountain height, and, let it be called 'Mt. Florence!'" This complimentary suggestion, through the kindness of friends, has been carried out; as one of the formerly unnamed peaks of the High Sierra now bears the name of "Mt. Florence." This is best seen and recognized from Glacier Point, and Sentinel Dome.

In less than six brief weeks after our daughter Florence had passed through the Beautiful Gate, the unwelcome angel again visited the old cabin, and this time carried away the devoted and beloved companion of my life, my beloved and devoted wife, after an illness of only a few hours. Without lingering too long upon these chastening experiences, let me add that her endearing qualities may be summed up in one expressive line:—

"Think what a wife should be, and she was that."

The beautiful gems of art that still adorn our cabin within are nearly all the work of her own hands and skill; and, with many other souvenirs, the creations of her own genius, are ever cherished as sacred memories, *memoriâ in æternâ.*

When the mystic ligature of love joins human hearts, and the vacant chair tells, silently, of the enforced absence of its once loving occupant, bringing back reminders of happy greetings ere you crossed the threshold, as of life's long summer's day of joy,

* The great Indian chief of antiquity.

to be yours with them no more—it is then, ah! *then*, that real loneliness strikes home to the heart.

Much of this, however, has been alleviated in past years by the many kindnesses of visitors who have honored and brightened the old cabin with their cheering and refining presence; and to its occupant have given unalloyed pleasure by their refreshing converse. It has been his acceptable pastime for many years to gather any fragmentary curios that were representative of mountain life and circumstances; such, for instance, as the cones and seeds of the different kinds of pine and fir, and other forest trees—including those of the Big Tree with its foliage and wood; specimens of our beautiful ferns, and flowers; Indian relics, with samples of their food; pieces of glacier-polished granite; snow-shoes (of home manufacture), for both valley use and mountain climbing; and those used upon horses for sleigh-riding and hauling over the mountains, and about which more will be said hereafter. In grateful return for the honor of a visit, he has tried to explain these, and given the why and the wherefore concerning them; and, moreover, still cherishes the hope of its indulgence for many years to come.

At the west end of the cabin is a small workshop (a necessary appendage to an isolated life and residence), which also answers for a wood-shed in winter. At the back is another lean-to, which comprises a kitchen, pantry, and store-rooms, and at the eastern end a bedroom. The attic, or roof-room, is sometimes also used as a sleeping apartment—and once, during a heavy flood (to be talked over by and by) as a place of refuge for ourselves and household wares, when the waters were at their highest.

A little west of north from this spot, apparently but a short distance off, while in reality it is nearly three-quarters of a mile away, the Yo Semite Fall makes a leap of over two thousand five hundred feet over the edge of the cliff, and in one bound clears fifteen hundred feet. The surging roll of the music from this fall is a constant and refreshing lullaby to slumber, and never wearies. With so many enduring charms, then, is it a wonder that one clings with admiring fondness to such a home?

CHAPTER XII.

CONGRESSIONAL AND STATE ENACTMENTS CONCERNING YO SEMITE.

Think that day lost whose low descending sun
Views from thy hand no noble action done.
—ROBART.

That action is best which procures the greatest happiness for the greatest numbers.
—HUTCHESON'S *Moral Good and Evil.*

I have always thought the actions of men the best interpreters of their thoughts.
—LOCKE'S *Human Understanding, Book I.*

While some of the occurrences narrated in preceding chapters were transpiring, the Hon. John Conness, U. S. Senator for California, in concert with Mr. I. W. Raymond and others, conceived a plan for the cession, by Congress, of the Yo Semite Valley, and its more immediate surroundings, with the Mariposa Big Tree Grove, to the State of California, for the purpose of setting them apart, and protecting them as public parks. Mr. Conness accordingly introduced the following bill in the United States Senate, which was promptly passed by both branches of Congress:—

An Act authorizing a grant to the State of California of the "Yo Semite Valley," and of the land embracing the Mariposa Big Tree Grove.

ACT OF CONGRESS GRANTING YO SEMITE TO THE STATE.*

Be it enacted by the Senate and House of Representatives of the United States of America in Congress assembled: That there shall be, and is hereby, granted to the State of California the "cleft" or "gorge" in the granite peak of the Sierra Nevada Mountains, situated in the county

---

* See United States Statutes at Large, for 1864, page 325.

(149)

of Mariposa, in the State aforesaid, and the headwaters of the Merced River, and known as the Yo Semite Valley, with its branches or spurs, in estimated length fifteen miles, and in average width one mile back from the main edge of the precipice, on each side of the valley, with the stipulation, nevertheless, that the said State shall accept this grant upon the express conditions that the premises shall be held for public use, resort, and recreation; shall be inalienable for all time; but leases not exceeding ten years may be granted for portions of said premises. All incomes derived from leases of privileges to be expended in the preservation and improvement of the property, or the roads leading thereto; the boundaries to be established at the cost of said State by the United States Surveyor-General of California, whose official plat, when affirmed by the Commissioner of the General Land Office, shall constitute the evidence of the locus, extent, and limits of the said cleft or gorge; the premises to be managed by the Governor of the State with eight other Commissioners, to be appointed by the Executive of California, and who shall receive no compensation for their services.

Sec. 2. *And be it further enacted:* That there shall likewise be, and there is hereby, granted to the State of California the tracts embracing what is known as the "Mariposa Big Tree Grove," not to exceed the area of four sections, and to be taken in legal subdivisions of one quarter section each, with the like stipulation as expressed in the first section of this Act as to the State's acceptance, with like conditions as in the first section of this Act, and to be taken in legal sub-divisions as aforesaid; and the official plat of the United States Surveyor-General, when affirmed by the Commissioner of the General Land Office, to be the evidence of the locus of the said Mariposa Big Tree Grove.

Approved, June 30, 1864.

The news of this generous donation was first made known to the California public through the columns of the San Francisco *Evening Bulletin* of August 9, 1864, as we had no railroads or telegraph lines across the continent in those days. In prompt responsive acknowledgement on the part of the State was issued

THE GOVERNOR'S PROCLAMATION.

State of California, Executive Department,
Sacramento, September 28, 1864.

Whereas, The United States, by an Act passed at the first session of the thirty-eighth Congress, has granted to this State the territory comprising the "Yosemite Valley and the Mariposa Big Tree Grove," to be held and used for the purpose mentioned in said Act; and whereas it is also provided in the Act that the management and control of the tracts of land shall be confided to a Board of Commissioners to be appointed by the Governor.

Now therefore, be it known, that I, FRED'K F. LOW, Governor of the State of California, by virtue of the authority in me vested, have appointed FRED. LAW OLMSTED, PROF. J. D. WHITNEY, WILLIAM ASH-BURNER, I. W. RAYMOND, E. S. HOLDEN, ALEXANDER DEERING, GEORGE W. COULTER, and GALEN CLARK, said Commissioners, to whom is confided the management of the aforesaid tracts of land. And I hereby warn and command all persons to desist from trespassing or settling upon said territory, and from cutting timber or doing any unlawful acts within the limits of said grant.

All propositions for the improvement of the aforesaid tracts of land, or for leases, should be made to the Commissioners, through FRED. LAW OLMSTED, Bear Valley, Mariposa County.

In testimony whereof, I have hereunto set my hand and caused the Great Seal of the State of California to be affixed, this twenty-eighth day of September, 1864.

[L. S.]   FRED'K F. LOW.
                                 Governor of California.

Attest: B. B. REDDING, *Secretary of State.*

By F. W. REDDING, *Deputy.*

During the sixteenth session of the State Legislature was enacted the following:—

ACT OF ACCEPTANCE

An Act to accept the grant by the United States Government to the State of California of the Yosemite Valley and the Mariposa Big Tree Grove, and to organize the Board of Commissioners, and to fully empower them to carry out the objects of the grant and fulfill the purposes of the trust. (Chap. DXXXVI of the Statutes of California passed at the 16th Session of the Legislature, 1865–66.)

WHEREAS, By an Act of Congress entitled an Act authorizing a grant to the State of California of the Yosemite Valley, and of the land embracing the Mariposa Big Tree Grove, approved June 30, A. D., 1864, there was granted to the State of California in the terms of said Act said Valley and the lands embracing said Grove upon certain conditions and stipulations therein expressed; now, therefore,

The people of the State of California, represented in Senate and Assembly, do enact as follows:—

SECTION 1. The State of California does hereby accept said grant upon the conditions, reservations, and stipulations contained in said Act of Congress.

SEC. 2. The Governor, and eight other Commissioners, Frederick Law Olmsted, Prof. J. D. Whitney, William Ashburner, I. W. Raymond, E. S. Holden, Alexander Deering, George W. Coulter, and Galen Clark, appointed by him on the twenty-eighth day of September, eighteen hundred and sixty-four, in accordance with the terms of said Act, are hereby constituted a Board to manage said premises, and any vacancy occurring therein from death, removal, or any cause, shall be filled by the appointment of the Governor. They shall be known in law as "The Commissioners to manage the Yosemite Valley and the Mariposa Big Tree Grove," and by such name they and their successors may sue and be sued, and shall have full power to manage and administer the grant made and the trust created by said Act of Congress, and shall have full power to make and adopt all rules, regulations, and by-laws for their own government, and the government, improvement, and preservation of said premises not inconsistent with the Constitution of the United States or of this State, or of said Act making the grant, or of any law of Congress or of the legislature. They shall hold their first meeting at the time and place to be specified by the Governor, and thereafter as their own rules shall prescribe, and a majority shall constitute a quorum for the transaction of business. They shall elect a President and Secretary, and any other officers from their number as their rules may prescribe.

SEC. 3. None of said Commissioners shall receive any compensation for their services as such. They shall have power to appoint a Guardian either of their number or not, of said premises, removable at their pleasure, to perform such duties as they may prescribe, and to receive such compensation as they may fix, not to exceed five hundred dollars per annum.

SEC. 4. The Commissioners shall make a full report of the condition of said premises, and of their acts under this law, and of their expenditures, through the Governor, to the Legislature, at every regular session thereof.

SEC. 5. The State Geologist is hereby authorized to make such further explorations on the said tracts and in the adjoining region of the Sierra Nevada Mountains as may be necessary to enable him to prepare a full description and accurate statistical report of the same, and the same shall be published in connection with reports of the Geological Survey.

SEC. 6. It shall be unlawful for any person willfully to commit any trespass whatever upon said premises, cut down or carry off any wood, underwood, tree, or timber, or girdle or otherwise injure any tree or timber, or deface or injure any natural object, or set fire to any wood or grass upon said premises, or destroy or injure any bridge or structure of any kind, or other improvement that is or may be placed thereon. Any person committing either or any of said acts, without the express permission of said Commissioners through said Guardian, shall be guilty of a misdemeanor, and on conviction thereof shall be punished by fine not exceeding five hundred dollars, or by imprisonment in the county jail not exceeding six months, or by both such fine and imprisonment.

Sec. 8. This Act shall take effect immediately.

Approved April 2, 1866.

ADVERSE ACTION TOWARDS THE SETTLERS.

This liberal and conservative concert of action between Congress and the State of California. was doubtlessly made with the implied understanding that no private rights were in any way invaded or jeopardized thereby. In this, however, subsequent proceedings proved that both the contracting parties were in error; inasmuch as the Board of Commissioners, created by the forgoing acts, notified Mr. J. C. Lamon and myself—the only *bona fide* settlers—that we must take a lease of the premises occupied by us from them, on or before a given time; or, failing to do this, they would lease them to other parties, "and, early in the ensuing spring, take all necessary measures for installing the new tenants into possession."

Under the beguiling hallucination that the Préemption Laws of the United States were a sacred compact between the Government and the citizen, I took the liberty of notifying the Secretary of the Board, in reply, that in my judgment it would be time enough for the Commissioners of the Yo Semite Valley to exercise authority over my house, or my horse, or anything that I possessed, *after* they had proven a better title to either than I had got, and that I remained very respectfully, etc.

SUIT OF EJECTMENT COMMENCED.

Believing that *bona fide* settlers were entrenched and fortified behind the bulwarks of National Law as well as of right, and, never doubting of ultimate success, the march of improvement kept commensurate progress with the constantly increasing

Photo. by S. C. Walker.   Photo-Typo by Britton & Rey, S. F.

THE YO SEMITE FALL—CHO-LOCK—IN EARLY SPRING.
(See page 377.)
Facing page 160 in edition one. Facing page 154 in all other editions.
The trees to the right of the lower fall have been retouched.

The Three Brothers—Pom-pom-pa-sa.

(See pages 395–96.)

Facing page 128 in edition one. Facing page 130 in all other editions.

army of visitors. But about a year after the service of the notice above mentioned, the terms of which had been declined, a legal bomb was thrown into our midst, in the shape of "a suit of eject- ment" against the writer, as a test case for all parties.

STATE ACTION IN THEIR BEHALF.

While this action was in abeyance in the District Court, a memorial to the State legislature was prepared, and numerously signed by a large majority of the prominent residents of the county of Mariposa, asking favorable legislation in behalf of the Yo Semite settlers. This was accorded by an Act passed in the Assembly by a vote of 55 to 9, and in the Senate with only two dissenting voices, surrendering to Mr. Lamon and myself all the State's right and title to each of our quarter-sections. Resolutions were also adopted memorializing Congress for confirmation of the same. This act not receiving the approval of the Governor, H. H. Haight, it was carried over his veto, by a vote of 41 to 11 in the Assembly, and by 27 to 10 in the Senate, thus making it a State law, notwithstanding the objections of the Governor. By some kind of clerical hocus pocus, however, this enactment was spirited away (?) and could not be found in time for its incorporation among the printed laws of that session; al- though it had received the necessary signature of the presiding officers of both Senate and Assembly! It was afterwards resur- rected from some vaulted recess of the State capitol, and is now among the archives of the Secretary of State.

Inasmuch as the State's favorable course in our behalf re- quired the indorsement of Congress, to give it full legal effect, and establish a perfect title in us to the land thus settled upon, the memorial adopted by the Legislature, and another numerously signed, from citizens, with a certified copy of the Act, were trans- mitted to Congress through the Hon. Geo. W. Julian, Chairman of the Committee of Public Lands, of the House of Representatives, asking Congressional action upon this question. Through the in- fluence of Mr. Julian—who has always been the uncompromising friend of the settler—and the unanimous vote of the Committee of Public Lands, an Act passed the House embodying the necessary provisions, without a dissenting voice. Owing, however, I deeply regret to say, to the most grossly unfair and untruthful representations of its enemies, when the measure was considered in the Committee of Public Lands of the United States Senate, a majority of one caused an unfavorable report to be adopted by that committee; and no action was taken upon it in the Senate, before Congress adjourned.

Be it remembered that until Congress had ratified the action of the legislature of California in our behalf, the homes we had founded in this wild gorge of the mountains, and every dollar expended here, were in jeopardy, notwithstanding the beneficent provisions of the United States Preëmption Laws. It is only just here to state that the Board of Commissioners considerately refrained from pressing their suit of ejectment, for a time, after State action in our behalf, pending that of Congress, for or against us; but, finally, calling it up for trial in the District Court, owing to its unquestioned equities, judgment was entered for defendant, and against the Board of Commissioners.

As notice of appeal to the State Supreme Court had been filed, and fearing that the same ruling might be made there in this as in the Suscol Ranch case, although widely differing to the latter in many of its conditions and merits, Congressional action was again sought. In hopes of preventing the defeat this time of so pre-eminently just a measure, by questionable if not positively dishonorable means, and to be present to meet any statement or inquiry, I visited Washington the ensuing winter, determined that the case should have fair play, if possible, whether it stand or fall thereby.

AN INCIDENTAL DIGRESSION ABOUT A VISIT TO WASHINGTON.

I hope to be forgiven for a short digression here, if only to show how an obliging act will sometimes secure for the doer the honor (!) of a title. During the summer of 1869—the year the great overland railroad was opened from Omaha to Sacramento—the "corps editorial" was largely represented from the Eastern States, as visitors to California and Yo Semite, and among them some from Washington, D. C. At that time the only turnpike-road nearing the valley still lacked twenty-five miles of completion, and the intervening space between the stage and the Valley being over a mountain trail, could only be traveled on saddle animals. As necessity required that I should supply these, and a certain kind of superintendence was needed, I had ridden to the western end of this intermission of country, and was returning, when I met a passenger far behind his companions, who was in trouble with his unpersuasive horse. I of course stopped, and asked the reason, when the following colloquy ensued:—

"Mr. H., I cannot induce this animal to keep up with the others. How is it?"

"He knows that you are a tourist, and is making the best of his knowledge."

"What am I to do? At the rate I am traveling I shall not be able to reach the station by midnight."

"Take my horse—he will carry you through, on time."

"What! Change animals, here, on the road?"

"Certainly. Mine will attend strictly to business, and, when yours finds out that I am his rider, he will also make the discovery that I am not a tourist, and will give *me* no trouble." The exchange was accordingly made, and, waving a hasty adieu, each started at a lively gait, in different directions. This gentleman proved to be one of the editors of a Washington evening paper.

Upon my arrival at the nation's capital, and accidentally meeting the before-mentioned editor, he gave me most cordial greeting, with invitations to dine with him, etc.; and in the issue of his paper of that evening there appeared a notice that "Colonel H—— of Yo Semite, had arrived, and would be warmly welcomed by his many friends," etc., etc. On the succeeding day we again met, and indulged in the following confab:—

"I see that I am promoted!"

"Yes! How is that?"

"I have always understood that I belonged only to the 'full privates;' but I see by your last evening's —— that you have promoted me to be a Colonel!"

With a mischievous twinkle lurking in the corner of his eye, came the courteous reply: "Ah! that's all right. When you have been a resident of Washington as long as I have, you will find that a stranger coming here, without a title, is placed, socially, at great disadvantage, and I thought you deserving of a good send off! Besides, whenever I have remembered that horse trade we made upon the mountain trail, I have laughed over the incident, many times. I am convinced that instead of promoting you to be a colonel, only, I ought to have made you a general—and will, next time(!)."

BEFORE THE UNITED STATES SENATE COMMITTEE OF PUBLIC LANDS.

Upon the reassembling of Congress, the Act which passed into the House of Representatives at its previous session, was again introduced by Mr. Julian, and again promptly passed by that body. Taking the usual course of similar measures, it was again referred to the United States Senate Committee of Public Lands. Deeply anxious that no act of omission or of commission on my part should endanger its successful consideration before that committee, (and let it not be overlooked that I was working in the interest of our little mountain homes) I first waited upon its chairman—then Senator Pomeroy, of Kansas—and explained to him the whole matter. Looking me straight in the eye, he thus addressed me:—

"Do you say, sir, that you are a settler in Yo Semite Valley?" "I do, Senator." "What is the actual date of your settlement there?" Responsive to this inquiry I supplied Senator Pomeroy, not only with the day of my settlement there, and that of those whose possessory rights I had purchased, but also with Mr. Lamon's—the time and circumstances of which are narrated in the preceding chapter—accompanying these with the substantiating testimonials of prominent Californians, well acquainted with the facts. After a long pause the Senator again addressed me as follows:—

REPREHENSIBLE REPRESENTATION IN THE UNITED STATES SENATE.

"Mr. Hutchings, sir, I am perfectly astounded at your statements, the proofs of which are positive and incontrovertible. Why, sir, I distinctly remember when the matter was under discussion in the United States Senate, putting this question to Senator Conness, the author of the Bill: 'Are there any settlers upon that land?'—accompanying the question with the remark—'because, if there are, their rights must be respected,' and the senator from California made answer, 'No. Not one(!).' With that assurance I gave my fullest support to the Bill."

But for this foundationless statement, then, there can arise but little doubt that the rights of settlers at Yo Semite, as elsewhere, would have been protected. Here originated the wrongdoing; and the successive troubles that beset and followed us in after years. And sacredly do I treasure, and would here most gracefully record, how steadfastly the sentiment and sympathy of the California public continued with us, to brighten and cheer us, even to the end. Subsequent action, also, abundantly proved that if the State, at any time, had desired the homesteads of the Yo Semite settlers, it would have made honorable provisions for acquiring them—not wrested them wrongfully away from them.

MISTAKEN "PUBLIC POLICY."

"Public policy" was the misleading and delusive key-note struck for prevaricating and unprincipled opposition to the measure. "It was a question between forty millions of people and two men," reasoned the adversary. (It is hoped that becoming credit will be accorded the "two men" for having pluck enough to "breast the breach" against "forty millions of people!") Conceding this, would not the "forty millions"—a few of the meaner ones excepted, perhaps—have preferred the equitable acquisition of our legally obtained lands—legally obtained, if the Preëmption laws mean anything, notwithstanding the technical rulings of the courts—than to wrest them wrongfully from us, even though it should have taken the one-thousandth part of one mill each, more or less, from the aforesaid "forty millions of people" to have accomplished this.

HOW INTERVALS OF LEISURE WERE EMPLOYED.

Of course necessary delays would continually occur in the action of Congressional Committees, and from other causes; delays that would have proven a heavy drain upon one's patience as well as finances, had I not devoted the interim to the apparently accepted mission of my life—the dissemination of knowledge on the charming realities of Yo Semite. To accomplish the one, and subserve the other, therefore, in addition to frequent visits to Washington for conferences with Congressional members, I gave some eighty-seven illustrated lectures on Yo Semite, sometimes to audiences of over three thousand. The results of this action were three-fold; first, in giving pleasant occupation to leisure hours; second, by assisting my finances (Mr. Lamon being too poor to contribute anything); and, third, by inviting the interested attention of the public to the marvelous grandeur of the scenery of Yo Semite, that afterwards induced many thousands to visit it: And who, I trust, were never sorry for so doing.

TAKING AN UNFAIR ADVANTAGE.

Notwithstanding these opposing forces from without, a majority of the United States Senate Committee of Public Lands expressed themselves to the writer as holding the above-mentioned views of the case, and for favorably reporting the Bill; yet, in the absence of some friends of the measure, when its consideration was entertained in that committee, a majority of one was secured against it, just as that session of Congress was closing; when it was assigned to the unfinished business of the Senate—and consequently again to defeat.

RULINGS OF THE SUPREME COURTS.

Meanwhile, the Board of Commissioners appealed from the decision of the District Court, to the State Supreme Court, where, under the ruling of the Supreme Court of the United States, in the Suscol Ranch Case, while admitting in its decision that I was a *bona fide* settler upon the land before it was donated to the State, had lived upon it ever since with my family, and was ready at any time to prove up my preëmption claim, and to pay the purchase money, whenever the land could have been surveyed, Ruled:—

"If a qualified preëmptioner enter upon a portion of the public domain, with the intention to preëmpt the same, and performs all the acts necessary to perfect his preëmptive right, except the payment of the purchase price, the government may, nevertheless, at any time before the price is actually paid, or tendered, devote the land to another purpose, and thereby wholly defeat the right of preëmption."—*California Reports, July, 1871, Vol. 41, pp. 658–9.*

Although this judgment was appealed, from the State Supreme Court to that of the United States, it was afterwards affirmed by that body, as their action could not be made retroactive from their decision in the Suscol Ranch Case.

POSSIBLY AN ARROGANT ASSUMPTION.

It may seemingly appear an act of supererogation, if not of arrogant assumption, on the part of any one, especially of lawyers who are eminent in their profession, to interpret the decision of the Supreme Court in the Suscol Ranch and Yo Semite cases— although not analogous in their equities—as traversing the well-understood and beneficent provisions of the Preëmption Laws, and subverting the covenantal principles of a general law to subserve a specific purpose, and one that could have been better provided for some other way. There is evidently a broad foundation for questioning the soundness of this ruling, as the settler has an abundant surplus of difficulties to overcome, without their unnecessary increase, involving the title to his land. The "unpardonable sin" assumed to have been committed by the settlers at Yo Semite was twofold—one, in choosing so wildly picturesque a portion of the public domain whereon to form a home; and the other to stand up manfully in its defense, after some one else wanted it. Herein lay the extent of their sinning, and the heinousness of their offenses. Had their choice fallen upon some shelterless desert, no envious motive would have prompted a wish for claiming it, or for their dispossession.

After the legal status of the question had been determined by the courts, and Congressional action circumstantially deferred, the writer received numerous letters from representative Californians, asking him to forego any further efforts before Congress, until the will and wishes of the California public could be consulted in the matter. This was acceded to. And when the Legislature of 1874 assembled, an appropriation was made of $60,000 for the purpose of compensating the Yo Semite settlers for any financial loss they might sustain, by surrendering all their right and title to the State. For the purposes of carrying out the provisions of this enactment, three special commissioners were appointed by the Executive of the State, Gov. Newton Booth, who repaired to Yo Semite to ascertain the relative proportion of the sum appropriated that should be paid to each.

It should here be explained that in addition to the two actual settlers, there were two others that claimed indemnity for improvements; and, in order to avoid any future controversies upon this subject, it was resolved that these claims should also be considered and disposed of at this juncture. In order to arrive at a just estimate of the relative expenditures of each claimant, an expert was employed, who reported as follows:—

Improvements made by J. M. Hutchings, $41,000; James C. Lamon, $11,000; A. G. Black, $8,350; Ira G. Folsom, $4,000. Notwithstanding this showing by the expert, the following awards were made by a majority of the special commission:—

J. M. Hutchings, $24,000; Jas. C. Lamon, $12,000; A. G. Black, $22,000. Mr. Black was to pay Ira B. Folsom out of his award, but as Mr. Black and Mr. Folsom could not agree upon the amount to be paid the latter, the whole matter was brought up before the State Board of Examiners, as provided by the statutes, when the expert was summoned, and the merits and demerits of each award that had been made, relatively examined and discussed, and finally adjudged as follows: J. M. Hutchings, $24,000; Jas. C. Lamon, $12,000; A. G. Black, $13,000; Ira B. Folsom, $6,000— total, $55,000. The balance of the $60,000 appropriated was returned to the State Treasury. When the sums awarded had been accepted, and paid to the parties in interest, a quit claim deed was given by each, of all claims to either land or improvements, to the State. Thus ended the unequal contest, of many years, between the old Board of Yo Semite Commissioners and the Yo Semite settlers. Comment would be superfluous, as facts not only tell their own story, but suggest their own inferences.

Before closing this unvarnished recital, however, I wish to give special prominence to the magnanimous action of the State in favor of the settlers; first, in declining to take the least advantage of the adjudgment of the higher courts against them; and, second, in its recognition of the equities of their claim, by procuring for them a becomingly liberal appropriation, as compensation therefor; thus proving that the State requires no injustice or wrong to be committed in her name or visited upon any of her citizens however plausible may be the excuse for attempting it.

Since the passage of the Acts introduced at the commencement of this chapter the following Governors have been *ex officio* Presidents of the Board of Commissioners: F. F. Low, H. H. Haight, Newton Booth, Romualdo Pacheco, William G. Irwin, George C. Perkins, and George Stoneman.

The following gentlemen constitute the present Board of Yo Semite Commissioners: His Excellency Geo. Stoneman, President; I. W. Raymond, Vice-President; Wm. B. May, Secretary and Treasurer; Wm. H. Mills, J. H. O'Brien, Thos. P. Madden, Jonathan Mentzer, E. W. Chapman, and J. M. Griffith.

CHAPTER XIII.

REMARKS IN OUTLINE ABOUT THE JOURNEY AND ROUTES TO YO SEMITE.

If thou art worn and hard beset
With sorrows, that thou would'st forget;
If thou would'st read a lesson that will keep
Thy heart from fainting, and thy soul from sleep—
Go to the woods and hills.

—LONGFELLOW.

The traveled mind is the catholic mind educated from exclusiveness and egotism.

—ALCOTT'S *Table Talk.*

Travel makes all men country men, makes people noblemen and kings, every man tasting of liberty and dominion.

—ALCOTT'S *Concord Days.*

The reader knows as well as I do that it is of little consequence, in point of fact, whether a spirit of romance, the love of the grand and beautiful in scenery, the suggestions or promptings of a fascinating woman—be she friend, sweetheart, or wife—the desire for change, the want of recreation, or the necessity for a restoration and recuperation of an overtasked physical or mental organization, or both—whatever may be the instrumentality that first gives birth to the wish for, or the love of, travel; when the mind is thoroughly made up, and the committee of ways and means reports itself financially prepared to undertake the pleasurable task—in order to enjoy it with luxurious zest, we must resolve upon four things: *first,* to leave the "peck of troubles," and a few thrown in, entirely behind us; *second,* to have none but good, suitable, and genial-hearted companions; *third,* a sufficient supply of personal patience, good humor, forbearance, and creature comforts for all emergencies; and, *fourth,* when it is possible, not to be in a hurry. To these both one and all, who have

(163)

ever visited the Yo Semite Valley and the Big Trees, I know will say—Amen.

According to the unimpeached testimony of nearly every traveler, there is not a country on earth, known to civilization, that possesses more of the beautiful and wildly picturesque than California. Her towering and pine-covered mountains; her wide-spread valleys, carpeted with flowers; her leaping water-falls; her foaming cataracts; her rushing rivers; her placid lakes; her ever green and densely timbered forests; her gently rolling hills, covered with blooming shrubs and trees, and wild flowers, give a voiceless invitation to the traveler to look upon her and admire.

The difficulties that generally beset the stranger are to learn how those that are the most noteworthy can be seen to the best advantage. This shall be the exclusive aim and object of this work. And at the outset I wish it to be distinctly understood that all route rivalry, or expressed preference, will be utterly ignored, my object being to present the most salient and attractive features of each and all routes, and leave it to the intelligent visitor to select for himself the one best calculated to give him the largest return of pleasure. Then, as tastes vary in different individuals, that which would be most enjoyable to one might prove altogether the reverse in another. It is true there may arise reasons, occasionally, in the interests of the traveling public, why suggestions, born of experience, should be freely offered, even though they should conflict somewhat with the interests and plans of private individuals, or companies; and, however this might be regretted, they will be fearlessly presented, and the results allowed to take care of themselves.

As many lovers of the sublime and beautiful will doubtlessly desire to visit the remarkable scenes that await their appreciative admiration in the High Sierra, and as I cannot in this brief outline present all the various routes thereto from every village, town, and city in the State—for they are almost as numerous as the different roads that Christians seem to take to their expected heaven, and the multitudinous creeds about the way and manner of getting there—I shall content myself with giving the principal ones, and after reciting the following quaint and un- answerable argument of a celebrated divine, to the querulous and uncharitably disposed members of his flock, proceed at once to delineate their principal characteristics:—

"There was once a Christian brother—a Presbyterian—who walked up to the gate of the New Jerusalem, and knocked for admittance, when an angel who was in charge, looked down from above and inquired what he wanted. 'To come in,' was the answer. 'Who and what are you?' 'A Presbyterian.' 'Sit on that seat there.' This was on the outside of the gate; and the good man feared that he had been refused admittance. Presently ar- rived an Episcopalian, then a Baptist, then a Methodist, and so on, until a representative of every Christian sect had made his appearance; and each alike ordered to take a seat outside. Before they had long been there," continued the good man, "a loud and familiar anthem broke forth, rolling and swelling upon the air from the choir within; when those outside immediately joined in the chorus. 'Oh!' said the angel as he opened wide the gate, 'I did not know you by your names, but you have all learned one song—come in! come in! The name you bear, or the way by which you came, is of little consequence compared with your being here at all.' As you, my brethren," the godly man went on—"as you expect to live peaceably and lovingly together in heaven, you had better begin to practice it on earth. I have done." As this allegorical advice needs no words of application either to the traveler or to the Christian, in the hope that the latter will take the admonition of Captain Cuttle, "and make a note on't," and an apology to the reader for this digression, I will at once enter upon my pleasing task.

THE SEVEN ROUTES TO THE YO SEMITE VALLEY,

All of which can now be traveled by rail and coach to the doors of each hotel there, spring principally from one main or trunk route, like branches from a young tree. This is the Central

Pacific Railroad from *San Francisco* to *Lathrop.* It is true, however, that two of the seven routes mentioned, being from Stockton, can be reached by steamboat. The seven branches, each
of which is to be hereafter briefly described—and they will be
given in the order determined by allotment, to avoid even the
semblance of favoritism—are as follows:—

First: The "Milton and Calaveras Big Tree Route." This is
from Lathrop to Stockton, by rail (or from San Francisco by
steamboat), thence to Milton, by rail;* thence *via* Murphy's,
Calaveras Big Tree Groves, Sonora, and Chinese Camp to Valley, by coach.

Second: The "Berenda Route *via* Grant's Sulphur Springs."
From Lathrop to Berenda (S. P. R. R.), thence to Raymond by
rail; thence to Gambetta Gold Mines, Grant's Sulphur Springs,
Wawona, and Mariposa Big Tree Groves, to Valley, by coach.

Third: The "Madera Route *via* Fresno Flats." From Madera
(S. P. R. R.) *via* Fresno Flats, Fish Springs, Wawona, and
Mariposa Big Trees Groves, to Valley, by coach.

Fourth: The "Coulterville Route *via* Modesto." From
Lathrop to Modesto (S. P. R. R.), by rail; thence *via* La Grange,
Coulterville, Dudley's, Bower Cave, and Merced Grove of Big
Trees, to Valley, by coach.

Fifth: The "Coulterville Route *via* Merced." From Lathrop
to Merced (S. P. R. R.), by rail; thence *via* Snellings, Merced
Falls, Coulterville, and Merced Grove of Big Trees, to Valley, by
coach.

Sixth: The "Mariposa Route." From Lathrop to Merced
(S. P. R. R.), by rail; thence *via* Hornitos, Princeton, Mariposa,
Wawona, and Mariposa Big Tree Groves, to Valley, by coach.

Seventh: The "Milton and Big Oak Flat Route." From
Lathrop to Stockton (C. P. R. R.), by rail, or by steamboat;
thence to Milton (S. & C. R. R.), by rail; thence *via* Copperopolis,

---

* There is also a narrow-gauge railroad in course of construction from Brack's Landing
on the Mokelumne River, to the Calaveras Grove—already completed to Valley Springs, and
running from Lodi on the C. P. R. R. to that point.

Chinese Camp, Moffitt's Bridge, Priests, Big Oak Flat, Crockers, and Tuolumne Grove of Big Trees, to Valley, by coach.

Each of these will be briefly outlined, and the different points of interest noted, in separate chapters, accompanied by a map that will indicate the diverging and connecting lines of each particular route—which, please consult—so as to enable visitors to travel understandingly, and, it is hoped, enjoyably, by whatsoever route they may elect to take. But, to make a journey thoroughly pleasurable, and its close a delightful memory, a limited amount of business caution should precede the start, and more or less accompany the traveler to the end.

Of course I will, if you please, assume that the object of the trip is at least twofold,—intellectual and physical gratification, and the gathering of impressions and facts that may be of use hereafter. With a desire to subserve such laudable purposes, permit me to make a few preliminary suggestions, tending somewhat to insure these results:—

First: Go in by one route, and out by another—remembering that all routes are picturesque and interesting while being equally safe. Should any one advise you to the contrary, you may be sure that he has some unworthy business "ax to grind;" therefore, heed him not.

Second: Having thoroughly made up your mind about the route that you prefer, see that your ticket, upon its face, exactly represents your wishes. Oral explanations are not always conveniently at hand, when they are perhaps most needed; and memory sometimes may be at fault, but written or printed testimony is always to the point, if presentable.

Third: Never be induced to leave a trunk, or a hat-box, or valise, or fish-rod, or rifle, or anything else, in any way calculated to compel you to return by that or any other route, contrary to your well-considered plans and intentions.

If, after what you read below, you have been induced to take something you do not need, either carry it along with you, or leave it at, or conveniently near, some juncture of the two roads.

PERSONAL BAGGAGE TO BE TAKEN.

This, you will allow, is a difficult matter for me to determine, and one that will require your generous forbearance and assistance. These questions settled, I will suppose that your good sense (no flattery is intended) will suggest at the start that all Saratoga trunks should be eschewed, even if their dimensions do not exceed those of an ordinary cottage or two. If you have one of moderate pretensions, be sure and carefully examine its contents with the view of laying aside everything that you know will not be wanted. Next, turn over your effects again, and reject everything you feel that you could conscientiously do without.

Now, if health and comfort are studied, gentlemen will see that they have one extra of each of the following articles: One pair of good serviceable boots (not necessarily very heavy) that have been broken to the feet; one complete outfit of underclothing; one woolen overshirt; three or four pairs of hose (woolen should be preferred); one suit of strong clothes (old ones, if not too easily torn, would be the best, as they will be good for nothing after your return); pocket-handkerchiefs, and a few other necessary articles; remembering that there are laundries in the Valley. Ladies would do well by taking some of the hints thrown out to gentlemen—in providing themselves with woolen dresses of suitable length, color, and texture, made in the Bloomer or other similar style, as such would be found to possess both comfort and adaptability; durable linen riding habit; boots that were made for wear more than for ornament; a warm shawl; and by making choice of such other articles as will best meet their wants, wishes, and tastes, without further enumeration from me. These should all be packed in as small a valise as possible; or, if an extended trip into the mountains is intended, in a pair of saddle-bags.

At best it will be difficult to give advice that will accord with every variety of condition and of circumstance. By way of illustration, we may mention that an estimable and intelligent lady correspondent of a San Francisco paper visited Yo Semite early in May; and, finding the weather cool, advised every lady to go there warmly clad. Other ladies, later in the season, taking that advice, and finding the climate pleasantly warm, remarked, "How could Mrs. H—— recommend us to come in such warm clothing? when we return we will tell all *our* lady friends to choose none but light summer dresses!"

Always look out for your baggage, and see that every piece is surely placed upon the conveyance you are about to take before leaving the hotel door. Careful attention to the above suggestions will, believe me, preserve you from many detracting annoyances in the future of your journey.

A WORD TO PARTIES CAMPING.

Supposing that you have wisely chosen your companions, of both sexes, from those you *know* possess kindred tastes and dispositions, each of whom expects to assume, cheerfully, his or her full share of all the duties appertaining to camp life— whether in song, a good story, recitation, or in the somewhat exacting attentions of the cuisine—you will then be in a position to consider how the enjoyments of the trip can be best subserved. Here permit me to make a few suggestions which originated in the laboratory of experience:—

ABOUT YOUR OUTFIT.

Let it consist, mainly, as follows: A light yet strong coach, sufficiently capacious to accommodate your party comfortably, especially if the weather is, like Bob Sawyer's apple (see Pickwick Papers), unpleasantly warm; horses that are known to be, not only true to the harness, but of about the same size and weight, and equal to every reasonable emergency of both load and road; bearing in mind that there are not less than from five to six thousand feet of altitude to be overcome, between the plains and Yo Semite, or Big Trees, the grade being heavy in some places. Do not overload with stores, for two reasons: First, it saps away the strength and spirit of your horses (to say nothing of your own), and consequently retards both speed and progress. Second, because every kind of article, almost, from a needle to a saw-horse, can be obtained upon arrival, and generally at fairly reasonable prices, considering their distance from the market. Still, enough should be taken for the necessities of the road. Provide a flattish sheet-iron, bottomless, cook-stove, of reasonably heavy iron, having two or four holes on top, and one length of stove-pipe, snugly fitted to the stove; a nest of camp-kettles (four or five) that fit into each other; baking, bread, and dish pans (one of the matrons of the party should select all such articles); frying-pan, bake-oven, coffee and teapots, granite-ware plates and cups; tea and table-spoons, and one large batter spoon; knives and forks, including a couple of good butcher knives; salt, pepper, sugar, tea and coffee bags, with extra ones for time of need. Then to these do not forget to add a whetstone, towels, soap, brooms, needles and thread, scissors, buttons, matches and candles, writing-paper, pens, ink, envelopes, postage stamps, etc. Then to these add three pairs of blankets for each couple, and as many for each one who prefers to sleep alone.

TENTS AND THEIR ARRANGEMENTS.

Suitable tents should always be provided for the ladies, and one long tent for general use, open at the front for its entire length, and consisting of one sheet of strong drilling, say three yards in width by five in length, with ends, resembling those of an old-fashioned Dutch-oven, as illustrated below. This, with the lower back edge fastened to the ground (suitable holes having been worked into the

sheet for picket-pins) is supported in front by a light pole-post, set under it at each front corner; over which a small cord (running the whole length of, and well sewed to, the sheet) is drawn tight, and fastened to a pin driven in the ground, in advance of the front line of the tent, by which the whole is made secure. A similar sheet, to form a kind of carpet, should be spread upon the ground, or over the improvised bedding of leaves, hay, pine needles, etc., to keep the blankets clean. These sheets, when carefully shaken, and folded once, make an excellent wrap for the blankets, sheets, pillows, and other articles requiring to be kept clean, especially if well tied up, to keep out the dust.

Contrivances like these add largely to the comfort of a party, by providing a place of shelter for themselves, and outfit, in all weathers, as well as a compartment for general rendezvous, and for social pleasures at all times. (Eleven of us—six ladies and five gentlemen—enjoyably occupied one of these in our mountain wanderings, for over three months.) In the Sierra Nevadas the summer winds generally blow from the east at night, and the open tent should be so pitched as to have the back of it towards that quarter; then the wind not only sweeps over it, but carries away all the camp-fire smoke, instead of driving it into the tent. For rainy weather in California it should be pitched towards the south, and the front open to the north. If the purposes of sight-seeing, or an outlook towards the horses, or wagon, can be sub-served by changing its direction a little, that can be done without interfering with any of its protective provisions. Be sure and select a dry place, as convenient as possible to wood and water, for your camp-ground. Now, although fine weather is the rule among the mountains of California, during summer, it should be borne in mind that nearly every rule has its exceptions, and this is one; therefore, it behooves every camping-party to be prepared for storms, should they come. Timely provision should according-ly be made for these, in order to avoid discomfort, and, possibly, severe colds. The old saying that "one ounce of prevention is better than pounds of antidotes," will, believe me, be found serv-iceable here, as elsewhere.

CHAPTER XIV.

THE MAIN OR TRUNK ROUTE TOWARDS YO SEMITE, SAN FRANCISCO TO LATHROP.

Speed the soft intercourse from soul to soul,
And waft a sigh from Indus to the pole.
—POPE'S *Eloise to Abelard.*

Traveling is no fool's errand to him who carries his eyes and itinerary with him.
—ALCOTT'S *Table Talk.*

Know most of the rooms of thy native country before thou goest over the threshold thereof.
—FULLER.

There are probably but few, if any, more exciting scenes in any part of the world than are to be witnessed on almost any day, Sunday excepted, at the Market Street Wharf, San Francisco, upon the departure of the various trains for the interior, or over-land. Men and women are hurrying to and fro; drays, carriages, express wagons, and horsemen dash past you with as much haste and vehemence as though they were carrying a reprieve to some poor condemned criminal, the last moments of whose life were fast ebbing away, and by the speedy delivery of that reprieve, they expected to save him from the scaffold. Indeed, one would suppose, by the apparently reckless manner in riding and driving through the crowd, that numerous limbs, if not necks, would be broken, and vehicles made into mince-meat! Yet, to your surprise, nothing of the kind occurs; for, upon arriving at the smallest obstruction, animals are reined in with a promptness that astonishes.

Interesting as this may be to you as a spectator, it should not be allowed to divert your attention sufficiently to prevent the timely checking of your trunk, or valise, to the very railway

(172)

terminus you are to leave by stage, or to cause your being the proverbial "last man," as he sometimes arrives too late. Presuming that all such matters have received becoming consideration; that your ticket, upon its face, provides for all emergencies of travel upon the route you have chosen; and, moreover, that you are safely aboard the ferry-boat that is speeding you towards the wonderful Valley and the Big Tree Groves; as you may be a stranger here, and somewhat unfamiliar with the scenes that will open before you, I will, in imagination at least, with your kind permission, be your traveling companion on this excursion, and explain such matters as most naturally will claim our attention.

As it is generally cool in summer, when crossing the Bay of San Francisco, please put on your overcoat, and let us take a cozy seat together on the north side of the boat; and while the black smoke is rolling in volumes from the funnels of numerous steamers, and we are shooting out from the wharf, past this or that vessel lying at anchor, or furling its sails from a voyage or spreading them for one; while numerous people are troubling about their baggage, and asking the porter all sorts of questions, let us have a quiet chat upon the sights to be seen around us. The first object of interest, after leaving the wharf and the city behind us, is

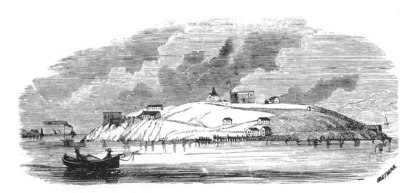

ALCATRACES, OR PELICAN ISLAND.

This is just opposite the Golden Gate, and about half way between the city and Angel Island. It commands the great land-locked Bay of San Francisco, and is but three and a half miles from Fort Point, on the southern side of the Golden Gate. This island (now generally called "Alcatraz") is one hundred and forty feet in height above low water mark, four hundred and fifty feet in width, and sixteen hundred and fifty feet in length; somewhat irregular in outline, and fortified on all sides. The large building on its summit is a defensive barrack, or citadel, three stories high, which in time of peace will, with other quarters, accommodate about two hundred men; and in war about three times that number. It is not only a shelter for the soldiers, capable of withstanding a respectable cannonade, but from its top a murderous fire could be opened upon its assailants at all parts of the island. There is, moreover, a belt of fortifications encircling the island, mounting guns of the heaviest caliber, and of the latest improved patterns.

Besides these there are stone guard-houses, shot and shell proof, protected by heavy gates and draw-bridges, and having embrasures for rifled cannon that command the approaches in every direction. Their tops, like the barrack, are flat, for the use of riflemen. In addition to these there are several bomb-proof magazines, and a large furnace for heating cannon balls.

Unfortunately, no natural supply of water has yet been discovered on the island, so that all of this element has to be carried there in tanks, and stored in a large cistern at the basement of the barracks. For washing purposes a sufficient quantity is obtained from the roofs of the principal buildings. At the southeastern end of the island is a fog-bell, of about the same size and weight as that at Fort Point, which is regulated to strike by machinery every quarter of a minute. There is also a light-house at the south of the barracks, with newly improved lenses, the glare from which can be distinctly seen, on a clear night, some twelve miles outside the Heads, and is of essential service in directing the course of vessels when entering the Bay. Northerly from Alcatraces, about two and a half miles distant, and five from San Francisco, is

ANGEL ISLAND.

This contains some eight hundred acres of excellent land, and is by far the largest and most valuable of any in the Bay of San Francisco. The wild oats and grasses that grow to its very summit, in early spring, give pasturage to stock of all kinds needed here; while several natural springs, at different points, supply good water in abundance, and at all seasons. A large portion of the island is susceptible of cultivation for all kinds of vegetables and cereals. Beautiful wild flowers grow in sequestered places from one end of it to the other. Live oaks *(quercus agrifolia)* supply both shade and firewood. Belonging, as it does, to the Government, it is a favorite place of residence for army officers stationed there, for whose accommodation a small steamer plies, regularly, between this island (calling at Alcatraces, Fort Point, and Point San Jose) and San Francisco.

From its almost inexhaustible quarries of hard blue and brown sandstone, nearly all the material for foundations of buildings in San Francisco were taken, in early times. The extensive fortifications at Alcatraces Island, Fort Point, and other places, have been faced with it, and the extensive Government works at Mare Island have been principally built with stone from these quarries. Clay, also, in abundance, and of excellent quality for bricks, is found here.

As Angel Island lies midway between Alcatraces Island and the main-land the guns from its fortifications completely sweep the bay, southerly, and Raccoon Straits, northwesterly, affording thorough protection on all sides. But for these not only would our Navy Yard at Mare Island be in jeopardy, but the city of San Francisco itself would be exposed; inasmuch as an enemy's war vessel could easily enter the harbor by Raccoon Straits, during a heavy fog, that frequently in summer hangs over the Golden Gate, if permitted to pass Fort Point in safety.

MT. TAMALPAIS

Is the highest point in the more immediate surroundings of the Bay of San Francisco, and is a more prominent landmark far out at sea. It stands northwesterly from the city of San Francisco, and its top is about fifteen miles distant, "as the crow flies." Its height above sea level is 2,610 feet. A good road to its summit from San Rafael now enables every one to view the comprehensive and beautiful landscape thence, not only with comfort but with positive enjoyment. We generally climbed it afoot, for exercise. The light-colored mark on its southern side was caused by a "cloud-burst," which literally tore out the earth and rocks to the depth of several feet, and for over forty feet in width by a hundred and fifty in length. This torrent-cut material, sweeping with impetuous force down a ravine, set bowlders free, tore out trees by their roots, snapped others in two, and made sad havoc from top to bottom. This event occurred in 1861. If I were to detain you here with descriptions of its madroñe, laurel, oak, and other trees; its fragrant shrubs, and numerous wild flowers, there is no telling when or where this theme would end. But while we have been chatting, and watching the receding city, with its seven hills—like Rome—all covered with buildings; or looking at the English, French, or German, and other ships-of-war that are now resting so peacefully at anchor, like sleeping giants; or admiring the daring of those little steam-tugs that shoot hither and thither, and take hold of vessels many dozen times their size, and push them wherever they may list; or interestedly note the craft of all sizes flitting across the seething wake of our boat, and glinting in the far-off sunlight; or listening to the beating paddles of numerous ferry-boats, starting in all conceivable directions; or observing that steamer with the stately sweep and build, whose prow so proudly cuts the brine, that is just now sailing for Panama, or Hong Kong *via* Japan, or Australia, or for one of the many Pacific Coast ports; while we have been observing these, and perhaps many other objects of interest, we have come abreast of a little green spot now known as

GOAT ISLAND.

When occupied by Mexicans it was called "Yerba Buena Island," from the generous supply of the "good herb"

(Micromeria Douglasii) found on its northern and sheltered side. It is now in the possession of the United States Government, and used mainly as a Fog-Horn Signal Station—a very necessary precaution in foggy weather, especially to the well-patronized ferries that ply between San Francisco and Oakland, or Alameda—and for the manufacture and storage of buoys, many of which can be seen lying on the landing there. Strenuous efforts were made several years ago for the possession of this island by the Central Pacific Railroad Company, as the western terminus of their great overland road, and for the accommodation of vessels loading with wheat, wool, argentiferous ores, or other California products; but the property owners of San Francisco saw the mental mirage of a rival city looming up, and successfully opposed its cession. Now the ship-loading business, intended for Goat Island, is carried on at Long Wharf, northwesterly from the Oakland pier, where vessels from all nations can be seen taking in cargo, for their respective destinations. But the ring of the bell responded to impatiently, apparently, by the passengers gives intimation that we have crossed the Bay of San Francisco, and are at

THE OAKLAND PIER.

The distance across, from the Market Street Wharf to the Oakland Pier, is three miles and sixty-three one hundredths, and has taken us just twenty minutes to accomplish it. Let us pause for a moment, if you please, and gaze at the hurrying stream of human life, flowing out from these commodious ferry-boats. If you and I could follow each and every one to his abiding place, enter into the secret heart-life of each and know their various plans and hopes, their sorrows, fears, and cares, I think our hearts would soften a little to the many. But, as we have to mix with the throng, or be left behind, we naturally cut short our reveries and walk ashore. Now a clear stentorian voice announces: "Passengers for Benicia, Sacramento, Stockton, Lathrop, and all intermediate points, please to step this way," and we flow with the outward-bound tide of humanity into the capacious depot, where there seems to be a bewildering number of trains, for all sorts of places; but as the destination of each is announced in large letters, "so that he who runneth can read," there is no danger of our selecting the wrong one.

As our course when leaving the ferry-boat has been to the left, we may have unintentionally passed

THE ELEGANT WAITING-ROOM,

Perhaps, without noticing it. This would be a regretable omission, as it is one of the most commodious, as well as most comfortable waiting-rooms, to be found in any country or clime; for as soon as it is entered by returning passengers, its spaciousness, and cheery brightness bespeak a cordial welcome that always impresses pleasantly. Photographs, paintings, and "live" advertisements make it fairly to glisten with sprightliness. But to our journey.

THE START FROM THE OAKLAND PIER.

With the waters of the Bay on each side of us, we speed along rapidly over a solid road-bed of rock, made through the shallow stretches of the Bay, instead of on piles and beams, as formerly, adding materially to the safety of the transit over it; the outlook broadening, and the interest deepening, as we advance.

There is something very exhilarating about the excitements of a journey through an unfamiliar country, and as soon as we have taken our seat in the railway car, and object after object, or scene after scene, opens up before us, we long for some one at our elbow, or by our side, to answer questions. This gratification is not always attainable. But, partly in anticipation of your wishes, it may be well to explain them briefly as we roll comfortably along. And, by way of commencement, when the cars stop at any particular station, as the conductor may be busy with his duties, and as you may like to know just how far we have traveled, the following table will explain the distances between San Francisco and Lathrop.—

WAY STATIONS.	DISTANCES IN MILES.		
	Between Consecutive Points.	From San Fran- cisco.	From Lathrop.
By Railway			
From San Francisco to—			94.34
Oakland Pier	3.69	3.69	90.65
West Oakland	2.20	5.89	88.45
Sixteenth Street, Oakland	0.60	6.49	87.85
Stock Yards	2.26	8.75	85.59
West Berkeley	1.67	10.42	83.92
Highland	1.26	11.68	82.66
Point Isabel	1.09	12.77	81.57
Stege	1.15	13.92	80.12
Barrett	2.20	16.12	78.20
San Pablo	1.47	17.59	76.75
Sobrante	3.23	20.82	73.52
Pinole	3.20	24.02	70.32
Tormey	2.74	26.76	67.58
VALLEJO JUNCTION	2.25	29.01	65.33
Valona	0.61	29.62	64.72
PORT COSTA	2.55	32.17	62.17
Martinez	3.47	35.64	58.70
Avon	3.51	39.15	55.19
Bay Point	3.09	42.24	52.10
McAvoy	3.26	45.50	48.84
Cornwall	4.39	49.89	44.45
Antioch	4.65	54.54	39.80
Brentwood	8.16	62.70	31.64
Byron	5.13	67.83	26.51
Bethany	8.81	76.64	17.70
TRACY	6.61	83.25	11.09
Banta	3.09	86.34	8.00
LATHROP	8.00	94.34	

Total from San Francisco to Lathrop. 94.34

On, on we ride, past the western suburbs of Oakland, the Stock Yards, and West Berkeley, various manufacturing establishments, catching a hasty glimpse of the California University buildings, the Deaf, Dumb, and Blind Asylum, and other State institutions, standing among the gently rolling foot-hills of the Contra Costa Range, the distance for many miles out being dotted with comfortable residences or prosperous farms. Back of and east of these rise the green yet almost treeless ridges of the Contra Costa Hills, covered to their summits in spring and early summer with a luxuriant growth of wild oats, which, in the fall, change to a rich golden brown, from very dryness.

WILD OATS, HOW PRESERVED FROM EXTERMINATION.

In early days, owing to carelessness, or to wantonness, miles of this parched surface would be ignited, and fire sweep over it in rolling waves, throwing its lurid light both far and near, and burning everything that was combustible—the wild oats included. Fortunately, however, nature had provided each grain with two slender extremities, as though anticipating the coming danger; and as the oats dropped down upon the ground, and became swollen by the dews of night, those extremities were contracted inwards towards the body of the grain, when their feet inserted themselves into the ground; the next day's warmth dried out the moisture, and in so doing straightened out the legs, so that by this process the grain itself was forced forward, until it dropped into one of the many sun-cracks near, and was entirely out of danger from the destroying element. The first heavy rains following, swell the earth sufficiently to cover the wild oats entirely up; when they stool out from among their hiding-places in the cracks; and when the tender shoots make their appearance, the whole surface presents a resemblance to some grotesquely woven, tessellated carpet.

Moving rapidly forward, and shooting past some stations without stopping, our course, for nearly thirty miles, lies along the southeastern margin of the charming bays of San Francisco and San Pablo; the light glinting upon their waters, and beyond which are the purple hills looming up in picturesque irregularity, indicating numerous spurs, or starting points of apparently different ranges, until we pass the Starr Co.'s flouring mills (where some two thousand five hundred barrels of flour are said to be manufactured daily) and arrive at Vallejo Junction. Now we lose those of our fellow-passengers who are bound for Vallejo, the Government works of Mare Island, Napa, and other prosperous settlements in these midland valleys.

Three miles farther on—the intermediate distance occupied mainly by grain warehouses and workshops—we reach the famous ferry landing of Port Costa, where all Eastern-bound passengers leave us for their multifarious destinations. Here we find

THE MONSTER C. P. R. R. TRANSFER BOAT "SOLANO."

This plies between Port Costa and Benicia, across the Straits of Carquinez, the distance between the slips being within a few feet of one mile. As this is the largest boat of her class afloat, the following description, kindly furnished by its owners, will be found interesting:—

The dimensions of the double-ender transfer boat *Solano* are: Length over all, 424 feet; length on bottom, 406 feet; height of sides, at center, 18 feet 5 inches; at ends, from bottom of boat, 15 feet 10 inches; moulded beam, 64 feet; extreme width over guards, 116 feet; camber, or reverse shear of deck, 2 feet 6 inches. Draught, light, 5 feet, loaded, 6 feet 6 inches. Registered tonnage, 3,541 31–100 tons.

She has two vertical beam engines: Cylinders, 60-inch bore, 11 feet stroke; wheels, 30 feet diameter, with 24 buckets each, 17 feet face.

Engines are driven by 8 steel boilers, each 28 feet long, 7 feet diameter of shells, containing 143 tubes, 4 inches diameter by 16 feet long. Total heating surface in 8 boilers, 19,640 square feet; grate surface 288 square feet, capable of driving engines with 2,000 horse-power each. The boilers are placed in pairs, on the guards, forward and abaft the paddle-boxes, connected with engines, so that one or all may be used at pleasure.

The engines are placed on the center line of the boat, fore and aft of the center of boat, 8 feet, making distance from center to center of shafts 16 feet, and not placed abreast of each other, as in the usual manner. The object of this arrangement is to give room on deck for four tracks—

and each wheel being driven by an independent engine, enables the boat to be more easily handled in entering slips.

Among other novelties in her construction are four Pratt trusses, arranged fore and aft, directly under tracks, varied in size to meet the strains upon them. These give longitudinal stiffness, and connect the deck and bottom of the boat, making her in reality a huge floating bridge. In addition there are eleven water-tight transverse bulkheads, dividing the hull into twelve compartments, rendering her absolutely secure from all danger of sinking, besides adding additional stiffness to the boat.

There are four balanced rudders at each end of boat, $11\frac{1}{2}$ feet long by $5\frac{1}{2}$ feet deep, coupled together and worked by hydraulic steering gear, operated by independent steam-engines and pumps. The steering gear is connected also with steering wheels in the ordinary manner—the pilot houses being 40 feet above deck, affording the helmsman a clear view, fore and aft.

There are four bridges running athwartship, and another fore and aft, connecting the pilot houses. Upon the deck are four tracks extending the entire length, with capacity for 48 freight cars, with locomotive, or 24 passenger coaches of the largest class.

The aprons connecting the boat with the slips at Benicia and Port Costa are each 100 feet long, with four tracks, so arranged so that freight and passenger trains are run aboard without being uncoupled from the locomotive. The aprons weigh, each, 150 tons, and are worked by a combination of pontoons and counter-weights, by hydraulic power.

In the hold of the boat are commodious quarters for the officers and crew; on deck, rooms for the transaction of railroad business.

THE STRAITS OF CARQUINEZ.

These form the only outlet for the entire water-shed of the Sierra Nevada Mountains, and the great basins of the Sacramento and San Joaquin Rivers, with their tributaries, comprising an area of nearly thirty thousand square miles. This, therefore, from necessity, forms the only inland, Golden Gate-like entrance, for all vessels needed for the commercial wants of the interior, outside and apart from the out-reaching railroad system of the State.

MARTINEZ.

Instead of crossing the Straits of Carquinez, however, we continue along its southern shore for some distance yet; and in about three miles arrive at Martinez, the county seat of Contra

Costa County. This, believe me, is one of the prettiest agricultural villages in any country. A week among its vineyards, gardens, groves, and farms, will convince the most skeptical of this.

COUNTRY NEAR MARTINEZ.

Here, too, the beautiful live oak *(Quercus agrifolia)* and the gracefully drooping white oak *(Q. lobata)* add their inviting attractions to the landscape. This, moreover, is the avenue by which Pacheco and other valleys are reached, and where the native Californians in early days enjoyed so many pastimes; which, like many of its people, have passed away forever. On this account I am tempted to briefly chronicle some of the most

POPULAR AMUSEMENTS OF NATIVE CALIFORNIANS.

Like their Mexican prototypes, they are very fond of amusements. They can endure any amount of enjoyment in every form, and at all times, and take as kindly to pleasure as though they were born to it. There is also another sympathetic characteristic between the two peoples—neither of them will do anything *today* in the form of work that they can, by any possibility, postpone until to-morrow. *Mañana esta siempre buena* (to-morrow is always good), where labor is concerned, because it never comes. On these accounts, mainly, every "saint's day," among these old settlers, was welcomed, because it brought a holiday.

NATIVE CALIFORNIANS RACING.

It used to be an interesting sight to watch these dusky-colored people issue from their humble, tile-roofed, adobe dwellings, in any of their dreamy towns, at sunrise, on any favorite saint's day, when the matin bell called to prayers. Then the señoritas and señoras, dressed in the brightest of colors; and the señores begirt themselves in the gayest of sashes; and all walked, saunteringly, side by side, to the shadow-filled house of devotion where, with low musical chantings, solemn ceremonials (and equally solemn countenances) they knelt together in seeming worship.

But no sooner was the church threshold recrossed than they felt "A change came o'er the spirit of my dream"[1] that almost amounted to an entire transformation; the muttered response was eversed to a merry laugh, and the kneeling posture to a lively, light-footed skip. Now the arrangements for the day's enjoyments were freely discussed, and every preparation made for insuring a general holiday. Wayside stalls, laden with fruits, cakes, sweetmeats, toys, and general refreshments, would spring up here and there; and be well patronized by juveniles, and friends that had come in from the neighboring ranches.

HORSE-RACING.

Every native Californian is as much at home on a horse, with or without a saddle, as a Sandwich Islander is upon a surf-board when he plays upon the waves; and, as horses are their particular pride (even while they excessively abuse them when in passion), skill in riding is the most esteemed of all accomplishments. Associated with this, and of which it forms a part, is the love of display; so that next to a beautiful animal the most costly of caparisons are preferred. A native Californian will, therefore, invest his last *real* (and go hungry) rather than forego the indulgence of expensive ornaments for his saddle, bridle, and spurs. And as horse-racing strikingly provides him with the opportunity for exhibiting these to the best advantage before the fair sex, and his envious companions, he indulges it to infatuation. Scarcely secondary to this, and for the selfsame reasons, follows the popular pastime of "snatching the rooster."

1. Byron, *The Dream.*

NATIVE CALIFORNIAN, WHEN AT FULL SPEED, SNATCHING THE ROOSTER.

As illustrated in the above engraving the body of the rooster is buried, so that nothing but the head is visible above ground. All of those who are mounted, and whose horses are prancing and dancing, about sixty yards distant, are to take part in the sport, and are impatiently awaiting their turn. The moment the signal is given for the start, the impetuous and expectant rider sets spurs to his horse, and dashes out at the top of his speed; and, when nearly opposite the would-be prize, he makes a dexterous swoop down to it; and, if he succeeds in clutching and unearthing the bird, he bears off the trophy in triumph, amid the applause of the concourse assembled. But, should he fail in the effort, as most frequently happens, he not only loses the favors he had looked forward to winning, but sometimes is unhorsed with violence, and dragged in the dust, at the risk of serious accident; and that, too, amid the derisive jeers and laughter of the spectators. Valuable horses, with their costly trappings, and sometimes large sums of money, and even ranches, are not infrequently staked upon the issue of "snatching the rooster."

Another source of amusement among native Californians, and this also was intended to illustrate their dexterity in horsemanship, is to place a rawhide flat upon the ground; and, when the horse is galloping swiftly, to suddenly check him in the moment his forefeet strike the hide. If, by any possibility, the horse is allowed to cross this before stopping, the rider is berated most unmercifully for his lack of skill, especially if he should be unseated in the effort. But the greatest of all sources of gratification, to all classes and to both sexes, were the

BULL, AND BULL AND BEAR FIGHTS.

After the discovery of gold, and before their grounds were acquired and much settled up by Americans, these people took increased delight in the cruel and dangerous recreation of bull-baiting, and bull and bear fighting, until 1852, when it was frowned down by the public, and prevented by the authorities. On one occasion thousands of persons had collected, in one of our populous valleys, to witness one of these disgraceful exhibitions, when twelve bulls, two large grizzly bears, and a considerable number of Indians were engaged at different times. In the second day's encounter four Indians and one horse were killed; and while the sharp horns of the infuriated bull were goring their voluntary victims, the band would strike up a lively tune to smother their cries and moans. Fortunately these, with cock-fighting and other debasing amusements, have, let us hope, forever ended, as they have been superseded by those which are progressive and refining.

The native Californians, with their half-dreamy and semi-religious teachings, seemed to have been a compromise between barbarism on the one hand and the æsthetical refinement of progress on the other; and, owing to their easy, "go-as-you-please" temperaments, and manners, have been despoiled, and sharply elbowed off the track in the great race of life, with a few tenacious and plucky exceptions; and, with their customs, for the most part, been retired into the irretrievable past.

Leaving the county seat of Contra Costa behind us, with the rolling hills that surround it, we emerge into an open country studded with farms that skirt the base of an imposing mountain on our right, known to the world as

MONTE DEL DIABLO.

Whether we are walking on the streets of San Francisco, or sailing on our bays and navigable rivers, or riding on the roads in the Sacramento and San Joaquin Valleys, or standing on the elevated ridges of the Sierras; in lonely boldness, at almost every turn, Monte Diablo stands prominently out as the great landmark of Central California.

Viewed from the northwest or southeast, it appears to have a double crown, with two elevated crests that are about three miles apart. The southwestern is the higher, with an elevation of three thousand eight hundred and fifty feet above sea level. From this lofty standpoint the country is spread out before you like an immense map, covering an estimated area of forty thousand square miles of land, and forming one of the most remarkable panoramas ever viewed by human eyes. To describe this in detail would of itself fill a volume. It is presumed that its name-givers, the early padres, having climbed it, and looked around upon its unspeakable wonders with awe, recalled to memory that passage of holy writ from Matt. 4: 8, 9: "The devil taketh him [Jesus] up into an exceeding high mountain, and sheweth him all the kingdoms of the world, and the glory of them; and saith unto him, All these things will I give thee, if thou wilt fall down and worship me," and that this suggested the name. Without even attempting an outline of the glorious view presented, let me counsel you to pay the summit of Monte del Diablo a visit, if you wish to revel in a scenic banquet, the memory of which will remain with you pleasantly forever. To accomplish this you leave the train at Martinez, and proceed to Clayton; whence you can ride to the very summit, by a fairly good road, and back again to Clayton, in a single day.

For the purpose of surveying the State into a network of township lines, three "meridians," or initial points, were established by the United States Survey, namely: Monte Diablo (Contra Costa County), Mount San Bernardino (San Bernardino County), and Mount Pierce (Humboldt County). Across the highest peaks of each of these a "meridian line" and a "base line" were run; the latter being from east to west, and the former from north to south. Of these three the Monte Diablo is by far the most comprehensive, as it includes all the lands lying between the Coast Range and the Sierras, and from the Siskiyou Mountains to the head of the Tulare Valley.

The geologic features of Monte Diablo are mainly primitive, although surrounded by sedimentary rock, abounding in marine shells. Near its summit gold-bearing quartz has been found in veins; on its western slope hornblende; and, in its numerous spurs, an inexhaustible supply of limestone. It is said that both copper and cinnabar ore has been found here, but with what truthfulness has not been determined. At the eastern base of Monte Diablo several veins of coal have been found, but this being strongly impregnated with sulphur, has been used, principally, for steamboats.

The cañons of this mountain are lined with stunted oak, and pines; and wild oats and chaparral, alternately, grow from base to summit. In the fall season, when the herbage and dead bushes are perfectly dry, the Indians have sometimes set portions of the surface on fire, and when the breeze is fresh, and the night dark, the lurid flames leap, and curl, and sweep, now to this side and now to that, and present a spectacle magnificent beyond the power of language to express.

But as time forbids a longer tarrying here, for the present at least, let us ride onward past farms, with cattle and horses on either side of the track; shoot under tramways from the Monte Diablo coal mines at Cornwall and Antioch; and, before long, arrive at Tracy, where the Western Division of the Central Pacific Railroad forms a junction with the main line. But a short time will elapse before crossing the San Joaquin River (which obtains its waters from the living glaciers of Mount Ritter, the Minarets, and other lofty peaks of the main chain of the Sierra Nevada Mountains) and, continuing about three miles beyond, we arrive at

LATHROP.

Here the trunk, or main line, forms a junction with its diverging branches, both north and south. This station—named in honor of Mrs. Leland Stanford (wife of Governor, now United States Senator Stanford, one of the founders and builders of the Central Pacific Railroad, and continuously its president) whose maiden name was Lathrop—from its establishment, has always been a general stopping-place for refreshments; and, when approaching it, you will still hear some resonant voice announce, "Lathrop—twenty minutes for meals." In recent years an opposition gong has rung out its unmusical clang, to tell to the hungry that there are other places at Lathrop, besides the station, where the hungry can be fed. Here, also, are workshops, engine houses, surplus cars, and all the usual paraphernalia of a central depot; so that "extras" of every kind needed in railroad transportation can be furnished without the least unnecessary delay. Railway officers, with their assistants, naturally make this quite a lively station; and, when the trains arrive with their passengers, all is bustle and excitement. Within the past few years this has grown somewhat into an agricultural settlement, which, with the conveniences needed by railway employes, has changed its formerly sleepy and forsaken look to one of wide-awake business prosperity, that augurs well for its future development and advancement.

If we are bound for Yo Semite *via* Modesto, Merced, Berenda, or Madera, we keep our seats in the car; but, if our ticket provides for entering the great Valley *via* Stockton, Milton, and the Calaveras Big Trees, or Milton direct, we change both ourselves and our baggage to the Stockton train. For particulars concerning routes beyond Lathrop, the reader is referred to one or other of succeeding chapters so that he may obtain the information desired on the one he has decided to take.

CHAPTER XV.

THE BAY AND RIVER ROUTES TOWARDS YO SEMITE.

Breathe soft, ye winds! ye waves, in silence sleep.

—Gay.

You know I say
Just what I think, and nothing more or less,
And, when I pray, my heart is in my prayer.
I cannot say one thing and mean another:
If I can't pray, I will not make believe!
—Longfellow's *Christus, Pt. III.*

The fall of waters and the song of birds,
And hills that echo to the distant herds,
Are luxuries excelling all the glare
The world can boast, and her chief favorites share.
—Cowper's *Retirement.*

About two hundred yards northerly of the Market Street Wharf lies that of Washington Street, whence sail the San Joaquin River steamboats bound for Stockton, on the Milton, Calaveras Big Tree, and Big Oak Flat routes to Yo Semite, with other destinations. If the freight is all aboard, they sail at five o'clock P. M.; but, if not, they generally delay starting until it is. As at the Market Street Wharf, the scene here is full of excitement, and of positive interest, although not partaking, altogether, of the same characteristics. The former is quiet and methodical; while this is irregular, and somewhat contentious; owing to the established rivalry between the two lines. Each has its friends; and both employ their own advocates. Eagerness to possess passengers, at any cost of eloquence, or of tact, is of more momentous consideration, at this juncture, than any rules of ordinary courtesy, or of personal convenience. But, once on board either of the boats, you are safely delivered from that vortex of contention, and peace reigns supreme. Polite attention

(191)

places you entirely at your ease; and, if the war of words is still raging below, it only becomes a source of amusement, to beguile the otherwise wearying moments of waiting. This, however, is of short duration, as orders are soon given by the captain to "Take in the plank," "Cast off your lines;" and, just as we are about to move out from the wharf, there is almost sure to be one or more passengers that have arrived, just too late to get aboard; and who, in their excitement, often throw their overcoat, or valise, or other articles on the boat (or overboard), yet neglect the only opportune moment of getting on themselves; and, consequently, are not only left behind, but are separated from their baggage; and which, perhaps, contains the only treasures they possess on earth! Not inconsiderately of this, let us hope,

AWAY WE SAIL.

Who, at such a season, does not recall the peaceful calm that uninvitedly steals over the spirit the very moment the boat has cast off her moorings, and sails out upon the placid waters of the Bay? All of the fatigues and wearying cares of the few last hours ashore—and something, kept to the last, is almost sure to go unaccomplished—are left, with it, behind; and, for the time being at least, are merged into absolute forgetfulness. Now comes the season of bewitching, perfect, unrestrained composure, as calm as the brine over which we are gliding. At such a befitting time for impressions, and mood for enjoyment, every object presenting itself reveals to us an exalted interpretation. The golden sheen of the setting sun, as it lights up the pathway of commerce through the Golden Gate, seems brighter and more golden as we pass it. Even the fog-banks that sometimes roll through the Golden Gate, in summer, have silvery edges; and the haze that drapes each mountain height, or dreamily sleeps in far-off cañons, is of a more ethereal purple when we thus preparedly commune with nature's mysterious wonders. Now we are sailing past, let us take

A GLIMPSE THROUGH THE GOLDEN GATE.

There is a peculiarly seductive charm that stealthily yet feelingly carries one into the far dreamy past, as he looks upon this scene; and recalls old-time memories, when this was almost the only entrance to the land of gold. How revertingly the sight again brings into review the golden-winged hopes, and heart-throbbing yearnings of the many who entered, or wished to enter, its charmed portals, "in days of auld lang syne," and make it the admission gate to fame and fortune; but who, perhaps, after coming through it, spent years of unremitting and unrequited toil; and yet hoped, aye, longed, to pass through it once again, to that place still endearingly called "home"—

"That spot of earth, by love supremely blest,
A dearer, sweeter spot, than all the rest."

With a chastened sadness in the heart, because they had hoped and yearned in vain. But to those whom success had crowned with its exhilarating laurels, how exultingly—and let us hope gratefully—welcome was their homeward passage through the Golden Gate; to share their fortunes with beloved ones, who, perhaps, had long been expectantly awaiting their return.

Many have supposed that the origin and meaning of the name given to this entrance to the Bay of San Francisco was suggested by the staple mineral of the country, gold. This is an error, as it was called "The Golden Gate" before the precious metal was discovered. It was probably used for the first time in a work entitled "A Geographical Review of California," by Col. J. C. Fremont, published, with a map, in New York, February, 1848; and as gold was discovered on the 19th of January preceding, the news could not have reached the office of publication, in those days, in time to influence this nomenclature. It is true there "may have been" some "spiritual telegrams" (!) sent to the author of the name, Col. J. C. Fremont, telling him of the glorious dawn of a golden day that had broken upon the world by the discovery of gold at Sutter's Mill, Coloma, and thus become suggestive of the golden age, about to be inaugurated, and

of the name. Its real origin was owing to the excessively productive lands of the interior, especially those around the Bay of San
Francisco. From whatever source the name "Golden Gate" has
sprung, its characteristic appropriateness will be unhesitatingly

PASSING THE GOLDEN GATE.

conceded. Having dwelt somewhat at length upon the name, let
us now briefly describe the place.

The Golden Gate, then, is the only entrance by sea to the
land-locked and magnificent harbor of San Francisco. It is
situated in the narrowest part of the channel, between Fort
Point and Lime Point. Its width is one thousand, seven hundred
and seventy-seven yards. Here the tide ebbs and flows at the
rate of about six knots an hour, and rises or falls some seven
feet. The center of the Gate is in longitude 122°30' from Greenwich. Through this flows the drainage of all the rivers from the
High Sierra, entering the valleys of the Sacramento and San
Joaquin, as well as from several tributaries of the Coast Range.

It has depth sufficient to float, safely, ships of the heaviest tonnage. Even the circular sand-bar at its entrance, seven miles in length, offers no obstacle to this, even at low tide; except, possibly, when the wind is blowing heavily from the northwest, west, or southeast; then it is scarcely safe for a vessel of the largest class to cross it at low tide. On the south side of the Golden Gate is Point Lobos (Wolves Point), from whence vessels at sea are signaled; and on the northern, Point Bonita, upon which is set a light-house; while opposite Lime Point stands the frowning fort, Winfield Scott.

THE FORT, NEAR VIEW.

You can see by its grim and defiant presence that it means business, when the order comes to "let loose the dogs of war." It is four tiers in height, the topmost of which is sixty-four feet above low tide, and is capable of mounting one hundred and fifty guns—including a battery on the hill at its back—of forty-two, sixty-four, and one hundred and twenty-eight pounders, besides rifled cannon of improved pattern. During an engagement, two thousand four hundred men can be accommodated here.

There is a light-house adjoining the Fort, that can be seen for some ten or twelve miles outside; connected with which is a fog-bell weighing eleven hundred pounds, that is worked by machinery, and strikes five consecutive taps ten seconds apart; then has an intermission of thirty-four seconds, when it re-commences the ten-second strike. This is carried on continuously in foggy weather.

At a convenient distance from Fort Point is the Presidio, which is the residence and head-quarters of both officers and men for this military district. Others are stationed at Point San Jose, formerly called Black Point. To outline these even, with their maneuverings, music, life, etc., would detain us too long; but it is hoped that this "mere mention" will induce you to pay each one of these a visit, to see and enjoy them at your leisure, upon your return.

But as the keel of our boat is speedily cutting its way through the water, we pass Alcatraz and Angel Islands; obtain glances of the snug little towns of Saucelito and San Rafael, catch a hasty sight of the State Prison at San Quentin; and, almost before we realize it, are opposite a gaudily stratified island known as

RED OR "TREASURE" ROCK.

This bright-colored little island was formerly called Treasure, and, in old charts, Golden Rock, from a traditionary report circulated that vast treasures had been buried there, by pirates and old Spanish navigators. Such stories were always sufficiently stimulating to induce the semi-demented adventurer, and dime novel reader, to attempt the securing of wealth with as little exercise as possible of his own. Hence the representative "treasure hunter" found occupation here, and, as elsewhere, went unrewarded for his pains.

It is now exclusively called "Red Rock," being composed of numerous strata, of an endless variety of colors, the prevailing one being red. There is an article found here that strikingly resembles one sometimes found upon a lady's toilet table (in early days, of course) known as rouge-powder (exclusively monopolized in these modern times by the theatrical profession). Besides this there are several veins of decomposed rock resembling clay, or pigment, from four to twelve inches in thickness, and from steel-gray to bright red in color. Upon the beach small red pebbles, resembling carnelian, are found in abundance. But on, on we sail; passing Maria Island, and

THE TWO SISTERS,

Both of which are covered with sea-birds, that seem to be tastefully and gracefully busy pluming their feathers; and who make this their roosting places at night, no matter where they may have wandered during the day.

Just beyond these we shoot by San Pablo Point (which juts out from the mainland) and enter the placid waters of the bay of San Pablo. The distant hills, with their lights and shadows, and varied verdure, encompassing us, are not less attractive upon water than on land for they seem to charm us into forgetfulness of the fact that, almost before we realize it, the hills are closing in upon us, and we are rapidly

ENTERING THE STRAITS OF CARQUINEZ.

The Straits of Carquinez connect the bays of San Pablo and Suisun; and, as mentioned in the foregoing chapter, are the only outlet for all the interior waters of the great basin of the Sacramento and San Joaquin Rivers, with all their tributaries. Our course lies through these straits; but, just before entering them, on our left-hand, we obtain a distant view of the Government Works at Mare Island, and the town of Vallejo; and, as we sail onward towards the hills, the impression comes, almost irresistibly, that we are certainly running into the bluffs ahead of us, and into trouble at the same time; but a slight deviation in our course, at just the right turn in the channel, proves that the knowledge and skill of the captain are superior to our own— which may be a little surprising!

When safely passing the narrowest part of the channel, we seem to be meeting "the leviathan of the deep," or some other huge monster that is coming down fearlessly upon us, and is about to swallow us up, as Jonah swallowed the whale (?); but just as we might suppose it to be opening its immense mouth for one easy effort, it shoots to one side (as we do to the other) as much as to say, "You needn't be afraid of me, I am only the C. P. R. R. transit boat *Solano*, on my way from Benicia to Port Costa!"

LOOKING TOWARD THE SACRAMENTO RIVER.

It would detain us too long to tell of the many interesting places to visit at Benicia—once the capital of the State—or the objects worthy of notice at Army Point, and Martinez (briefly outlined in the last chapter); so, if you please, we will regretfully pass these, just as the moonlight is silvering the waters of

THE BAY OF SUISUN.

This, with its numerous islands (almost level with the surface at high water), is nearly as large as the bay of San Pablo. At one time, "in the uninterpretable past," it must have resembled a small inland sea, inasmuch as the broad expanse of the tule lands, now covering several thousands of square miles, once formed a portion of the bay. An apparently interminable sea of tules extends nearly one hundred and fifty miles northeasterly up the valley of the Sacramento, and for more than half that distance southerly, up the valley of the San Joaquin, with an average width of thirty miles; and as nearly all of this land is overflowed during high water there can be but little doubt of its once having formed an immense lake.

SALMON FISHING—PAYING OUT THE SEINE.

THE SAN JOAQUIN RIVER.

Deriving its main source from the living glaciers of Mt. Ritter, the Minarets, and other lofty peaks of the High Sierra, whence it hurries rapidly to the plains, but runs sluggishly through these tules, and forms one of the most serpentine of all rivers out-of-doors. It is navigable for somewhat commodious steamboats and large schooners to Stockton, and some seventy miles beyond for smaller craft. It makes its *debouchure* into the bay of Suisun just above Cornwall and Antioch, landings for the Monte Diablo coal mines.

SALMON FISHING—HAULING IN THE SEINE.

Were we passing this earlier in the day, the scene would possibly be enlivened by the sight of sundry small boats, and men engaged in salmon fishing, which still forms quite an important industry here, and at the junction of the Sacramento River with the Bay of Suisun; interesting, however, as it might be to linger here, and watch the *modus operandi* of taking in this valuable fish, we must now forego it.

SALMON FISHING—A GROUP OF SALMON.

After touching at the latter settlements for the disembarkation of passengers and cargo, we are soon sailing upon the turbid waters of the San Joaquin. But for the overshadowing mountain of Monte Diablo, whose omnipresence still asserts itself here as elsewhere, the scenery would prove to be very uninteresting. But, as the evening is calm (and sultry, perhaps) the mosquitoes may offer a little divertisement; as, possibly, this may be their harvest season; and, as a consequence, a large representation may be out, on a free-booting excursion. Now, although their harvest-home song may be very musical to those who can enjoy its feeling refrain, it becomes penetratingly evident to any disinterested observer, that but few persons on board seem to have an appreciative ear for their music! In order, however, to show that they have no idea of being overlooked, or neglected, the mosquitoes take real pleasure in impressing their embossed notes upon the hands, faces, or foreheads of all unwatchful sleepers— even though their slumbers may have been involuntary from exhaustion, or in combating their musical enemies. While this unequal warfare is going on, and for one carcass slain a dozen mourners come to the funeral, we may as well do something more than fight these little bill-presenting, tax-collecting tormentors; so, please permit me to relate an incident that occurred, just as I was leaving my Southern home, on the banks of the "Father of waters," the old Mississippi, in the spring of 1849:—

A gentleman arrived from "Merry England," with excellent letters of introduction, and was at once admitted a member of our family circle. Now, however strange it may appear, this gentleman had never looked upon a live mosquito—there being no such insect in England—and as a sequence was as unfamiliar with a mosquito-net and its uses, as the average office-holder might be with politeness. The *femme de charge* being unaware of this, had omitted to call his attention to the arrangements there for passing a comfortable night. In the morning, when he presented himself at the breakfast-table, his face was nearly covered with wounds from the enemy's proboscis; without seemingly noticing this, the lady of the house politely inquired if he had slept pleasantly; "Ye-yes," he replied with some hesitation "ye-yes, tol-er-a-bly pleasant, the bed was sufficiently comfortable, but, *a—a—small—fly* annoyed me somewhat." At this confession the assembled company could not refrain from a good hearty laugh, in which the English gentleman most cordially joined, although it was at his expense. The good-natured hostess, after duly suppressing her risibility, explained the uses and arrangements of the mosquito-bar, to insure comfort in mosquito-infested countries, to the entire satisfaction of her guest. But the *small fly* was a source of considerable mirthfulness in our social circles there for a long time afterwards.

"Boxing the compass" in every conceivable direction, on a sea of tules; stopping here and slowing there, to avoid a jutting point of tules, or compass a bend of the circuitous river, upon which we are supposed to be sailing; our attention is attracted by a bright light in the distance, accompanied by the startling information that

THE TULES ARE ON FIRE.

To those who are unfamiliar with the water-plant, well known in California as the *tule*, or, more generally called, *tules*, a briefly outlined sketch may not be unacceptable, especially as the word is not to be found in "Worcester," or in "Webster Unabridged." Its botanical name is *Scirpus palustris*, var. Californica. In form and habit it resembles the eastern flag, with this difference; the flag is flat, while the tule is round for two-thirds of its height, tapering to a point, and flattening as it tapers, like a sailor's needle. Although perennial in character, its growth is annual, and from six to twelve feet. Owing to the inexhaustible quantities and the vast area covered by this plant, efforts have not been wanting to press it into useful service; for paper, encasing of bottles, life-preservers, underlying for carpets, etc., and, for life-preservers it is worth four to one of cork. This, when closely interwoven and stretched upon a frame, then covered with pitch, is said to make a boat as light as a bark canoe.

Let it be remembered that there are slightly elevated grounds, and islands, in this sea of tules, that they are not only inhabited, but which are susceptible of high cultivation; and are of marvelous productiveness, after the native plant is subdued; from three to four crops a year having been harvested therefrom. An intelligent gentleman, well known to the writer, reliably informed him that, while gathering one crop of wheat, yielding sixty-five bushels to the acre, a neighbor of his was just sowing the adjoining lands; and harvested his crop in sixty days thereafter! One cultivator has six thousand acres of potatoes in a patch, on Roberts' Island. Most of the vegetables used in Stockton are procured from the tule lands. But from the uncertainties and dangers of occasional high water, these tule lands would become exceedingly valuable—and will be when a thoroughly efficient system of leveeing and drainage are adopted.

And let us, if you please, suppose that a flood-proof protective levee has been constructed around two hundred thousand acres of this productive land; with drains, waste-gates, and every other contrivance to insure its being thoroughly done, at an estimated cost of $20,000,000. Then let us, if you please, suppose that this area has been put into successful cultivation, and will yield sixty-five bushels to the acre, the total product for a single crop (and two can be easily raised) would be thirteen million bushels; which, at the low estimate of sixty cents per bushel, would aggregate $7,800,000 annually, and of course would double that amount should two crops be realized.

But, while we have been talking, our steamboat has been drawing nearer and nearer to the conflagration, so that we can see the broad sheet of devouring blaze leaping into the air, and with tongue of flame licking up everything that is combustible, like a prairie on fire; and which, with the black smoke surging hither and thither, its edges and masses covered with a lurid

THE SAN JOAQUIN RIVER AT NIGHT—TULES ON FIRE.

glare, presents a scene of fearful grandeur, that becomes suggestive of some earthly pandemonium. In admiration, we forget the
mosquitoes, and even the discordant and hoarse shriek of the
so-called "steam-whistle," that is now announcing our approach to
a landing.

Whenever a dry season comes upon California the succulent
pastures found here, by stock, supplies the needed forage. But as

ENTERING THE STOCKTON SLOUGH.

we are now at the junction of the Stockton Slough with the San
Joaquin River, we proceed up the former for three miles, and are
at the end of our voyage, and the wharf of the city of Stockton.

CHAPTER XVI.

THE MILTON AND CALAVERAS BIG TREE ROUTE.

And those that paint them truest praise them most.

—ADDISON'S *Campaign.*

Thought is deeper than all speech;
  Feeling deeper than all thought;
Souls to souls can never teach
  What unto themselves was taught.

—C. P. CRANCH.

So nature deals with us, and takes away
  Our playthings one by one, and by the hand
  Leads us to rest so gently, that we go,
Scarce knowing if we wish to go or stay,
  Being too full of sleep to understand
  How far the unknown transcends the what we know.

—LONGFELLOW'S *Nature.*

Having arrived at Lathrop by the main or trunk line of the Central Pacific Railroad, and having arranged to journey *via* the Calaveras Big Tree Route, we enter the train bound for Stockton; and, the run being only some nine miles, it is very soon accomplished. As the country is comparatively level, there is but little to excite interest, except to those who delight in pastoral loveliness, until we are near that city. Then the suburban residences, peeping out from the umbrageous oaks, and the church spires towering above them, tell that we shall soon enter its hospitable precincts. Acting upon the suggestion made in a former chapter, "when it is possible not to be in a hurry," with your permission, we will allow the train to depart without us this morning, and take a stroll through

THE CITY OF STOCKTON.

This flourishing commercial city is advantageously situated at the head of a deep navigable slough, or arm of the San Joaquin

(207)

River, about three miles above its junction with that stream. The luxuriant foliage of its trees, the thrifty growth of its shrubs, and plants of every kind, give voiceless commendation to its founders for choosing so desirable a situation. It is true that, as this was the head of navigation for all supplies needed in the proverbially rich gold mines of Tuolumne and Mariposa Counties, and intermediate points, it became a natural landing place; and, as such, was therefore suggestive of the suitability of this location for the building of a city. As a result, tents and cloth houses sprung up like mushrooms; but the fire of December 23, 1849, entirely swept away the last vestige of this city of cloth, and destroyed other property to the value of over two hundred thousand dollars. Almost before its ruins had ceased smouldering, however, a new and cleaner city, composed of an admixture of cloth and wood, was erected in its place. In the following spring nearly all the cloth houses were superseded by wooden ones, and as this embrio city was now in steam communication with its base of supplies at San Francisco, assurance was given of its future stability and permanence, and justified the removal of wooden structures, and their replacement by those of brick.

On the 30th of March, 1850, the first weekly newspaper was published by Messrs. Radcliffe and White, conducted by Mr. John White—afterwards well known by newspapermen in the Bay City. On the same day the first theatrical performance was given in the Assembly Room of the Stockton House, by Bingham and Fury. The first election was held on the 13th of May following, the population at that early day numbering over two thousand. The Stockton Fire Department was organized June 20 (1850), and James E. Nuttman (afterwards associated with the fire department of San Francisco) was elected chief engineer. On the 25th of July, ensuing, Stockton was incorporated as a city. May 6, 1851, another fire swept away nearly every building, and destroyed property valued at a million and a half of dollars. Nothing daunted, a new city sprung up, Phœnix-like, from its ashes; and from that day to this the march of improvement has kept

THE "PRAIRIE SCHOONER."

commensurate progress with the spirit of the age, and the requirements of its steady development. Owing to the general healthiness of its climate, and the convenience of its location, Stockton was chosen, by an Act of the Legislature of 1853, for the erection here of a State asylum for the insane; and this, with greatly enlarged accommodation, has been continued here ever since.

PRAIRIE SCHOONERS.

One of the most striking features of the commerce of this city in early days, and one that well deserves to be commemorated, was the large number of heavily laden freight wagons that used to leave it for the mines. These, owing to their huge bulk and enormous carrying capacity, were, not inappropriately, denominated "Prairie Schooners," and "Steamboats of the Plains." They would average twenty-five thousand pounds per trip. The cost of wagons was from $900 to $1,100, and they were generally over twenty feet in length. Large mules, having the requisite strength, used to cost $350 each; and some, the finest and best, $1,400 per span. The main advantage of these large teams was the economy in teamsters, as one man could drive and tend as many as fourteen animals, always guiding them with a single line. They were drilled like soldiers, and were almost as tractable; and when a teamster cracked his whip its report was like that of a revolver.

The unusually large number of windmills are suggestive of the preferred method of

NORTH DOME—TO-COY-AE
(See page 383)
Fiske #431. Facing page 208 in edition one.
Facing page 210 in all other editions.

THE VERNAL FALL—PI-WY-ACK

(See pages 441–42.)

Fiske #341. Facing page 288 in edition one. Facing page 290 in all other editions.

irrigation and of water supply. Notwithstanding this, Stockton can boast of having

THE DEEPEST ARTESIAN WELL IN THE STATE.

It is one thousand and two feet deep, and throws out two hundred and fifty gallons of water per minute, or three hundred and sixty thousand gallons every twenty-four hours, and to the height of nine feet above the city grade. In sinking this well, ninety-six different strata of loam, clay, micaceous sand, soft green sandstone, gravel, etc., etc., were passed through. Three hundred and forty feet from the surface, a stump of one of the big trees was found imbedded in the sand, from whence a stream of water issued to the top, although not in sufficient quantities to afford the supply desired, hence its continuance to the depth mentioned. The temperature of the water was 77° Fahrenheit.

The various strata bored through, indicate beyond question, that not only this, but nearly all other valleys were at one time inland lakes, that have been filled up and formed by the denudation and lowering of the contiguous mountains, in the unrecorded ages of the far distant past. The siliceous sediment constantly floating down all our rivers, especially during high water, is incontrovertible proof that continuous denudation is still an active force in lowering mountains, and in forming valleys.

It would make our advent here extremely interesting could we visit the tanneries, carriage factories, agricultural implement manufactories, canning establishments, the two flouring mills, woolen and paper mills, schools, free library, etc., not omitting the State asylum for the insane, which would be found a model of cleanliness and good management. After this brief outline of Stockton and its attractions, with your permission we will now resume our journey.

Almost before we are fairly seated in the car, we shoot out from the station at Stockton, leaving the Central Pacific Railroad, and taking the Stockton and Copperopolis Railroad for Milton; and as we are rolling out from among the tasteful suburban residences of the city, under the gracefully pendant white oaks

THE CALAVERAS BIG TREE ROUTE,

From San Francisco, via Lathrop, Stockton, Milton, Murphy's, Calaveras Big Tree Grove, Sonora, Chinese Camp, and Big Oak Flat, to Yo Semite Valley.

Stations marked (*a*) are stopping places at night for stage passengers; those marked (*b*) are hotels, or where meals can be had; those marked (*c*) are where hay and grain are obtainable; those marked (*d*) are stage stations.

STATIONS.	Between consecutive points.........	From San Francisco..	From Yo Semite Valley	Altitude, in feet, above Sea Level........
		DISTANCES IN MILES.		
By Railway.	.....	.....	133.05	
From San Francisco to—				
Lathrop, junction of the Central Pacific with the Southern Pacific Railroad (*b c*)	94.03	94.03	39.02	28
Stockton, on Central Pacific Railroad (*a b c*)	9.02	103.05	30.00	29
Milton, on the Stockton and Copperopolis Railroad (*b c d*)	30.00	133.05	.....	376
By Carriage Road.			152.53	
From Milton to—				
Reservoir House (*b c*)	6.13	6.13	146.40	1,013
Gibson's Station (*b c d*)	10.87	17.00	135.53	1,570
Altaville (*b c*)	5.50	22.50	130.03	1,520
Murphy's (*b c d*)	7.50	30.00	122.53	2,195
Half-way House (*b c*)	8.11	38.11	114.42	3,358
Calaveras Big Tree Grove Hotel (*a b c d*)	7.31	45.42	107.11	4,730
Half-way House, returning (*b c*)	7.31	52.72	99.80	3,358
Murphy's (*a b c d*)	8.11	60.84	91.69	2,195
Vallecito (*b c*)	4.16	65.00	87.53	1,748
Trail to Natural Bridge	3.32	68.32	84.21	.....
Parrott's Ferry, Stanislaus River	2.27	70.59	81.94	834
Gold Spring	3.17	73.76	78.77	2,014
Columbia (*b c*)	1.15	74.91	77.62	2,157
Sonora (*b c d*)	4.17	79.08	73.45	1,816
Chinese Camp (*a b c d*)	11.00	90.08	62.45	1,299
Priest's Hotel—for full details see "Big Oak Flat Route" (*a b c d*)	12.11	102.19	50.34	2,558
Tuolumne Big Tree Grove	33.43	135.62	15.84	5,794
Leidig's Hotel, Yo Semite Valley (*a b c d*)	15.84	151.46	1.07	3,851
Cook's Hotel, Yo Semite Valley (*a b c d*)	0.30	151.76	0.77	.....
Barnard's Hotel, Yo Semite Valley (*a b c d*)	0.77	152.53	.....	.....

RECAPITULATION.

By railway .... 133.05 miles.
By carriage road .... 152.53 "

Total distance .... 285.58 miles.

(Q. lobata), and past the fertile farms of this portion of the valley of the San Joaquin, a quiet, gentlemanly person, whose name is Mr. Robert Patton, politely introduces himself to us by inquiring, "May I ask what is your proposed destination, beyond Milton? I am the agent for the different stage lines leaving there for all the various points beyond." Receiving satisfactory replies, our names are entered on the way-bill; and, upon arrival at Milton, we find a row of stages backed up against the platform, and awaiting us; with every coachman on his box, and the reins in his hand, ready for the start, the moment Mr. Patton gives him the signal. As we are supposed, on this occasion, to have chosen the route *via* the Calaveras Big Trees Groves, the agent has seen that ourselves and baggage are safely placed upon the Murphy's stage, Murphy's being *en route* for that point, when "All set" is shouted to the coachman, and away we go.

As every one knows, the most desirable of all places on a stage coach is that known as the "box-seat." This is with the coachman; for, if he is intelligent, and in a good humor, he can tell you of all the sights by the way; with the personal history of nearly every man and woman you may meet; the qualities and "points" of every horse upon the road; with all the adventures, jokes, and other good things he has seen and heard during his thousand and one trips, under all kinds of circumstances, and in all sorts of weather. In short, he is a living road-encyclopedia, to be read and studied at intervals, by the occupant of the "box-seat."

You saw that look and motion of the coachman's head? That was at once a sign of recognition and of invitation to the privileged seat at his side, as we are old acquaintances. But, as you are a stranger, and as every excursion of real pleasure—like the happiest experiences of social life—become dependent to a very great extent upon little courtesies and kindnesses, that cost nothing, we will, if you please, set the good example of foregoing selfishness by trying to secure that seat for *you*. No thanks are needed, as every pleasure is doubled by being shared. Now, suppose that you are the occupant of the "box-seat," we will make one suggestion—invite the driver to accept one of your best cigars; and, as its smoke and fragrance are rising on the air, he will gradually soften to you, and both will become better acquainted before you have traveled far.

There is a feeling of jovial, good-humored pleasurableness that steals insensibly over the spirit when the secluded residents of cities leave all the cares of a daily routine of duties behind, and the novelty of fresh scenes forms new sources of enjoyment. Especially is it so when seated comfortably in an easy-going coach; with the prospect before us of witnessing many of the most wonderful sights to be found in any country, either in the Old or New World; and, more especially, if we have learned to take a journey, as it is said that a Frenchman does his dinner, thereby enjoying it three times; *first,* in anticipation; *second,* in participation; and *third,* on retrospection!

For several miles before arriving at Milton, as for two or three beyond, the entire country is covered with sedimentary deposits, and water-washed gravel; and, as there are no such elemental forces at work in the present day, they offer conjectural revelations of very different conditions in the past while being suggestive of pertinent inquiries for the time and cause of change.

It is over these, for the most part treeless and rolling hills, that our road now lies. It is true there is one clump of white post oaks *(Quercus Douglasii)* about half a mile from Milton; remarkable only for its being the favorite resort of a species of bird, somewhat scarce in California, known as the magpie. Leaving the gravelly hills, we enter upon a graded road up a deep ravine, where shrubs and trees begin to add an interest to the landscape. At the top of the hill we reach the Reservoir House (so named from a large reservoir near, built for mining purposes), where the horses rest, and where both man and beast take water, (the former, occasionally, something a little stronger). Here are seen the first pine trees *(Pinus Sabiniana).*

Beyond this for many miles the country is gently undulating, yet is sparsely timbered with post oaks. At Gibson's Station horses are exchanged, and the hungry can eat. Five miles beyond this we find ourselves at Altaville; a sprightly little mining camp, in a gold-mining district, where we cross flumes and ditches, filled with water made muddy by washing out the precious metal, and where can be witnessed all the *modus operandi* of gold mining. Still our course is upward as well as onward, until we are over two thousand feet above sea level, and

THE MINING VILLAGE OF MURPHY'S.

Now, although the gold mines here have been among the richest, Murphy's was but little known, beyond its more immediate surroundings, until the discovery of the Big Tree Groves of Calaveras (the first of this species ever found); and, more recently, the adjacent remarkable cave. Its proximity to, and the starting-point for, the new wonders, lifted it into world-wide notoriety, almost at a bound. It is deserving of record, however, that the discovery of those enormous trees must be credited, in a degree, to the business men of Murphy's, through whose enterprise, incidentally, they were first seen; as the sequel, obtained from the writer from the discoverer himself, will abundantly show:—

HOW AND WHEN THE BIG TREES OF CALAVERAS WERE FIRST DISCOVERED.

In the spring of 1852, Mr. A. T. Dowd, a hunter, was employed by the Union Water Company, of Murphy's, Calaveras County, to supply the workmen engaged in the construction of their canal, with fresh meat, from the large quantities of game running wild on the upper portion of their works. While engaged in this calling, having wounded a grizzly bear, and while industriously pursuing him, he suddenly came upon one of those immense trees that have since become so justly celebrated throughout the civilized world. All thoughts of hunting were absorbed and lost in the wonder and surprise inspired by the scene. "Surely," he mused, "this must be some curiously delusive dream!" But the great realities indubitably confronting him were convincing proof, beyond question, that they were no mere fanciful creations of his imagination.

Returning to camp, he there related the wonders he had seen, when his companions laughed at him; and even questioned his veracity, which, previously, they had considered to be in every way reliable. He affirmed his statement to be true; but they still thought it "too big a story" to believe, supposing that he was trying to perpetrate upon them some first-of-April joke.

For a day or two he allowed the matter to rest; submitting, with chuckling satisfaction, to their occasional jocular allusions to "his big tree yarn," but continued hunting as formerly. On the Sunday morning ensuing, he went out early as usual, but soon returned in haste, apparently excited by some great event, when he exclaimed, "Boys, I have killed the largest grizzly bear that I ever saw in my life. While I am getting a little something to eat, you make every preparation for bringing him in; all had better go that can possibly be spared, as their assistance will certainly be needed."

As the big tree story was now almost forgotten, or by common consent laid aside as a subject of conversation; and, moreover, as Sunday was a leisure day, and one that generally hangs the heaviest of the seven on those who are shut out from social or religious intercourse with friends, as many Californians unfortunately were and still are, the tidings were gladly welcomed, especially as the proposition was suggestive of a day's intense excitement.

Nothing loath, they were soon ready for the start. The camp was almost deserted. On, on they hurried, with Dowd as their guide, through thickets and pine groves; crossing ridges and cañons, flats, and ravines, each relating in turn the adventures experienced, or heard of from companions, with grizzly bears, and other formidable tenants of the mountains, until their leader came to a halt at the foot of the immense tree he had seen, and to them had represented the approximate size. Pointing to its extraordinary diameter and lofty height, he exultingly exclaimed,

"Now, boys, do you believe my big tree story? That is the large grizzly I wanted you to see. Do you now think it a yarn?" By this ruse of their leader all doubt was changed into certainty, and unbelief into amazement; as, speechless with profound awe, their admiring gaze was riveted upon those forest giants.

But a short season was allowed to elapse before the trumpet-tongued press proclaimed abroad the wonder; and the intelligent and devout worshipers, in nature and science, flocked to the Big Tree Groves of Calaveras, for the purpose of seeing for themselves the astounding marvels about which they had heard so much. In a subsequent chapter will be found full particulars concerning the naming, habits, characteristics, and comparative area of this species, to which the reader is referred.

ROAD TO THE MAMMOTH TREE GROVE.

Leaving the mining village of Murphy's behind, we pass through an avenue of trees; and, about half a mile from town, enter a narrow cañon, up which we travel, now upon this side of the stream, and now on that, as the hills proved favorable or otherwise, for the construction of the road. If our visit is supposed to be in spring or early summer, every mountain-side, even to the tops of the ridges, is covered with flowers and flowering shrubs of great variety and beauty; while, on either hand, groves of oaks and pines stand as shade-giving guardians of personal comfort.

As we continue the ascent for a few miles our course becomes more undulating and gradual; and, for the most part on the top or gently sloping sides of a dividing ridge; often through dense forests of tall, magnificent pines that are from one hundred and seventy, to two hundred and twenty feet in height; slender, and straight as an arrow. We measured one that had fallen, that was twenty inches in diameter at the base, and fourteen and a half inches in diameter at the distance of one hundred and twenty-five feet from the base. The ridges being nearly clear of an undergrowth of shrubbery; and the trunks of the trees, for fifty feet upward, or more, entirely clear of branches, the eye can wander, delightedly, for a long distance, among these captivating scenes of the forest.

At different distances upon the route, the canal of the Union Water Company winds its sinuous way on, or around, the sides of the ridge; or its sparkling contents rushed impetuously down the water-furrowed center of a ravine. Here and there an aqueduct, or cabin, or saw mill, gives variety to an ever-changing landscape. When within about four and a half miles of the Mammoth Tree Grove, the surrounding mountain peaks and ridges are boldly visible. Looking southeast, the uncovered head of Bald Mountain silently announces its solitude and distinctiveness; west, the Coast Range of mountains forms a continuous girdle to the horizon; extending to the north and east, where the snow-covered tops of the Sierras form a magnificent background to the glorious picture.

The deepening shadows of the densely timbered forest through which we are passing, by the awe they inspire, impressively intimate that we are soon to enter the imposing presence of those forest giants, the Big Trees of Calaveras, and almost before we realize our actual nearness, we catch the inviting gleam of the Calaveras Big Tree Grove Hotel. On our way to it, the carriage road passes directly between the

TWO SENTINELS,

Each of which is over three hundred feet in height, and the larger one of the two is twenty-three feet in diameter at the base. But as no one can thoroughly enjoy the wonderful, or beautiful, with a tired body, or upon an empty stomach, let us, for the present at least, prefer the refreshing comforts and kindly hospitalities of this commodious and well-kept inn, to a walk about the grove.

According to Capt. Geo. M. Wheeler's U. S. Geographical Survey Reports, the Calaveras Big Tree Grove Hotel is 2,535 feet above Murphy's, and 4,730 feet above sea level. It stands in latitude 38° north, and in longitude 120°10' west from Greenwich. The forest in which the Big Trees stand was so densely timbered

Photo by J. C. Scripture.

Moss Engraving Co., N. Y.

THE CALAVERAS BIG TREE GROVE HOTEL.

THE CALAVERAS BIG TREE GROVE HOTEL

The photo is a very close companion to the one from which the engraving on the opposite page was made. That one appears to have been taken from a spot a few feet forward and to the right.

Photo by Geo. Fiske.

Courtesy, The Bancroft Library

ISLAND RAPIDS, FROM TIS-SA-ACK BRIDGE

Made from a Britton & Rey photo-typo.

Facing page 192 in edition one.

that many hundreds of trees had to be cut down "to let in a little sunlight" to the hotel site. Here, in a gently sloping declivity, or hollow, of the main divide, separating San Antonio Creek on the north, and the north fork of the Stanislaus River on the south (two favorite trouting streams), is located this remarkable grove.

After refreshment and rest we are in better condition to examine the different objects of interest that have attracted us hither. One thought, one feeling, one emotion, that of vastness, sublimity, profoundness, pervades the soul; for there, in awful presence—

"The giant trees in silent majesty,
Like pillars stand 'neath Heaven's mighty dome.
'Twould seem that, perched upon their topmost branch,
With outstretched finger, man might touch the stars."

Within an area of about fifty acres there are ninety-three trees of large size, twenty of which exceed twenty-five feet in diameter at their base, and will consequently average about seventy-five feet in circumference. These would look still more imposing in proportions but for the large growth of sugar pine (*Pinus Lambertiana*), and the yellow pine (*Pinus ponderosa*). One of the latter to the southwestward of the hotel exceeds ten feet in diameter. But let us first take a walk to the

BIG TREE STUMP.

This is the stump of the original Big Tree discovered by Mr. Dowd. We can see that it is perfectly smooth, sound, and level. Its diameter across the solid wood, after the bark was removed (and which was from fifteen to eighteen inches in thickness), is twenty-five feet; although the tree was cut off six feet above the ground. However incredible it may appear, on July 4, 1854, the writer formed one of a cotillion party of thirty-two persons, dancing upon this stump; in addition to which the musicians and onlookers numbered seventeen, making a total of forty-nine occupants of its surface at one time! The accompanying sketch was made at that time, and, of course, before the present pavilion was erected over it. There is no more strikingly convincing proof, in any grove, of the immense size of the big trees, than this stump.

A COTILLION PARTY OF THIRTY-TWO PERSONS DANCING ON THE STUMP OF THE MAMMOTH TREE.

This tree was three hundred and two feet in height; and, at the ground, ninety-six feet in circumference, before it was disturbed. Some sacrilegious vandals, from the motive of making its exposition "pay," removed the bark to the height of thirty feet; and afterwards transported it to England, where it was formed into a room; but was afterwards consumed by fire, with the celebrated Crystal Palace, at Kensington, England. This girdling of the tree very naturally brought death to it; but even then its majestic form must have perpetually taunted the belittled and sordid spirits that caused it. It is, however, but an act of justice to its present proprietor, Mr. James L. Sperry, to state that, although he has been the owner of the grove for over twenty years, that act of vandalism was perpetrated before he purchased it, or it would never have been permitted.

The next act in this botanical tragedy was the cutting down of the tree, in order to accommodate those who wished to carry home specimens of its wood, as souvenirs of their visit. But how to do this was the puzzling conundrum! If one could fittingly imagine so ludicrous a sight as a few lilliputian men attempting to *chop* down this brobdingnaggian giant, his contempt would reach its becoming climax. This, therefore, was given up as altogether too chimerical and impracticable. Finally, the plan was adopted of *boring it off with pump-augers*. This employed five men twenty-two days to accomplish; and after the stem was fairly severed from the stump,

BORING DOWN THE ORIGINAL BIG TREE WITH PUMP-AUGERS.

the uprightness of its position, and breadth of its base, prevented its overthrow; so that two and a half of the twenty-two days were spent in inserting wedges, and driving them into the butt of the tree, by logs suspended on ropes, thereby to compel its downfall. While these slow and apparently hopeless attempts were being undertaken, and the workmen had retired for dinner, a gust of wind took hold of its top, and hurled it over without the least seeming effort; its fall causing the earth to tremble as by an earthquake. Thus this noble monarch of the forest was dethroned, after "braving the battle and the breeze" for nearly two thousand years. Verily, how little real veneration does the average man possess.

THE PAVILION.

This was erected over the stump as a protection against the elements; for use on Sundays in public worship; and on weekday evenings for dancing, although I have heard that ladies complain "that there was no 'spring' to that floor!" Theatrical performances and concerts have taken place upon it; and, in 1858, the *Big Tree Bulletin* was printed and published here.

Near to the pavilion and stump still lies a portion of the prostrate trunk of this magnificent tree. Of course the butt-end

Photo by J. C. Scripture.
TRUNK OF BIG TREE, AND PAVILION.

Photo by J. C. Scripture   Peter E. Palmquist

The "original" Big Tree. Diam. 32 Feet.

Visiting the Mammoth Tree Grove and climbing onto the trunk of the "original"
Big Tree was a standard thing to do in the 19th century. It was also the norm
for every photographer to take a standard picture.
(Scripture #3123. No copy of the Scripture photo, opposite, could be found.)

Published by Thomas Houseworth & Co.   Peter E. Palmquist

Father of the Forest. 112 feet circumference.
Entrance to the Horseback Ride, Mammoth Grove.

Another standard photograph was one demonstrating that the trees were
so big you could ride a horse into them. See the engraving on page 226.

of the trunk is of the same diameter as the stump, where the auger marks make silent explanations of the method used in felling it.

WALK THROUGH THE GROVE.

Now, if you please, let us seek the dark recesses of this primeval forest, in spirit with uncovered head from reverential awe, feeling that we are entering the stately presence of trees that have successfully withstood the climatic changes, and storms, of more than thirty centuries. It is true that many of these grand old representatives of the dreamy past have been assailed by fire, and still proudly bear the marks of that resistless enemy; although the new growth has, in many instances, sought to cover up the scars, and renew the vigorous growth of each, as much as possible. So Nature, like a gentle mother, neglects no opportunity to heal all wounds; and, where that is impossible, covers up even deformity and decay with mosses or lichens. We can see that nearly every tree has a name (many most worthily given) and an individuality of its own; that, like human faces, are suggestive of conflict with hidden forces, that have inscribed their characteristics in every line; and were we to pause at every one, and paint the peculiarities of each, I fear that it would prove a somewhat tedious task. If you please, then, we will pass to such as are most noteworthy.

Among these once stood a most beautiful tree, graceful in form, and unexcelled in proportions; hence (as in human experiences) those very qualities at once became the most attractive to the eyes of the unfeeling spoliator. This bore the queenly name of

THE MOTHER OF THE FOREST.

In the summer of 1854, the bark was stripped from its trunk, by a Mr. George Gale, for purposes of exhibition in the East, to the height of one hundred and sixteen feet. It now measures in circumference, at the base, without the bark, eighty-four feet; twenty feet from base, sixty-nine feet; seventy feet from base, forty-three feet six inches; one hundred and sixteen feet from base, and up to the bark, thirty-nine feet six inches. The full circumference at base, including bark, was ninety feet. Its height was three hundred and twenty-one feet. The average thickness of bark was eleven inches, although in places it was about two feet. This tree is estimated to contain five hundred and thirty-seven thousand feet of sound inch lumber. To the first branch it is one hundred and thirty-seven feet. The small black marks upon the tree indicate points where two and a half inch auger holes were bored, and into these rounds were inserted, by which to ascend and descend while removing the bark. At different distances upward, especially at the top, numerous dates and names of visitors have been cut. It is contemplated to construct a circular stairway around this tree. When the bark was being removed, a young man fell from the scaffolding—or, rather, out of a descending noose—at a distance of seventy-nine feet from the ground, and escaped with a broken limb. The writer was within a few yards of him when he fell, and was agreeably surprised to discover that he had not broken his neck. The accompanying engraving, representing this once symmetrical tree, is from a daguerreotype taken in 1854, immediately after the bark was removed, and correctly represents the foliage of this wonderful genus, ere the vandal's

> "Effacing fingers
> Had swept the lines where beauty lingers."

Now, alas! the noble "Mother of the Forest," dismantled of her once proud beauty, still stands boldly out, a reproving, yet magnificent ruin. Even the elements seemed to have sympathized with her, in the unmerited disgrace, brought to her by the ax; as the snows and storms of recent winters have kept hastening her dismemberment, the sooner to cover up the wrong. But a short distance from this lies the prostrate form of one that was probably the tallest sequoia that ever grew—

THE FATHER OF THE FOREST.

This tree, when standing in its primitive majesty, is accredited with exceeding four hundred feet in height, with a circum-

"MOTHER OF THE FOREST"
(321 feet in height, 84 feet in circumference, without the bark.)

ference at its base of one hundred and ten feet; and, although limbless, without bark, and even much of its sap decayed and gone, has still proportions that once could crown him king of the grove. In falling, it struck against "Old Hercules," another old time rival in size, by which the upper part of his trunk was shivered into fragments, that were scattered in every direction. While fire has eaten out the heart of "The Father of the Forest," and consumed his huge limbs, as of many others, the following measurements, recently taken, will prove that he was among the giants of those days, and, that "even in death he still lives."

Photo by J. C. Scripture.
HORSEMAN EMERGING FROM THE FATHER OF THE FOREST.

From the roots, to where the center of the trunk can be reached on horseback, it is ninety feet. The distance that one can ride erect through it on horseback is eighty-two feet six inches. Height of entrance, nine feet four inches; of arch to floor, ten feet nine inches. Across the roots it is twenty-eight feet; to where one would have an idea of standing to chop it down, twenty-three feet two inches; ten feet from the roots its diameter is twenty feet eight inches; one hundred feet from roots, twelve feet one inch; one hundred and fifty feet from roots, ten feet four inches, extreme length, to where any sign of top could be found, three hundred and sixty-five feet.

But no one can approximately realize the immense proportions of this prostrate forest sire, without climbing to its top, and walking down it for its entire length; by this, moreover, he will ascertain that it was nearly two hundred feet to the first branch. At the end of the burnt cavity within, is a never-failing spring of deliciously cool water. The handsome group of stately trees that encompass the "Father of the Forest," make it an imposing family circle; and probably assisted in originating the name.

And this is only one of the numerous vegetable giants that Time's scythe has laid low, for, near here, lies "Old Hercules," the largest standing tree in the grove until 1862, then being three hundred and twenty-five feet in height, by ninety-five feet in circumference, at the ground; this was blown down that year during a heavy storm; "The Miner's Cabin," three hundred and nineteen feet long by twenty-one in diameter, thrown over by a gale, in 1860; and "The Fallen Monarch," which has probably been down for centuries.

THE LIVING AND REPRESENTATIVE TREES IN THE CALAVERAS GROVE.

Consist of ten that are each thirty feet in diameter, and over seventy that measure from fifteen to thirty feet, at the ground. Were we to linger at the foot of every one, and indulge in the portrayal of all the characteristics, size, and peculiarities of each, fascinating as they are when in their immediate presence, they would detain us too long from other scenes, and some that are especially inviting our attention; such, for instance, as

THE SOUTH GROVE.

This stands about six miles southeasterly from the Calaveras Grove, and is, without doubt, the most extensive of any within the ordinary range of tourist travel; as it contains one thousand three hundred and eighty *Sequoias*, ranging from one foot to thirty-four feet in diameter, and as the route thither is extremely picturesque, as well as varied and interesting, let us pay it a visit.

Threading our way through a luxuriant growth of forest trees, with here and there a long vista, which conducts the eye to scenes beyond, and gives grateful leafy shadows, and occasional patches of sunlight on our path, about a mile from the hotel we reach the top of the Divide separating the Calaveras Grove from the north fork of the Stanislaus River. Here a remarkably fine view of the Sierras is obtained, one of whose peaks, the "Dardanelles," is twelve thousand five hundred feet above sea level. By an easy trail, with all sorts of attractive turnings upon it, the north fork of the Stanislaus River is crossed. This is the dividing line between Calaveras and Tuolumne Counties, giving the South Grove to the latter county. This river, from the bridge, is a gem of beauty. Now we wind up to the summit of the Beaver Creek Ridge, and soon descend again to Beaver Creek (where the trout-fishing is excellent); and from this point wend our way to the lower end of the grove. Here the altitude above sea level is four thousand six hundred and thirty-five feet, and the upper end, four thousand eight hundred and twenty feet.

The large number of these immense trees, from thirty feet to over one hundred feet in circumference, at the ground, and in almost every position and condition, would become almost bewildering were I to present in detail each and every one; a few notable examples therefore, will suffice, as representatives of the whole.

The first big tree that attracts our attention, and which is seen from the ridge north of the Stanislaus River, is the "Columbus," a magnificent specimen, with three main divisions in its branches; and standing alone. Passing this we soon enter the lower end of the South Grove, and arrive at the "New York," one hundred and four feet in circumference, and over three hundred feet in height. Near to this is the "Correspondent," a tree of stately proportions, named in honor of the "Knights of the Quill." The "Ohio" measures one hundred and three feet, and is three hundred and eleven feet in height. The "Massachusetts" is ninety-eight feet, with an altitude of three hundred and seven.

Near to a large black stump, above this, stands a tree that is seventy-six feet in circumference, that has been struck by lightning, one hundred and seventy feet from its base; where its top was shivered into fragments, and hurled in all directions for over a hundred feet from the tree; the main stem being rent from top to bottom, the apex of this dismantled trunk being twelve feet in diameter. The "Grand Hotel" is burned out so badly that nothing but a mere shell is left. This will hold forty persons. Then comes the "Canal Boat"; which, as its name implies, is a prostrate tree; the upper side and heart of which have been burned away, so that the remaining portion resembles a huge boat; in the bottom of which thousands of young big trees have started out in life; and, if no accident befalls them, in a thousand or two years hence, they may be respectable-sized trees, that can worthily take the places of the present representatives of this noble genus, and, like these, challenge the admiring awe of the intellectual giants of that day and age.

"Noah's Ark" was another prostrate shell that was hollow for one hundred and fifty feet; through which, for sixty feet, three horsemen could ride abreast; but the snows of recent winters have broken in its roof, and blocked all further passage down it. Next comes the "Tree of Refuge," where, during one severe winter, sixteen cattle took shelter; but subsequently perished from starvation. They found protection from the storm, but their bleaching bones told the sad tale of their sufferings and death from lack of food. Near to this lies "Old Goliath," the largest decumbent tree in the grove; whose circumference was over one hundred feet, and, when erect, was of proportionate height to the tallest. During the gale that prostrated "Hercules," in the Calaveras Grove, this grand old tree had also to succumb. One of his stalwart limbs was eleven feet in diameter.

There is another notable specimen, which somewhat forms a sequel to the above, known as

Photo by J. C. Scripture.   Peter E. Palmquist
SMITH'S CABIN.

On account of its having been the chosen residence of a trapper and old mountaineer named A. J. Smith—Andrew Jackson Smith—who made the charred hollow of this burnt-out tree his lonely home for three years. There is no telling what these old denizens of the mountains can or will do when they have made up their minds to anything. The diameter of his cabin—which was to him a bedroom, sitting room, kitchen, and, sometimes, during stormy weather, a stable for his horse—was twenty-one feet by sixteen. Being one of the tallest, and consequently one of the most exposed, whenever the wind was upon one of its "high jinks," it seemed to take especial delight in playing, wantonly, with the top of this tree, so as to make it creak and tremble from stem to stern—not that it had any particular spite against its tenant—yet, upon such occasions, Smith would listen to its ominous music with a somewhat foreboding watchfulness, lest these pranks should be carried too far, and thus endanger his personal safety, as well as comfort. On one occasion a regular "southeaster" was on the rampage, hurling down trees, twisting off branches, tossing about tree-tops, and limbs, in all directions. As the old trapper dare not venture out, he sat listening, with unquestionable interest, to ascertain whether the wind or "Smith's Cabin" was becoming the better wrestler of the two. At this juncture, an earth-trembling crash came with nerve-testing force, that made his hair to stand on end, when he jumped to his feet, using certain emphatic words (the synonyms of which can be found in "holy writ," or elsewhere), thinking, as he afterwards expressed it, "that it was all u-p with him." As this was the downfall of "Old Goliath," he began to fear that old Boreas was getting the best of the match, if he did not claim the gate-money, and that "Smith's Cabin" would be the next giant thrown. But, being a brave man—and who could live such a life as his if he were not?—and knowing well that he could not do better, concluded to look this danger unquailingly in the face, as he had done many a one before it; stay where he was, and take the best, or worst, that might befall him. This proved Mr. A. J. Smith to be not only a hermit-trapper, but a philosopher as well. I am glad to say that this hero still lives, and makes himself both useful and entertaining, by acting as guide between the Calaveras and South Park Groves, and it would be difficult to find one more careful or more obliging.

"Adam" and "Eve" we did not see, but were assured that

the former has a circumference of one hundred and three feet; and that the latter was a fitting helpmate to Adam, at least in correlative magnitude, with breast-like protuberances seven feet in diameter, at an altitude of one hundred and fifty feet from the ground.

Before taking leave of the South Grove, it may be well to mention, that it is three and a half miles in length, situated in a beautifully formed, valley-like hollow, that not only contain the number of "big trees" already mentioned, but, like the Calaveras Grove, has magnificent colonnades of other trees, such as the sugar pine *(Pinus Lambertiana);* the two yellow pines *(Pinus ponderosa* and *P. Jeffreyi);* three silver firs *(Abies concolor, A. grandis* and *A. nobilis);* the red spruce *(A. Douglasi);* the cedar *(Libocedrus decurrens),* with other genera; and an almost endless variety of beautiful shrubs and flowers. Indeed, there is a richly supplied banquet, as endless in variety as it is unique in loveliness and grandeur, upon which appreciative minds can feast the whole of the ride. Upon the return a glimpse can be had, westwardly, of the Basaltic Cliff; and which forms the destination of one of the many enjoyable rides from the hotel.

As we must soon bid a pleasant adieu to the Calaveras Groves, before saying our parting "good-by," it may be well to state that the "Calaveras" and "South Groves" are both owned by Mr. James L. Sperry, who is also the proprietor and landlord of the Calaveras Grove Hotel;[1] and who has the good fortune of uniting the attentive considerations of "mine host," with the intuitive qualities of a gentleman—not always met with when traveling. And, for the information of the public, I most unreservedly state that here will be found a good table, cleanly accommodations, polite service, and reasonable charges; to which I deem it my duty to add, that the air is pure and invigorating; the climate exhilarating and renewing; and the trout-fishing in adjacent streams most excellent. Months should be spent here instead of a few brief hours, or days.

Now, if you please, in the quiet of the evening, we will return

1. The hotel was destroyed by fire in August 1943.

to Murphy's; and, after we have had a good dinner, and a brief rest, will visit

THE NEWLY-DISCOVERED CAVE.

This, believe me, is one of the greatest natural curiosities of this section. It is situated about a mile from town, and can be reached either by carriage or afoot; and, moreover, can be seen as well by night as by day.

The moment it is entered, intense darkness envelops you like a mantle; so that even the candles, carried by visitors, seem barely sufficient to more than "make darkness visible." Soon, however, the eyes become adjusted to the circumstances, and objects become more or less recognized, although indistinctly at first, then to reveal themselves more clearly to our astonished gaze.

The first chamber reached is about two hundred feet from side to side, its roof stretching far upward into semi-darkness some seventy or eighty feet; and, like the side wall, is slightly curvilinear in form, and at an angle of about 50°. Its uneven sides are partially covered with grotesquely formed stalactites, in masses, closely resembling white fungus. Some hang pendent, like icicles that have run into each other, and broadened as they formed; yet are suspended, in some instances, by a slender, tape-like stem, that one would expect to be broken almost by a breath. From among the seams of the rock overhead hang slender bunches of dark chocolate-colored moss, that are from ten to sixteen feet in length.

Proceeding downwards, the sides of the chamber resemble the folds of massive curtains, the edges or binding of which are, in appearance, very closely akin to the delicate white coral of the South Seas. Here and there are stalagmites that appear like inverted icicles, somewhat discolored, from a few inches to over seven feet in height, and from three inches to two feet in diameter. In one spot stand "The Cherubim," united by a ligature like the once celebrated Siamese Twins. These are about three feet in width by four in height, white as alabaster, and glistening with frost-like crystals.

Still descending, one threads his way among narrow corridors and chambers, the walls of which are draped with coral-like ornaments of many beautiful patterns, until he reaches "The Angels' Wings." These are some eight feet in length by three in breadth, while not exceeding half an inch in thickness, and which are seemingly cemented to the nearly vertical wall of the chamber. From top to bottom of these "wings," are numerous irregular bands, about one and a half inches broad, and of various tints of pink; which show to great advantage when a light is placed at the back of these translucent, wavy sheets. When gently touched—and they should be gently touched, if at all—they give forth sweetly musical notes that resound weirdly through those silent halls of darkness. Nature, as though intending the protection of these delicate forms from vandal hands, has surrounded them with stone icicles.

Other portions of the walls, especially near the roof-ceiling (if so it may be called), have the appearance of an inverted forest of young pines, that, having been dwarfed in their growth, were afterwards turned into stone. Still others resemble moss, lichens, or dead trees in miniature. Occasionally the entire side wall has a resemblance to sugar frosting, which is sufficiently delusive to the eye for tempting children to wish for a piece of it to eat!

The lowest chamber, two hundred and twenty-six feet below the entrance, is the most singular and beautiful of all. If imagination for a moment could come to our assistance, and picture the most exquisitely delicate of coral, arranged in beautiful tufts, and masses, the entire surface covered with silvery hoar frost, and that surface extending up a wall over thirty feet in height, we could obtain some approximating idea of this gorgeous spectacle. There is no language that can approximately portray this fairy-like creation of some chemical genii for the simple reason that it is utterly indescribable.

Specimens of human remains, and those of other animals, have been exhumed from this cave, some of which were embedded on the alabaster formation.

STILL ANOTHER CAVE

Exists seven miles north of Murphy's, and which is probably in the same belt of limestone. This is on "McKinney's Humbug Creek" (what a name!), a tributary of the Calaveras River. As you enter, the walls are dark, rough, and solid, rather than beautiful; but you are soon ushered into a chamber, the roof of which is for some time invisible in the darkness, but where the whole formation has a resemblance to a vast cataract of waters, rushing from some inconceivable height in one broad sheet of foam.

Descending through a small opening, we enter a room beautifully ornamented with pendants from the roof, white as the whitest feldspar, and of every possible form. Some, like garments hung in a wardrobe, every fold and seam complete; others, like curtains; with portions of columns, half-way to the floor, fluted and scalloped for unknown purposes; while innumerable spear-shaped stalactites, of different sizes and lengths, hang from all parts, giving a beauty and splendor to the whole appearance

VIEW OF THE BRIDAL CHAMBER.

surpassing description. Once, as the light was borne up along a glorious fairy stairway, and back behind solid pillars of clear deposits, and the reflected rays glanced through the myriads of varying forms, the whole—pillars, curtains, pendants, and carved work, white as snow, and translucent as crystal—glistened, and shone, and sparkled with a glory that surpassed in splendor all that we had seen in art, or read in fable. This is called

THE BRIDAL CHAMBER.

Immediately at the back of this, and yet connected with it by different openings, is another room that has been, not inappropriately, named "The Music Hall." On one side of this is suspended a singular mass, that resembles a musical sounding-board, from which hang numerous stalactites, arranged on a graduated scale like the pipes of an organ; and if these are gently touched by a skilled musician's hand, will bring out the sweetest and richest of notes, from deep bass to high treble.

FROM MURPHY'S TO CHINESE CAMP.

If time would permit, it would repay us, before leaving Murphy's, to visit the productive gold mines of Central Hill and Oro Plata; see the deep excavations made between the fissure-like formations of the limestone here, for the purpose of extracting the gravel therefrom, which contains the precious metal; or, to watch the various processes used in separating the gold from the gravel and pay dirt; but, as the stage leaves at 7 o'clock A. M., this will be impossible, unless we decide to remain behind for a day or two for that purpose.

It may be interesting for the stranger to know that after leaving Murphy's, our course, for nearly thirty miles, is substantially over the bed of an ancient river, that once ran parallel with the main chain of the Sierra Nevada Mountains. There is no telling how much this stream could reveal to us if it had the power, inasmuch as the fossil remains of mastodons, mammoths, and other animals have been found here. The late Dr. Snell, of Sonora, had several hundred specimens of these. Then, gold in fabulous quantities has been taken from among the bowlders and gravel forming the under-stratum of this stream. In 1853 the writer saw a nugget of solid gold extracted near Vallecito, four miles from Murphy's, that was shaped like a beef's kidney, and weighed twenty-six pounds.

But soon after leaving Vallecito, our course winds down among the hills to Cayote Creek, upon which, about five hundred yards below the road, are two

NATURAL BRIDGES,

Beneath which all the waters of the creek make their exit. The upper side of the upper natural bridge to its arch is thirty-two feet, and the breadth of the arch, twenty-five feet; but as we walk beneath it, the height increases to fifty feet, and the

THE UPPER SIDE OF UPPER NATURAL BRIDGE.

breadth to forty. The roof reminds one of the vaulted arches of some old cathedral, supported by innumerable columns. The sides in places are suggestive of the flowing of a stream whose waters had suddenly turned to ice; and in others to urns and basins; all formed by the action of water, by which they are filled to the brim. The distance from the upper to the lower end of this bridge is two hundred and seventy feet.

About half a mile below the lower side of the upper bridge,

THE UPPER SIDE OF LOWER NATURAL BRIDGE.

there is another that is equally singular and grotesque. One spot beneath the roof and supporting walls presents the appearance of a beautifully worked rotunda, sixty feet in width, with a height of fifteen. It would be impossible to fully describe the many wonderful forms that ornament the arches and walls of these bridges; but as they are of the same general character as the cave, imagination can readily fill out the picture.

Soon we reach Parrot's Ferry at the Stanislaus River, where we find a kindly-hearted old hermit, after whom the ferry is named, who takes us safely across.[1] This stream, transversely crossing the general trend of the ancient river, has cut the old bed away, and formed a channel through it nearly one thousand feet in depth; but, when we have ascended the hill, we are again upon its course.

The auriferous treasures that were there found, stimulated the effort and rewarded the energy of many thousands of miners, and the thriving settlements of Gold Spring (a bounteous spring having here supplied water for washing out the gold), Columbia, Springfield (where another spring gushes out), Shaw's Flat, Sonora, Jamestown, and others sprang into life. It is no exaggeration to say that, within a radius of eight miles, not less than ten thousand miners found employment in unearthing the precious metal, from 1849 to 1854. And although it was supposed by many that these diggings were long since "all worked out," a population still numbering thousands obtains profitable returns from it, directly or indirectly. But while we have been talking, we find ourselves passing down the main street of one of the prettiest mining towns in California, euphoniously named

SONORA.

I like Sonora, and like and believe in its wide-awake, energetic, and large-hearted people; with whom I frankly confess to feel most thoroughly at home. And if time only permitted, I should desire to introduce them, personally; knowing that you would be gratified and honored with their acquaintance. As this, however, is impracticable, I cannot forego the opportunity of saying, that Sonora is not only the county seat of Tuolumne County, but is still the center of a rich mining district. Only a few years ago the "Piety Hill" ledge (since named the "Bonanza Mine"), alone, yielded over half a ton of gold in a single week; and this is only one of many claims still profitably worked. Wood's Creek, upon which Sonora and other towns are located, has produced more gold, for its length, than almost any other stream on the Pacific Coast; and it is questionable if any mule team in existence could haul away in a single load all the

1. Thomas H. Parrott inaugurated his ferry service here in 1860, and ran it until 1903. The present bridge is named "Parrotts Ferry Bridge."

precious metal that has been taken from these rich mines. Nor is gold the only product, by any means; inasmuch as the very finest of fruit, and that in untold abundance, is grown here; with all kinds of vegetables, and cereals. Its altitude, as given by the Wheeler U. S. Survey, is, at the post-office, one thousand eight hundred and sixteen feet above sea level.

As the climate is temperate, healthy, and exceedingly invigorating; its people kindly-natured and enterprising; the gold mines and mining interests instructive to the student, and diverting to the invalid, with abundant educational advantages provided for the young, there can exist but little doubt that the entire section, in and around Sonora, at a very early day, will become not only a favorite place to visit, but whereon to found permanent homes.

A few miles above Sonora, upon or near the great highway which here crosses the main chain of the Sierra Nevada Mountains, are several very productive gold-bearing quartz ledges, that give profitable employment to hundreds of men, and yield rich returns of the precious metal to their fortunate owners.

Upon our departure from this prosperous town, we follow the course of Wood's Creek, past suburban residences and gardens, machine shops and foundries, flouring mills and quartz mills, orchards and vineyards; down to the once famous mining camp of Jamestown (affectionately called by old residents "Jimtown"— consult Bret Harte and Prentice Mulford on this); and as we now drive through its principal street, and revert to its exciting past, it requires quite an effort to overcome the sadness which the contrast inspires, and which, uninvitedly, prompts the soliloquy, *sic transit gloria mundi.* Still, there is more or less prosperity lingering here, owing to its proximity to the gold mines of Poverty Hill, Quartz Mountain, and others. From Jamestown, through Montezuma, to Chinese Camp, evidences are abundant that this extensive district was once thronged to overflowing with miners, and full to the brim with mining life. But as we are now in Chinese Camp, and our route here intersects with the Milton and Big Oak Flat, our course hence will be outlined in a future chapter.

CHAPTER XVII.

THE BIG TREES IN GENERAL.

Their age unknown, into what depths of time
Might Fancy wander sportively, and deem
Some Monarch-Father of this grove set forth
His tiny shoot, when the primeval flood
Receded from the old and changed the earth.
—Mrs. S. C. Connor's *Legend of California.*

The whole creation is a mystery.
—Sir Thomas Browne's *Religio Medici.*

Our best impressions of grand or beautiful sights are always enhanced by their communication to sympathetic and appreciative minds.
—Abel Stevens' *Life of Madame de Staël, Chap. XXII.*

As four different routes to the Yo Semite Valley pass through, or near, one or other of the Big Tree Groves; and inasmuch as all who are fond of botanical studies would like to consider the peculiarities of this interesting genus, I have thought that it would probably be most acceptable to devote this chapter exclusively to their discussion.

As stated in the preceding chapter, it is to Mr. A. T. Dowd, a hunter, to whom the honor is due of discovering this remarkable species, in 1852. Shortly after their discovery was made known, the California Academy of Sciences of San Francisco obtained and transmitted illustrative specimens of its cones and foliage to Prof. Asa Gray, of Cambridge, Massachusetts; and to Dr. John Torrey, of Columbia College, New York; but these were lost on the voyage. The next year Mr. William Lobb, an English botanist, was sent to California, by Mr. James Veitch, of the Royal Exotic Nursery, Chelsea, England, as a collector of plants; who

CONE AND FOLIAGE OF THE BIG TREES—ORDINARY SIZE.

forwarded specimens of the seeds, cones, and foliage of the Big
Trees, to the firm he represented; who placed them in the hands
of the eminent English botanist, Dr. Lindley, for examination and
classification. As Dr. Lindley was the first to describe them (in
the *Gardener's Chronicle* of December 24, 1853), thinking it a new
genus, he named it *Wellingtonia gigantea,* after His Grace the
Duke of Wellington, then recently deceased. Apart from the questionable taste of naming a purely American tree, discovered by an
American, after an English nobleman, however exalted he might
deservedly be in the estimation of his countrymen, subsequent

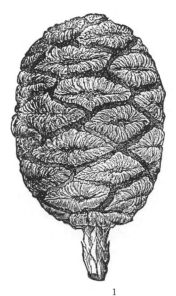

closer analysis proved that it belonged to a genus already classified, and named, by the famous botanist, Endlicher, and known as the Redwood, *Sequoia sempervirens* (the *Taxodium sempervirens* of Lambert). The generic similarity between the Big Tree and the Redwood deter-

1   2

No. 1 represents the cone of the *Sequoia gigantea*, and No. 2 that of the *Sequoia sempervirens*. Natural size.*

1   2

No. 1 represents the male flower of the *Sequoia gigantea*, and No. 2 that of the *Sequoia sempervirens.* Natural size.*

mines them to belong to the same genus, *Sequoia.* Outside of England, therefore, the Big Tree is now known as the *Sequoia gigantea;* that and the *Sequoia sempervirens* being the only representatives of the genus, the flowers and cones of which differ in nothing except size, as clearly indicated in the above engravings.

Although botanical investigation claims that nearly all pines require two years for flowering and the ripening of their fruit, for seed-bearing purposes, and the *Sequoias* three, Mr. W. M. Whitley, for several seasons a resident as well as visitor of the Mariposa Big Tree Grove, after closely watching the annual progress and development of different clusters of cones, contends that the *Sequoia* requires *four*, instead of three years, to bring it to perfection.

* Veitch's Manual of Coniferæ.

WHY NAMED "SEQUOIA."

Sequoyah was the name of a Cherokee Indian chief, of mixed blood, who lived in Will's Valley, at the northeastern corner of Alabama; and who became famous to the world as the inventor of an alphabet of eighty-six characters, each representing a syllable, for the purpose of supplying his tribe with a written language. This language is still in use among the Cherokees. He died in 1843, at the age of 73 years. His intellectual and inventive prominence exalted him as far above his people as the lofty redwoods of the Coast Range towered above other forest trees; and this coincidence suggested to Endlicher the propriety of honorably perpetuating the name of this memorable chief, through one of the most valuable and imposing productions of the vegetable kingdom. Hence the name, *Sequoia,* now made generic by its application to both species of the genus.

THEIR DISTRIBUTION.

The Big Trees do not grow in one continuous belt, like the pines and firs, for instance; but in groups, some of which, as the South Grove and Tuolumne, are nearly forty miles apart; and generally in sheltered hollows, below the tops of ridges. These groups are ten in number; and, commencing northerly at the one first discovered, run southerly, as follows: The Calaveras, South Grove, Tuolumne, Merced, Mariposa, Fresno, Dinky, King's River, New King's River, and Kaweah or Tule Group. The latter, being scattered over low ridges and valleys, only separated by deep cañons, for over sixty miles, and having a breadth of five, might more correctly be called a belt; with a vertical range of nearly two thousand five hundred feet. Their altitude, like the upper timber-line of the Sierras, is more or less climatic, and regulated somewhat by latitude; for, while some of the Calaveras group are less than five thousand feet above sea level, the Grizzly Giant in the Mariposa Grove, by no means the highest in location, is nearly six thousand, and those of the Tule Grove over eight thousand. This applies to the native habitat of all forest trees of the Sierras, even when having a range, in altitude, of from two to three thousand feet, as in the Tule Grove; for, while the upper edge of the timber forest at Mt. Shasta is only eight thousand feet, that immediately east of Yo Semite is eleven thousand, while on the ridges near Fishermen's Peak (the proposed new Mt. Whitney) it is twelve thousand two hundred feet above sea level. Latitude, therefore, as well as altitude becomes an important factor in the distribution of species, in the forests of the Sierras, and should be allowed due consideration when determining their habitat.

PROBABLE AGE OF THE BIG TREES.

If, as generally conceded by botanists, the concentric rings of trees interpret their annual growth, they at once suggest an interesting inquiry as to the probable age of the *Sequoias.* The distance of the rings between is sometimes very marked; inasmuch as, while some do not show more than six or eight to the inch, others will give forty. Rich soil and favorable location may account for the former, and the reverse for the latter. The concentric rings of the stump of the original Big Tree in the Calaveras Grove, prove its annual growth to have been more than double that of others in the same group; therefore, while intimating that it was cut down in its youth, perhaps a thousand years before it had attained its full development, it is suggestive of the possibility of many eminent scientists having been misled in their estimate of the approximate age of these vegetable giants. I have a piece of wood in my Yo Semite cabin, taken from one of the decumbent trees in the Mariposa Grove, that will average thirty-four rings to the inch. I have counted such in numerous specimens, and am satisfied that the average number of concentric rings in the *Sequoias*, would be about twenty-four to the inch; supposing, therefore, the diameter of the tree to be twenty-five feet (the distance across the stump in the Calaveras Grove), measuring from the heart to the outer edge of the sap, the half being twelve feet six inches, would make its astonishing age three thousand six hundred years; and, if thirty feet in diameter (there are many of these), it would be four thousand three hundred and twenty years.

There is no apparent probability of this species ever becoming extinct, as its fecundity exceeds that of any other forest tree in the Sierras.

Notwithstanding the striking resemblance between the two species of this genus, in habit, form, wood, cones, and foliage, the "Redwood" has never been found growing in the Sierra Nevada Mountains, or the "Big Tree" in the Coast Range.

RAPID GROWTH.

There can be no question of the very rapid growth of the *Sequoia gigantea*, inasmuch as the species was unknown until 1852, and no seeds from it were sent to England before 1853; yet trees have been grown there that have attained an altitude and circumference that are remarkable: For instance, at the country seat of the Earl of Devon, at Powderham Castle, near Exeter, England, there is one specimen that exceeds sixty feet in height and ten in girth, at three feet from the ground; and that growth has been attained in less than one-third of a century. There are many other notable examples in Kent, Devon, Gloucester, Sussex, and other counties of England, where this species seems thoroughly to acclimatize.

There is one striking difference between the *Sequoia gigantea*, and the *Sequoia sempervirens*, in habit; the former grows only from seeds, and the latter from both seeds and suckers, and mainly from the latter, in their native forests.

DURABILITY OF THE WOOD.

Notwithstanding the exceeding softness, lightness, and fineness of texture of its timber, its durability is unequaled. In the Fresno Grove there lies an immense *Sequoia*, within three feet of whose sides there sprung up a thrifty young giant, which, when it reached the prostrate tree, as it could not thrust it out of its way, grew over it; so that when last seen by the writer it had grown across it six feet and ten inches; yet the heart-wood of that prostrate tree was as sound as the day that it fell. This species, therefore, will, at no distant day, be cultivated for its valuable qualities as a timber tree; both from its durability, fineness of texture, and general excellence for finishing purposes.

There is a dense resinous gum that exudes from the body of the tree in considerable quantity, where fire has consumed the wood, and much of this has run into the burned cavity; and which, becoming ignited, has largely contributed to the destruction of the tree. This gum is of a crimson-tinted chocolate color; but its relative uses, or commercial value, have not yet been determined. A similar substance drops from the cone in fragmentary crystals, when it is ripe.

Although especial prominence has been given here to the *Sequoia gigantea* or Big Tree, owing to its being one of the remarkable forest products of the Sierras, and within the circle or round of Yo Semite travel, there can exist no possible intention of slighting its big twin brother of the Coast Range, the *Sequoia sempervirens*, or Redwood; inasmuch as, although separate in habitat, there is but little inequality between the two species, either in stature, texture, imposing presence, or other valuable qualities. They are, therefore, twin representatives of the finest genus of forest trees yet known to man. Yet, notwithstanding this, and their being the new wonder of the world, found within a limited area on this coast only, humiliating confession has to be made, that, from business greed and lack of foresight in the government, these glorious Sequoian forests are so rapidly disappearing that, within a quarter, or at most a third of a century, they will have been swept from off the earth.

FOSSILIZED BIG TREES.

The *Sequoias* are proven to have existed in the Tertiary Period, as fossil remains of its cones and foliage are in the possession of Mr. Carruthers, Curator of Botany at the British Museum, London; and fossil specimens have also been recently found in the Calaveras Grove. The so-called "Petrified Forest," near Calistoga, Napa County, represents the fossiliferous condition of *Sequoia sempervirens*.

CHAPTER XVIII.

THE BERENDA ROUTE TO YO SEMITE.

> Go forth under the open sky, and list
> To Nature's teachings.
> —BRYANT'S *Thanatopsis.*

> O what a glory doth this world put on
> For him who, with a fervent heart, goes forth
> Under the bright and glorious sky, and looks
> On duties well performed, and days well spent!
> —LONGFELLOW'S *Autumn.*

> One contented with what he has done, stands but small chance of becoming famous for what he will do. He has laid down to die. The grass is already growing over him.
> —BOVEE'S *Summaries of Thought.*

Spinning out from the Lathrop depot on our way to Berenda, by the Southern Pacific Railroad, that being the route we have now elected to take, our course lies up the valley of the San Joaquin; past farms, and stock, and towns; with the snow-capped Sierras on our left hand, the Coast Range on our right, and both in the far-away distance until we reach Berenda. Here we leave the Southern Pacific and take the Yo Semite branch railroad to Raymond, twenty-two miles distant.

Our course lies easterly; and, for the first eight or ten miles, over a treeless tract of country, of the peculiar formation designated by people generally as "hog wallows;" consisting of little flat hills, nearly round, about twenty feet in diameter, and from one to three feet in elevation, only divided from each other by narrow hollows. As there are hundreds of square miles of these, all sorts of theories upon their origin have been formulated, but none, as yet, satisfactorily so. Some think them the creations of an immense number of rodents; others, by shrubs around which the wind has carried soil, and left it; others, by the action of

(248)

water; but, as all these know as much about their cause as we do, there is something left over for all to inquire into and think about. Uninviting, however, as these may at first sight appear, for agricultural purposes, as the land is comparatively cheap, easily reclaimed, and the soil productive, they are rapidly being taken up by colonies of settlers.

THE BERENDA ROUTE.

From San Francisco, via Lathrop, Merced, Berenda, Raymond, Grant's Sulphur Springs, Wawona, and Mariposa Big Tree Grove, to Yo Semite.

Stations marked (a) are stopping places at night for stage passengers; those marked (b) are hotels, or where meals can be had; those marked (c) are where hay and grain are obtainable; those marked (d) are stage stations.

STATIONS.	Between consecutive points...	From San Francisco......	To San Francisco	Altitude, in feet, above sea level.
By Railway.	. . . . .	. . . . .	200.03	
From San Francisco to—				
Lathrop, junction of the Southern Pacific with the Central Pacific Railroad (b c)	94.03	94.03	58.00	28
Merced, on Southern Pacific Railroad (b c)	58.00	152.03	26.00	171
Berenda, on Southern Pacific Railroad (a b c d)	26.00	178.03	22.00	280
Raymond, on Yosemite Branch Railroad (b c)	22.00	200.03	. . . . .	350
By Carriage Road.	. . . . .	. . . . .	60.90	
From Raymond to—				
Gambetta Mines	13.00	13.00	47.90	1,900
Crook's Ranch	4.50	17.50	43.40	1,800
Grant's Sulphur Springs (b c d)	5.50	23.00	37.90	2,850
Summit of Chow-chilla Mountain	6.50	29.50	31.40	5,605
Wawona (Clark's)* (a b c d)	4.50	34.00	26.90	3,925
Eleven Mile Station (b c)	10.76	44.76	16.14	5,567
Chinquapin Flat (d)	2.20	46.96	13.94	5,908
El Capitan Bridge, Yo Semite Valley	10.31	57.27	3.63	3,926
Leidig's Hotel, Yo Semite Valley	2.56	59.83	1.07	. . . . .
Cook's Hotel, Yo Semite Valley (a b c d)	0.30	60.13	0.77	. . . . .
Barnard's Hotel, Yo Semite Valley (a b c d)	.77	60.90	. . . . . .	3,934

*From Big Tree Station (Clark's) to and through the Mariposa Big Trees and back to Station, 17 miles.

RECAPITULATION.

By railway . . . . 200.03 miles
By carriage road . . . . 60.90 "
To Big Tree Groves and return . . . . 17.00 "

Total distance . . . . 277.93 miles.

Leaving the railroad at Raymond our road now winds around oak-studded ridges, or across flats and low knolls, which, in spring, are garnished with an endless variety of flowers and flowering shrubs. Of the former, from a single square yard, carefully measured off, a botanical enthusiast informed the writer that he picked over three thousand plants! Journeying over the same ground in the fall, nothing but a just and discriminating imagination could realize how beautifully these hills were then garnished.

While changing horses at the station, there can sometimes be seen a horny-backed, and point-armored little reptile that attracts attention by the singularity of his appearance. It is called

THE HORNED TOAD.

This quaint little member of the lizard family is generally found on dry hills, or sandy plains; never in swamps or marshes. There are six different species, and all perfectly harmless. Owing to this, and their slow movements making them easy of capture, with their singular appearance, they have been carried off by curiosity-hunters, as pets; so that, although quite numerous some years ago, they are now becoming scarce. They possess the wonderful power of adapting their color to that of the soil; and change from one hue to another in from twenty-four to

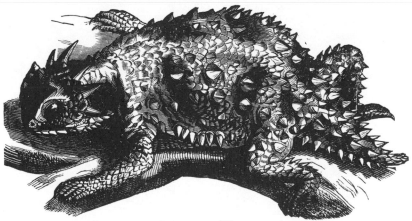

THE HORNED TOAD *(Phrynosoma).*

forty-eight hours.* They sometimes simulate death when handled, and will puff themselves into a nearly spherical shape. Their aversion to dogs is very great; and, when one approaches, they raise themselves to their full height, puff out their body, and hiss aloud. They will completely bury themselves out of sight in the sand in a few moments. Their food consists of flies and other insects, which they capture by quickly thrusting out the tongue, coated with a viscid saliva.

When a resident of the mines, in 1849–50, the writer had a pair picketed out in front of his cabin for three over months; when, strange to say, at the end of that time, the male, which was the smaller of the two, wound himself around his picket-pin one morning, and strangled himself; and, on the evening of the same day the female followed his suicidal example. Upon making a *post-mortem* examination of the latter, a cluster of fifteen eggs

was found, as represented in the accompanying engraving. Upon a visit to any Chinese pharmacy, the Horned Toad will be found dried and ground into powder, or infused in a decoction, for certain fevers, and diseases of the skin.

EGGS OF THE HORNED TOAD,
NATURAL SIZE

As we keep ascending, the scenery becomes more picturesque, and the shrubs and trees more interesting. There are two of the former that are very marked in their attractiveness: one is the "Leatherwood," *Fremontia Californica*, which is from eight to twelve feet in height, covered with bright yellow blossoms; and the other the "Buckeye," *Æsculus Californica*, having an erect panicle of pinkish-white blossoms, from six to twelve inches in height, and two or more in thickness. But were we to examine every flower, shrub, and tree, found upon our way, our task would be endless; as the late Dr. Torrey assured me that he saw over three hundred

* See Lieutenant Wheeler's U. S. Survey, vol. v, page 512.

different species, not to mention varieties, in a single day's ride, on his way to Yo Semite.

Just as we are coming to another station, the "lump-e-tump-thump" of machinery in motion tells us that we are near

THE GAMBETTA GOLD MINES.

That which is nearest the road, and most easily seen, is the "Shore Pride," owned by J. M. McDonald & Bro. This is situated on "Grub Gulch" (the name of the post-office); so called from the fact that, whenever men grew too poor to exist elsewhere, they returned here, and "dug out a living." To the left of this, and a little farther on, is the Haley or Gambetta Mine. This is a rich vein of ore that steadily yields a given sum (I must not tell you how much, as the amount was named confidentially; but it would take you and I many thousand years to starve to death upon it if we did not spend over $5,000 per month). If you wish to see a neat and cozy home, a well-arranged mill, and an excellent gold-bearing quartz ledge, do not fail to call here. These works are about thirty-three miles from Berenda, and are one thousand nine hundred feet above sea level.

But, threading our way among cultivated fields, over low hills covered with oaks and pines, we find ourselves at

GRANT'S SULPHUR SPRINGS.

Here you will find what New Englanders would call a "chipper," brisk, go-ahead, wide-awake, and kindly-hearted man; who, as "mine host," will make you feel at home; and, as proprietor, that he has spared neither money, time, nor energy to compel a forest-wilderness to "blossom as the rose." He raises the largest crops, the biggest water-melons, the nicest strawberries, and the finest fruit to be found anywhere. More than this, he will praise his chicken, and chicken salad, or roast beef, or home-raised hams, and everything else upon his table; if for no other purpose than to help you to find an appetite to eat it. Almost before you know it, therefore, you find that you have not only eaten a hearty meal, but have thoroughly enjoyed it. If there could be found a single stingy hair in Judge Grant's head, light as the crop is becoming, I believe he would pull it out.

Then, there are the "Sulphur Springs," rolling out thirty-three inches of strong sulphurous water every second; and said to be fully equal to the celebrated springs of Arkansas, and Saratoga. These, with the mountain air, conveniences of access, and wildly picturesque surroundings, will bring hither many an invalid, who can here take out a new lease of life, with Judge Grant to assist in "drawing up the papers."

Leaving this attractive spot, our road winds along the shoulders of Chow-chilla Mountain; and, while his bold brow of granite is frowning above us, there is a broad and marvelously beautiful landscape smiling below and beyond us, and one that it would be difficult to excel anywhere. Be sure and induce your coachman to "hold up" for a few moments to obtain this view.

That satisfying and intensely gratifying prospect only prepares us for the contrast so soon to follow; for, having reached the summit of Chow-chilla Mountain, and an altitude of five thousand six hundred feet, we enter a glorious forest of pines, which continues all the way down the mountain, some four and a half miles, to

WAWONA.

Wawona (the Indian name for Big Tree), formerly called "Clark's," is the great central stage station, where the Berenda, Madera, and Mariposa routes all come together; and which also forms the starting-point for the Mariposa Big Tree Groves. The very instant the bridge is crossed, on the way to the hotel, the whole place seems bristling with business, and business energy. Conveyances of all kinds, from a sulky to whole rows of passenger coaches, capable of carrying from one to eighteen or twenty persons each, at a load, come into sight. From some the horses are just being taken out, while others are being hitched up. Hay and grain wagons; freight teams coming and going; horses with or without harness; stables for a hundred animals; blacksmiths' shops, carriage and paint shops, laundries and other buildings, look at us from as many different stand-points. That cozy-looking structure on our left is Mr. Thos. Hill's studio; but that which now most claims our attention, and invites our sympathies, is the commodious and cheery, yet stately edifice in front known as the Wawona Hotel.

The moment we reach its platform, and are assisted in alighting by one of the three brothers, Mr. A. H., Mr. E. P., or Mr. J. S. Washburn, we feel at home. And while one or the other of these gentlemen are seeking to divest our garments of the little dust that has gathered on them, and the servants are performing a similar service to our baggage, let me introduce these gentlemen to you. Mr. A. H. Washburn is one of the principal owners of the Wawona Hotel, with its extensive grounds and pastures; and also of the Yo Semite Stage and Turnpike Company's stage lines, of which he is the efficient superintendent. If he gives you his word for anything, you may rest assured that it will be accomplished, very near to programme, or proven to be utterly impossible. Mr. Edward Washburn, and Mr. John Washburn with his accomplished wife, will do their best to make our stay here enjoyable. To their kind and courteous care, therefore, we confidently commit ourselves.

After dinner the first place generally visited is

HILL'S STUDIO.

Here will be found quite a number of beautiful gems of art, the merits of which are assured from the fact that Mr. Thos. Hill took the first medal for landscape painting at the Centennial Exhibition of 1876, and also the Temple Medal of the Academy of Fine Arts, of Philadelphia, for 1884, with numerous others. The paintings, therefore, will speak for themselves. We shall, moreover, find Mr. Hill a very genial gentleman, who has been everywhere, almost—if not a little beyond—seen about as much as most men, and can tell you what he has seen pleasantly, including his haps and mishaps. So that apart from the delight given by an inspection of his beautiful creations (and he loves Art for her own sake), our visit will meet with other rewards.

Drawn by T. Hill.

THE WAWONA HOTEL.

Moss Engraving Co., N. Y.

EXCURSION TO THE MARIPOSA BIG TREE GROVE.

This, deservedly, forms one of the attractive pilgrimages around Wawona, and a sight of these botanical prodigies has probably been one of the many inducements to the journey hither. The trip is generally undertaken in the early afternoon; but, if time will allow, the entire day should be devoted to it. There is so much to be seen upon the way; its flora, and fauna (not much of the latter), and sundry "what nots," that will otherwise beguile us into the regretful wish that we had more time to spend, lingeringly, among them. And, after all, what is time for, but to use well, and to spend pleasantly?

But before setting out for them, it may be well to state that this grove of big trees was discovered about the end of July, or the beginning of August, 1855, by a young man named Hogg; who passed by, however, without examining them. Relating the fact to Mr. Galen Clark and others, Mr. Clark and Mr. Milton Mann, in June, 1856, united forces, for the purpose of visiting and exploring the newly discovered grove; in order to definitely ascertain its location, with the number and size of its trees. These gentlemen, therefore, were the first to make known the extent and value of this new discovery. Finding that its position was near the southern edge of Mariposa County, it was thenceforward called the "Mariposa Grove of Big Trees."

How renewing memory brings back the treasures of old-time experiences; when, in company with Mr. Galen Clark, three years later, we shouldered our rifles, carrying our blankets and provisions at the backs of our saddles, and started on my first jaunt to this grove, over the old Indian trail. How well and how pleasantly do I remember it, Mr. Clark; since which time you and I have both grown older, and learned many of the instructively suggestive lessons of life.

THE DRIVE TO THE GROVE

Is through a vast forest of stately pines, firs, and cedars, and among blossoming shrubs, and bright-faced flowers. On the way,

Sketched from Nature by G. Tirrel.

THE GRIZZLY GIANT.

however, there is one immense sugar pine, which, had it been found in the grove of Big Trees, we might have supposed that there was the pride of rivalry in its heart, as its circumference is about thirty-three feet. About five miles from Wawona we find the first cluster of Big Trees, which are of goodly proportions; although the driver, by way of answer to our inquiring exclamations, responds, "Oh! they're nothin,' we throws those little chaps in, without countin'." These our aneroid barometer placed at an altitude of five thousand six hundred and thirty feet. But once fairly within the impressive precincts of the grove, we are soon brought face to face with one of the oldest, most storm-tossed, and grizzled, of this entire family of Brobdingnags. It is called

THE GRIZZLY GIANT,

And it looks at you as defiantly as the oldest veteran grizzly bear ever could. By careful measurement we found its dimensions to be, at the ground, including a jutting spur, ninety-one feet; and three feet six inches above the ground, seventy-four feet six inches. Professor Whitney places its circumference, eleven feet from the ground, at sixty-four feet three inches; with its two diameters at base thirty, and thirty-one feet; and, eleven feet above base, twenty feet.

But a mere statement of dimensions and altitudes of these trees can give no realizing sense of their idealistic presence and magnitude. It is the grandeur of their exalted individuality and awe-inspiring presence that thrills through the soul, and fills it with profound and speechless surprise and admiration; and not merely of one tree, but of whole vistas formed by their stately trunks. Who, then, by pen or pencil, can picture these as they are seen and felt? But we must not linger here, as there are just as many big trees in this grove as there are days in the year; so let us see a few of those which are most remarkable.

The coach generally halts at a large and deliciously cool spring near the cabin, where those who have come to spend the day will probably take lunch. Here, too, we shall have the pleasure of meeting the guardian of the grove, Mr. S. M. Cunningham, who knows every tree by heart; with its history, size, and name, and who can tell us more about them in ten minutes than many men could in an hour, who are perhaps quite as familiar with them, and he will do it cheerfully. I can see his bright and genial look, and can watch his wiry form and supple movements, while I write. There is one thing especially noticeable about Mr. Cunningham, he never gets discouraged; and always sees the bright side of things; so that when a storm is swaying the tops of the trees until they bend again, he can listen, interestedly, to their music; and can tell you laughable incidents until your sides shake.

Two beautifully perfect *Sequoias* stand on either side the cabin, one named the "Ohio," and the other "U. S. Grant." The former is seventy-six feet in girth at the ground, and six feet above the ground is fifty-five feet; and the latter sixty-five feet six below, and forty-five feet above. Within thirty yards of these is the "General Lafayette," thirty feet in diameter. Near this is the "Haverford" (named after the "Friends" College, Philadelphia), in which sixteen horses have stood at one time. It is burned into three compartments; across two of the spurs of which the distance is thirty-five feet; and, transversely, thirty-three feet. "Washington" has a girth of ninety-one feet, at the base; is round and very symmetrical. Although burned out somewhat near the ground, the new growth, as usual, is rapidly healing the wounds that fire has made. This is an especially excellent provision of nature for preserving and perpetuating this grand species, when in its prime; inasmuch as while restoring the ravages of the elements by the new growth, a much-needed support is added to the abutments, which intercepts and prevents its premature downfall.

The "Mariposa" is eighty-six feet in circumference, at the ground; and seven feet above it, is sixty-six feet. This tree seems to have been badly burned by two consuming fires, at different periods; after each of which the new growth has, visibly, attempted its restoration. Near to this are four beautifully symmetrical trees, named, respectively, "Longfellow," "Whittier," "Lyell," and "Dana," a quarto of great natures, whose companionship is suggestive of poetry and geology going hand in hand with each other; and almost adjoining these is the "Harvard," a tall and gracefully tapering tree of fine proportions, which seems to derive much strength of purpose from so congenial an association. The "Telescope" is an erect, burnt-out chimney-like trunk about one hundred and twenty feet in height, and which, although a mere shell, has still a growth of cone-bearing foliage upon it. The "Workshop" is an immense living giant with a capacious hollow at its base, which forms a room twelve by sixteen, in which all sorts of little souvenirs are made from broken pieces of the big tree.

But, "Wawona," the "Tunnel Tree," through the heart of which the road passes, is one of the most attractive in the grove.[1] At the base this tree is twenty-seven feet in diameter;

---

1. In 1881 an old burn scar in the tree was enlarged to create the "tunnel." The Wawona Tunnel Tree fell in 1969.

while the enormous trunk through which the excavation is made is in solid heart-wood, where the concentric rings, indicating its annual growth, can be readily seen and counted, and its approximate age determined by actual enumeration, and thus satisfactorily settle that interesting fact beyond the least perad-

Photo by Geo. Fiske.

DRIVING THROUGH LIVING TREE, "WAWONA."

Wawona, Diam. 30 ft. Mariposa Grove.

Fiske #376, the photograph from which the engraving on the opposite page was made.

Photo. by L. Wagoner.

Photo-Typo by Britton & Rey, S. F.

MOFFITT'S TUOLUMNE CAÑON BRIDGE, NEAR JACKSONVILLE.
(See pages 318–19.)
Facing page 320 in edition one. Facing page 322 in editions two and three.

venture. The arch, or "tunnel" as it is called, is ten feet in height, by a width of nine feet six inches at the bottom, and six feet six inches at the top. "Driving through a living tree," one would suppose to be as great a feat as Daniel O'Connell's, who boasted that he could "drive a 'coach and four' through any Act of Parliament ever made in the British House of Commons!"

Just below this is a very large prostrate tree, in possession of the questionable name of "Claveau's Saloon," through which, in former years, two horsemen could ride abreast for eighty feet; but, another "big tree" falling across it, has broken in its roof; yet, above this, people can ride through, for thirty feet. The few noticeable examples here presented can be but barely sufficient to illustrate the peculiarities and immense proportions of this extraordinary genus; and when our delighted vision can be feasted upon such magnificent representatives as the "Queen of the Forest," "Monadnock," "Keystone," "Virginia and Maryland," "Board of Commissioners," the "Diamond Group," and many other equally perfect trees, varying in circumference from sixty to ninety feet, and in altitude from two hundred and fifty to two hundred and seventy-five feet, we become satisfied that, like the Queen of Sheba's opinion of the wisdom of Solomon, "The half hath not been told," and never can be; and these become suggestive of the rich banquet in store for those who can here worship nature for her own glorious sake.

And, be it remembered, that the "big trees," large as they are in themselves, are but a small proportion of this magnificent forest growth, intermixed and interwoven, as they are, with the drooping boughs of the white blossoming dogwood, *Cornus Nutallii;* or the rich purple flowers of the ceanothus, *Ceanothus thyrsiflorus;* or the feathery bunches of white California lilac, *Ceanothus integerrimus*, and other species of this beautiful plant; and to which must be added, the ever fragrant masses of blossom which adorn the azaleas, *Azalea occidentalis*, or the spice bush, *Calycanthus occidentalis*, with its long, bright green leaves, and singular, wine-colored flowers; and from among all of these will be seen peeping the large white bells of the "Lady Washington Lily," *Lilium Washingtonianum;* or the Little Red Lily, *Lilium parvum,* with the gorgeously bright red and orange-colored Tiger Lilies, *Lilium pardalinum,* and *L. Humboldtii;* and other flowers *ad infinitum.*

But, reluctantly as the word "good-bye" may sometimes fall upon the ear, or strike home to the heart, it must occasionally be spoken; yet, before doing this, let us take just one outlook from

WAWONA POINT.

Here is a jutting ridge that stands boldly out from the grove, but a short distance from the road; and, as this affords us a comprehensive bird's-eye view of the surrounding country, with its distant mountain ranges, and long lines of trees; and more especially of the grassy meadows and numerous buildings which constitute the Big Tree Station, "Wawona," two thousand five hundred feet below us, we shall feel that we are well repaid for our trouble.

It may be well here to state that the Mariposa Big Tree Grove, with the Yo Semite Valley, was donated to the State of California in 1864, as recorded in Chapter VIII of this volume.

THE FRESNO GROVE OF BIG TREES.[1]

As this is only about ten miles distant from the Mariposa Grove; and will, without doubt, at an early day, form one of the many delightful excursions from Wawona, a brief outline concerning it may not be unacceptable. On a warm summer evening in July, 1856, Mr. Galen Clark was riding along the ridge which divides the waters of Big Creek from the Fresno, and caught sight of a large group of trees similar to those found in the Mariposa Grove. Two days afterward, Mr. L. A. Holmes, of the Mariposa *Gazette,* and Judge Fitzhugh, while on a hunting excursion, saw the tracks of Mr. Clark's mule as they passed the same group; and as both these parties were very thirsty at the time, and near the top of the ridge at sundown, without water for themselves and animals, they were anxious to find this luxury,

---

1. So named because it was, at that time, in Fresno County. Madera County— where the grove is—was created out of Fresno County in 1893. The grove is now named Nelder Grove, for John A. Nelder, a gold-miner of 1849, who in 1886 homesteaded 156 acres, which encompassed part of the grove.

and a good camping-place, before dark. Consequently, they did not deem it best to tarry to explore, intending to pay it a visit at some early time of leisure in the future. This interesting task, however, seemed to be reserved for Mr. Clark—to whom the world is indebted for this new discovery—and the writer, on the second and third days of July, 1859.

With our fire-arms across our shoulders, and our blankets and a couple of days' provisions at the back of our saddles, we proceeded for a short distance through the thick, heavy grass of the meadow, and commenced the gradual ascent of a well-timbered side-hill, on the edge of the valley, and up and over numerous ridges, all of which were more or less covered with wild flowers. About six o'clock the same evening, we reached the first tree of that which has since been known as the "Fresno Grove" in safety; but as the sun was fast sinking, we deemed it prudent to look out for a good camping-ground before darkness precluded the opportunity, and postpone exploration for the present. Fortunately we soon found one, and at the only patch of grass to be seen in several miles, as afterwards discovered.

As we were making our way through the forest towards it, thinking and feeling that probably we were the first whites who had ever broken the profound solitudes of that grove, we heard a splashing sound, coming from the direction in which we were heading. This, with the moving and rustling of bushes, and the snapping of dead sticks, reminded us that we were possibly invading the secluded home of the grizzly bear, and might, almost before we knew it, have good sport or great danger, to add variety to our experiences. Hastily dismounting and unsaddling, we at once picketed our animals on the grass-plat; still wet with the spurtings of bear's feet, that had hurriedly made tracks across it; then, kindling a fire, to indicate by its smoke the direction of our camp, we started quietly out

ON A BEAR HUNT.

Cautiously peering over a low ridge, not over a hundred yards from our horses, we saw two large bears moving slowly

BEAR HUNT IN THE FRESNO GROVE.

away. Their attention had evidently been attracted by our movements, as they had paused, and were looking towards us in a
listening and somewhat defiant attitude. Mr. Clark was just raising his rifle for a shot, when I whispered a request for permission
to be allowed "the first shot at that immense fellow yonder?" who
was not over thirty-five yards off. "Certainly, with pleasure," was
my companion's prompt and courteous rejoinder. In an instant a
charge of buck-shot was sent, just behind the shoulder; when he
made a quivering leap towards us, as though he would pay us
back for our temerity; but a ball, from the unerring rifle of Mr.
Clark, determined him to make a hasty retreat after the other
one, already scampering off in the distance.

We immediately started in pursuit; and although their course could be easily followed by the tracks made, as well as the blood from the wounded bear, they reached the shelter of a dense mass of chaparral, before we could overtake them, even by a shot; as they traveled much faster than we could, and were there securely hidden from sight. Deeming it impolitic and unwise to follow them, by creeping under and among the bushes forming their place of refuge, if not their lair, we walked around upon the lookout, until the deepening darkness, as if in sympathy with bruin, completed their hiding, and admonished our return to camp without the expected prize; and where, when supper was ended, we soon found forgetfulness in sleep. After a very early breakfast we again renewed our search for the hoped-for game; but, although we ventured into the chaparral, and I looked under this and that heavier clump of bushes, in the hopes of finding it; we never saw either of them afterwards. Finding nothing larger than grouse, we bagged a few of those, and then commenced our explorations.

We spent the whole day wandering through the dense forest which forms this splendid grove; looking at this one, admiring that, and measuring others, without attempting to ascertain the exact number of *Sequoias* found here; yet concluded that there were about five hundred of well developed Big Trees, on about as many acres of gently undulating land. The two largest we could find measured eighty-one feet each in circumference, were well formed, and straightly tapering from the ground to their tops. Many others that were equally sound, and as symmetrically proportioned, were from fifty-one feet to seventy-five feet in girth. The sugar pines were enormously large for that species; as one that was near our camp measured twenty-nine feet six inches in circumference, and two hundred and thirty-seven feet in length. None of the trees in this grove were badly deformed by fire.

But now, if you please, let us imagine that we have taken the delightful, forest-arched ride, from the Mariposa Big Tree Grove, down to Wawona; as, before we leave its enjoyable precincts, there are many points of interest still to visit, and among them

Drawn by T. Hill

THE CHIL-NOO-AL-NA FALLS.

NEAR WAWONA.

CHIL-NOO-AL-NA.

Hail me, dashing Chil-noo-al-na!
  O'er the cliffs and crags I'm leaping,
Where the wild bear, and the lion,
  From their lairs are stealthy creeping.

Here I love to shout and clamber,
  O'er the rocky heights and steepness,
As with misty mantle covering
  Every nook and cave-like deepness.

Here I dwell with nymphs and dryads;
  Here, so high perched on the mountains;
While my everlasting waters
  Flutter down in ceaseless fountains.

Dashing into space so grandly,
  Naiad streams are dancing lightly,
With a million scintillations,
  Spangling all the air so brightly.

In the Sylvan Grotto hiding,
  See my bride; her bright hair tosses,
Shim'ring down in glist'ning meshes,
  'Mong the lovely ferns and mosses.

Lo! the Frost King brings his shackles,
  Ties my limbs with strength and power,
While his elves are deftly weaving
  Shroud, and wreath, and snowy flower.

Though he tries with deathly stillness,
  But to hush my voice forever,
I leap forth from his embraces,
  And his manacles I sever.

For I'm Monarch of these forests,
  From my great throne high and lonely,
Shouting out to lesser streamlets,
  I reign o'er these waters only.

I am mighty in my power.
  I am splendid in my glory.
What care I for Neptune's oceans,
  Famed in song, and ancient story.

—Mrs. Fannie Bruce Cook.

THE CHIL-NOO-AL-NA FALLS.

The beautiful pen drawing on the adjoining page, kindly made by Mr. Thos. Hill for this work, will tell how richly a visit there will be repaid, by either walking or riding the two miles of distance from the hotel.

Another compensating and satisfying sally from Wawona is to

SIGNAL PEAK,

The name given to the highest point of the Chow-chilla Mountains, lying westerly from the hotel. This suggestive nomenclature was given to it owing to the Indians having made choice of that point as a signal station, from which to telegraph, by fire and smoke, to all their Indian allies, both far and near, any message they might wish to send. Its commanding outlook will at once commend their choice for the selection. The accompanying engraving, also from a sketch by Mr. Hill, significantly indicates the wonderful panorama rolled out before us from that glorious scenic standpoint, when looking east. On any clear day every deep gorge, and element-chiseled furrow, every lofty peak, and storm-defying crag, of the great chain of the Sierras, for a radius of nearly one hundred miles, is distinctly visible to the naked eye. It is one vast sea of mountains, whose storm-crested waves tell of their billowy upheaval by elemental forces, and suggest that they were afterwards suddenly cooled, and solidified into rock, when in most violent ebullition; and that while the impressive individuality of each culminating crest is measurably dwarfed by distance, the general effect of the whole is inexplicably enhanced by the wonderful combination.

Looking west how suddenly the scene changes from storm to calm; for, while the near mountain ridges, which form the foreground to the picture, remind us of the former, the receding foot-hills, and broad valleys peacefully stretching to the horizon, tell only of the latter; so that the one by contrast, exalts the impressiveness of the other, and provides, as a whole, a satisfying "feast of good things, of wines on the lees, well refined," that will be

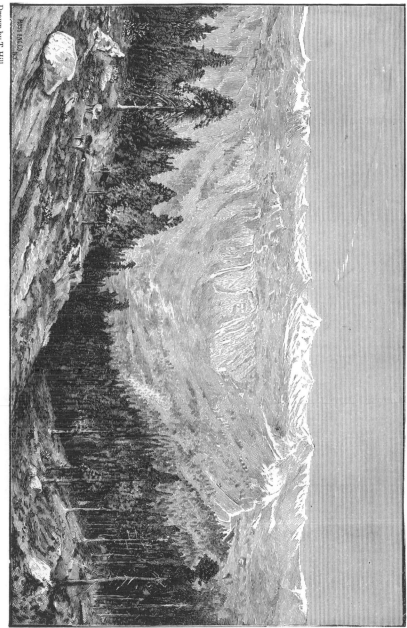

Drawn by T. Hill.

THE SIERRAS FROM SIGNAL PEAK.

pleasantly remembered as long as memory reigns queen upon her throne.

LESSER POINTS OF INTEREST AROUND WAWONA.

Such as the excellent trout fishing in the south fork of the Merced, that runs directly past the hotel; the walk to the Fish Pond, and boat ride upon it; visit to Hill's Point, for the distant view of Chil-noo-al-na Falls; the Soda Spring, and grove of young *Sequoias* near; and other places of interest, which not only enable visitors to spend their time pleasantly here, but become sufficiently attractive to induce many to tarry months at Wawona, and some for the whole summer. The cheery liveliness of its constantly changing throng of visitors; its salubrious and exhilarating climate; the balmy fragrance of its surrounding pine forests, and charming variety of scenery, would seem to unite in making this a most delightful resort for invalids.

But as the glorious scenes of the Yo Semite are in immediate prospect, and as anticipation has long been on tiptoe to enter their sublime precincts, let us cross the South Fork Bridge at Wawona, and start at once upon our deeply interesting journey.

Following the eastern bank of that stream for about a mile, we commence the gradual ascent of a long hill, the outlook from which is everywhere full of inspiriting pleasure. On both sides of the road the gossamer, floss-like blossoms of the Mountain Mahogany, *Cercocarpus ledifolius;* the Manzanita, *Arctostaphylos glauca* (What a name for such a beautiful shrub!) with its pinkish-white, wax-like, and globe-shaped blossoms, hanging in bunches, challenge our admiration. But, on we roll, the landscape broadening and the gulches, like our interest, deepening as we ascend, until we come to "Lookout Point." Here grandeur culminates, and an admonition spontaneously finds its way to the lips, "Oh! driver, please to stop here just one minute for this marvelous view." This is five thousand five hundred and sixty feet above sea level.

Before long the darkening forest shadows we are entering remind us that we shall soon be at Eleven Mile Station, and at "West Woods." West Woods is the name given to Mr. John W. Woods, an open-faced and kindly-hearted hunter, who makes this his lonely abiding-place both winter and summer. A short distance beyond this we attain the highest point on the road, six thousand one hundred and sixty feet above the sea. About half a mile further on we arrive at Chinquapin Flat, where the diverging road for Glacier Point, fourteen miles distant, leaves the main one. From here every step towards Yo Semite is constantly alternating and changing in scenic grandeur; now we emerge from forest shades to open glades; then look into the deep cañon of the Merced River; then upon the leaping tributaries of Cascade Creek; until, at last, we come to that unspeakably glorious view which suddenly breaks upon us at

INSPIRATION POINT.

Here language fails; for neither the pencil's creative power, the painter's eliminating art, photography, pen, or human tongue, can adequately portray the scene of unutterable sublimity that is now out-rolled before us. Longfellow's beautiful thought seems uppermost: "Earth has built the great watch-towers of the mountains, and they lift their heads far into the sky, and gaze ever upward and around to see if the Judge of the World comes not"—even while we are entrancedly waiting.

Deep down in the mountain-walled gorge before us sleeps the great Valley. Its beautiful glades, its peacefully glinting river, its dark green pines, its heavily timbered slopes; all hemmed-in, bounded, by cliff-encompassing domes, and spires; with crags and peaks, from three to five thousand feet in height, and over which there gracefully leap the most charming of water-falls, from nine hundred to three thousand feet in height above the meadows. While "the laurel-crowned king of the vale," grand old El Capitan, with a vertical mountain cleavage of three thousand three hundred feet, stands out most nobly defiant, and asserts the impressive individuality of his wonderful presence; while over all of these an atmospheric veil of ethereal purple haze is enchantingly thrown, with the whole bathed in sunshine, to heighten the general loveliness of the scene. No change of time or circumstance can ever efface from memory this glorious first glimpse of Yo Semite.

CHAPTER XIX.

THE MADERA ROUTE TO YO SEMITE.

Go abroad
Upon the paths of Nature, and, when all
Its voices whisper, and its silent things
Are breathing the deep beauty of the world,
Kneel at its simple altar, and the God
Who hath the living waters shall be there.

—N. P. WILLIS.

Pleasures lie thickest where no pleasures seem;
There's not a leaf that falls upon the ground
But holds some joy, of silence or of sound,
Some sprite begotten of a summer's dream.

—BLANCHARD'S *Hidden Joys.*

This route, like the Berenda, lies up the great valley of the San Joaquin, seven miles beyond the former starting-point, to Madera, a town probably of about five hundred inhabitants. We are now upon historic ground, as here the famous Fresno Indian Reservation was founded; and, about nine miles above where Madera now stands, was the place of general rendezvous for all the Indians gathered in, after the Mariposa Indian War of 1851–52; for the Indian Commission, and the officers and men forming the Mariposa Battalion. Then, it was one vast stretch of country without a building upon it, or any other sign of civilization—if we except those made necessary by the needs of reservation life—now it is dotted in all directions with farm-houses and gardens, orchards and vineyards, with cultivated fields, and succulent pastures, on every hand; with the Southern Pacific Railroad running through and among them. Let their enemies say what they may, these railroads are rapidly assisting development, and progress, wheresoever their iron bands may extend.

(272)

THE MADERA ROUTE,

From San Francisco, via Lathrop, Merced, Madera, Fresno Flats, and Mariposa Big Tree Station (Clark's), to Barnard's Hotel, Yo Semite Valley.

Stations marked (*a*) are stopping places at night for stage passengers; those marked (*b*) are hotels, or where meals can be had; those marked (*c*) are where hay and grain are obtainable; those marked (*d*) are stage stations.

STATIONS.	Between Consecutive Points.	From San Francisco.	To San Francisco.	Altitude, in feet above Sea Level.
By Railway.	......	......	185.03	
From San Francisco to—				
Lathrop, junction of the Southern Pacific with the Central Pacific Railroad (*b c*)	94.03	94.03	91.00	28
Merced, on Southern Pacific Railroad (*b c*)	58.00	152.03	33.00	171
Madera, on Southern Pacific Railroad (*a b c d*)	33.00	185.03	.....	280
By Carriage Road.	......	......	95.35	
From Madera to—				
Adobe Station, Stitts' (*b c*)	9.25	9.25	86.10	
Mudgett's Ranch (*b c*)	9.25	18.50	76.85	
Green's Ranch (*b c d*)	6.50	25.00	70.35	1,100
Kron's, Coarse Gold Gulch (*b c d*)	13.50	38.50	56.85	2,085
Fresno Flats (*b c*)	6.50	45.00	50.35	2,192
Bufford's (*b c*)	5.00	50.00	45.35	3,260
Board Ranch (*b c d*)	8.00	58.00	37.36	4,639
Summit of Chowchilla Mountain	3.60	61.60	33.76	5,005
Forks of road to Mariposa Big Tree Groves	3.33	64.43	30.43	5,062
Big Tree Station, Clark's (*a b c d*)*	3.47	68.40	26.96	3,925
Eleven Mile Station (*b c d*)	10.76	79.16	16.20	5,567
El Capitan Bridge, Yo Semite Valley	12.57	91.73	3.63	3,926
Leidig's Hotel, Yo Semite Valley (*a b c d*)	2.56	97.29	1.07	.....
Cook's Hotel, Yo Semite Valley (*a b c d*)	0.30	97.59	0.77	.....
Barnard's Hotel, Yo Semite Valley (*a b c d*)	0.77	98.36	.....	3,934

*From Big Tree Station (Clark's) to and through the Mariposa Big Trees and back to station, seventeen miles.

RECAPITULATION.

By railway .... 185.03 miles.
By carriage road .... 95.35 "
To Big Tree Groves and return .... 17.00 "

Total distance .... 298.32 miles.

THE TOWN OF MADERA.

After the completion of the Southern Pacific Railroad through this section, the California Lumber Company was organized, for the purpose of tapping the extraordinary growth of timber that was found to exist in the Fresno Grove, and for bringing its lumber down to the market created by the railroad. Sawmills were accordingly erected in that vicinity; but, as its great distance from market precluded the possibility of its successful delivery there by ordinary conveyance, a V flume was constructed, fifty-four miles in length, at an original cost of $375,000, for the purpose of floating it down. This will readily be seen at numerous points on the route. As soon as this was completed, the mills were put working to their fullest capacity; and lumber, to the extent of one hundred thousand feet per day, was started upon its meandering voyage to the depot. The business connected with this enterprise became the inception of the now prosperous town of "Madera"—*Madera* being Spanish for lumber. And for the purpose of meeting the wants of the people settling along the line of the railroad from here to New Mexico, the sugar and yellow pine, fir, and big tree wood, were converted into doors, blinds, sashes, etc. Here it may be said, in parenthesis, that the largest of the Big Trees, being found altogether too large for advantageous handling in lumber manufacturing, were allowed to remain undisturbed? Two hundred men are employed in this industry. They saw off the trees at the ground with the ordinary cross-cut saw, instead of chopping them down, as formerly.

There is a lumber yard of forty acres, through which there are roads and railroads in all directions, and to lumber piles of all sizes and kinds. Near the terminus of the flume it is divided into two branches, each of which is provided with a separate reservoir, into which the lumber is floated from the mountains; although most of it is removed directly from the flume, placed upon trucks, and then run upon tramways to the location desired. The wastewater, after being relieved of its cargo, is distributed in different directions, and sold for irrigation purposes.

This enterprise naturally formed the stimulating nucleus for the commencement of others; and farms and farm buildings sprung into existence; and with them the store and hotel, the blacksmith shop, and other creations of industrial development. So that now there are numerous stores, post-office, Wells, Fargo & Co's. express office, a commodious hotel, saloons; and long lines of business places of all kinds needed in a thriving community, including a printing office and newspaper.

For many years Madera was the principal station on the Southern Pacific Railroad, for the departure of tourists for the Yo Semite Valley and Mariposa Big Tree Groves; but, since the construction of the Yo Semite branch railroad, from Berenda to Raymond, that business has naturally transferred thither. Owing, however, to its convenience of location, and the excellence of the mountain roads leading therefrom to the great sights beyond, Madera will continue to be the principal place of departure for all persons traveling by private teams. A short distance above this was once a very favorite place for *rodeos** and for rancheros.

LASSOING AND BRANDING THEIR CATTLE.

Before gold was discovered in California its main wealth seemed to consist in its cattle and horses, the former being slaughtered almost exclusively for their hides and tallow, which then formed about the only articles of export. As there were no fences in those days, all animals were allowed to roam wheresoever they chose; generally between defined bounds, as between rivers, or mountain ranges; and every spring their different owners, with their *vaqueros* (all well mounted), would sally out on a given day, scour the whole district assigned to them, and drive every animal found within it to the spot designated for the *rodeo*. Others would do the same for districts assigned to them, until every animal ranging at large was collected together.

This accomplished, all would assemble around a large camp-fire for social pleasures, and spend the remainder of the day in

---

* *Rodeo* is a Spanish word, generally applied to the place and annual gathering in of cattle and horses, for the purpose of counting and branding them.

RANCHEROS LASSOING CATTLE

frolicking or feasting. Sometimes these indulgences would continue for a number of days, before commencing upon the business which had brought them together. Finally, however, they would settle down to their exciting work. Every ranchero had and knew the particular brand which belonged to him, and which was well understood and conceded by every one present. But, whenever there was a single doubt about that, the animal in question was immediately lassoed, as shown in the accompanying illustration, thrown upon the ground, and examined. This satisfactorily determined, every calf or colt that followed its mother, was unhesitatingly conceded to belong to the same owner, and was accordingly branded with the red-hot iron which formed the brand. Sometimes this was a character (somewhat after the Chinese pattern) and at others a letter—generally the initial of the family name. After the counting and branding, each drove would be driven back to its usual range, and there left to look out for itself until the next spring. Occasionally there would be two *rodeos* a year, but not often.

As our road lies over gently undulating hills near the Fresno River, we have frequent and refreshing glances of its willows and cottonwoods; and the bright green verdure of its meadow land, confessedly somewhat limited; with the V flume on its sinuous course at our side, bearing its freight of lumber down to the railroad.

Soon the white post oaks and numerous shrubs, begin to dot the landscape. Then we enter the cañon of Coarse Gold Gulch— one of the historic places of early days—and find the music of its gurgling waters, and the shadow of its alder and black oak trees, most pleasantly diverting until we reach the little village of the same name, and its hotel, where the inner man can be regaled and the outer man refreshed. Here we have attained an altitude of two thousand and eighty-five feet above the level of the sea.

After climbing a dividing ridge of the Fresno River, nearly a thousand feet above the gulch, we again descend to a pretty little hill-encompassed town, known everywhere as Fresno Flats. This is supported, mainly, by lumbering, farming, mining, and stock-raising. Being the business center of a number of small settlements around it, the principal street is fairly alive with teams, saddle-horses, bustling men and men of leisure; with the customary complement of Indians and dogs, found at nearly every foothill outpost of civilization throughout the State. More recently a number of gold-bearing quartz ledges have been found in the adjacent hills, which, when developed, will make an acceptable addition to the prosperity of the town. But,

"Onward, and upward, let our course be."

Before advancing far upon our journey, we enter the glorious forests of the Sierra, which deservedly attract the wondering admiration of every traveler; these, diversified by broad openings and impressive glimpses of landscape, continue every foot of the way to Wawona. The highest portion of the Chow-chilla Range crossed upon this road is near the saw-mill at Fish Springs, which is five thousand one hundred and seven feet above sea level. This entire section is remarkably attractive to camping parties, desirous of exchanging the hot air of the plains for the deliciously cool atmosphere of the mountains, owing to the dense growth of its forests, the little patches of grassy meadows, and the leaping waters of Big Creek being literally alive with trout. Some families spend the whole summer here, at the Big Tree Groves, and on the mountains bordering the Yo Semite. The only detraction to this, as of other mountain fastnesses, is from the immense droves of sheep passing over, eating up every green thing (including beautiful lilies, and other flowering plants), and leaving a desert behind them. Nor is this all, for as neither deer nor any other game will feed after sheep, they naturally and necessarily seek other pastures. Then to this must be added the infamous practice of sheep-herders setting the forests on fire—the unprincipled return for being allowed to pasture their flocks upon the public domain, free of every kind of charge. This route intersecting those of Berenda and Mariposa, as before stated, at Wawona, they are thence necessarily continued conjointly.

CHAPTER XX.

THE COULTERVILLE ROUTES.

Nature never did betray
The heart that loved her.
—Wordsworth's *Tintern Abbey.*

Converse with men makes sharp the glittering wit,
But God to man doth speak in solitude.
—John Stuart Blackie.

He prayeth best, who lovest best
All things, both great and small.
—Coleridge's *Ancient Mariner.*

As on the Berenda route our course lies up the valley of the San Joaquin, to either Modesto or Merced. We can make either of these towns the place of departure for Coulterville and Yo Semite. If we have chosen the former, the first place reached, we shall find it a goodly-sized town, full of energetic people; and the usual accompaniments of a very prosperous business community of about seventeen hundred inhabitants, including good hotel accommodations (an important consideration just now, as we have to spend the night here). Modesto is the county seat of Stanislaus County.

But, if we have preferred to take the Coulterville Route to Yo Semite *via* Merced, we keep our seat in the railroad car for about an hour and a half longer, and then alight at the El Capitan Hotel, Merced, where we shall forget ourselves in sleep. This is the county town of Merced County, and a thriving city of one thousand nine hundred inhabitants; with all the usual accessories of business, amusement, and education; and is the center of a remarkably fertile farming district.

Leaving the Southern Pacific at either Modesto or Merced, by stage, we pass over a farming region and rolling country,

(279)

THE COULTERVILLE ROUTE,

From San Francisco, via Lathrop, Merced, or Modesto, Coulterville, and Merced Grove of Big Trees, to Yo Semite Valley.

Stations marked (*a*) are stopping places at night for stage passengers; those marked (*b*) are hotels, or where meals can be had; those marked (*c*) are where hay and grain are obtainable; those marked (*d*) are stage stations.

STATIONS.	Between consecutive points.	From San Francisco.	From Yo Semite Valley.	Altitude, in feet, above Sea Level.
	DISTANCES IN MILES.			
By Railway.	. . . . . .	. . . . .	152.03	
From San Francisco to—				
Lathrop, junction of the Southern Pacific with the Central Pacific Railroad (*b c*)	94.03	94.03	58.00	28
Merced, on Southern Pacific Railroad (*a b c d*)	58.00	152.03	. . . . .	171
By Carriage Road.	. . . . .	. . . . .	93.66	
From Merced to—				
Halfway House, watering place (*b c*)	6.35	6.35	87.31	215
Snelling's (*b c*)	12.60	18.95	74.71	252
Merced Falls (*b c*)	4.58	23.53	70.13	260
Junction Station (*b c*)	5.81	29.34	64.32	578
Lebright's Ranch (*b c d*)	5.53	34.87	58.79	995
Herbeck's (*b c*)	5.74	40.61	53.05	1,621
Coulterville (*b c*)	5.57	46.18	47.48	1,665
Dudley's Hotel and Ranch (*a b c d*)	7.58	53.76	39.90	2,959
Bower Cave (*b c*)	4.69	58.45	35.21	2,360
Wenger's Ranch (*b c*)	3.23	61.68	31.98	3,218
Watering trough	4.00	65.68	27.98	4,120
Hazel Green (*b c d*)	5.51	71.19	22.47	5,550
Forks of road to Crane Flat	0.36	71.55	22.11	5,502
Merced Grove of Big Trees	2.80	74.35	19.31	5,327
Big Meadows (*b c d*)	8.45	82.80	10.86	4,237
Junction of Coulterville Road with Merced River Trail	4.59	87.39	6.27	3,352
Forks of Coulterville and Big Oak Flat Roads	2.61	90.00	3.66	. . . .
Leidig's Hotel (*a b c d*)	2.59	92.59	1.07	. . . .
Cook's Hotel (*a b c d*)	0.30	92.89	0.77	. . . .
Barnard's Hotel (*a b c d*)	0.77	93.66	. . . . . .	3,934
By Railway.				
From San Francisco to—				
Lathrop, junction of Southern Pacific with Central Pacific R. R.	94.03	. . . . .	. . . .	. . . .
Modesto, on Southern Pacific Railroad	20.00	114.03	. . . .	. . . .
By Carriage Road.				
From Modesto to—				
Waterford	.12	.12	. . . . . .	. . . .
Horr's Ranch	.08	.20	. . . . . .	. . . .
La Grange	.08	.28	. . . . . .	. . . .
Lebright's	.10	.38	. . . . . .	. . . .
Coulterville	.12	.50	. . . . . .	. . . .

RECAPITULATION.

By railway to Merced . . . . 152.03 miles.
By carriage road from Merced to Yo Semite . . . . 93.66 "
    Total distance *via* Merced . . . . 245.69 miles.

By railway to Modesto . . . . 114.03 miles.
By carriage road, Modesto *via* Coulterville to Yo Semite . . . . 99.46 "

    Total distance *via* Modesto . . . . 212.44 miles.

devoted mainly to the raising of wheat; with the great chain of the Sierras in full view before us. On the Modesto branch we cross the Tuolumne River near La Grange, and on the Merced branch cross the Merced River at Snelling. A few miles above the former village the fossil remains of an immense mastodon were found, imbedded in the auriferous gravel of the mine, some ten feet below the surface, beneath an oak tree three feet in diameter. The accompanying illustration, sketched from nature, will indicate its character.

This tooth measured six inches and three-quarters across it, by eight and a half inches from front to back; and the longest

FOSSILIZED MASTODON'S TOOTH, AND PORTION OF JAW.

fang, or root, was eight and a quarter inches in depth, from the upper to the lower surface of the jaw, reaching nearly through the jaw-bone. The tooth stood above the upper surface of the jaw about two inches. The knee-joint of this huge animal was about four times the size of that of the largest ox.

Soon after crossing both the Tuolumne and Merced Rivers, the beautiful natural parks of the foot-hills of the Sierra, lying between the two rivers, are entered, consisting mostly of "digger" or "bull" pines, *Pinus Sabiniana;* white post oaks, *Quercus Douglasii;* and black oaks, *Quercus Kelloggii;* with numerous shrubs and flowers interspersed between, until our arrival at Coulterville, a mining town of Mariposa County, one thousand eight hundred feet above the sea. But a few miles before arriving there, near to the Dutch Boys' Ranch, as it is called, there is frequently to be seen a very singular bird, that invites special attention, and which is known as

THE CALIFORNIA ROAD-RUNNER, *Geococcyx Californianus.*

This strange and rare bird, peculiar to California and some portions of Mexico, is sometimes called the Ground Cuckoo, to which family it belongs. At first sight it might be supposed to be a new kind of pheasant, so striking is the resemblance in color and pattern of plumage to that genus; but upon closer examination it is soon discovered to be unlike it in every particular. Owing to its exceeding shyness and uncommon scarcity, there is probably less known about this singular species than almost any other. The late Mr. A. J. Grayson, a loving student of ornithology, succeeded in catching, unobserved, the expression of eye and attitude of this bird just when preparing to spring, and kindly sent me the sketch and accompanying notes:—

So far as I am acquainted, the Road-runner, or, as it is called in Spanish, *Courier del Camino,* or *Pisano,* has not been described by any ornithologist. It is a distinct and isolated species from all other birds, roaming about over barren plains and hills in search of lizards, snakes, and other reptiles, upon which it preys. It is almost always seen upon the ground, seldom in trees, unless pursued very closely, when it has been seen to spring from the ground to the branches, a height of from ten to fifteen feet, at a single bound, but prefers running along a road or path; from which habit it derives its name. When discovered, it instantly runs off, with remarkable fleetness, to the nearest thicket or hill, where it generally escapes its pursuers, either by hiding, or by sailing from one hill to another. It is very quick in its motions—active and vigilant; indeed its remarkable swiftness enables it to outstrip a horse.

The most remarkable feature about it is its feet, these being more like those of clinging birds, such as the woodpecker or parrot, having two toes before, and two behind, armed with sharp claws. Its legs being strong and muscular, make it well adapted for running.

Its plumage is rather coarse and rough, of a dusky hue, marked with white and brownish specks on the neck and upper parts, while underneath, it is of a dirty white. The tail is long, the bill strong and slightly curved, eye of a greyish brown, the pupil encircled by a light-colored ring. A bare space extends from the eye to the back of the neck, of a pale bluish color tinged with red. The specimen I have now before me measures twenty-three inches from the tip of his bill to the end of his tail. The tail is eleven and a quarter inches, the bill two and a half inches. I have frequently met with this bird in my travels over the country, and I have never seen one in company with any other bird, either of its own or any other kind. It is excessively shy and solitary, inhabiting the wildest and most unfrequented places. It has no song to cheer its solitude. At times it utters a harsh note, not unlike the sudden twirl of a watchman's rattle.

One of these birds in my possession is becoming quite tame, and readily feeds upon any kind of raw meat; but prefers lizards and small birds, which it swallows whole—feathers and all. If given to him alive, he will play with them awhile before swallowing them, just as a cat will do with a mouse. I have seen him devour three sparrows, one lizard, and a portion of the breast of a coot, for his breakfast, without experiencing any inconvenience. It is exceedingly ravenous; and, like all birds of that class, has a disagreeable odor; and should, I think, be placed in the order of rapacious birds.

Just before entering Coulterville, some three miles north-westerly, the croppings of an immense gold-bearing quartz ledge stand boldly out at Peñon Blanco (a mountain of white rock); and the vein is crossed within rifle-shot of the hotels. This lode is the most remarkable one, in size and lineal extent, of any one yet found in California, as it can be distinctly traced from the middle of Amador County to the center of Mariposa County, a distance of seventy-five miles, by its stupendous croppings. It is estimated that the various quartz mines on this lode, within the limit stated, have yielded $40,000,000 in gold. As this "Mother Vein," as it is called, crosses Maxwell's Creek just below the town of Coulter-ville, a visit can be paid it while the coach is stopping for the assortment of the mail.

TARANTULAS, *Aranea Tarentula.*

Here, too, perhaps some enterprising boy or man may bring a tarantula's nest to show us; and as we examine the peculiarly

A TARANTULA'S NEST.

unique manner of its construction, we naturally wish to know more concerning its architect and builder. The tarantula, then (so called from Taranto, in Italy, from whence the first specimens were obtained by entomologists), evidently belongs to the spider family, although the nest is out of the ordinary style of such insects. I have seen specimens of this genus that measured five inches from the tip of one of its hairy legs to that of the other; with a body two and a half inches in length, by one inch in diameter. Their appearance is both formidable and forbidding; and they are quite venomous in their bite. It has eight legs, four on each side. Between the two fore legs there is a pair of sharp, serrated nippers, which they use when seizing their prey; and in their head, between these, are two horny, sharp, and hollow fangs, curved inwardly, through which a poisonous fluid is projected when striking an enemy.

They live in nests formed of clay; which is provided with an ingeniously constructed trap-door, made out of about thirty layers of silk and dirt (the former spun from their own body), the inner side of which is also covered with silk, and made water and air tight. The springy strength of the silken hinges of this trap-door is sufficient to instantly close it, the moment the nest is entered. As an additional security to those within there are holes made in the edges of the door, into which the tarantula can insert its fangs, and bolt himself in.

The tarantula, like every living tenant of this world, has its enemy, in a large, hornet-like fly called the *pepsis*, whose dark blue body, and bright reddish-orange colored wings, enable the curious to closely study his movements; as, with unrelenting vindictiveness, he encompasses the helplessness of his victim. When the *pepsis* catches sight of his prey, he swoops down upon it with a viz-z-z-zip, viz-z-z-zip, which he continues until the tarantula is utterly paralyzed—not killed. This accomplished, he leaves the defenseless body where it fell, and flies away for assistance. Sometimes it is an hour or more (I once watched for nearly two hours without results) before the victor returns, when he brings with him from three to five coadjutors, who push or pull the body forward until they reach their nest (always built in the ground), into which the tarantula is unceremoniously dropped, and then stowed away on one side. It has generally been supposed that this is simply a provision made for food purposes; but this is incorrect, inasmuch as when the female *pepsis* has carefully placed the paralyzed tarantula into the corner desired, she then punctures the body, deposits her eggs in the punctures; and the warmth of the paralyzed body continues until the hatching process is completed; then the tarantula dies, and his decomposing body supplies the pabulum needed for the larvæ and pupæ of the *pepsis*, until they can fly abroad in the earth to seek their living elsewhere. One singular feature of the enemy of the tarantula, the *pepsis*, is, that the male dies immediately after sexual contact.

Following up Maxwell's Creek beyond Coulterville for about

two miles, we commence the ascent of a long hill, whence a panorama of the town, the foot-hills, and the distant plains opens up before us. But, once upon its summit, the first grand view of the snow-clad peaks of the High Sierra, the sources of the Tuolumne and Merced Rivers, beyond Yo Semite, is obtained, and an altitude gained of three thousand five hundred feet.

Now the elevated table-like flats, extending for miles, are either under settlement and cultivation, or are occupied by a bounteous forest growth of yellow pine, *Pinus ponderosa*, and the first seen upon this route. Busy saw-mills, and the wood-man's ax and frow here, once gave both lumber and "shakes" (split boards) for the mines and farms, that necessarily depended upon the mountains for their supplies of these; now, however, as the demand has nearly ceased, the supply has correspondingly dwindled away.

Winding our way among timber-clothed hills we soon arrive at

DUDLEY'S RANCH.

Where we can spend the night. And the moment we have felt the grip of Mr. Dudley's manly hand, and looked into his open countenance; or received the undemonstrative welcome of his pleasant wife, there promptly comes a confidence that everything they may or can do for our comfort, will be a spontaneous and cordial act. I have entered many more pretentious way-side inns than this, but have never been better cared for, or kindlier treated than here. If I can say more, why please to consider it said, and I will thank you. Four miles above this we come to

BOWER CAVE.

This is a natural cleft in a great vein of limestone, of a singular grotto-like formation, one hundred and nine feet in depth and length, and ninety in width, which is entered by a passage between rocks, not more than three and a half feet wide, at the northern end of an opening in the roof, some seventy feet long by thirteen feet wide. The sides of this great cavity are draped with wild grape-vines, while through it peep the tops of tall maple trees that grow deep down in the cave. When the boughs of these are drawn aside, you look into the abyss below, where sleeps a small pool of water that is forty feet deep, made shadowy and mysterious by overhanging rocks. There is a boat

upon the pool for the convenience of visitors. Side caverns opening into the main cave, unite to make this unique spot a very desirable one to visit. This is owned by Mr. Louis Pechart, a Frenchman, who is already the happy father of some thirteen living children.

BOWER CAVE.

CONSTRUCTION OF THE COULTERVILLE AND YO SEMITE TURNPIKE.

Here the public road ends; but not so the enterprise of the Coulterville people. Desirous of sharing the patronage of the Yo Semite travel, "The Coulterville and Yosemite Turnpike Company" was formed in 1859, and the road extended, by this company, to Crane Flat, some eighteen miles distant, at a cost of about $15,000.

But, as Yo Semite lay still far beyond, and both passengers and freight had to be transported thither on the backs of horses and mules, and over rough and precipitous trails; and although it was deemed impracticable, if not impossible, to construct a wagon road down to the floor of the valley, from the high cliffs that margined it in; and this work could only be accomplished by the aid of the best engineering skill, after the expenditure of large sums of money, the Coulterville and Yosemite Turnpike Company, stimulated to this action by Dr. John T. McLean, its President and largest stockholder, under an agreement between said company and the Yo Semite Commissioners that the Coulterville Company should have the exclusive rights to construct, and to maintain for ten years, a toll road into the valley, on the north side of the Merced River, undertook the construction of such a road and completed it, in accordance with the agreement above named, on June 18, 1874, at an expense, over and above the expense of that part of the road from Bower Cave to Crane Flat, of over $50,000. Subsequent, however, to the agreement above mentioned being made, and to the commencement of the survey and construction of the Coulterville Road to Yo Semite under it, the Big Oak Flat and Yo Semite Turnpike Company applied to the Yo Semite Commissioners for the privilege of extending their road (already completed to Gentrys, on the northwestern boundary of the Yo Semite grant), down to the floor of the valley. The Commissioners declined to grant this privilege to build a second road into Yo Semite, on the north side of the Merced River, because of the agreement they had previously made with the Coulterville Road Company, under which that company had expended money and acquired vested rights.

The Big Oak Flat and Yo Semite Turnpike Company, applied to the State Legislature, at its next session, for the privilege of extending its road from Gentrys to the level of the Yo Semite Valley, when the Act was passed and approved by the Governor, giving this company the privilege asked, under which it built its road to the level of the valley.

While this Act of the legislature may be regarded as an act of simple justice to the Oak Flat Road Company, which had previously completed its road to the very edge of the Yo Semite grant, there is no doubt that it worked great pecuniary damage and loss to the Coulterville and Yo Semite Turnpike Company, which, under its agreement with the Yo Semite Commissioners for an exclusive privilege for a road into Yo Semite on the north side of the Merced River, had expended many thousands of dollars in the construction of its road, and had it nearly completed, when this Act of the Legislature, allowing a competing road to be built, was passed. But the fact remains, and it is worthy of special and honorable mention, that to Dr. John T. McLean, the President of the Coulterville and Yo Semite Turnpike Company, belongs the honor of making the Yo Semite Valley accessible to wheeled vehicles, by the construction of the first wagon road into it. This road, built and maintained by him at great pecuniary loss, by reason of unexpected competition from the Big Oak Flat Road, is an enduring monument to his energy and enterprise.

SCENERY ON THE ROAD.

After leaving Bower Cave, as we ascend the hill beyond, the scenery grows wilder and more beautiful. Long lines of heavily timbered ridges, intersecting each other like waves of the sea, stretch to the horizon on every hand, with here and there a treeless peak that seems like a desert island in an ocean of pines. There is one very noticeable feature in the scenery of the Sierras, it never grows monotonous or commonplace, as new views open up at every turn in the road. For ten miles from Bower Cave the rise is very gradual on the southern slopes of Pilot Peak Ridge, crossing numerous streamlets, until the pass is reached, and an altitude gained of five thousand three hundred and fifty feet.

PILOT PEAK

Is the boldly defiant cone-shaped landmark of the section, rising to the height of seven hundred feet above the pass, with an elevation of six thousand two hundred feet above sea level. From its summit, to which a branch road is built, all the deep cañons of the Middle Sierras, flanked by high ridges that are covered with dense forests, are in full view, while eastward are seen all the great peaks on the main crest of the Sierras, whence rise the Tuolumne and Merced Rivers; and to the westward extends the broad San Joaquin Valley and the Coast Range; the whole forming a panorama of remarkable grandeur that fully compensates for the short climb from the main road.

From the Pilot Peak Pass the road is built on the backbone of the ridge, affording outlooks on either side, until we enter the dark, tree-formed shadows of Hazel Green, where, owing to its grassy meadows, magnificent timber, and convenience of location, Mr. James Halstead has established a way-side inn.

The forests of the Sierra have their finest development in an elevation ranging from three thousand to seven thousand feet above the sea, and for three miles east and west of Hazel Green, some of the noblest specimens of yellow or pitch pines, *Pinus ponderosa;* sugar pine, *Pinus Lambertiana;* red cedar, *Libocedrus decurrens;* and Douglas spruce, *Abies Douglasii,* are found. Sugar Pine Pass, two miles southeasterly of Hazel Green, is six thousand eight hundred feet in altitude, and is the highest point on the Coulterville and Yo Semite road. Gently descending for about three-quarters of a mile beyond this we find ourselves in

THE MERCED GROVE OF BIG TREES.

This grove, five thousand four hundred feet above the sea, is worthy of special mention, as containing some of the best preserved of any of the big tree species. It is directly on the line of the road, the survey having been made with special reference to these attractive studies for the Yo Semite tourist. It contains over fifty *Sequoias,* the half of which number measure from forty-five to ninety feet in circumference. The largest are remarkably well preserved and beautifully symmetrical, only two or three in the whole grove having been injured by fire. From

BUENA VISTA GAP,

Four miles easterly of the Merced Grove, at an altitude of five thousand one hundred feet, the first glimpse of the Yo Semite Valley is obtained on this road. El Capitan, Three Graces, The Sentinel, and Sentinel Dome, with Glacier Point, loom grandly up in the distance; and, going down the eastern side of the ridge, others of the great Yo Semite cliffs and domes unveil their awful majesty, the Half Dome being the most prominent. Jogging along we soon come to

THE BIG MEADOWS.

As the name implies, these are extensive grassy flats, that

afford excellent pasturage for stock, and where much of the grain-hay used in Yo Semite is produced. How pleasantly does the writer recall the kindly treatment he has received here from its proprietors, Messrs. Meason and Myers, when out upon some of his rambles, and found this a cordial hospice and place of refuge. This is four thousand three hundred and twenty feet above the sea, and only eleven miles from the hotels at Yo Semite. Thought and feeling become enlisted as we draw near the glorious realization of our day-dreams, the present end of our wonderful pilgrimage; and this measurably prepares us for the impressive view before us when we reach the edge of the cliff, and obtain our first look down into the marvelous depths of the Merced Cañon, and of the river, after making its hurrying exit from the valley.

DESCENT TO THE MERCED CAÑON.

This is made by a safe and excellent road, portions of the way having been blasted from the solid granite walls of the cañon. The passage of "Devil's Gulch," and other points of the bluff tell how formidable were the obstructions to be overcome when building this road. There is a cranny little spot at the foot of the hill, known as "The Blacksmith's Shop," which consists of an irregular chamber formed entirely of huge bowlders that have toppled off and down from the surrounding cliffs, in the "long, long ago."[1] Here the forge and anvil rung out their merry peals, while picks and drills and crow-bars needed on the road, were being sharpened. No matter how high the thermometer stood upon the outside, this shady, rock-formed retreat, fanned by the rippling frolics of the leaping water of the river, was always refreshingly cool. A slight delay for inspecting this nature-built blacksmith's shop will be both gratifying and compensating. Once down on the river we begin to realize the height and massiveness of the bluffs that stand, frowningly, on either side of us; and while we are thinking about it, almost before we realize our nearness to it, we pass a leaping rivulet, and are then at the Cascade Falls; but as this forms one of the many delightful excursions of the Valley, further description of this scene now will be unnecessary.

---

1. On April 3, 1982 another fall of boulders, at this same location, closed the old Coulterville Road forever.

CHAPTER XXI.

THE MARIPOSA ROUTE TO YO SEMITE.

> We live in deeds, not years; in thoughts, not breaths;
> In feelings, not in figures on a dial.
> We should count time by heart throbs. He most lives
> Who thinks most, feels the noblest, acts the best.
> —BAILEY'S *Festus.*

> A land of promise flowing with the milk
> And honey of delicious memories.
> —TENNYSON'S *The Lover's Tale.*

> Tis pleasant through the loop-holes of retreat
> To peep at such a world.
> —COWPER'S *Task, Bk. IV.*

As recorded in earlier chapters, this was the first and original route ever traveled to the Yo Semite Valley; and its fearless people the first to enter it, in pursuit of the marauding and murderous Indians in 1851; and afterwards to make the existence of such a marvelous spot known abroad. The great public, therefore, throughout the civilized world, owe an agreeable, enduring, and never-to-be-canceled debt of gratitude to the people of Mariposa, for the glorious heritage they were thus instrumental in conferring upon them. Unlike any other ordinary indebtedness, however, its remembrance will impart none but pleasurable emotions. In winding our way among its rich and beautiful hills, then, the memory of the early struggles of its people with the foe, and the boon of the remarkable discovery which followed, will bespeak for our journey over this historic ground far more than mere ordinary interest.

The accompanying table of distances and altitudes, with the map of routes, will indicate that the place of departure for Yo Semite on the Mariposa route, is, like the one *via* Coulterville, from Merced, on the Southern Pacific Railroad.

(292)

THE MARIPOSA ROUTE,

From San Francisco, via Lathrop, Merced, Mariposa, Mariposa Big Tree Station (Wawona), and Mariposa Big Tree Groves, to Yo Semite Valley.

Stations marked (*a*) are stopping places at night for stage passengers; those marked (*b*) are hotels, or where meals can be had; those marked (*c*) are where hay and grain are obtainable; those marked (*d*) are stage stations.

STATIONS.	Between consecutive points	From San Francisco .	From Yo Semite Valley	Altitude, in feet, above Sea Level
	DISTANCES IN MILES.			
By Railway.	. . . . .	. . . . .	152.03	
From San Francisco to—				
Lathrop, junction of the Southern Pacific with the Central Pacific Railroad (*b c*)	94.03	94.03	58.00	28
Merced, on Southern Pacific Railroad (*a b c d*)	58.00	152.03	. . . .	171
By Carriage Road.	. . . .	. . . .	93.95	
From Merced to—				
Half-way House, watering station (*b c*)	6.35	6.35	87.60	215
Forks of Road to Snelling's	0.87	7.22	86.73	225
Lava Bed Station (*c d*)	7.26	14.48	79.47	446
Griffith's Ranch	3.63	18.11	75.84	473
Hornitos (*b c*)	4.35	22.46	71.49	847
Forks of Road to Indian Gulch	1.52	23.98	69.97	898
Smith's Ranch	2.44	26.42	67.53	1,047
Corbett's Ranch (*b c*)	1.91	28.83	65.62	1,075
Toll House	1.81	30.14	63.81	1,598
Toll House	2.83	32.97	60.98	1,780
Princeton (*b c*)	2.65	35.62	58.33	2,104
Lewis' Ranch (*b c*)	3.54	39.16	54.79	2,112
Mariposa (*a b c d*)	1.70	40.86	53.09	1,932
Mormon Bar (*b c*)	1.89	42.75	51.20	1,630
Sebastopol Flat (*b c*)	2.76	45.51	48.44	2,210
Thompson's Ranch (*b c*)	3.51	49.02	44.93	2,114
Turner's, formerly De Long's (*b c*)	3.93	52.95	41.00	2,741
Cold Spring (*b c d*)	4.36	57.31	36.64	3,126
Summit of Chowchilla Mountain	5.24	62.55	31.40	5,605
Wawona* (*a b c d*)	4.50	67.05	26.90	3,923
Eleven Mile Station (*b c d*)	10.76	77.81	16.14	5,567
El Capitan (lower iron) Bridge, Yo Semite Valley	12.51	90.32	3.63	3,843
Leidig's Hotel, Yo Semite Valley (*a b c d*)	2.56	92.88	1.07	. . . . .
Cook's Hotel, Yo Semite Valley (*a b c d*)	0.30	93.18	0.77	. . . . .
Barnard's Hotel. Yo Semite Valley (*a b c d*)	0.77	93.95	. . . . .	3,934

*From Wawona (Clark's) to and through the Mariposa Big Tree Groves, and back to Big Tree Station, 17 miles.

RECAPITULATION.

By railway	152.03 miles.	
By carriage road	93.95	"
Big Tree Groves and back to station	17.00	"
Total distance	262.98 miles.	

INDIAN WOMAN PANNING OUT GOLD.

As on other routes, our course for the first few miles after leaving the railroad is among fertile farms and bounteous crops; then over gently undulating and treeless gravelly hills; then across or around oak knolls, intermixed with flowering shrubs and flowers; among which is the charming Mariposa, or "Butterfly Tulip," *Calochortus venustus* (Mariposa being Spanish for butterfly).

From the great abundance of this beautiful lily, the county, with its county town, received its musical name "Mariposa."[1]

Once among the more abruptly formed uplands of the county, evidences of gold mining are on every hand; and the irrepressible prospector for gold is met hunting for hidden treasures. The world owes much to the undiscouraged energy of this class of men; as, but for their labors, much of the wealth of the world would have been undiscovered. Good luck then to the prospector; as blessings from the gold he may discover will, let us hope, bring prosperity and happiness to himself and family, and be more or less shared in by all.

As much of the way, on any route we

"THE PROSPECTOR."

1. This seems to have been the popular notion of how the name arose—that the flower was named first, and the town derived its name from the flower. But in fact the name *Mariposas* was given to an unknown location in the San Joaquin Valley in September 1806 by an expedition led by Gabriel Moraga, because they encountered great swarms of butterflies there. The name "Mariposa" was applied to two land grants, and eventually to the town, the county, and a grove of Sequoias.

may elect to take for Yo Semite, passes directly through some portions of the mining region, where the principal occupation of its people consists in extracting the precious metal; and inasmuch as the stranger, who has perhaps never looked upon gold-mining scenes, feels a thrill of fascination in the thought of seeing people "digging out gold" from the earth, it creates the temptation to give a brief outline of the method by which this is accomplished. And by way of commencement let me explain that there are two distinctly different sets of conditions, or of circumstances, under which gold is found, and which necessarily require two different systems of treatment; one being in surface soils or gravels, and the other in a ledge or vein formation; the former is called "Placer Mining," and the latter "Quartz Mining."

After the discovery of gold upon a bar of the American River, Coloma, California, January 19, 1848, and for several years thereafter, it was supposed that the precious metal was only to be found in rivers, gulches, and ravines; then, experience revealed the fact that gold was also to be found in flats, and gravelly hills, away from existing water-courses; then, advancing knowledge presented scientific certainty that even the gold found everywhere in placer diggings, had come, mainly, from quartz veins, or ledges—quartz being the principal matrix for its production. Let us, therefore, follow the earliest and most primitive methods, and see how gold was then taken out of surface mines.

PANNING OUT GOLD.

The prospector having arrived at a spot that looked inviting, at once cleared away the rocks and rubbish that might cover up the "pay dirt;" then he would fill his pan, and carry it to the nearest pool or stream of water, set it down into it, and, when immersed beneath the surface, would commence an oscillatory and slightly tipping and rotary motion forward, by which the finer particles of soil were induced to float away, and the pieces of rock or pebbles near the top to become washed; these were picked out and thrown away; this process was repeated until there was nothing left in the pan but the gold, and which, being the heaviest of all, would keep settling down into the lowest inside edge, and was thence taken out.

By this process thirty-five to fifty pans of pay dirt were washed out per day, sometimes more; the remuneration being in proportion to the richness of the material washed—sometimes "only the color" would be obtained, and at others, vary from a few cents to many dollars. The writer once found $137.50 in a single pan of dirt. This method of digging gold was the earliest and most primitive; the batea, or broad, wooden bowl of the Mexican, excepted.

THE BATEA, OR MEXICAN BOWL.

"Panning out" gold was soon discovered to be altogether too slow a process to the impetuous American, and was, accordingly, superseded by the "Cradle."

THE CRADLE AND MANNER OF USING IT.

This, as will be seen by the illustration (for it is still in use among

CHINAMEN WASHING OUT GOLD WITH A CRADLE.

the Chinese), was a wonderful improvement upon panning; as two men, one to procure and carry the pay dirt, and the other to wash it, could readily average a hundred bucketfuls per day each.

The plan of using the cradle will be very clear; as the pay dirt, whether of soil or gravel, was emptied into the "hopper" at the top of the machine, the bottom of which was perforated with holes half an inch in diameter; and while water was being poured in upon the dirt with one hand the cradle was rocked with the other. This complex movement was about as difficult of attainment to the novice, as that of the school-boy's attempt to rub his nose with one hand while patting his chest with the other. By this process, however, all the gold would pass through the bottom of the hopper, to be caught upon an apron immediately beneath it, and there saved; or, escaping the apron, would lodge in one or other of the divisions across the bottom. Any pieces of gold too large to pass through the hopper (and there have been many of these) were joyfully picked out, exulted over, and then dropped into the "lucky buckskin purse" and there taken care of.

Great as was the advance made from the pan to the cradle, that in turn had to give way to the "Long Tom," by which thousands of bucketfuls (the only method of counting or of estimating quantities in those days) would be washed in a single day. But this again had to fall into desuetude, and be superseded by

SLUICE MINING, AND GROUND SLUICING.

The accompanying illustration will give a general outline of this method, almost at a glance. Long troughs, called "sluices," about twelve feet in length, are made to fit into each other at the end; the number used depending upon the clayey toughness of the dirt to be washed, or the fineness of the gold to be saved; and varying from half a dozen to over one hundred lengths. Across the bottom of these sluice-boxes bars are placed, partly to intercept the too rapid passage of the material shoveled into them, but, principally, to form a riffle and an eddy, wherein to provide a place of settlement for the gold being washed out. These troughs

SLUICE MINING.

are set at a sufficient slant to
insure the rapid passage of
water down them; the auriferous soil, or gravel, is then
shoveled in; when all the finer
material, including the precious metal, passes down the
sluice, the gold settles into the
riffles; or, falling to the bottom, is there saved; while the
soil is carried off by the water.

GROUND SLUICING.

There is always one man needed to "tend sluice," whose duties
consist in throwing out the largest of the rocks, and in having a
general supervision of its working, to prevent mishaps.

"Ground sluicing" consists of turning a stream of water into
a mining claim, by which all the light and worthless material,
assisted by miner's picks, is made to float away; when the gold
settles down among the rocks or gravel; and with the better

quality of earth remaining, is there saved, and afterwards shoveled into the sluice for gathering in and cleaning up.

GRAVEL, OR HILL MINING.

This is generally carried on by what is known as the "Hydraulic Method." For the better apprehending of this, perhaps it will be desirable to explain that in nearly all the mining districts there are immense deposits of water-washed gravel, forming whole ridges and hills many hundreds of feet high. These have been placed there by agencies not existing in the present day; but how they came, or when, is left entirely to the geologist or mining expert. I do not know this, nor do I know any one that does.

WATER FLUME ACROSS A HOLLOW BETWEEN RIDGES.

That they are there, and that they contain auriferous gravel in untold abundance, is beyond any doubt; and it is with these, and the methods of extracting the precious metal therefrom, that we now have to do. Additional interest may accrue from the fact that, owing to the wonderful efficiency of hydraulic mining, and the accredited filling up of navigable streams from the "slickens" or gravel floated therefrom, their working has been legally estopped by the courts.

Water, being the great working force in all placer mines, was especially needed to tear down these mountains of gravel, and wash out the gold; consequently, all sorts of canals, flumes, and ditches were constructed, for conveying that invaluable element from living streams to the mining districts, at an enormous expense. Once upon the ridge it was distributed from the main canal by hose, or in smaller ditches, to the different mines, where it was run into a sheet-iron pipe, largest at the upper end, and there confined; so that the entire weight of the inclosed water, frequently having hundreds of feet of vertical pressure, escaping through a nozzle at the lower end, like a fireman's pipe, tore down the gravel with tremendous force, and caused immense masses, frequently many scores of tons in weight, to "cave down," and not only to break themselves to pieces by the fall, but frequently to bury the too venturesome miner underneath them. Sometimes tunnels are driven far into these gravelly deposits, and hundreds of kegs of blasting powder are simultaneously exploded, to shake the banks into pieces, so that the gravel may be more effectually washed by the water. Frequently over a thousand miner's inches of this element are brought to play, steadily, upon these "Hydraulic Mines." After several weeks have been consumed at this, a "clean up" is made, the results "bagged," and sent by express to the San Francisco Mint. It can readily be seen what vast quantities of this material would be annually run into the beds of tributary streams, the tendency of which would be to choke them up, and force an overflowing flood both of water and sediment upon the low adjacent lands.

QUARTZ MINING.

This consists in extracting the precious metal from quartz, which is the principal matrix for gold (although not the only one), the ledges or veins of which sometimes extend several thousand feet down into the earth. Indeed it is more than probable that from this source nearly all the gold found in placer mining has originally come; as the action of air, water, sunshine, frost, and other elements have disintegrated the matrix containing the gold, and set the precious metal free. Heavy rains and great floods have washed the lighter silica into the water-courses, and thence to the valleys, thus forming the soil and gravel that has buried up the gold; and it was here that the early gold miner found his rewarding treasures.

Quartz ledges, or veins, are readily discoverable by their white crests or belts cropping above or mapping the hills; it must not, however, be supposed that each and every one of these possesses an inexhaustible mine of untold wealth; far from it. Like true worth in humanity, it is not self-assertive prominence that is the unerring augury of excellence, as the boldest fronted are proverbially of the least intrinsic value. The richest of gold-producing veins are those which are generally without distinguishing features outwardly, and are composed of what miners call "rotten quartz." From this material (but not from this only by any means) much of the wealth in and from California, and elsewhere, has been and is being produced.

When gold is found in bits of quartz lying on the surface (and

MINER'S PAN AND HORN SPOON.

by these nearly all the richest veins have been discovered), they are ground fine in a mortar, and washed in a horn spoon, or miner's pan; and when the "prospect" is deemed encouraging, its fortunate discoverer, under the uniformly (though not invariably) correct impression that quartz ledges grow richer in proportion to the depth attained, commences.

SINKING A SHAFT.

To "sink a shaft" (this being a perpendicular opening in the earth, usually from four to six feet in width) the same appliances are used as in sinking a well, which it very much resembles. As

MINERS SINKING A SHAFT.

quartz ledges are seldom vertical, instead of the so-called shaft, an opening is frequently made on the top, and the work continued directly upon it, as here illustrated. Of course these were the earlier and more primitive plans for obtaining gold from the matrix, whether it be quartz, talcose or schist slate, greenstone, soapstone, or any other gangue; and only prepared the way for the vast enterprises which subsequently followed, whose results were known only by the millions of dollars extracted annually from a single mine.

The principle of separating the precious metals from the matrix in which they are found, is, substantially, the same in all cases; their treatment only differing according to the presence and extent of the baser metals; and it is simply this: The matrix, whether it be quartz or any other, is reduced to as fine a powder

FOLLOWING DOWN THE LEDGE.

as possible by pulverization, when the gold naturally falls out; this being also fine, might be carried off by the water used in a wet battery, to assist its manipulation there; but, to prevent it, as quicksilver and gold (and other metals also) have a remarkable affinity for each other, the former metal is placed within the battery, on copper plates below it, and on other places where the connection with the two affinities can be assured, and the gold retained. The quicksilver is then separated from the gold by forcibly squeezing it through buckskin, where the gold is retained. This is now called "amalgam," from which any quicksilver still remaining is separated by retortion, before the gold is melted into bars. The explanatory digression, here presented, is intended to assist the stranger in traveling, understandingly, through the gold mining districts; and, it is hoped, give additional interest to the sights to be witnessed while passing over it.

Hornitos (Spanish for little oven), is the first mining town entered in Mariposa County; which, being originally settled by Mexicans, and still having numerous representatives of that nationality, has more the appearance of a Spanish than an American town. Its quartz ledges, however, are now attracting other classes of residents thither, who are gradually changing its characteristics. Whatever changes may come to its people there will never be any serious questioning as to the appositeness of its name—unless it could be made to express something a little hotter! This place is only about eight hundred and fifty feet above sea level.

A few miles easterly of Hornitos we enter upon the once famous "Fremont's Mariposa Grant;" and, as one passes through the various settlements that have been made upon it, how memory reverts to the busy hum of mining and of mining life that once pulsated through the great arteries of this mineral aorta, giving to it a strength of purpose that brought a prosperity which became proverbial. It has long been a subject of legitimate discussion, however, whether or not the best interests of this entire region would or would not have been best subserved, had the Fremont grant never been floated upon this mining district; notwithstanding the large sums of money that have been expended here at different times, by the various companies that have represented that ownership (for it has always been in some kind of financial or managerial trouble). From the Benton Mills on the Merced to Mormon Bar on Mariposa Creek, such towns as Bear Valley, Agua Fria, Princeton, and Mariposa, prove that the elements of success have been, and there can be no doubt are still here, and only await favorable development to bring back the halcyon days of yore, although much of the cream has been taken from the placer mines.

As we ride along we can see that every gulch, ravine, or flat upon the way, bears the unmistakable scars of an active mining life, and gives unmistakable evidence that a miner's labors, if they bring prosperity to himself and family, and make acceptable addition to the country's wealth, invariably bring desolation to the landscape; yet, even this, is relieved by cultivated gardens, orchards and vineyards, near and among the settlements; while Mount Bullion, "the backbone of the county," and its timbered spurs, attract attention by their scenic boldness. From the northern crest of this ridge some of the vertical cliffs of the Yo Semite are distinctly visible, although some forty miles distant.

But here we are in the county town of Mariposa; its court house, hotels, stores, livery stables, printing offices, schools, churches and numerous shops, tell at once that it is still the active center of business for the main portions of the county. And although its people have had to contend with marauding Indians, submit to the desolating losses of fire at sundry times, and bear their share of the customary ups and downs of life, they never seem to have been discouraged. That the reward may come in the increase of business a thousand-fold is the writer's heartiest and most devout wish. After saying a pleasant good-bye (and I never knew any other), as soon as we reach the lower end of town we pass a quartz mill of some forty stamps, now unused; and at the outskirts of the town, we can see covies of quail running hither and thither in every direction.

THE CALIFORNIA QUAIL *(Perdix Californica).*

This beautiful bird abounds throughout California; if we except districts destitute of shrubbery, and the higher mountain region. It is a little larger than the quail of the Northern and Western States, but as a tid-bit for the epicure is not fully its equal, its habits making the flesh harder and tougher. From their great plentifulness, in many sections, there is no difficulty in procuring them in large numbers for market. They can be partially tamed, when kept in capacious cages, or in inclosures where they can get to the ground; they will they then lay their eggs, and rear their young, like the common fowl. Their fecundity is remarkable; a single female, domesticated by a friend of mine, in a single summer, laid the astonishing number of seventy-nine eggs. She was, moreover, very tame, and would eat from the hand of her mistress, although invariably shy to strangers. Sometimes the male bird was very pugnacious for several days together, when her ladyship had to take refuge in a corner, or seek the protection of a tea-saucer, from which they were daily fed.

The valley quail must not be confounded with that of the

PAIR OF CALIFORNIA VALLEY QUAIL.

mountain, or with the large mountain quail, as there are three species, the former being the smallest, and the latter the largest of the three, and very rare. The former, moreover, carries his tremulous top-knot, which generally consists of six feathers, though appearing as one, forward; while those of both the other two trend backward; and it is not a little singular that while California quail carry their top-knots as indicated, that of the Mexican quail spreads out like a fan on the center of the head. In autumn they become gregarious, as numerous distinct flocks or families unite; the aggregate of which sometimes amounts to over one hundred; but, even then, as in spring, they always go in pairs.

Our road now runs down Mariposa Creek, past quartz ledges, and placer mines, to Mormon Bar; where it commences to ascend the hills at an easy grade, for several miles, among buckeye bushes, *Æsculus Californica;* greasewood, *Ceanothus cuneatus;* leatherwood, *Fremontia Californica;* and white post oaks, *Quercus Douglasii.*

Just about dark one evening as three of us were jogging along this road (we had a camping outfit with us), and anxious to obtain necessary feed for our animals for the night, we stopped at the gate of a wayside house, at which stood a boy who had

evidently, on that very day, been invested in a new suit of clothes, and felt the dignity of such a rare event correspondingly. One of our party, in the most conciliatory of tones, inquired of this scion of the household, "Has your father any barley or oats he can sell us?" "Don't know." "Is he anywhere about that we could ask him?" "Don't know." "Is there any one in the house— your father or mother, or sister, or brother— that we could ask?" "I don't know—I don't

THE BOY THAT "DIDN'T KNOW NUFFINK."

know nuffink." Being such a remarkable boy we took his portrait, and herewith present it, for his own recognition and future study!

When riding upon nearly every highway in California, there can be seen a brilliant-coated woodpecker, flitting hither and thither; the red, white, and black of his plume glinting brightly in the sunshine. It is the red-headed woodpecker *(Melanerpes formicivorus).* The Spanish people here call it *El Carpintero,* or Carpenter Woodpecker, from his singular habit of boring into the bark

THE RED-HEADED WOODPECKER *(Melanerpes formicivorus.)*

and dead wood of trees for the purpose of storing away acorns. The rapidity with which his busy head moves, and the rattling scrape of the sound given out, tell of his unmistakable earnestness in taking care of the harvest. The entire trunks of pine trees, to the height of thirty feet, are sometimes dotted with the result of their labors. And it is not a little singular that, after the hole is made in the bark or wood, its exact measure is so carefully taken that, when an acorn is selected to insert in it, a mistake is seldom made in the size, to insure its fitting so snugly that not even the pilfering jays can take it out, when once driven in.

The red-headed woodpecker, contrary to the habits of birds, provides for future emergencies; and from instincts of its own, anticipates some coming want, and prepares for it accordingly. It is an open question, however, whether or not the acorn forms part of its food; or is only the treasury of an insect possessing essential qualities for the woodpecker's existence, when such are unattainable elsewhere; some contending for the former, while others as persistently insist upon the latter. The same habit is possessed, though not to the same extent, by the *Melanerpes erythocephalus,* east of the Rocky Mountains.

Our ride for many miles now is among or over gently rolling gravelly hills, covered with a light growth of shrubbery and white post oaks; where nearly all the available flats, or small valleys on streams, have been converted into grain fields, or gardens and orchards, so that numerous little tenements add variety to the journey. Farther on, the stately pines once tempted the erection of saw-mills, one of which, White and Hatch's, became famous for its excellence as a lunch house for Yo Semite tourists. These industries made the road lively by the coming and going of teams, either with supplies up for mining settlements and ranches, or with lumber down for the cities and towns.

Finally we reach Conway's at Cold Spring (where an excellent meal and good bed can always be obtained), and here commence the ascent of Chow-chilla Mountain. In five and a quarter miles, from Conway's to the summit, we make a rise of two thousand four hundred and seventy-nine feet. But the many beautiful live oaks, *Quercus chrysolepis;* black oaks, *Q. Kelloggii;* yellow pines, *Pinus ponderosa;* sugar pine, *P. Lambertiana;* and red cedar, *Libocedrus decurrens,* that throw their welcome shadows on the road, or allow of openings between them to afford glimpses of the charming scenery beyond, beguile every mile and moment of the way. And when once upon the summit what a tree feast is here provided, which continues all the way to Wawona.

Reveling in memories of such a luxuriant growth one cannot wonder that the great newspaper genius, Horace Greeley, should thus write about it:—

Here let me renew my tribute to the marvelous bounty and beauty of the forests of this whole mountain region. The Sierra Nevadas lack the glorious glaciers, the frequent rains, the rich verdure, the abundant cataracts of the Alps; but they far surpass them—they surpass any other mountains I ever saw—in the wealth and grace of their trees. Look down from almost any of their peaks, and your range of vision is filled, bounded, satisfied, by what might be termed a tempest-tossed sea of evergreens, filling every upland valley, covering every hill-side, crowning every peak, but the highest, with their unfading luxuriance. That I saw, during this day's travel, many hundreds of pines eight feet in diameter, with cedars at least six feet, I am confident; and there were miles of such, and smaller trees of like genus, standing as thick as they could grow. Steep mountain-sides, allowing these giants to grow, rank above rank, without obstructing each other's sunshine, seem peculiarly favorable to the production of these serviceable giants. But the Summit Meadows are peculiar in their heavy fringe of balsam fir, of all sizes, from those barely one foot high to those hardly less than two hundred, their branches surrounding them in collars, their extremities gracefully bent down by the weight of winter snows, making them here, I am confident, the most beautiful trees on earth. The dry promontories which separate these meadows are also covered with a species of spruce, which is only less graceful than the firs aforesaid. I never before enjoyed such a tree-feast as on this wearing, difficult ride.*

* Mr. Greeley being in a hurry (this had become habitual with him), and anxious to see as much as possible in the limited time he had allowed himself, rode from Bear Valley to Yo Semite, over sixty miles, in a single day, or thereabouts; thirty-eight of which were on the back of one of the hardest trotting mules in America; and as he had not been in the saddle for thirty years, was somewhat inclined to portliness, and the possessor of a cuticle as tender as that of a child, there was but little of the unabrased article left, when he arrived in the valley at one o'clock the next morning. His suffering, must, therefore, have been intense; and, being utterly helpless, he was carefully lifted from the saddle, his comfort cared for as much as possible under the circumstances, and, at his own request, put supperless to bed. Just before noon of the day of his arrival, he was assisted from his couch, and, as he had speaking engagements to fulfill, after a light breakfast, taken as distinguished guests are honored with a toast, he was again lifted into the saddle, and without seeing any of the great sights beyond the hotel, made a returning ride of twenty-four miles, to Clark's. He was seen by the writer, in San Francisco, some three weeks afterwards shuffling along the sidewalk, slowly; and when allusion was made to his too evident lameness the response came: "Oh! Mr. H., you cannot realize how much I have suffered from that jaunt to the Yo Semite." To speak glowingly, therefore, of anything, after such an experience, proves Mr. Greeley to have been more than an ordinary man.

CHAPTER XXII.

THE MILTON AND BIG OAK FLAT ROUTE TO YO SEMITE.

Know the true value of time; snatch, seize, and enjoy every moment of it.
Never put off till to-morrow what you can do to-day.
                        —EARL OF CHESTERFIELD'S *Letters to his Son.*

Wherefore did Nature pour her bounties forth
With a full and unwithdrawing hand,
Covering the earth with odors, fruits, and flocks,
But all to please and sate the curious taste?
                        —MILTON'S *Comus.*

Age cannot wither her, nor custom stale
Her infinite variety.
                        —SHAKESPEAR'S *Anthony and Cleopatra.*

A glance at the outline map of routes will show that our course is *via* Stockton and Milton; just the same, so far, as that *via* the Calaveras Big Tree Groves; but, just beyond the Reservoir House and reservoir, our road trends to the right, through Copperopolis—so named from the immense deposits of copper ore once found here, the extraction of which employed many hundreds of men. Now its deserted streets and decaying buildings tell the sad story that the copper mines are no longer worked; and suggest the business stagnation that ensued. But the coachman's cheery "All aboard" will cut short any sympathetic reveries at the change, and keep us rolling on among white post oaks and bull pines, until we reach Byrne's Ferry at the Stanislaus River. It is simply presumed that the name "Byrne's Ferry" will ever be continued, although a substantial bridge made this a polite fiction of the past a score or more years ago.[1]

Here, however, we see disconnected parts of a mountain of volcanic origin, which to appearance is "as level as a table," and which is called by everybody living near it, Table Mountain.

(311)

1. Patrick O'Byrne had a ferry in pioneer days where the road from Copperopolis to Mountain Pass crossed the Stanislaus River. In 1852 he built a bridge. That was washed away in a flood, and was replaced by a covered bridge in 1862, which was removed in 1957 when Tulloch Dam was constructed. The site is now beneath the waters of Tulloch Lake.

BIG OAK FLAT ROUTE,

From San Francisco, via Stockton, Milton, Chinese Camp, and Big Oak Flat, to Yo Semite Valley.

Stations marked (*a*) are stopping places at night for stage passengers; those marked (*b*) are hotels, or where meals can be had; those marked (*c*) are where hay and grain are obtainable; those marked (*d*) are stage stations.

STATIONS.	Between consecutive points	From San Francisco	From Yo Semite Valley	Altitude, in feet, above Sea Level
	DISTANCES IN MILES.			
By Railway.	. . . . .	. . . . .	133.05	
From San Francisco to—				
Lathrop, junction of the Central Pacific with the Southern Pacific Railroad (*b*)	94.03	94.03	39.02	28
Stockton, on Central Pacific Railroad (*a b c d*)	9.02	103.05	30.00	29
Milton, on Stockton and Copperopolis Railroad (*b c d*)	30.00	133.05	. . . . .	376
By Carriage Road.	. . . . .	. . . . .	91.28	
From Milton to—				
Reservoir House (*b c*)	6.13	6.13	85.15	1,013
Copperopolis (*b c d*)	8.70	14.83	76.45	1,015
Byrne's Ferry Bridge, Stanislaus River	7.00	21.83	69.45	475
Goodwin's, Table Mountain Pass (*b c d*)	3.50	25.33	65.95	1,050
Chinese Camp (*a b c d*)	3.50	28.83	62.45	1,299
Moffitt's Bridge	4.18	33.01	58.27	602
Keith's Orchard and Vineyard	1.03	34.04	57.24	612
Stevens' Bar Ferry	1.24	35.28	56.00	614
Culbertson's Vineyard (*c*)	3.45	38.73	52.55	980
Priest's Hotel (*a b c d*)	2.21	40.94	50.34	2,558
Big Oak Flat (*b c*)	1.07	42.01	49.27	2,823
Groveland (*b c*)	2.24	44.25	47.03	2,828
Second Garrote	2.15	46.40	44.88	2,857
Sprague's Ranch (*b c*)	4.97	51.37	39.91	2,950
Hamilton's Ranch (*b c d*)	3.98	55.35	35.93	2,978
Colfax Spring, Elwell's (*b c*)	2.55	57.90	33.38	3,022
South Fork Tuolumne, Lower Bridge	0.93	58.83	32.45	2,654
Hardin's Ranch (*c*)	4.39	63.22	28.06	3,396
South Fork Tuolumne River, Upper Bridge	1.37	64.59	26.69	3,420
Crocker's Ranch (*b c*)	3.34	67.93	23.35	3,970
Hodgdon's Ranch (*b c*)	2.00	69.93	. . . . .	4,506
Tuolumne Big Tree Grove	. . . . .	74.37	16.91	5,794
Crane Flat (*b c*)	1.00	75.37	15.91	6,054
Tamarack Flat	5.07	80.44	10.84	6,234
Gentry's (deserted)	2.81	83.25	8.03	5,627
Junction of Big Oak Flat and Coulterville Roads	4.37	87.62	3.66	3,949
Leidig's Hotel, Yo Semite Valley (*a b c d*)	2.59	90.21	1.07	. . . .
Cook's Hotel, Yo Semite Valley (*a b c d*)	0.30	90.57	0.77	. . . .
Barnard's Hotel, Yo Semite Valley (*a b c d*)	0.77	91.28	. . . . .	3,934

RECAPITULATION.

By railway . . . . .133.05 miles.

By carriage road . . . . 91.28 "

Total distance . . . . .224.33 miles.

TABLE MOUNTAIN.

It is a superincumbent mass of volcanic trap that is supposed to have commenced its outpour near Shaw's Flat, Tuolumne County; and, flowing into the channel of an old river, followed its sinuous

From Near Byrne's Ferry.

TABLE MOUNTAIN.

course for over twenty miles; but since that time, the hills that once formed the banks of the stream have been washed and worn down many hundreds of feet, so that they are far below the surface of the lava, forming the top of Table Mountain, leaving its bold and vertical walls towering far above all. Immense rifts, shaken in it at sundry times, have enabled the present Stanislaus River to force openings through it, and to tear away whole sections; hence the broken links in this chain of lava.

Many years ago some very rich auriferous gravel was found in the old river bed underneath this singular volcanic deposit, and tunnels were run into it in every direction for the purpose of "tapping" the paying strata, (one of which was driven nine hundred feet through solid rock, and upon which three thousand

Photo by Geo. Fiske   Courtesy, The Bancroft Library

WALL OF TABLE MOUNTAIN

(See page 313)

Facing page 313 in edition one. Facing page 314 in all other editions.

HYDRAULIC MINING
(See pages 299–300.)
The original photograph is entitled MALAKOFF DIGGINGS,
Nevada County, California 1418 WATKINS' New Series.
Facing page 304 in edition one. Facing page 306 in all other editions.

Photo by Carleton E. Watkins

seven hundred and fifty-six days' labor were expended, additional to the cost of tools, blasting powder, etc.). How far these enterprises became remunerative is still wrapped in mystery; but sufficient information was allowed to escape to induce a numerous following of such examples.

After crossing the Stanislaus River our road winds gradually up the hill, whence fine views are obtained of that picturesque stream, and the numerous broken walls and bolder points of Table Mountain, among which Goodwin's vineyard is most charmingly situated. Just before arriving at the entrance gate, however, we shall find the portrait of a Chinaman and his pack, upon their travels, painted upon a sign, containing this inscription—ME GO CHINESE CAMP—3 MILE ONE HALF. Now

GOODWIN'S

Is a beautiful orchard and vineyard, fenced in mainly by volcanic bombs from Table Mountain, by which it is surrounded. Its well-kept and weed-free grounds bespeak a becoming pride in their owner; and the temptingly bright oranges, luscious peaches, large and delicious grapes, pure home-made California wine, and the refreshing shade of umbrageous fig-trees, are suggestively inviting of a brief yet delightful visit. From the ridge beyond this a large, plain-like country, once covered with miners, stretches far away in every direction, on one side of which stands

CHINESE CAMP.

Now it must not be supposed that the name found to belong to this once prosperous mining settlement implies that it is in the exclusive possession of natives of the Flowery Kingdom. Far from it, inasmuch as they are now largely in the minority. It is true, however, that nearly every mining town in California has a liberal representation of this class, and it is also true that the number found here in early days was far in excess of that generally found elsewhere; as it was a kind of head-quarters, especially on Sundays, for all Chinamen living within a radius of many miles. This gave the town its name.

Every village, town, or city in California, moreover, wherein the Chinese congregate, has its "Chinese Quarter." They never attempt, socially, to intermix; and, unlike other nationalities, a Chinaman never drops his distinctive habits, manners, customs, dress, or manner of living, to adopt those of a people by whom he is surrounded. A Chinaman, therefore, is always a Chinaman, no matter where he may be. His contract with one or other of the

A CHINESE COUPLE.

"Six Companies," to which every Chinaman belongs, always provides that should death come to him in this strange land, his bones shall be taken back to his native country. In this he is as true a patriot as any man on earth. Whatever else he may believe,

CHINESE FEAST TO THE DEAD.

or disbelieve, he never wavers in his allegiance to the land that gave him national birth. Whatever else, therefore, we may deny him, let us not withhold from him the just respect that such a noble trait commands.

A CHINESE BELIEF WORTHY OF ADOPTION.

Whatsoever the Chinese may believe about God, they hold to the idea, whether they carry it out in practice or not, that the principal duty of man is to perform kindly services to each other, upon earth, and thus bespeak the personal good offices of their friends, especially of their parents, in the hereafter. A little of this kind of philosophy incorporated into the Christian system, would not be (as an English gentleman once expressed himself) "half bad." Let us try a few good heavy doses of it as an experiment. Their "Feast to the Dead" probably originated in this idea, as, according to Mr. Williams, in his book upon the Middle Kingdom, they thus address the departed at the grave: "My trust is in your divine spirit. Reverently I present thee five-fold sacrifices of a pig, a fowl, a duck, a goose, and a fish; also an offering of five plates of fruit, with libations of spirituous liquors."

INDIAN SOLUTION OF A DIFFICULT PROBLEM.

When the Indians in California first saw the Chinese, there arose a dispute among the former as to the country to which the latter belonged, some contending that the Chinese were an inferior race of Indians from beyond the sea; and others, with equal pertinacity, asseverating that their eyes and facial expression were utterly unlike the Indians; and that, therefore, there could be no tribal relationship between them. This question they all determined should be effectually settled, and at once; and as they were agreed upon one point, viz., that if the new-comers *were* Indians, they could all swim; a water test was accordingly accepted as thoroughly satisfactory and conclusive to both parties.

When the spring snows were rapidly melting, and the angry streams were booming, a tree having been fallen across by which to form a foot-bridge, at an understood signal between the contestants, they met a couple of Chinamen upon this bridge; and, pushing them into the angry current, drowned them both! It is stated that this was a perfectly demonstrative settlement of the doubtful point between the contestants, and decided that *Chinamen were not Indians!* but it is not stated, authoritatively, that this process of determination was equally satisfactory to the Chinamen?

Owing to convenience of location Yo Semite bound passengers, as well as many others, generally tarry for the night at Chinese Camp, where they will find a brick hotel, clean beds, attentive service, and an obliging, wide-awake landlord, in the person of Count Solinsky, who has been Wells, Fargo & Co.'s express agent here for over thirty-five years. Then there are numerous stores, and one of the best wheelwright shops to be found in any country. Here, too, once lived the large-hearted and gifted physician, Dr. Lampson, whose genial face, so sadly missed by old-timed friends, will never be looked upon again.

Leaving "the cloud-capped towers and gorgeous palaces" of Chinese Camp behind us, our journey lies over rolling hills and flat ravines to the western side of Wood's Creek, down which our well-graded road winds and turns, affording grand views of a wildly picturesque country in every direction, until we reach the Tuolumne River.

Formerly our course lay past Jacksonville,[1] where its resplendent oaks gave acceptable shade while watering the horses, and for having a pleasant chat with one of its oldest pioneers, whom everybody familiarly called "Dave Ackerman." This little village is supported, mainly, by river mining (mostly monopolized now by Chinamen) and the placer diggings of Wood's Creek. Within a stone's throw of the hotel was "Smart's Garden,"[2] where once grew the earliest and finest of fruit; but which is now a desert waste, owing to its having been "worked out" by Chinese miners, for the rich placers of gold found there, and which, following the course of all gold dug out by these people, was exported to China. A short distance above this, Keith's Orchard and Vineyard, one of the best cultivated in the State, and producing some of the choicest of fruit, were passed; and a mile farther on, the river was crossed by the Steven's Bar Ferry. Now all this is changed, through the enterprise of Mr. J. R. Moffitt, who has had a splendid combination truss bridge thrown across the Tuolumne River Cañon, near Jacksonville, capable of supporting a weight of one hundred tons. This is called

MOFFITT'S TUOLUMNE CAÑON BRIDGE.

It is three hundred feet in length (having a single span of one hundred and sixty-five feet), twelve feet in width, is fifty

1. Jacksonville still had ten or twelve buildings, including a quaint cafe, into the 1970s. The site is now at the bottom of Don Pedro Reservoir.

2. The name "Smarts Gulch" is on the road to Jamestown, about a mile north of state route 120 and the reservoir.

feet above low water mark; and its floor is six hundred and fifty feet above the sea.[1] As we stand upon this we are for a moment at a loss which to admire most, the skill and pluck of its builder and owner, or the beautiful scenes to be witnessed from it on every hand. When we see how a broad road has been hewn out of the mountain's side, and in all its turnings and windings preserved its uniformity of breadth and excellence; and then note how the chasm forming the river's channel has been spanned by so fine a structure, we are ready to accord due and admiring credit to the originator of the undertaking, and yet not forego the pleasure of looking at the beautiful scenery. By the commodious and comfortable residence erected near a deliciously cold spring, it would seem that Mr. Moffitt expects to make his permanent home in this wild cañon.

After relieving one's conscience concerning the bridge, the road, and their builder, a clearer outlook can be had of the country, and a concise summary of the whole will be embodied in Mr. John Taylor's expressive sentence concerning it: "Skirting the Tuolumne River for three miles, the scenery becomes picturesque in the extreme, the grand panorama ever changing, so as to keep tourists and lovers of nature's pristine grandeur in one continual ecstasy of delight."

Leaving the main stream our course is now up one of its tributaries, for three and a half miles, known as Moccasin Creek; past vineyards, mines, and miners. This entire section becomes noteworthy from its prodigality in children's faces, seen at the doors and windows of its humble dwellings. One family numbers thirteen, another only eleven, and so on, exclusive of their fathers and mothers! Soon after crossing the bridge we come to Newhall and Culbertson's Vineyard (for although the former has passed home to the spirit-land, the name is still retained in the firm). This is another of those wayside tarrying places where fruit of the finest quality is in abundance, and where we can obtain a glass of the most delicious white wine to be had in any portion of the State, It is but simple justice to these people to

1. This site is also under water.

say that their charges are not only very reasonable, but always low. Here the altitude above the sea, as given by the U. S. (Wheeler's) Survey, is nine hundred and eighty feet.

For the next two and a quarter miles our road is on the side of a mountain, covered with a dense mass of shrubbery, among which will be found manzanita, buckeye, mountain mahogany, pipe wood, Indian arrow, granite wood, and numerous other kinds; all of which, if cut in the proper season,—November to March—are hard and useful furniture woods, susceptible of a very high polish.

You will think this quite a mountain climb—and it is. It will be well, however, to bear in mind that, before commencing the descent toward Yo Semite, we have to attain an altitude of near-ly seven thousand feet from our starting point; we must, there-fore, commence ascending somewhere, and why not here? It will be a task upon our patience, perhaps, but as it seems to be a trial of both wind and muscle to the horses, we may surely console ourselves with the thought that we can stand it—if they can. Up, up we toil, many of us on foot, perhaps, in order to ease the faithful and apparently overtasked animals, which puff and snort like miniature locomotives, while the sweat drops from them in abundance. In two and a quarter miles there is a clear gain in altitude of one thousand five hundred and seventy-eight feet, between Culbertson's Vineyard and Priest's Hotel.

One quiet evening, in the height of summer, after the sun had set, and the deep purple atmosphere peculiar to California had changed to somber gray, we (the passengers) were wending our way up the mountain on foot, and a little ahead of the stage, when a rustling sound, just below the road, startled us with its singular and suspicious distinctness, and dark shadowy forms were seen gently threading their way among the bushes. Our hearts beat uncomfortably fast, and we instinctively felt for our revolvers, but they were in the stage! It should be told that at this time numerous robberies had been committed upon the highway by Joaquin, Tom Bell, and their respective gangs. "We are caught," whispered one. "They will rob, and perhaps murder us," suggested another. "We can die but once," bravely retorted a third. "Let us all keep close together," pantomimed a fourth. "Who goes there?" loudly challenged a fifth. "A friend," exclaimed the ringleader of a party of miners who were climbing the steep sides of the mountain just at our side, with their blankets at their backs, all walking to town, and who had caused all our alarm; and as he and his companions quietly seated themselves by the road-side, they commenced wiping off the perspiration, and gave us cordial salutation in good plain English. "Why, bless us, these men, who have almost frightened us out of our seven senses, are fellow-travelers!" "Couldn't you see that?" now valorously inquired one whose knees had knocked uncontrollably together with fear only a few moments before. At this we all laughed; and the coachman having stopped his stage, said, "Get in, gentlemen"; and we had enough to talk of and joke about until we reached Priest's Hotel, at the top of the hill.

PRIEST'S HOTEL.

Travelers in many lands have made frequent confessions to the writer, that this unpretentious wayside inn is among the most comfortable and enjoyable they have ever found in any country. Could commendatory volumes written upon it therefore say more? Many, many times have I tested it, and can both conscientiously and emphatically indorse every sentiment uttered in its praise. For although it will not, I trust, be deemed out of place to say, in all kindness, that no traveler should expect to find meals and accommodations in the mountains of California equal to those of the Palace Hotel, the Grand, the Baldwin, the Occidental, or the Lick House of San Francisco, no one will leave this hospice without carrying away with him the conviction that these people are among the too limited number of those "who know how to keep a hotel;" and regretfully riding away from its hospitable door, leave the best of good wishes behind them. What more then can be said?

A DOG STORY.

Now Priest's at one time had a very remarkable dog (there is no doubt about that fact), which writers have accredited with the wonderful intelligence of knowing the exact time the up-ward-bound passengers were due for dinner; when he would start off with a bound down the hill, and, meeting the stage, would look steadfastly at the inside for a few moments, as though counting the number of people to be found there, and then scamper back up the hill. Instead of lying down in front of the hotel (his usual and favorite pastime, as well as that of other dogs), he would deliberately make for the poultry yard; and, seizing the youngest and plumpest of its tenants, would carry it at once to the cook, repeating this until the requisite number was provided! Now, it might seem to be a wanton, and, perhaps, an envious act on my part to attempt to destroy the effect of a good story by questioning its reliability in the smallest degree; yet, I cannot resist the temptation of submitting, whether or not the tenderness, juiciness, and flavor of the well-cooked chicken found upon the table, might not be somewhat in conflict with placing implicit confidence in that statement? But this I do know, that he would at any time, unharmedly, seize any fowl pointed out to him, and take it direct to his master.

The commanding view from the porch, and especially that from the hill at the back of the house, not only presents the broad valleys below, with their glinting streams, and clumps of oaks, but the bold outline of the Coast Range bordering the Pacific Ocean, and all the intermediate landscape. Frequently, too, the whole country seems flooded with billowy clouds, over the tops of which peaks and mountain ranges stand boldly out in the transparent atmospheric strata above them.

BIG OAK FLAT.

When leaving Priest's we must not omit to notice the evi-dences of mining on every hand, even if we forget the unplea-sant fact that a miner's labors invariably bring desolation to the landscape. Nor must we pass unseen the sturdy, branch-lopped, and root-cut veteran trunk of a noble and enormous oak, *Quercus lobata;* some eleven feet in diameter, now prostrate, on our right; as it was from this once famous tree that "Big Oak Flat," the village through which we pass, and the route, received their names. Then, however, its immense branch-crowned top gave refreshing shadow to the traveler, and beauty to the scene. We fear that many a year will have made its faithful record before our virtues become sufficiently Christian to confess personal forgiveness to those who committed, or even permitted, the vandal act of its destruction. We take real comfort in the thought that its storm-beaten, dead, limbless, and prostrate form must daily administer stinging reproofs to every one whose act, or silence, gave sanction to the deed.

As we spin along among pines and firs, the deliciously bracing "champagne atmosphere" (as a lady friend so naively expresses it), is quaffed with a delightful and thrilling zest that makes itself felt through every nerve tissue of our being. Even the brief delay at Groveland (a bustling little mining town) to change the mail, only postpones the pleasure, that is renewed the moment we advance.

CHAFFEY AND CHAMBERLAIN'S.

The gardens, vineyards, and orchards that are passed only add agreeable variety. But, speaking of orchards; at Garotte (such name-givers deserve to be garroted!), the last mining town passed on the journey (there are several), let me caution you against stopping at Chaffey and Chamberlain's (two affectionate and noble-natured old bachelors who have lived and mined together for over thirty years); for the large and luscious fruits they take so much pride in producing will be sure to tempt you to eat again (and so soon after leaving Priest's, you know), and it is a long way to the doctor's! Before leaving here, let me call especial attention to two species of beautiful oaks; one is the weeping white oak, *Quercus lobata;* and the other a live oak,

Quercus chrysolepis, as they are among the best representatives of that family that I have ever seen, anywhere.

A COSTLY PIECE OF ENGINEERING.

A short ascent up a somewhat steep hill, brings us to the ups and downs of a ridge road, with timber and shrubbery on both sides. The large ditch we cross several times is that of the Golden Rock Water Company, constructed for the purpose of supplying the mining towns below with water for mining purposes. This work will be seen at different times until we pass the "Big Gap"; where still lie the burnt fragments of a flume, once the pride of its engineers, as the finest wooden structure of the kind in the State, with a height of two hundred and sixty-four feet above the Gap, and a length of two thousand two hundred feet; costing the snug little amount of pocket-change of eighty thousand dollars. A strong wind one night told the sad story, that "the best laid plans of mice and men gang aft agley," and made it a total wreck. Now, a large iron tube placed upon the ground answers the purpose of the flume. This only cost some twelve thousand dollars. An immense deposit of "tailings" at the "Little Gap" we are now passing, with the water-torn banks of a gravelly hill standing near, tell that the work of hydraulic mining has but recently ceased here.

HAMILTON'S.

A little beyond this we come to a bright little home-like spot called "Hamilton's"; and, while the horses are being changed, the opportunity will be afforded of making the acquaintance of its owners. Mrs. Hamilton, who is the presiding genius of the household (her husband probably being busy on the farm), can cook as nice a meal as almost any one, and by adding a little spice of praise to this or that upon the table (not to the cooking, remember, as she is too modest for that), induce you to find an appetite to eat it; but as the stage arrangements may not allow of such a test, she will be sure to have some kind of fruit to offer; and, if that is out of season, has always a kindly word, and a refreshing glass of water to give you. Try it.

As we advance it is evident that the timber becomes larger and the forest land more extensive. The gently rolling hills begin to give way to tall mountains; and the quiet and even tenor of the landscape changes to the wild and picturesque. An occasional deer may shoot across our track; or coveys of quail, with their beautiful plumage and nodding "topknots," whirr among the bushes. The robin, and meadow-lark, and oriole may prove to us that they still have a love and a voice for music; and the "too-coo-"ing of the dove tells us that its sweetly mournful voice "is still heard in our land."

A FORETASTE OF GRAND SCENES.

But who, in feeble language, can fully disclose the grandeur of the scenery that opens before us a short distance east of the Big Gap? When the painter's art can build the rainbow upon canvas so as to deceive the sense of sight—when simple words can tell the depth and height, the length and breadth of a single thought—or the metaphysician's skill delineate, beyond peradventure, the hidden mysteries of a living soul—then, ah! then, it may be possible.

Deep down in an abyss before us is a gulf—a cañon—of more than two thousand feet. The gleaming, silvery thread, seen running among bowlders, is the Tuolumne River, a hundred feet in width. Its rock-ribbed sides, in places, show not a vestige of a tree or shrub. In others, its generous soil has clothed the almost perpendicular walls with verdure. As the eye wanders onward and upward, it traces the pine-clad outlines of distant gorges, whose tributary waters compose and swell the volume of the stream beneath us. To the right, surrounded by noble trees, can be discerned a bright speck—it is a water-fall a hundred feet in height and thirty feet in width. In the far distance, piercing the clouds, the snow-covered peaks of the Sierras lift their glorious heads of sheen, while a beautiful purple haze casts its broad, softening mantle over all. Our road, shaded by lofty pines and umbrageous oaks, and cooled by a delicious breeze, lies safely near the edge of the precipice; the whole panorama rolled vividly out before us. It is such scenes as this that introduce such grateful changes to such a journey.

Just beyond this we arrive at Elwell's, Colfax Springs; another pleasant little wayside house, and soon thereafter cross the south fork of the Tuolumne River, at the lower bridge; then wind our way up a long hill, over to Hardin's Ranch; and after recrossing the south fork by the upper bridge, ascend another long hill, and are then at the justly famous lunch house of

CROCKER'S.

The pretty little garden, bright with flowers, bespeaks a cheery welcome almost before we alight, and the look of cleanliness everywhere apparent prepares the way for an appetizing meal. There is no hurry, no excitement; a quiet wash, followed by the quiet announcement that "lunch is ready," and we are ushered into a room where a most elegant repast awaits us. It is but simple justice to Mr. and Mrs. Crocker, to say that their table is loaded with creature comforts, and in such abundance and variety that even the most delicate or fastidious can find something they can relish and enjoy. There are but few places upon earth, if there are any, where a more excellent refection can be obtained, or one be more pleasantly served.

Still our course is upward, until we have reached a long stretch of elevated table-land that, for timber, is not excelled in any portion of the State. Large sugar-pine trees, *Pinus Lambertiana*; from five to ten feet in diameter, and over two hundred feet in height, devoid of branches for sixty or a hundred feet, and straight as an arrow, everywhere abound. Besides these there are thousands of yellow pines, *Pinus ponderosa*; Douglas firs, *Abies Douglasii*; and cedar, *Libocedrus decurrens*; that are but little, if any, smaller or shorter than the sugar-pines. These forests are not covered up with a dense undergrowth, as at the East, but give long and ever-changing vistas for the eye to penetrate.

Mr. George McQuesten, of East Boston, measured one of the prostrate sugar-pines in this grove, with the following results: Circumference, three feet from base, twenty-one feet ten inches; fifty feet from base, fourteen feet six inches; one hundred feet from base, eleven feet three inches; one hundred and fifty feet from base, eight feet six inches; two hundred feet from base, four feet three inches; two hundred and nine feet from base, two feet three inches. This might have been from twenty feet to forty feet higher when standing. It contained nineteen thousand five hundred and sixty running feet of lumber, or one thousand seven hundred and eighty cubic feet, after deducting ten per cent for saw scarfs. Value in Boston, less cost of carriage and sawing, $195. While thinking, and almost dreaming of forest scenes, we have arrived at

THE TUOLUMNE GROVE OF BIG TREES.

These are of the same genus, *Sequoia gigantea*, as those of Calaveras, Mariposa, and other groves; many fine specimens of which stand by the road-side, or can be readily seen without leaving the coach; but none can realize their large proportions without standing up against one, or walking around it. Besides, it rests us to walk a little, and adds much to the interest to touch their enormous sides. There are about thirty in this group, well proportioned, and excellent representatives of the class. Two of them which grew from the same root, and unite a few feet above the base, are called the "Siamese Twins." These are about one hundred and fourteen feet in circumference at the ground, and, consequently, about thirty-eight feet in diameter—of course including both. The bark has been cut on one side of one of them and has been found to measure twenty inches in thickness. Near the "Twins" there are two others which measure seventy-four feet around their base.

THE DEAD GIANT.

One of the most striking examples of the extraordinary growth of this species is found in the immense stump called "The

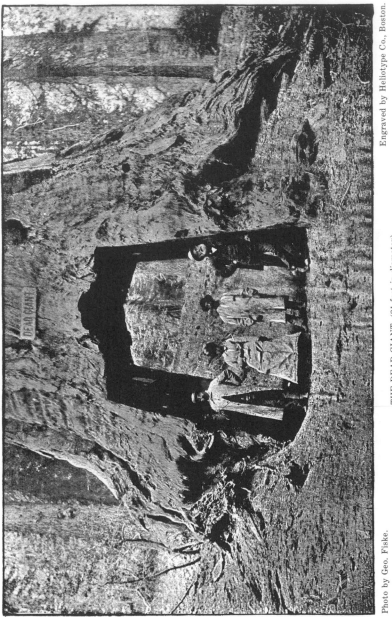

Photo by Geo. Fiske.

THE DEAD GIANT (31 feet in diameter)

Engraved by Heliotype Co., Boston.

Photo by Geo. Fiske

Courtesy, The Bancroft Library

THE DEAD GIANT

Although the image on the opposite page is called an engraving, it looks like an early halftone—one of the first attempts at using the now common method for printing photographs. The man on the right in the photo is James M. Hutchings.

Photo. by Geo. Fiske.

Photo-Typo by Britton & Rey, S. F.

The Sentinel—Loya,—El Capitan and Valley
From Glacier Point Trail (See pages 467–68.)
Facing page 368 in all editions, but in edition one a vertical photo was used.

Dead Giant," for, although fire has entirely denuded it of its bark, and largely reduced its proportions, it is even now thirty-one feet in diameter. By the earthy ridges that form around almost every forest tree, it is plainly evident that this, at one time, must have had a circumference of over a hundred and twenty feet. For the purpose of enabling visitors more easily to apprehend its enormous size, a "tunnel" has been cut through it which is ten feet in width by twelve in height, and through which the stage coach passes when either going or returning to Yo Semite. There is no more convincing evidence of size than this in either of the groves—if we except the "Stump" at Calaveras. Within a few yards of this grows one of the finest and most symmetrical representatives of this wondrous family.

"Excelsior" being our motto, we shall soon reach "Crane Flat." These flats are grassy meadows, interspersed among the mountain districts, and are generally the heads of creeks or rivers, being almost always "springy." Of late years they are fed off by bands of sheep, brought from the plains when the feed there has become short or dry. Running upon or over trails, they are apt to obliterate all traces of the traveler's course, and where a short turn is made, great care is needed, by the inexperienced, to prevent being lost. Crane Flat, kept by Mrs. Gobin, was once celebrated for the excellence of its meals, when horseback riding was the only method of reaching Yo Semite. Its wrecked buildings now tell their own story of the effects of deep snow. Here the stage possibly changes horses, and thirsty passengers take a drink with Mr. Hurst (whom nearly all the old-timers affectionately call "Billy Hurst").

One of the obstacles to be overcome for early season travel to Yo Semite on the Big Oak Flat Route was the deep snow belt of some ten miles, lying between the Tuolumne Big Tree Grove and Gentry's; the highest part of the road being seven thousand feet above sea level. Here snow would be from six to twenty feet deep. To shovel all this out was a herculean and expensive undertaking, while building walls of snow that reached far above the tops of stage coaches. Then, the glaring sheen of the sunshine on a white surface was exceedingly trying to the eyes of the shovelers, and frequently brought "snow-blindness;" attended with the discomfort, and unhealthiness, of working in wet snow that chilled their lower limbs while the entire upper part of their body was steaming with perspiration. These difficulties, therefore, must be conquered by other means. But, how? That query brought forth another: Why not put

SNOW-SHOES ON THE HORSES?

This experiment was accordingly tried, and proven to be most eminently successful. A glance at the accompanying engraving will give an idea of their form, and the manner of their use.

HORSE ON SNOW-SHOES.

Photo by Geo. Fiske NPS, Yosemite Collections

Prince on Snowshoes

The image on the opposite page is intended to show a horse wearing
snowshoes appropriately—on snow. But it was achieved by deleting
the background. It probably is in Yosemite Valley, on grass.
"Pictures don't lie."
Fiske #251

Photo. by Geo. Fiske.

Photo-Typo by Britton & Rey, S. F.

THE DOMES OF YO SEMITE.
(See page 385.)
A wandering photograph. It faced page 194 in edition two,
page 13 in edition three, and page 322 in edition four.

The horse snow-shoe is made of one inch ash plank, thirteen inches long by eleven wide. It is rounded at the corners to prevent striking, or chafing; and a hollow is cut at the back to allow full play to the shoe, without cutting or bruising the leg. There are three holes mortised in the upper surface of the snow-shoe, the exact size and shape of the horse-shoe calks, and which are inserted therein, to keep the foot in its place, and give solidity to the tread. To make the snow-shoe clutch the horse's hoof snugly, well-fitting flat bands of Norway iron, lined with thick india-rubber cloth, are placed across and clip it; these meet in the center of the foot, where they are brought together by an adjustable screw-bolt; the lower ends of these bands pass through the snow-shoe, to which they are fastened by a bolt and nut, and become assistant tighteners of the clip. On the under side of the snow-shoe, and additional to the bolt and nut, an irregular and almost heart-shaped flange of steel, about half an inch in depth, is riveted, nearly covering the bottom of the shoe, and which prevents sliding in any direction, while adding to its strength. To prevent the snow-shoe from splitting, a fine bolt is run through each end.

When every foot is equipped with one of these, each of the four horses forming the team is ready for the start. Now the interesting essay of using them commences. Each animal seems to have an intuitive knowledge of what they are for, as of the duties expected of them; for, carefully lifting the foot higher than he would under ordinary circumstances, with a somewhat rotary and semi-oscillatory movement, he throws the foot forward, and one shoe over the other, with such intelligent dexterity that they rarely touch each other; and invariably manages to take the front snow-shoe out of the way, before setting the hind one in its place. There is no confusion or even awkwardness in their use, although there is in appearances when seeing horses in such ungainly-looking appendages.

I speak from personal observation, after several delightful sleigh rides over that snow-belt with Joe Mulligan (we all know him by that unpretentious and familiar cognomen only), whose patient care, skill, and watchful management of his horses, under the most trying circumstances, occasionally, elicited my warmest admiration. The gait uphill was a quiet walk, at the rate of about three miles an hour, performed with no more excitement or friction than a heavily-laden team would use, in moving its load upon a level road. Downhill we frequently took a short trot, and which, like the walk uphill, was accomplished without clumsiness. The time generally consumed in crossing the ten miles of snow was about three and a half hours.

To illustrate how much such pioneer path-finders over snow have sometimes to endure, it is only necessary to sketch a single "first trip of the season." There were three strong men, Mulligan, Billings, and Wood, who left Crocker's early one April morning for Crane Flat, some six miles distant, with a coach and four good horses, sleigh, horse snow-shoes, shovels, axes, ropes and other desirable accessories for such an enterprise. Deep new snow had made progress exceedingly slow and difficult. At two o'clock on the following morning they succeeded in reaching the point designated, but no signs of buildings were visible in all the snowy waste. They could see large hillocks of snow, but no place wherein to shelter themselves and horses. Finally, as day was breaking, they found the bearings of the stable door; and, weary as they were, commenced shoveling away the feathery element in front, in order to give their tired animals a place of refuge, and necessary food. An entrance to the stable was eventually secured; but, as the snow was some eighteen feet in depth, and a passageway down to the floor would be the work of many industrious hours, they led each horse, separately, as near as possible to the opening effected; when, by fastening one rope around the head, and another to the tail of each animal, they lowered them into their quarters for the night, by sliding them down over the snow; and, being too tired to eat, the men rolled themselves up in their blankets, and forgot the fatigues of the day in refreshing sleep.

About ten o'clock A. M., they found themselves outside of

their breakfasts (as they expressed it), and were again upon the snow—one might have said *the road*, but *that* lay from sixteen to twenty feet below the surface. Spending this day also in wearying and unflinching effort, they only broke the way to the top of the ridge, some two and a half miles distant, and then returned to their inhospitable quarters at Crane Flat for that night also. On the following day they again, undauntedly, set their own and horses' faces towards Yo Semite, still some sixteen miles distant. Its mountain peaks, and cheery open fire-places, far down out of the snow, became delightfully stimulating day-dreams to them; and, about nine o'clock P. M., Tamarack Flat had been gained, and five additional miles overcome, leaving eleven only to be conquered. Here, also, the snow was as deep as at their stopping-place of the two preceding nights; and similar experiences in snow-shoveling, and horse-sliding down to the stable floor, had to be indulged in until long after midnight. Hungry as wolves, most of the remaining portion of the night was spent in cooking and eating, and the residue only devoted to renewing slumber.

Notwithstanding these protracted wrestlings with their white-faced enemy, their motto, "There's no such word as fail," was not only inscribed upon their determined faces, but was written deeply in their wills and hearts; and as soon as a passage way out for their horses could be dug through the snow, and the snow-shoes were adjusted to the animals, they made the crisp air ring with the shout, "Ho! for Yo Semite," and again started forward. On reaching Cascade Creek Bridge they found the snow piled upon it as deep and steep as the roof of a Swiss cottage; but, with shovels in hands, as defiant of obstacles as ever, they dug a pathway across it, led the horses over in single file, pulled over the sleigh with ropes, and again set out for the Valley. Before noon they reached the lower edge of the snow-belt, and the solid earth; where they left their sleigh, and horse snow-shoes, and by three o'clock P.M. were safely at the hotels at Yo Semite. Pluck, human endurance, and determination, had conquered a victory. All honor to such noble and unremitting exertion.

Nor were these by any means the only efforts that were made to overcome the elemental forces in antagonism to early tourist travel to Yo Semite; inasmuch as Mr. A. H. Washburn, the energetic superintendent of the Yo Semite Stage and Turnpike Company, and assistants, had pressed every available man into service on the southern side of the great chasm; to shovel snow, chop out limbs and trees that had fallen across the road, drain and repair the road-bed, rebuild road walls and bridges, and perform all sorts of other and similar services, before coaches could safely and expeditiously carry passengers into the great Valley. Those who make the journey later, and find everything just as it should be, can form but a very inadequate idea of the difficulties that have been surmounted, the labor performed, and money expended in these necessary enterprises.

Two and a half miles above Crane Flat the highest portion of the road is reached, being seven thousand feet above sea level; and which, lying upon the dividing ridge which separates the waters of the Tuolumne River from those of the Merced, the outlook from it is strikingly bold. From this ridge magnificent views of distant landmarks, and the snow-covered peaks of the Sierras open at brief intervals before us; while timber-covered ridges and gorges stretch farther and farther away to the verge of the distant horizon; with an occasional mountain of verdureless rock, standing gloriously out as if to defy the further encroachments of those evergreen masses of pines. There does not seem to be a foot of ground over which we are passing that has not some novelty to charm us.

The apparently omnipresent forest overarches our way; and beautiful firs, *Abies concolor* and *A. grandis*, the magnificent pines, *P. Jeffreyi*, *P. ponderosa*, and *P. Lambertiana;* and "tamaracks," *Pinus contorta*, stand sentinel guard on every hand; while patches of stunted manzanita, *Arctostaphylos glauca*, with its evergreen leaves and fragrant waxy-like blossoms; and several different species of *Ceanothus* literally loading the air with their perfume, and brightening the landscape with their plumes of white and blue, attract our attention, until, by a gentle declivity, we pass Tamarack Flat, down to Cascade Creek, where the water is dashing itself to atoms, that scintillate and sparkle in the sun; and arriving at Gentry's, commence the descent of the mountain-side on the Yo Semite Turnpike Road. Looking down upon the great cañon of the Merced River from this point, there opens before us one of the most magnificent and comprehensive scenes to be found anywhere; as not only can the numerous windings of the river be traced for miles, as it makes its exit from the valley, but its high bluffs and distant mountains stand boldly out. At another turning of the road we look into the profound and haze-draped depths, and up toward the sublime and storm-defying heights, with feelings all our own, and behold Yo Semite.

Before closing this chapter it becomes my pleasant duty to chronicle the historical fact, that the Big Oak Flat and Yo Semite Turnpike Road Company was the first ever organized for the purpose of extending wagon road facilities beyond the settlements in the direction of the Yo Semite Valley. When the great overland railroads, the Central Pacific and Union Pacific, were nearing completion, in 1869, the question was very properly considered of providing easier transit for the large class of visitors that might be attracted hither; and who, unlike old Californians, were unaccustomed to horseback riding. In this emergency the residents of Big Oak Flat and vicinity were waited upon, and as a business lethargy had fallen upon that district, in the hope of its revival somewhat by such an enterprise, these people formed a company; and the road was completed that year to Hardin's, leaving but about twenty-five miles to be traversed on saddle animals. Encouraged by the liberal patronage bestowed, this was extended the following year to Hodgdon's; and, during the next two years, to Gentry's, the northwestern corner of the Yo Semite Grant. As the company was not financially strong enough then to complete it to the valley, this became the terminus of the road, and so continued until its completion to Yo Semite, July 17, 1874, on which occasion over five hundred persons passed over it, in a kind of triumphal procession.

CHAPTER XXIII.

SCENES TO BE WITNESSED FROM THE FLOOR OF YO SEMITE VALLEY.

Who doth not feel, until his failing sight
Faints into dimness with its own delight,
His changing cheek, his sinking heart confess
The might, the majesty of loveliness?
—BYRON'S *Bride of Abydos, Canto I.*

How massively doth awful Nature pile
The living rock.
—THOMAS DOUBLEDAY'S *Literary Souvenir.*

All are but parts of one stupendous whole,
Whose body Nature is, and God the soul.
—POPE'S ESSAY *on Man.*

Once within the encompassing walls of the glorious Valley, and the broad shadows of its mighty cliffs are thrown over us like some mystic mantle, fatigued as we may be, every jutting mountain, every pointed crag, every leaping water-fall, has a weird yet captivating charm, that makes us feel as though we were entering some fictitious dreamland. Even the rainbow hues, which are playfully toying with the mists and sprays and beautiful rocket-like forms of the Pohono, or Bridal Veil Fall; or the manifold pearly lights and shades that are intermixing and commingling on that marvelous promontory of vertical granite, known as El Capitan, distributed broadcast as they are, only enhance the delusion. There comes a feeling over us akin to sympathy in the thought-painted picture of Mr. Greeley, when entering the Valley on the eventful first moonlighted night of his visit:—

That first full, deliberate gaze up the opposite height! can I ever forget it? The valley is here scarcely half a mile wide, while its northern wall, of mainly naked, perpendicular granite, is at least four thousand feet high—probably more [since demonstrated by actual measurement to be

(336)

three thousand three hundred]. But the modicum of moonlight that fell into this awful gorge gave to that precipice a vagueness of outline, an indefinite vastness, a ghostly and weird spirituality. Had the mountain spoken to me in audible voice, or begun to lean over with the purpose of burying me beneath its crushing mass, I should hardly have been surprised. Its whiteness, thrown into bold relief by the patches of trees or shrubs which fringed or flecked it whenever a few handfuls of its moss, slowly decomposed to earth, could contrive to hold on, continually suggested the presence of snow, which suggestion, with difficulty refuted, was at once renewed. And, looking up the valley, we saw just such mountain precipices, barely separated by intervening water-courses of inconsiderable depth, and only receding sufficiently to make room for a very narrow meadow, inclosing the river, to the furthest limit of vision.

ENTERING RIDE UP THE VALLEY.

Our road up the Valley to the hotels, for the most part, lies among giant pines, or firs, and cedars, from one hundred and seventy-five to two hundred and twenty feet in height, and beneath the refreshing shade of outspreading oaks. Not a sound breaks the impressive stillness that reigns, save the occasional chirping and singing of birds, or the low, distant sighing of the water-falls, or the breeze in the tops of the trees. Crystal streams occasionally gurgle and ripple across our path, whose sides are fringed with willows and wild flowers that are almost ever blossoming, and grass that is ever green. On either side of us stand almost perpendicular cliffs, to the height of nearly thirty-five hundred feet; on whose rugged faces, or in their uneven tops and sides, here and there a stunted pine struggles to live; and every crag seems crowned with some shrub or tree. The bright sheen of the river occasionally glistens among the dense foliage of the long vistas that continually open up before us. At every step, some new picture of great beauty presents itself, and some new shapes and shadows from trees and mountains, form new combinations of light and shade, in this great kaleidoscope of nature; and as we ride along, in addition to the Bridal Veil Fall and El Capitan, we pass the Ribbon Fall, Cathedral Spires, the Three Brothers, and the Sentinel; while in the distance glimpses are obtained of the Yo Semite Fall, Indian Cañon, North Dome, Royal Arches, Washington Tower, Cloud's Rest, and the Half, or South Dome; all of which expressively suggest the treat there is in store for us, when we can examine them in detail, and enjoy a nearer and more satisfying view of their matchless wonders.

Now, notwithstanding the many objects of interest we have passed, one thought has probably obtruded itself, and it is this, "Shall we ever come up to this or that mountain?" and the length of time consumed in the attempt would seem to give back the nonchalant and unfeeling answer, "Never!" There is, however, no greater proof of the unrealized altitudes of these mountain walls than this—the time it takes to come up with or to pass them. But amidst all these we can possibly hear one ejaculation that seems to contain more real satisfaction in it than any amount of sight-seeing just now. It is this: "Thank goodness, here is the hotel!" Commending ourselves to its most generous hospitalities, we wish our traveling companions a temporary good-by, and prepare for the repast that awaits us.

Our creature comforts having supposably been well cared for at one or other of the hotels, it is natural to infer that the journey, having been more or less fatiguing, has prepared us for a sweet and refreshing sleep; yet experience may prove that the excitement attending our glorious surroundings has cast over us a stronger spell even than that of Morpheus, and charmed us into wakefulness, that we may listen to the splashing, dashing, wash-ing, roaring, surging, hissing, seething sound of the great Yo Semite Falls, just opposite; or has beguiled us into passing quietly out of our resting-place, to look up between the lofty pines and outspreading oaks to the granite cliffs, that tower up with such majesty of form and boldness of outline against the vast ethereal vault of heaven; or to watch, in the moonlight, the ever-changing shapes and shadows of the water, as it leaps the cloud-draped summit of the mountain, and falls in gusty torrents on the un-yielding granite, to be dashed to an infinity of atoms. Then, when prudential reasons have wooed us back again to our couch, we may even there have visions of some tutelary spirit of immense proportions, who, in the exercise of his benignant functions, has vouchsafed to us his protecting genius, and admonished the water-fall to modulate the depth and height of its tones somewhat, so that we can sleep and be refreshed, and thus become the better prepared to quaff the delicious draught from this perennial fountain, that only awaits our waking to satisfy all our longings.

There is a possibility, however, that for some time before we are prepared to sing,

"Hail! smiling morn, that tips the hills with gold,"

The sun (hours in advance of a good honest look upon us, perhaps, deep down as we are in this awful gorge) may have been up, and painting the rosiest of tints upon the surrounding domes and crags; burnishing up their ridges; gilding trees with bright effects; etching lights and shadows in the time-worked furrows of the mountain's face, as though he took especial pride in bringing out, strongly, the wrinkles which the president of the hour-glass and scythe has been busily engaged upon for so many thousands of years.

A SUGGESTION WORTH ADOPTING.

And while we are looking admiringly upon them, please permit me to hazard a suggestion that is born of the experience and teachings of a quarter of a century at Yo Semite. It is this: If it is among the possibilities (and there may exist such a possibility when the subject is well weighed), no matter how tempting the surrounding influences may be—and there is almost sure to be some restless, impetuous, and irrepressible spirit in nearly every party—if you would make your visit healthful, restful, and thoroughly enjoyable, and an ever-present pleasing after-thought, *do not attempt any very fatiguing excursion the first day after arrival.* Devote it to day-dreaming and to rest; not absolutely, perhaps, inasmuch as a modicum of exercise is really better, in a majority of cases, than total inaction; but let it be an easy jaunt among some of the attractive scenes not very far from the hotel.

Before satisfying our expectant curiosity, or gratifying a love for the sublime and beautiful through a closer communion with the marvelous grandeur which surrounds us, permit me to explain what this great Valley is, how it was possibly formed, and the various natural phenomena connected with it; as these may form interesting themes for reflection and conjecture, while we are wandering about among its wonderful scenes.

WHAT THE YO SEMITE VALLEY IS.

It is a deep, almost vertical-walled chasm, in the heart of the Sierra Nevada Mountains—here about seventy miles in breadth—about one hundred and fifty miles due east of San Francisco, and thirty from the main crest of the chain. Its sides are built of a beautiful pearl-gray granite of many shades and colors, and are in an infinite variety of forms. These are from three thousand three hundred to six thousand feet in perpendicular height above their base. Over these vertical walls vault numerous water-falls, that make a clear leap of from three hundred and fifty to two thousand feet; besides numerous bounding cascades.

The altitude of the floor of the Valley is nearly four thousand feet above the level of the sea, and the measurements given of the surrounding cliffs and water-falls are mostly from this basis. Its total area within the encompassing walls, according to the report of the Commissioner of the General Land Office, Washington, D. C., comprises eight thousand four hundred and eighty acres, three thousand one hundred and nine of which are meadow land. The entire grant to the State, however, embraces thirty-six thousand one hundred and eleven acres, and includes one mile beyond the edge of the precipices throughout their entire circumference. The Valley proper is about seven miles in length, by from three-quarters to one and a half miles in width; yet the distance between the face of the cliff at the Yo Semite Fall and the Sentinel, according to the measurements of Prof. J. D. Whitney, is two and a half miles. The Merced River, a beautifully transparent stream, full of delicious trout, runs through it, with an average width of

THE NEVADA FALL—YO-WI-YE

(See page 447)

Fiske #349. Facing page 336 in edition one. Facing page 338 in all other editions.

Photo by Charles L. Weed   NPS, Yosemite Collections

SCENE ON THE MERCED RIVER

Half of a stereo made in 1859 (Weed stereo #31)—
the model for the engraving on the opposite page.

SCENE ON THE RIVER.

one hundred feet, and whose banks are ornamented with azaleas and syringas, and overarched with balm of gileads, alders, black oaks, pines, cedars, and silver firs. This has numerous tributaries, which, after leaping the cliffs, join it in its general course down the Valley.

The general trend of the Valley is northeasterly and south-westwardly, a fortunate circumstance indeed, inasmuch as the delightfully bracing northwesterly trade-winds, which sweep the Pacific Ocean in this latitude during summer, course pleasantly through it, and keep it exceedingly temperate on the hottest of days; so that there is no sultry oppressiveness of atmosphere felt here, as sometimes in the East. Besides this, the sun is afforded the opportunity of looking into the Valley from before six o'clock in the morning until nearly five in the afternoon, during summer, instead of only an hour or two at most, had its bearings been transversely to this. In the short days of winter, however, as the hotels and other buildings are for the most part approximately nearest to the southern wall of the Valley, when Apollo goes farthest on his southern rambles, he looks down upon them over the mountain about half past one in the afternoon, and vanishes at half past three; thus deigning to show his cheerful face only about two hours out of the twenty-four; so that the hotel side of the Valley, so to speak, is mapped in mountain shadow, while the opposite or northern side is flooded with brightness.

THEORIES ABOUT ITS FORMATION.

Prof. J. D. Whitney, for many years State Geologist, thus expresses his views:*—

Most of the great cañons and valleys of the Sierra Nevada have resulted from aqueous denudation, and in no part of the world has this kind of work been done on a larger scale. The long-continued action of tremendous torrents of water, rushing with impetuous velocity down the slopes of the mountains, has excavated those immense gorges by which the chain of the Sierra Nevada is furrowed, on its western slope, to the depth of thousands of feet. . . .

The eroded cañons of the Sierra,† however, whose formation is due to the action of water, never have vertical walls, nor do their sides present the peculiar angular forms which are seen in the Yosemite, as, for instance, in El Capitan, where two perpendicular surfaces of smooth granite, more than three thousand feet high, meet each other at a right angle. It is sufficient to look for a moment at the vertical faces of El Capitan and the Bridal Veil Rock, turned down the Valley, or away from the direction in which the eroding forces must have acted, to be able to say that aqueous erosion could not have been the agent employed to do any such work. The squarely cut re-entering angles, like those below El Capitan, and between Cathedral Rock and the Sentinel, or in the Illilouette Cañon, were never produced by ordinary erosion. Much less could any such cause be called into account for the peculiar formation of the Half Dome, the vertical

* The Yosemite Guide Book, page 81.

† Ibid., pages 82, 83, 85.

portion of which is all above the ordinary level of the Valley, rising two thousand feet, in sublime isolation, above any point which could have been reached by denuding agencies, even supposing the current of water to have filled the whole Valley. . . .

In short, we are led irresistibly to the adoption of a theory of the origin of the Yosemite in a way which has hardly yet been recognized as one of those in which valleys may be formed, probably for the reason that there are so few cases in which such an event can be absolutely proved to have occurred. We conceive that, during the process of upheaval of the Sierra, or, possibly, at some time after that had taken place, there was at the Yosemite a subsidence of a limited area, marked by lines of "fault" or fissures crossing each other somewhat nearly at right angles. In other and more simple language, *the bottom of the Valley sunk down to an unknown depth*, owing to its support being withdrawn from beneath.*

The late Prof. Benjamin Silliman, of Yale College, thought that it was caused through some great volcanic convulsion by which the mountains were reft asunder, and a fissure formed.

Now although I entertain the deepest respect for both those gentlemen, and their views, I am unable to concur in their opinions, for the following reasons: The natural cleavage of the granite walls is not, for the most part, vertical, but at an acute angle of from seventy to eighty-five degrees, as at Glacier Point and the Royal Arches; and that of the Yo Semite Fall is not by any means vertical, to say nothing of the intermediate shoulders between such points as Eagle Tower and the Three Brothers. And although the northern and western sides of El Capitan are more than vertical, as they overhang over one hundred feet, the abutting angle of that marvelous mountain is at an angle of say eighty degrees; while its eastern spur consists of glacier-rounded ridges that project far into the Valley. With this uniform angle of cleavage how could the bottom of the Valley sink down, any more than the key-stone of an arch? unless by the displacement of its supporting base; and, to concede this possibility, is to admit the theory of Professor Silliman of the violent rending of the mountains asunder by volcanic co-action, which, in my judgment, is unsupported by convincing data.

* The italics are my own to emphasize the substance of Professor Whitney's views.

To admit this contingency, moreover, is to pre-suppose the entire uplifting and rending of a large proportion of the solid granite forming the great chain of the High Sierra; and then of its having left only this particular fissure to mark the co-action that then took place—a possible but not probable result. It is even more than improbable, from the fact that the solidified granite crossing every one of its side cañons, even near to the Valley, is everywhere completely and visibly intact, so that there is not the slightest semblance of any disjunction whatsoever. To my convictions, therefore, the evidences that the Yo Semite Valley was ever formed by either subsidence, or volcanic rending, are not only unsatisfactory, but are entirely absent.

Nor is it altogether clear why Professor Whitney, after giving his emphatic opinion that "the long-continued action of tremendous torrents of water, rushing with impetuous velocity down the slopes of the mountains, has excavated those immense gorges by which the chain of the Sierra Nevada is furrowed, on its western slope, to the depth of thousands of feet," should make the Yo Semite Valley an exception; especially when the premises are so abundantly clear that it was created by precisely similar agencies as those of other cañons—that of erosion. To illustrate this, let me call attention to some interstices in the face of a jutting spur of the southern wall of the Valley, about midway between the Sentinel and Cathedral Spires (see engraving), known as

THE FISSURES.

One of these is several hundred feet in depth, and yet not over three and a half feet across it. But for its rounding edges one could stand upon its top, look into its mysterious depths, and then step across it to the other side. There can exist no doubt that this has been formed from a soft stratum of granite, just the width of the fissure; and as that there is not the smallest stream of water running through it (except when it rains), as the elements have disintegrated the demulcent rock, every storm of wind, or rain, or snow, had kept constantly removing the friable particles and left only the hard walls standing.

Photo by S. C. Walker.   Pen drawing by Mrs. Brodt.

THE FISSURE.

Making this a basis of conclusions, is it not reasonable to suppose that there once existed similar strata where the Valley now is, and that as the disintegrating agencies completed their work upon it, the denuding torrents of the Sierra swept over or through it, and carried off the disintegrated material to build the plains and valleys below? Stand upon any of the bridges which now span the Merced River, during high water, and the floating silica with which it is laden will be conclusive evidence that the same forces, on a comparatively limited scale, are still actively going on.

ITS FORMATION ASSISTED BY GLACIER ACTION.

Nor has water, in its liquefied form at least, been the only potential agency for cutting down and hewing out chasms like this among the High Sierra, inasmuch as its polished valley floors, burnished mountain-sides and tops, and vast moraines, many thousands of feet in altitude above the Valley, prove, beyond peradventure or question, that glaciers of immense thickness once covered all this vast area; filling every gorge, roofing every dome, and overspreading every mountain ridge with ice; the trend of whose striations is unmistakably towards the channel of the Merced River, mainly through its tributaries. As the Yo Semite Valley is but four thousand feet above sea level, and these glacial writings are distinctly traceable not only on the walls of the Valley and the cliffs above it, but nearly to the summits of the highest mountains east of it (here over thirteen thousand feet in altitude) there can be but little doubt that a vast field of ice had pre-existence at Yo Semite that was *over a mile and a half in absolute thickness and depth!* Who, then, can even conceive, much less estimate, the cyclopean force, and erosive power, of such a glacier? It would seem that plowing into soft rock, tearing away of projections, loosening seamy blocks, detaching jutting precipices, grinding off ridges, scooping out hollows for future lakes, and forcing everything movable before it, would be a mere frolicsome pastime to so irresistible and mighty a giant. And, when that pastime has been indulged in for countless ages, its results may be imagined, but cannot be comprehended.

This, then, in my judgment, has been no insignificant factor in broadening and deepening the chasm first cut here, as elsewhere, by water; and indicating, if not proving, that *the Yo Semite Valley was formed by erosion, and not by volcanic action.*

UNCERTAIN TIME OF THE GLACIAL PERIOD.

In a personal conference with Prof. Wm. H. Brewer, formerly first assistant of the State Geological Survey of California, now of Yale College, New Haven, Connecticut, the question was asked him, "In about what age of the world was the glacial period supposed to have existed?" and the answer was, "This has not been positively agreed upon by scientists, as some think it was about twenty or thirty thousand years ago, others from fifty to eighty thousand, and some contend that nearly one hundred and fifty thousand years have elapsed since that time, and it may have been even more." As something will be said about this, and about the moraines of the High Sierra when we take our mountain jaunts beyond the Yo Semite, further present mention will be unnecessary.

NATURAL PHENOMENA.

The thermometer seldom reads higher than eighty-six degrees in summer, or lower than sixteen degrees in winter, although it has been ninety-five degrees (and even then the heat was not oppressive, owing to the rarefaction of the atmosphere), and nearly to zero—never below it. The usual ice-harvesting season is from December 15th to 25th, when the days are clear, and the temperature at night ranges from sixteen to twenty-five degrees; at which time ice forms from six to eleven inches in thickness, and is then taken from the sheltered eddies of the river. A good quality of ice is seldom attainable after the rains and snows of winter have fairly set in.

The first fall rain generally occurs about the time of the autumnal equinox, in September; but does not continue more than a day or two; when it usually clears up and continues fine for several weeks. It is after this rain that the first frost generally pays its timely visit, and commences to paint the deciduous trees and shrubs in the brightest of autumnal colors. Early in November the first snow generally begins to fall, when it will probably not deposit more than a few inches in the Valley, but prove more liberal in the mountains, where it sometimes will leave fifteen or twenty inches. It was in one of these storms that Lady Avonmore, better known as the Hon. Theresa Yelverton, was caught, alone, and being lost and benighted, came near losing her life. A few days thereafter the delightfully balmy Indian summer weather sets in, and continues to near the end of December; when old Winter, he with the hoary locks and unfeeling heart, swoops down in good earnest; and, turning his frosty key, keeps the inhabitants of Yo Semite—generally about forty in number—close prisoners until the benignant smiles of the gentle angel, Spring, unlocks the snowy doors, and again sets them free.

The pluvial downpour of an average winter in Yo Semite is usually from twenty to thirty-three inches, and of snow from nine to seventeen feet. It must not, however, be supposed that this falls all at once, or that it ever aggregates so great a depth, as it keeps melting and settling more or less all the time; so that I have never known it to exceed an average depth over the Valley of more than five and a half feet. Snow possesses the wonderful quality of keeping the temperature of anything upon which it falls, about the same as it finds it; so that if the ground which it covers is warm, it is kept in that condition, and the snow melts rapidly from beneath; but, should the earth be frozen, it retains that temperature, and liquefies mostly from above.

IMPROVED PROVISIONS FOR REACHING SCENIC STANDPOINTS.

To enable visitors to see every point of interest to the greatest advantage, the State, through its Board of Yo Semite Commissioners, has constructed a most excellent carriage road throughout the entire circumference of the Valley; and which, including that to Mirror Lake and the Cascade Falls, opens up a drive of over twenty-one miles, that has not its equal in scenic grandeur and beauty anywhere else on earth.

In addition to this, broad, safe, and well-built trails for horseback riding have been made up the cañon of the Merced River to the Vernal and Nevada Falls; over old moraines, to the summit of Cloud's Rest, and to the foot of Half Dome; up the mountain-sides to Union Point, Glacier Point, and Sentinel Dome, to Columbia Rock, the foot and top of the upper Yo Semite Fall, and Eagle Peak, so that impressive views may be enjoyed of these by an actual visit to and among them. Earlier enterprises of this kind were inaugurated by private individuals, and tolls collected for passing over them; but they were all subsequently purchased by the State and made free. To each and all of which it is proposed to make excursions in due season; so that when the traveler has journeyed so far to witness these glorious scenes, nothing of importance may be omitted, that could in any measure tend to insure their being visited understandingly, and as intelligently as possible.

As there are frequently moments of leisure that visitors desire to utilize, besides having wants that need to be supplied, perhaps it may be as well here, as elsewhere, to enumerate the various interests represented in the little settlement of Yo Semite. Of course the first to be mentioned are the

THREE HOTELS AND THEIR LANDLORDS;

Four when the new one now building is completed. These are kept by Mr. J. K. Barnard, Mr. J. J. Cook, and Mr. and Mrs. G. F. Leidig, each of which is generally called after the name of its proprietor; as, "Barnard's," "Cook's," and "Leidig's." The latter is the first reached, Cook's the next, and Barnard's is the farthest up the Valley, near to the iron bridge.[1] The latter can accommodate about one hundred guests; Mr. Cook, about seventy-five; Mr. Leidig, forty; and the new hotel is sufficiently commodious to take care of one hundred and fifty. All of these are comfortable, and the prices charged are reasonable,

1. Leidig's Hotel and Cook's Hotel were successors of the pioneer Lower Hotel; both were built in 1869 and torn down in 1888. Cook's Hotel was also known as "Black's Hotel." Barnard's Hotel had the formal name of "Yosemite Falls Hotel," but since Barnard was the lessee the hotel was known by his name. It was built in 1876 by George W. Coulter and A. J. Murphy, and was renamed the "Sentinel Hotel" in 1893. It was destroyed in 1940.

THE BIG TREE ROOM, BARNARD'S.

Photo. by Geo. Fiske

BIG TREE ROOM, BARNARD'S HOTEL, YOSEMITE

The photograph from which the engraving on the opposite page was made. Fiske's photos, including an earlier version of this photo, are for sale on the table at the left. The hotel is long gone, but the huge cedar tree still stands. Fiske #594.

especially considering their distance from market, and the short-
ness of the business season.

When you are within this room, and your eye falls upon any
one of the creations of his genius, you can see at a glance that Mr.
Sinning has the rare gift of uniting the taste of the artist with the
skill of the workman. His choice specimens of various woods,
found in this vicinity, most admirably joined, and beautifully
polished, are so arranged that one colored wood is made complimentary to that of the other adjoining it. They are simply
perfect, both in arrangement and mechanical execution. Then, it
gives him such real pleasure to show you, and explain all about his
work, that his eyes, seen through a single pair of glasses, actually
double in brightness when you admire it. Nor need you be afraid
of offending him if you do not purchase, as he readily sells all that
he can make, notwithstanding he is at his bench on every working
day, both winter and summer, making and finishing the most
beautiful of ladies' cabinets, glove-boxes, etc., etc.

ART STUDIOS.

Of these, there are two, Mr. Thomas Hill's, and that of Mr.
Charles D. Robinson; the former is near Cook's Hotel, and the latter
adjoins the Guardian's office. The moment that either studio is
entered, the works of each pleasantly impresses visitors with their
unquestioned excellence and faithfulness to nature. And while
every true artist is in thought and feeling more or less a poet, and
these ethereal essences are noticeably present in, and breathe
through every line and color of his touch, there is frequently as
wide a difference in their treatment of the subject, as there is
between the poetry of Shakespeare and that of Tennyson. And it is
well that it is so, for in art, as in food, it is the rich variety that
makes pleasing provision for all. The thought-coloring of Mr. Hill
may differ widely from that of Mr. Robinson, and it does; but in that
very difference lies the secret of the measurable success of both.
The beautiful creations of either will worthily occupy any picture

gallery, or drawing-room on earth, should visitors desire to live these scenes over again when within their own far-off homes, by leaving with Mr. Hill, or Mr. Robinson, their orders for pictures.

PHOTOGRAPHIC.

Of course photographs have become one of the popular luxuries of the age, and there is scarcely an intelligent visitor that enters the Valley, who does not wish to carry home, for himself or friends, some souvenir of his visit; and to renew pleasant memories of its marvelous scenes. To supply this want there are two galleries established; one, conducted by Mr. Geo. Fiske—to whom I am largely indebted for so many of the beautiful illustrations that appear in this book—who, as a man, a gentleman, and an artist, is in every way worthy of the most liberal patronage that can be extended to him; and the other is kept by Mr. G. Fagersteen, who, while being devoted to his art, is among the best residents of Yo Semite, and who, like Mr. Fiske, takes groups of visitors which embody the views around, as a background to the picture. There are also two other places where photographic views of the surrounding scenery are sold, Mr. J. J. Cook's, and at the Big Tree Room, Barnard's; the former having Taber's, and the latter Fiske's.

THE STORE

For general merchandise is kept by Mr. Angelo Cavagnaro, an Italian; and who, you will find, has on hand almost any article that may be desired, from a box of paper collars to a side of bacon; and probably many others that neither you nor any one else may want.

MRS. GLYNN'S.

Mrs. Glynn is an industrious woman, who, finding it impossible to breathe the air of a lower altitude, has prolonged her useful life by making choice of Yo Semite as a home; and, being a good cook, ekes out a frugal living by selling bread, pies, and such things, to transient customers; and by keeping two or three boarders.

LIVERY STABLES, CARRIAGES, AND SADDLE HORSES.

These are kept by Messrs. Wm. F. Coffman and Geo. Kenney, two wide-awake, square men, who wait upon guests at the hotel every evening to learn their wishes concerning the rides around the Valley in carriages, or up the mountains on horses, for the next day. When they present themselves, it will be well for visitors to have considered their plans for the morrow, and give to them their order accordingly; as, by so doing, all delays, and many annoyances, are avoided in the morning. The charges for saddle horses and carriages are determined by the Board of Commissioners. Should any irregularity of any kind occur it should be promptly reported to the Guardian. Additional to the gentlemen above mentioned, Mr. Galen Clark (one of the oldest pioneers of this section, and who for sixteen years was the Valley's Guardian) has also the privilege of conveying passengers in his carriage to every point of interest around Yo Semite. He will be found intelligent, obliging, and efficient in everything he undertakes.

THE GUIDES.

Of course when any one wishes to witness the scenic grandeur visible from the mountain-tops which surround the Valley, he is at liberty to elect whether these trips shall be taken on horseback or afoot. If on foot, he avoids all care and expense for either himself or his horse; but finds it very fatiguing. If on horseback, a guide is needed, not only to explain the different objects of interest to be found, but to look out for the safety and comfort of those in his care; and to insure these, saddles have to be carefully watched, and adjusted, on all mountain trails. These form important parts of a guide's duty. The day's expense for a guide (which includes his horse, board, and wages) is $3.00, divided between the different members of the party. For instance, to a party of six—and none should be larger than this if a guide is expected to do his full duty by it—the *pro rata* for each person would be fifty cents for his day's service.

To mention even the names of the many whose kindly attentions and really valuable services as guides, have been more or less before the Yo Semite visiting public for the last twenty-five years, would make many a visitor's heart warm with grateful emotion; and to recall to memory the faces, and with them the obliging acts and excellent qualities of those who were thus personally useful to them, in the "long, long ago." Many of these could be given, but the restraining fear that a treacherous memory might cause some to be omitted, that were equally worthy of a place, is suggestive of possible yet unintentional injustice, that is sufficiently strong to tempt me to forego the record altogether.

Still, there is one of the present guides whose peculiar characteristics, singular ways, and husky voice, make him "the observed of all observers," whose name is Nathan B. Phillips, but who is better known to all the world as "Pike." Being among the oldest and longest in the service of any now acting in the capacity of guide, permit me to introduce him:—

If, when you present this letter of introduction, he should not recognize the fact that you are addressing him by his own name, you have only to add the proud cognomen of "Pike," to convince him that, for the moment at least, he was a little absent-minded! Now when Pike is himself (as once in a while he gets "socially" inclined) no better guide ever took care of a party; as he is polite, studiously attentive without seeming so, patient, thoughtful, careful; and there is not a peak or gorge, valley or cañon, in the whole range of the High Sierra, within view, that is not "as familiar to him as household words." Besides, he can trail a bear, track a deer, bag a grouse, and work off agonizing music from a violin with the best. I do not say that there are not others equally good, as either hunter, guide, or violinist, for that would not be true; and would, moreover, be begging the question. I never saw him angry but once, and that was when a miserable wretch, sometimes inappropriately called a man, was abusing a horse. Then, in language, he "made the fur fly;" and I said, Amen! Once he was asked by a lady how the huskiness of his voice was brought about. "Ah," he good-naturedly responded, "telling so many 'whoppers'

MR. NATHAN B. PHILLIPS.

to tourists, I expect!" Pike is a Yo Semite character, and one worth meeting.

BUTCHER, AND BLACKSMITH'S SHOPS.

When meal-times come we should feel it a great omission had the former been overlooked; and when traveling on our own horse tells us he has lost his shoe, or in our own conveyance we find that a spring has broken, a bolt is gone, or a nut lost, how gladly we welcome the blacksmith and his shop. Both of these are found in Yo Semite.

HARRIS'.

This is near the camp-ground set apart by the Board of Commissioners for the accommodation of those who leave the scorching plains below for the respite and comfort of recuperation in such a charming spot as Yo Semite, and come in their own conveyances; generally bringing their own tents and supplies with them, and camp out. As Mr. A. Harris grows and keeps an abundant supply of fodder, besides stabling for animals, his place is deservedly popular with camping parties. Milk, eggs, and other farm products are obtainable here; and, should the bread burn at the camp-fire, and the yeast become sour, Mrs. Harris has always the remedy on hand to help strangers out of their difficulty, and that most cheerfully. Then, next to the Leidig's, the Harris' have the largest family in the Valley; both being a source of pleasurable pride to the parents. Speaking of children, it must not be forgotten that there is here

THE PUBLIC SCHOOL.

It is situated on the margin of a small meadow just above Barnard's; with the North Dome, Royal Arches, Washington Tower, and Half Dome, lifting their exalted proportions heavenward, just in front of the school-house door. Then there is

THE YO SEMITE CHAPEL.

This neat little edifice, devoted to the worship of God amid the marvelous creations of His hand, was built by the California State Sunday School Association, in the summer of 1879; partly by subscriptions from the children, but mainly from the voluntary contributions of prominent members of the Association. Mr. Charles Geddes, a leading architect of San Francisco, made and presented the plans; and Mr. E. Thomson, also of San Francisco, erected the building, at a cost of between three and four thousand dollars. It will seat an audience of about two hundred and fifty. Mr. H. D. Bacon, of Oakland, gave the bell; and when its first notes rung out upon the moon-silvered air, on the evening

Photo by Geo. Fiske.   Engraved by J. M. Hay, S. F.

THE YO SEMITE CHAPEL.

of dedication, it was the first sound of "the church-going bell" ever heard in Yo Semite. Let us hope that it will assist to

> "Ring out the false, ring in the true,
> Ring in the valiant man and free,
>   The larger heart, the kindlier hand;
>   Ring out the darkness of the land,
>   Ring in the Christ that is to be."*

Miss Mary Porter, of Philadelphia, donated the organ, in memorium of Miss Florence Hutchings, the first white child born in

* TENNYSON'S *Ring Out, Wild Bells.*

YOSEMITE CHAPEL

The engraving on the opposite page was made from this photograph, which is
Fiske's #361. The engraver was completely faithful to the original—except
that he deleted the outhouse at the right rear of the chapel.

Nathan B. "Pike" Phillips

In a photographer's studio, deprived of gun, steed, and cheroot, Pike Phillips presents a different appearance—rough-hewn but respectable. See the photograph on page 354.

Yo Semite, who passed through the Beautiful Gate, September 20, 1881 (as recorded on pages 145, 146), to whom she had become devotedly attached while visiting the Valley the preceding year.

The Yo Semite Chapel is for the free use of Christians of every denomination.

THE GUARDIAN

Is a State officer, appointed by the Board of Commissioners, for the purpose of watching over the best interest of the Valley, and superintending the local details connected with its management, under the Board. To him, therefore, all irregularities of every kind should be promptly reported, to insure their abatement. From him, moreover, can be obtained information, not only concerning the rules and regulations adopted by the Board of Commissioners, for the management of the Valley in the interests of the public; but the best places to camp, the points most noteworthy to see, and the best time and manner of seeing them; with answers to every reasonable question intelligent persons may ask concerning this wonderful spot. In short he will, to the best of his ability, be the living embodiment of a cyclopedia of Yo Semite; and that politely, cheerily, and pleasantly. The present Guardian of the Valley is Mr. Walter E. Dennison, to whom all communications concerning it should be addressed. His office is on the south bank of the Merced River, near the upper iron bridge.

WELLS, FARGO & CO'S EXPRESS, AND THE POST-OFFICE.

Both of these invaluable institutions, of especial interest to the traveling public, as well as residents, have been established at Yo Semite. The former opens and closes with the business season, but the latter maintains connections with the outside world all the year—in summer, daily, and in winter, by a semi-weekly mail. Notwithstanding the unquestioned efficiency of Wells, Fargo & Co.'s Express for the conveyance of valuable packages, Yo Semite should be made a "Money-order Office" of the postal service, as the wants of tourist visitors, as well as residents, would be much subserved thereby.

Before the establishment of a postal route to, and post-office at Yo Semite, all letters and papers were carried thither by private hands; but the late U. S. Senator Howe, of Wisconsin, afterwards Postmaster-General of the United States, secured this great boon for the Valley. Through him the writer became its first postmaster, at the enormously extravagant salary of $12.00 per annum, besides perquisites of uncalled-for old papers and quack advertisements! But as there was then no winter service, and he sometimes paid his Indian mail carrier ten dollars for a single winter trip, besides board and old clothes for trudging through and over snow, in the dead of winter, without snow-shoes, to bring in the precious missives; strange as it may seem, it was not deemed a sufficient sinecure to incite and tempt the envious longings of needy politicians for its possession!

TELEGRAPHIC CONNECTIONS.

For many years the Valley was in telegraphic communication with the outside world, *via* Sonora and Groveland; but as it was not sufficiently patronized after 1874 to pay for repairing the line and running the office, in a few years thereafter it went un-repaired, and was consequently unused. In 1882, however, a new one was constructed, by the Western Union Company, which is still maintained, *via* Berenda, Grant's Sulphur Springs, and Wawona to Yo Semite; so that now telegrams can be sent thence to every nook and corner of civilization.

THE FOREST TREES OF YO SEMITE.

There are four different species of pine growing here: Two "Yellow Pines," *Pinus ponderosa*, and *P. Jeffreyi*, with three needles to each leaf; "Sugar Pine," *P. Lambertiana*, having five needles to a leaf; and the "Tamarack Pine," *P. contorta*, with only two to a leaf: "Red, or Incense Cedar," *Libocedrus decurrens:* Three "Silver Firs," *Abies concolor, A. grandis*, and *A. nobilis*.

There is but one more of this genus found in the State, and that one only in a single locality (the Santa Lucia Mountains, Monterey County), but, owing to its beauty, and rarity, I am

THE SILVER FIR, *Abies Bracteata*, Santa Lucia Mountains.

tempted to introduce engravings of it here. All the cones of the silver fir grow upwards,—not downwards, like the pines.

Of the coniferæ, the next in importance, perhaps, is the "Red" or "Douglas" Spruce, *Psudo tsuga Douglasii*. Then, in resemblance of foliage, its single leaves sharp as a needle, and fruit like a nutmeg, whence comes the name "California Nutmeg," *Torreya Californica*. Then follows the "Black Oak," *Quercus Kelloggii*, upon the acorns of which the Indians mainly depend for their staple bread-stuff;* and a few of the "Quaking Aspen," *Populus*

* See Chapter on Indian manners and customs.

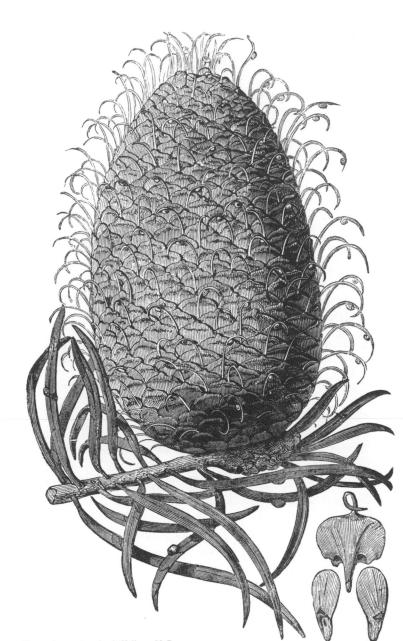

Drawn from nature by A. Kellogg, M. D.
CONE OF THE SILVER FIR, *Abies Bracteata, Santa Lucia Mountains.*

tremuloides which came down from the mountains in the flood of 1867. The "Balm of Gilead" Poplar, *Populus balsamifera:* "Alder," *Alnus viridis:* "Rock," or "Oregon, Maple," *Acer macrophyllum:* "California Laurel," *Umbellularia Californica:* "Dogwood," *Cornus Nuttallii*, with its large white blossoms. Then follows the most beautiful of all the "Live Oaks," the golden-cupped *Quercus chrysolepis*.

THE SHRUBBERY OF YO SEMITE.

The most attractive of all, on account of the bright green of its leaves, its dwarf, bell-shaped, and waxy bunches of pinkish-white blossoms, and the red olive-green of its smooth stems, the bark of which peels off annually, is the "Manzanita," *Arctostaphylos pungens*. Next comes the "California Lilac," *Ceanothus integerrimus*, whose large feathery plumes of white flowers, redolent with perfume, that become so inviting to both the eye and nostril; with its bright sap-green bark: The "Azalea," *Azalea Occidentalis*, the fragrant masses of whose pinkish-white or yellowish-white blossoms can be "scented from afar:" The "Spice Plant," *Calycanthus Occidentalis*, that grows in such rich abundance on the way to Cascade Falls, and whose large deep-green and pointed ovate leaves shine in striking contrast to its wine-colored flowers. Nor must we overlook the "Chokecherry," *Prunus demissa*, with its gracefully depending blossoms, and fruit so valuable an edible to the natives; or the "Wild Coffee," *Rhamnus Californica*, whose root-wood makes such beautiful veneers. These, with some few others, are the principal representatives of the interesting shrubbery of the Valley.

THE FLOWERS OF YO SEMITE.

These are so numerous and so varied that but a few only can here be mentioned. Perhaps the first claiming attention, not only for its graceful tulip-like cup, and richly colored butterfly wing-formed petals, but from its being the flower after which this county was named, "Mariposa," or "Butterfly Tulip," *Calochortus venustus:* The "Penstemon," *Penstemon lœtus*, with its bright purplish-blue flowers: "Pussy's Paws," *Spraguea umbellata,* whose attractive, radiating bunches clothe even sandy places with beauty; *Hosackia crassifolia,* with its singular clover-like blossoms and vetch-like leaves, the young shoots of which form such tender and delicious greens for the Indians; the "Evening Primrose," *Œnothera biennis,* that brightens the meadows at eventide with its golden eyes of glory, but which closes when the sun looks too steadfastly into them at midday; or its dark-purplish rose-colored twin sister, the *Godetia,* that forsakes the moist meadow land to grow on sandy slopes. But there is such a fascinating charm in these delicate creations that one may be easily tempted to linger too long in their delightful company.

THE FERNS OF YO SEMITE AND ITS SURROUNDING MOUNTAINS.

Mr. J. G. Lemmon, of Oakland, and his talented wife, who have made this interesting family a loving and special study, have kindly sent me the following carefully prepared list of those found here:—

Common Polypody, *Polypodium vulgare;* California Polypody, *P. Californicum;* California Lip Fern, *Cheilanthes Californica;* Graceful Lip Fern, *C. gracillima;* Many-leaved Lip Fern, *C. myriophylla;* (Prof.) Brewer's Cliff-brake, *Pellœa Breweri;* Heather-leaved Cliff-brake, *Pellœa andromedœfolia;* Wright's Cliff-brake, *Pellœa Wrightiana;* Short-winged Cliff-brake, *Pellœa brachyptera;* Bird-foot Cliff-brake, *Pellœa ornithopus;* Dwarf Cliff-brake, *Pellœa densa;* Bridges' Cliff-brake, *Pellœa Bridgesii;* Rock-brake, *Cryptogramme acrostichoides;* Common bracken, *Pteris aquilina,* var. *lanuginosa;* Venus' hair, *Adiantum Capillus-veneris;* California Maiden hair, *Adiantum emarginatum;* Foot-stalked Maiden hair, *Adiantum pedatum;* Greek Chain fern, *Woodwardia radicans;* Lady fern, *Asplenium Filixfœmina;* Alpine Beech fern, *Phegopteris alpestris;* Rough Shield fern, *Aspidium rigidum,* var. *argutum;* Armed Shield fern, *Aspidium munitum;* Naked Shield fern, *Aspidium munitum,* var. *nudatum;* Over-lapped Shield fern, *Aspidium munitum,* var. *imbricans;* Sharp-leaved Shield fern, *Aspidium aculeatum;*

Sierra Shield fern, *Aspidium aculeatum,* var. *scopulorum;* Delicate Cup fern, *Cystopteris fragilis;* Hairy Woodsia, *Woodsia scopulina;* Oregon Woodsia, *Woodsia Oregana.*

FERN ALLIES.

Simple Grape fern, *Botrychium simplex;* Southern three-parted Grape fern, *Botrychiumternatum,* var. *australe;* Virginia Grape fern, *Botrychium Virginianum;* Common Adder tongue, *Ophioglossum vulgatum.*

To those who are interested in this attractive family, the above complete synopsis, which embraces every species and variety yet found within and around the Valley, will be especially acceptable

TROUT-FISHING.

"Are there trout in that pellucid and beautiful stream flowing past us?" inquired a somewhat fancifully dressed young gentleman with a *distingue* air, equipped with the latest patented fishing-rod, and a large book well filled with flies of the most approved color and pattern.

"Yes, sir, speckled mountain trout. There are but two kinds of fish found in this river, or in any of its tributaries, speckled trout and sucker; the former swim near the surface, ready to catch the first fly that comes along, and the latter float near the bottom of the stream, upon the lookout for worms, or offal of any kind that may be drifting down. Trout, as you find, are a delicious table fish; but no one, except Indians, will think of eating sucker."

"Is there any good place near here for a little sport of that kind? as I think I should like to try my hand at that sort of thing, you know."

"Oh! yes, almost anywhere; they are just where you can see and find them; but, if they should *see you first* you had better move on to the next pool or riffle, as you would be wasting your time there."

"Oh! I thank you very much, as trout-fishing is such delightful sport, you know."

Apparently full of ruminating anticipation, our hero of the

rod and line sauntered leisurely along, occasionally testing the
flexibility of his pole by whipping it after some imaginary trout,
until he disappeared behind a clump of young cottonwoods, to
be seen no more until dinner-time. But "when the evening
shades prevail"-ed, the would-be disciple of Isaac Walton could
be seen advancing slowly, and somewhat disconsolately, towards
the hotel, with one small, deluded trout dangling at the end of
a twig. Simultaneously, as if with mischievous "malice
aforethought," an Indian walked briskly up with about as large
a string of trout as he could conveniently carry. Now this was
the additional feather that broke the camel's back, and our crest-
fallen friend looked bewildered and dumbfounded. Placing his
solitary eyeglass firmly in front of his left eye, he fixed the
discomfited gaze of that one eye (glass) alternately upon the
Indian, and then upon the successful "catch" that was hanging at
the Indian's side; and as soon as he could discover that he could
find a voice, he falteringly inquired, "What do you use for bait?"

.Nature·versus·Art.

An artist friend being present, made the accompanying graphic sketch of this soul-harrowing scene.

The general absence here of what is termed "good luck" among anglers, has fabricated the trite aphorism among visitors that, "It takes an Indian to catch trout at Yo Semite." And this is in a great measure true; yet, it must not be supposed that his uniform success in the art is altogether attributable to his superior skill. By no means. It is to be accredited more to his knowledge of the haunts and habits of trout, which that wonderful mother, Necessity, has persistently taught him from childhood; and by which he learns where to find them at the different seasons of the year, and in the varying stages of water. This is an advantage that is unshared by the stranger. Then, the old proverb, that "practice makes perfect," has not a little to do with an Indian's invariable success, especially as his bread and dinner depend upon it. Admitting, however, that skill and practice go hand in hand with an Indian, to bring fish to his string, I have seen white adepts in the art that could largely discount an Indian's best efforts.

The most matter-of-fact manner of catching trout among unskilled and unpracticed anglers, is, to cover up the hook completely with a good-sized worm, and then cause it to float gently down to where he can see some suckers apparently resting on the bottom of the stream; and, when he sees the tempting morsel fairly in the mouth of his intended victim, to suddenly jerk in the line. Thus captured the sucker is laid carefully away until night-fall, when he is cut up into pieces about a quarter of an inch in thickness and half an inch square; and which, when placed snugly on the hook, become an inviting bait to trout, which it readily seizes, and is himself seized in turn, to supply breakfast for the angler and his guests. Good fishing places, free from roots and sticks, and well stocked with trout, should be sought quietly out in the day-time.

In early days the Indians fished only with the spear (in which some were adepts), and with the worm; but in these latter days they avail themselves of the lessons taught them by the whites, of using sucker as bait, and fishing at night; by which they are enabled to bring such large strings of trout to the hotels, for which they invariably receive twenty-five cents per pound.

As it is reasonably presumable that every one before starting out upon any of the many interesting trips within and around the Valley, will be desirous of ascertaining not only their particular direction and location, but the distances thereto, the following tables, and accompanying map, are herewith submitted.

BASIS OF MEASUREMENTS.

Before setting out upon any of our excursions around or beyond the Valley, it seems desirable to state that, according to Lieutenant Wheeler's U. S. Survey, from which much of this data concerning altitudes here is taken, its elevation above sea level as computed from the floor of the upper iron bridge, near Barnard's, is three thousand nine hundred and thirty-four feet; and that all the measurements of the cliffs and water-falls about the Valley are calculated from this basis, except where otherwise stated.

For the purpose of enabling visitors to make their respective jaunts understandingly, I have thought it desirable to present the various points of interest somewhat in detail, and in the order they are generally preferred to be seen; but which order can, of course, be changed according to circumstances, or to individual taste and preference. With the reader's permission, therefore, we will suppose that we are now prepared to set out upon our glorious pilgrimage among the marvelous scenes which surround us, and are standing upon the floor of the upper iron bridge, three thousand nine hundred and thirty-four feet above sea level, and looking into the transparent waters of

THE MERCED RIVER.

This musical and suggestive name was given to it by the old Spanish padres, by whom it was called *Rio de la Merced*,[1] the River of Mercy. And, by the way, we are much indebted to the poetical taste of those old missionaries for a number of apposite

1. The expedition under Gabriel Moraga, including the diarist Fray Pedro Muñoz, crossed the river in the San Joaquin Valley and named it *El Rio de Nuestra Señora de la Merced* on September 29, 1806, five days after the feast day of Our Lady of Mercy.

TABLE OF DISTANCES.

From the Guardian's Office, near the Upper Iron Bridge, to Different Points of Interest in and Around Yo Semite Valley, California.

POINTS OF INTEREST.	Between Consecutive Points.	From Guardian's Office.	To Guardian's Office.	Altitude in feet above Yo Semite.	Altitude in feet above Sea Level.
To Mirror Lake (by carriage road).	....	....	2.91	....	3,934
From Guardian's Office to —					
Indian Cañon Bridge	0.65	0.65	2.26	....	.....
Harris' Residence	0.56	1.21	1.70	....	.....
Forks of Tis-sa-ack Avenue Road	0.95	2.16	0.75		
Mirror Lake	0.75	2.91	......	174	4,108
If the return is made via Tis-sa-ack Avenue, the distances from Mirror Lake are—	....	....	3.70	....	.....
Upper Forks of Tis-sa-ack Avenue Road	0.61	0.61	3.09	....	.....
Ten-ie-ya Creek Bridge	0.17	0.78	2.92	....	.....
Tis-sa-ack Bridge	0.89	1.67	2.03	....	.....
Guardian's Office	2.03	3.70	....	....	3,934
Tis-sa-ack Avenue Drive.	....	....	5.18	....	.....
From Guardian's Office to—					
Tis-sa-ack Bridge	2.03	2.03	3.15	....	.....
Ten-ie-ya Bridge	0.89	2.92	2.26	....	.....
Harris' Residence	1.05	3.97	1.21	....	.....
Guardian's Office	1.21	5.18	....	....	3,934
To Bridal Veil Fall, Artist Point, and New Inspiration Point (by carriage road)— From Guardian's Office to—	....	....	7.19	....	.....
Cathedral Spires Bridge	2.50	2.50	4.69	....	.....
El Capitan (lower iron) Bridge	1.13	3.63	3.56	....	3,925
Bridal Veil Fall	0.41	4.04	3.15	....	.....
Forks of Pohono Avenue Road	0.28	4.32	2.87	....	.....
Artist Point	1.48	5.80	1.39	800	4,651
Cabin	0.43	6.23	0.96	1,000	4,851
New Inspiration Point	0.96	7.19	....	1,500	5,371
To the Cascade Falls (by carriage road). From Guardian's Office to—	....	....	7.67	....	.....
Forks of Big Oak Flat Road	3.66	3.66	4.01	....	3,944
Black Springs	0.69	4.35	3.32	....	.....
River View	0.19	4.54	3.13	....	.....
Pohono Bridge	1.29	4.83	2.84	....	.....
Cascade Falls	2.84	7.67	....	....	3,225
The Pohono Avenue Drive. From Guardian's Office to—	....	....	10.45	....	.....
Yo Semite Creek Bridge	0.49	0.49	9.96	....	.....
Rocky Point	0.96	1.45	9.00	....	.....
Indian Camp	0.37	1.82	8.63	....	.....
Ribbon Fall	2.17	3.99	6.46	....	.....
Forks of Big Oak Flat Road	0.07	4.06	6.39	....	3,949
Black Springs	0.69	4.75	5.70	....	.....
River View	0.25	5.00	5.45	....	.....
Pohono Bridge	0.29	5.29	5.16	....	.....
Fern Spring	0.19	5.48	4.97	....	.....
Moss Spring	0.06	5.54	4.91	....	.....
Forks of Big Tree Station Road	0.59	6.13	4.32	....	.....
Bridal Veil Fall	0.28	6.41	4.04	....	.....

TABLE OF DISTANCES—Continued.

POINTS OF INTEREST.	Between Consecutive Points.	From Guardian's Office.	To Guardian's Office....	Altitude in feet above Yo Semite Valley....	Altitude in feet above Sea Level....
El Capitan Bridge	0.41	6.82	3.36	.....	3,925
Cathedral Spires Bridge	1.13	7.95	2.50	.....	.....
Leidig's Hotel	1.43	9.38	1,07	.....	3,934
Cook's Hotel	0.30	9.68	0.77	.....	3,934
Cosmopolitan Billiard Hall	0.73	10.41	0.04	.....	3,934
Barnard's Hotel	0.04	10.45	.....	.....	3,934
The Round Drive on the Floor of the Valley.					
From Guardian's Office, via Merced, Ten-ie-ya, Yo Semite, and Pohono Bridges, and back	15.06	.....	.....	.....	.....
Including Mirror Lake and Cascade Falls	21.32	.....	.....	.....	.....
To Foot of Lower Yo Semite Falls.	....	.....	0.90	.....	....
From Guardian's Office to—					
Yo Semite Creek Bridge	0.49	0.49	0.41	.....	.....
Foot of Fall	0.41	0.90	.....	.....	.....
To Top of Yo Semite Fall and Eagle Peak, by Trail.	....	.....	6.59	.....	.....
From Guardian's Office to—					
Columbia Rock	1.98	1.98	4.61	1,154	5,088
Foot of Upper Yo Semite Fall	0.69	2.67	3.92	1,114	5,048
Forks of Trail for Top of Yo Semite Fall	1.21	3.88	2.74	.....	.....
Top of Yo Semite Fall	0.45	4.33	2.26	2,550	6,484
Eagle Meadow	1.36	5.69	0.90	.....	.....
Eagle Peak	0.90	6.59	.....	3,818	7,752
To Snow's Hotel, by Trail.	....	.....	4.63	.....	.....
(Between the Vernal and Nevada Falls.)					
From Guardian's Office to—					
Opposite Merced Bridge	2.02	2.02	2.61	.....	.....
Too-lool-a-we-ack (South Branch) Bridge	0.60	2.62	2.01	.....	.....
Register Rock	0.62	3.24	1.39	.....	.....
Snow's Hotel	1.39	4.63	.....	1,366	5,300
If the return is made via Glacier Point, the distance from Snow's will be:	....	.....	12.35	.....	.....
Bridge, above the Nevada Fall	0.82	0.82	11.53	.....	.....
Glacier Point	7.08	7.90	4.45	3,257	7,191
Guardian's Office	4.45	12.35	.....	.....	3,934
To Glacier Point and Sentinel Dome, by Trail	....	.....	5.57	.....	.....
From Guardian's Office to—					
Cook's Hotel	0.77	0.77	4.80	.....	3,934
Foot of Glacier Point Trail	0.27	1.04	4.53	.....	.....
Union Point	2.09	3.13	2.44	2,356	6,290
Glacier Point	1.32	4.45	1.12	3,257	7,191
Sentinel Dome	1.12	5.57	.....	.....	.....
If the return is made via Snow's Hotel, the distances from Glacier Point are:	....	.....	12.53	.....	.....
Bridge, above the Nevada Fall	7.08	7.08	5.45	.....	.....
Snow's Hotel	0.82	7.90	4.63	1,366	5,300
Guardian's Office	4.63	12.53	.....	.....	3,934

TABLE OF DISTANCES—Continued.

POINTS OF INTEREST.	Between Consecutive Points.	From Guardian's Office.	To Guardian's Office.	Altitude in feet above Yo Semite Valley.	Altitude in feet above Sea Level.
To Summit of South Dome, by trail.	....	....	10.00	....	.....
From Guardian's Office to—					
Snow's Hotel	4.63	4.63	5.37	1,366	5,300
Forks of Glacier Point Trail	0.82	5.45	4.55	....	.....
Forks of Cloud's Rest Trail	2.58	8.03	1.97	....	.....
Anderson's Cabin	0.60	8.63	1.37	3,514	7,448
Foot of Lower Dome	1.00	9.63	0.37	3,964	7,898
Top of Lower Dome	0.19	9.82	0.18	4,530	8,404
Top of South Dome	0.18	10.00	....	4,953	8,887
To Summit of Cloud's Rest, by trail.	....	....	11.81	....	.....
From Guardian's Office to—					
Snow's Hotel	4.63	4.63	7.18	1,366	5,300
Forks of South Dome Trail	3.40	8.03	3.78	....	.....
Hopkin's Meadow	1.26	9.29	2.52	4,339	8,273
Summit of Cloud's Rest	2.52	11.81	....	5,921	9,885
To Soda Springs and Summit of Mt. Dana by trail.	....	....	40.34	....	.....
From Guardian's Office to—					
Snow's Hotel	4.63	4.63	35.71	1,366	5,300
Forks of Cloud's Rest Trail	4.44	9.07	31.27	....	.....
Top of Sunrise Ridge	3.23	12.30	28.04	5,648	9,582
Cathedral Meadow Ridge	5.20	17.50	22.84	....	.....
Forks of Lake Ten-ie-ya Trail, Tuolumne Meadows	4.14	21.64	18.70	4,724	8,658
Soda Springs	0.90	22.54	17.80	4,737	8,671
Junction of Mt. Dana and Mt. Lyell Creeks	0.70	23.24	17.10	....	.....
Camping ground for Mt. Dana	8.90	32.14	8.20	5,849	9,783
Saddle, between Mt. Gibbs and Mt. Dana	5.20	37.34	3.00	7,759	11,963
Summit of Mt. Dana	3.00	40.34	....	9,376	13,310
To Summit of Mt. Lyell, by trail.	....	....	38.20	....	.....
From Guardian's Office to—					
Soda Springs	22.54	22.54	15.66	4,624	8,558
Forks of Mt. Dana Trail	0.60	23.14	15.06	....	.....
Head of Tuolumne Meadows	9.41	32.55	5.65	5,098	9,032
Summit of Mt. Lyell	5.65	38.20	....	9,340	13,274
To Soda Springs, via the Eagle Peak and Lake Ten-ie-ya Trail, by trail.	....	....	24.50	....	.....
From Guardian's Office to—					
Forks of Eagle Peak Trail	4.64	4.64	19.86	3,219	7,153
Forks of Mono Trail	1.36	6.00	18.50	....	.....
Lake Ten-ie-ya	10.00	16.00	8.50	4,120	8,054
Soda Springs	8.50	24.50	....	....	8,671
To the Summit of the Obelisk, or Mt. Clark, by trail.	....	....	15.82	....	.....
From Guardian's Office to—					
Glacier Point	4.45	4.45	11.37	3,257	7,191
Too-lool-a-we-ack Creek	2.12	6.57	9.25	....	.....
Camping Ground	7.00	13.57	2.25	6,179	10,113
Summit of Obelisk	2.25	15.82	....	7,444	11,378

names that embellish the California map; such, for instance, as the *Rio de Sacramento*, the River of the Sacrament; *Rio de las Plumas*, the River of Feathers; *Ciudad Los Angeles*, the City of the Angels, and many others. The view, easterly, reveals the "Half Dome," framed by a vista of overarching pines, cedars, oaks, and balm of gileads, that stand on the margin of the river; westerly the lofty, sky-piercing crest of "Eagle Peak" is seen through a similar portal, about both of which more will be said hereafter.

COMPREHENSIVE PANORAMA FROM MEADOW AVENUE.

When about midway of the avenue, which here crosses the meadow, directly in front of us, looking northerly, "Yo Semite Point" stands boldly out, the apex of which is three thousand two hundred and twenty feet above us, and the view from which, looking down into the Valley, is very impressive. This, when associated with the Giant's Thumb, is called by the Indians, "Hum-moo," or the Lost Arrow, and connected with which is the following characteristic

LEGEND OF THE LOST ARROW.

Tee-hee-neh was among the fairest and most beautiful of the daughters of Ah-wah-ne. Her tall yet symmetrically rounded form was as erect as the silver firs, and as supple as the tamarack pines. The delicately tapering fingers of her small hand were, if possible, prettier than those of other Indian maidens; and the arched instep of her slender foot was as flexile as the azalea when shake by the wind. The tresses of her raven hair, unlike that of her companions, was as silky as the milkweed's floss, and depended from her well-poised head to her ankles. Her movements were as graceful and agile as the bound of a fawn. When she stepped forth from her wigwam in the early morning, accompanied by other damsels of her tribe, to seek the mirrored river and make her unpretentious toilet, there can be but little wonder that the admiring gaze of captivated young chiefs, and the envious looks of less favored lassies, should follow her every footstep.

Then, knowing this, who could wonder at, or blame, the noble Kos-soo-kah,—the tallest, strongest, swiftest-footed, bravest and most handsome in form and face, of all the young Ah-wah-ne chiefs,—for allowing the silken meshes of devoted love to intertwine around his heart, and bring him a willing captive to her feet? Or marvel that the early spring flowers which she plucked for him were always the most redolent with perfume? Or that the wild strawberries which she picked, and the wild plums that she gathered, were ever the sweetest, because transfused by love? Then, who could censure him for not resisting the silvery sweetness of her musical voice, when she raised it in song by the evening camp-fire; or, for not withstanding the fascinations of her merry laugh, as its liquid cadences rung out at night-fall upon the air, when every note was in delicious and accordant sympathy with the pulsations of his own glad heart?

And that which filled both their souls with an intense and beatified joy was the consciousness that the tender passion was unreservedly reciprocated by each. Nothing, therefore, remained, but to select becoming presents for the parents of the bride, in accordance with Indian custom,* provide a sumptuous repast, and celebrate their auspicious nuptials with appropriate ceremonies. To do this, Tee-hee-neh and her companions would prepare the acorn bread, collect ripe wild fruits and edible herbs in liberal abundance, and garnish them with fragrant flowers; while Kos-soo-kah, pressing the best hunters of his tribe into his service, should scale the adjacent cliffs for grouse, and deer, that right royal might be the feast.

Before taking their fond and long-lingering adieus, it was agreed that Kos-soo-kah, at sunset, should go to the edge of the mountain north of Cholock,† and report the measure of his success to Tee-hee-neh (who was to climb to its foot to receive it), by fastening the requisite number of grouse feathers to an arrow thereby to indicate the quantity taken; and from his

* See chapter on Indian manners, customs, etc.

† The Yo Semite Fall.

strong bow shoot it far out that she might see it, and watch for its falling, and thus be the first to report the good tidings of his success to her people.

After a most fortunate hunt, while his young braves were resting, preparatory to the exacting task of carrying down their game, Kos-soo-kah repaired to the point agreed upon, prepared the arrow for its tender mission, and was about to send it forth, when the edge of the cliff began to crumble away, carrying the noble Kos-soo-kah with it.

Long did the loving Tee-hee-neh wait, and longingly watch for the signal; nor would she leave her watchful post for many weary hours after darkness had settled down upon the mountain, although restless premonitions and forebodings were bringing a deeper darkness to her heart, that were intensified by the sounds of falling rock she had heard. But thinking, at last, that his ambitious wishes might have tempted him to wander farther than he had intended, and finding that his signal-arrow could not be seen in the darkness, at that very moment he might be feeling his uncertain way among the blocks of rock that strewed the Indian Cañon, down which he was to come; that possibility gave wings to her thoughts, and speed to her tripping feet, as she hurriedly picked her difficult way from ledge to ledge; passing this precipice, lowering herself rapidly over that, where a misstep must necessarily have proven fatal, until at last she reached the foot of the cliff.

Finding upon her advent there that her beloved Kos-soo-kah had not yet arrived, her anxious yearnings for his safe return, made more poignant by a kind of uncontrollable prescience, led her to the spot where he must first emerge. Hoping against hope, she could hear as well as feel the beatings of her own sad heart, as she listened through the lagging hours for the sound of his welcome footfall, or manly voice. And as she impatiently waited, pacing the hot sand backwards and forwards, she sang in the low, sweet, yet impassioned cadences peculiar to her race, that which, when translated, should be substantially rendered as follows:—

"Come to the heart that loves thee;
  To the eyes that beam in brightness but to gladden thine;
Come, where fond thoughts in holiest incense rise;
  And cherished memory rears her altar-shrine.
Dearest—come home!"

But, alas! finding that when the dark gray dawn of earliest morning brought not her beloved one, like a deer she sprang from rock to rock up the steep ascent, not pausing even for breath, nor delaying a moment for rest; she hastened towards the spot whence the expected signal was to be given. Tracks—his blessed tracks—could be distinctly seen, and followed to the mountain's edge; but, alas, not one was visible to indicate his return therefrom. When she called, only the echo of her own sad voice returned an answer. Where could he be? The marks of a new fracture of the mountain disclosed the fact that a portion had recently broken off; and memory, at once, recalled the sounds that she had heard, when on the ledge below. It could not be that her heart-cherished Kos-soo-kah could have been standing there at the time of its fall! Oh! No. The Great Spirit would not be so unmindful of her burning love for him as to permit that. With agonized dread she summoned sufficient courage to peer over the edge of the cliff, and the lifeless and ghastly form of her darling was seen lying in the hollow, near that which has since been designated the Giant's Thumb.

Spontaneously acting with a clearness and strength that despair will sometimes give, she kindled a bright fire upon the very edge of the mountain, that thereby she might telegraph her wants and wishes to those below, in accordance with a custom that every Indian learns to practice from childhood;* and slow as the hours ebbed away, the entreated relief came at last, for the hoped-for recovery of her soul's jewel, even though now sleeping in the cold embrace of death. Young sapling tamaracks were lashed endwise together, with thongs cut from the skin of the deer that were to form part of the wedding feast; and, when these

* See pages 25, 26.

were ready, Tee-hee-neh, springing forward, would permit no hands but her own to be the first to touch the beloved one. She would descend to recover him, or perish in the attempt. Finding that no amount of persuasion could change her resolve they reluctantly, yet carefully, lowered her to the prostrate form of Kos-soo-kah; and, as though strength of purpose had converted her nerves into steel, defiant of all danger, she first kissed his pale lips, then unwound the deer-skin cords from around her body, fastened them lovingly, yet firmly, to his, and gave the signal for uplifting him to the top. This accomplished, gently, yet efficiently, a reverent anxiety could be seen engraved upon the faces of those performing that kindly act, for the safe deliverance of the heroic Tee-hee-neh; but, the same undismayed fearlessness, and apparent nerve, that had enabled her to descend, did not forsake her now, and before the self-imposed task she had so unfalteringly set herself had been accomplished. Firmly fastening her foot, to prevent slipping, without other support or protection, she nervously clutched the pole with one hand, and as a signal of her wishes waved the other; and in a few moments was again at the side of her adored, though lifeless, Kos-soo-kah. Silently, tearlessly, she looked for a moment into those eyes that love had once lighted, and at the colorless lips from which she had so delectably sipped the nectar of her earthly bliss; then, noiselessly, quiveringly, sinking to her knees, she fell upon his bosom; and, when lifted by gentle hands a few moments thereafter, it was discovered that her spirit had joined that of her Kos-soo-kah, in the hunting grounds of the hereafter. She had died of a broken heart.

As the arrow that had so unexpectedly, yet so ruthlessly, brought on this double calamity, could never be found, it is believed that it was spirited away by the reunited Tee-hee-neh and Kos-soo-kah, to be sacredly kept as a memento of their undying love. The heavenward-pointed thumb, still standing there, in the hollow near which Kos-soo-kah's body was found, is ever reverently known among all the sons and daughters of Ah-wah-nee, as Hum-moo, or "The Lost Arrow."

Photo by C. Roach   NPS, Yosemite Collections

NORTH DOME, ROYAL ARCHES, AND WASHINGTON TOWER

I believe that the photographer's name is correctly Thomas C. Roche.
The photograph is the model for the engraving on page 384.
It was published as a stereo view by E. & H. T. Anthony.

Photo by Charles L. Weed · Peter E. Palmquist

Indian Cañon

Half of a stereo made in June 1859. This is the model
for the engraving on the opposite page.
Published by E. and H. T. Anthony.

On the right of Hum-Moo, or Yo Semite Point, is Indian Cañon.

It was up this cañon that the Indian prisoners escaped in 1851, as related in Chapter V, pages 68, 69; from which circumstance originated the name; and it was down this that the avenging Monos crept, when they substantially exterminated the Yo

INDIAN CAÑON.

Semite tribe in 1853, as recorded in Chapter VI, pages 76, 77, and 78. This cañon, therefore, is invested with historical interest. For the purpose of enabling visitors to obtain views of the sublime scenery of the Sierras from the high ridge westerly from the crest of Yo Semite Point, and look upon the top of the Yo Semite

Fall, before making its leap into the Valley, the writer had a horse-trail constructed up it, in 1870. The small stream leaping in at the side is called the Little Winkle.

Bearing to the right from this standpoint can be seen the North Dome, beneath which are the Royal Arches and Washington Tower; and, following in succession, are the Half Dome, Grizzly Peak, Mount Starr King, Glacier Point, Union Point, the Sentinel, Cathedral Peaks, Eagle Peak, Eagle Tower, and the Yo Semite Fall, all forming a glorious panorama of Valley celebrities. But, advancing toward the latter, on our right we pass the orchard, the Hutchings' cabin (described in Chapter XI, pages 138, 139, 140 and 141), and are soon at the Yo Semite Creek Bridge, and can there see the large volume of water that forms

THE YO SEMITE FALL.

Looking at the full stream that is hurrying on, in the early spring at least, we can scarcely realize that all this water has just made the leap of nearly two thousand six hundred feet; or that the apparently small fall we had seen from the opposite side of the Valley, could develop into so imposing a spectacle. Noticing this on a recent occasion, when in company with a civil engineer, the inquiry was made, "About how much water do you suppose there is now rolling over the edge of that mountain yonder, judging from the size and speed of this stream?" "I will tell you this evening," was the prompt rejoinder. At the promised time I received the following:—

When at the little red bridge which spans the stream, which I understood you to be supplied entirely by the Yo Semite Fall, this afternoon, I made a rough measurement of the quantity of water flowing, and found it to be as follows: Width 40 feet, mean depth 5 feet, mean velocity about 4 feet per second. Quantity 40x5x4=800 cubic feet per second, or about 6,000 gallons per second.

I understood you to say that you had found the width of the stream at the top of the Yo Semite Fall to be 34 feet. If the velocity there be 15 feet per second, this quantity would require a mean depth of 1 foot 7 inches.   Very respectfully yours,

HIRAM F. MILLS, *Civil Engineer.*

Before advancing far beyond the Yo Semite Creek Bridge, let me call attention to an apparently small pine tree that stands alone, at the top of the shrub-covered slope that extends to the foot of the upper Yo Semite Fall wall, and seemingly beneath it. Now that tree, small as it appears, by careful measurement is a little over one hundred and twenty-five feet in height, by eight feet seven inches in circumference. By noticing the comparatively insignificant proportions of that tree, we may be assisted in comprehending the otherwise unrealized altitudes of these immense cliffs. The large pine growing on the ledge below that, had a circumference, at the base, of twelve feet nine inches. Hum-moo, or the Giant's Thumb, stands prominently up and out when seen from this standpoint; and whose height is said to be two hundred and three feet above the hollow where Kos-soo-kah's body was reputed to be found, according to the legend of the Lost Arrow.

FOOT OF THE LOWER YO SEMITE FALL.

The nearer we approach the Yo Semite Fall, the more fully do we realize its astonishing attractions. Those who content themselves by viewing this magnificent scene only at a distance, must have about the same apprehension of its impressive attraction as they would of a very beautiful woman, or handsome man, when seen about half a mile off. The same comparison will appositely apply to seeing the Vernal and Nevada Falls *only* from Glacier Point. It is *nearness* that places us in appreciative communion with Nature and her manifold and unspeakable glories. I have accompanied hundreds, aye, thousands, to the foot of the Lower Yo Semite Fall, and this, without an exception, has been the spontaneous confession of every one. So that every step that we take after crossing the Yo Semite Creek Bridge puts us into closer relationship with the impressive majesty of this wonderful fall. "How it *grows* upon us," is a most frequent ejaculation that is born of apprehensive and appreciative feeling. How we watch the bold leap that it is making over the cliff, more than two thousand five hundred feet above our heads, and follow the

vaulting masses of its rocket-shaped and foaming waters with
the eye, down to the seething caldron into which it bounds, at
the base of the upper fall; its eddying mists fringed by the sun
with iridescent colors, that are constantly changing and reform-
ing. At the right of the fall, just below its crest, a dark mass of
shadow reveals the portrait of the "Gnome of the Yo Semite,"
with his badge of rank hanging across the shoulder.

The oaks, dogwoods, alders, pines, and cedars now begin to

Photo by C. L. Weed.

VALLEY FORD OF THE YO SEMITE.

form an arcade of great beauty over the sparkling, rippling,
foaming, singing, bowlder-strewn foreground of the stream;
while in the background the lower Yo Semite is leaping down in
one broad sheet of white sheen, the main body of which seems

composed of immense icicles fringed with snow, falling from behind a dark middle distance of pines and firs. If the snow fields
are rapidly melting beneath the fiery strength of a hot summer's
sun, a large body of water will be seen rushing and bounding
over and among blocks of granite; then, spreading out afterwards, to form numerous streams that can readily be forded, if
the ford is prudently selected, and thus afford a strikingly picturesque scene.

It must not be supposed that the cloud-like spray that descends is the main fall itself, broken into infinitesimal particles
and thus becomes nothing but a broad sheet of cloud. By no
means; for, although this stream shoots over the margin of the
mountain, nearly five hundred feet above, it falls almost in a
solid body; not in a continuous stream exactly, but having a close
resemblance to an avalanche of snowy rockets that appear to be
perpetually trying to overtake each other in their descent, and
commingling one with the other, compose a torrent of indescribable power and beauty.

As we advance, a change of temperature becomes very perceptible, so that the warmth experienced in the open Valley upon
the way, is gradually changed to chilliness. Soon we feel that a
breeze, about equal in strength to eight knots an hour, is meeting
us directly in the face, and bringing with it a heavy shower
of finely comminuted spray, that falls with sufficient force to
saturate our clothing in a few moments. From this a beautiful
phenomenon is observable, inasmuch as, after striking our hats,
the diamond-like mist shoots off at an angle of about thirty-five or
forty degrees, and as the sun shines upon it, a number of miniature rainbows are formed all around us. In early days, when
conveniences were few, this cold draught of air was pressed into
service as a meat-safe, and answered very well, in the absence
of all others. The philosophy which explains the cause of this
cold current is, that the water-fall leaping into the air naturally
displaces it by driving it downward, and thus creates a vacuum;
and the air from above rushing in to fill that vacuum, causes this

constant wind. It will be noticed that even the trees which stand in the current are prevented from forming branches on their windward side. It will also be noticed that the trunks of these trees are denuded of branches for from fifty to eighty feet up them; the cause of which, probably, arises from the heavy deposits of snow which form here during some winters (I have crossed bridges of snow here that were over seventy feet in thickness), and as its melting is mainly from beneath, when the snow settles down it breaks off all the branches, and carries them down with it.

Drawing still nearer, large masses of sharp, angular rocks, are scattered here and there, forming the uneven sides of an immense and apparently ever-boiling caldron; around, and in the interstices of which numerous dwarf ferns, weeds, grasses, and flowers are ever growing; where not actually washed by the falling stream. Hastily rushing through the spray, and taking shelter behind a buttress of the mountain, we can see two of the divisions which make this water-fall apparently forming into one.

It is beyond the power of language to describe the awe-inspiring majesty of the darkly frowning and overhanging mountain walls of solid granite that here hem us in on every side, as though they would threaten us with instantaneous annihilation, did we for a moment attempt to deny their power. If man ever feels his utter insignificance, it is when looking upon such a scene of appalling grandeur as the one here presented.

The point whence the photograph was taken from which the accompanying engraving was made, being directly near the foot of the lower fall, might lead to the supposition that the lower section, embracing, as it does, about three-fourths of the whole, was the highest of the two, when the relative heights of the three are, as given by

PROF. J. D. WHITNEY, *State Geologist:*		LIEUTENANT WHEELER, *U. S. Survey.*	
Upper Fall	1,500	Upper Fall	1,436
Middle (including cascades)	626	Middle (including cascades)	626
Lower	400	Lower	488
Total	2,526	Total	2,550

But Professor Whitney makes this observation:—

Photo. by S. C. Walker.   Photo-Typo by Britton & Rey, S. F.

HALF DOME AND CLOUDS' REST, FROM GLACIER POINT.
Men standing on a precipice of 3,257 feet.
(See page 469.)
Facing page 400 in all editions.

Photo by Charles L. Weed   NPS, Yosemite Collections

NEAR VIEW OF YO SEMITE FALL

The first photograph ever taken in Yosemite Valley, on June 18, 1859.
See the engraving on the opposite page, the upper portion of which was
derived from this photograph. This is half of a stereo view published
by E. & H. T. Anthony.

Photo by C. L. Weed.

NEAR VIEW OF YO SEMITE FALL.

The vertical height of the lip of the fall above the Valley is, in round numbers, 2,600 feet, our various measurements giving from 2,537 to 2,641, the discrepancies being due to the fact that a near approach to, or a precise definition of, the place where the perpendicular portion of the fall commences is not possible. The lip or edge of the fall is a great rounded mass of granite, polished to the last degree, on which it was found to be a hazardous matter to move. A difference of a hundred feet, in a fall of this height, would be entirely imperceptible to most eyes.

The stream which forms this fall flows mainly from the melting snows near Mt. Hoffmann, some eighteen miles distant. When the trip is taken to Eagle Peak, as the trail passes sufficiently close to the foot of the upper Yo Semite Fall to afford the opportunity of a closer examination, we can then see more of its varied and interesting features.

JAUNT TO MIRROR LAKE.

This is one of the most delightful and most satisfying of pilgrimages that could possibly be made within the walls of the Valley; but, to see the lake at its best, when the reflected shadows are strongest, and the beautiful mirror upon its glassy bosom is in the greatest perfection, it should be seen before the sun rises upon it. This will enable the visitor to witness the interesting phenomena of "sunrise on the lake," and afford the opportunity of its repetition several times on the same morning! Between ten and twelve A. M., the sea breeze generally sweeps across it, and breaks the mirror into as many pieces as there are ripples upon it. Therefore make the visit early, say about seven o'clock; but this, of course, differs according to the season of the year; yet the proper time for leaving the hotel can always be ascertained from the landlord, or from the carriage proprietors. On account of the early time desirable for setting out on this trip, it is better to postpone it until the second day after arrival, as a premature departure from our couch on the succeeding morning of our advent, will generally bring on premature fatigue, and a consequent decrease in the amount of our enjoyment.

Leaving the hotel early, then, we cross Meadow Avenue to

the oak-studded low ridge on the northern side, and threading our way through the grove, have glimpses of our unspeakably sublime surroundings from between the trees. On our left we pass the revered spot where dear ones are sleeping; and soon find ourselves at the old Indian camp ground, near Indian Cañon; the bright sunlight and somber shadows winking and twinkling from between the trees, upon the gurgling streams that intersect the road. While on our right lie luxuriant green fields, first fenced and cultivated by Mr. J. C. Lamon; and the old cabin where he once spent his winters, as narrated on page 137. These are now occupied, and well cared for, by Mr. A. Harris and family.

ROYAL ARCHES, AND WASHINGTON TOWER.

But a few yards beyond these we cross the streams that form the Royal Arch Cascades, a diamond-lighted, wavy, musical rivulet, that drops gently down some two thousand feet over the Royal Arch wall. This is so called from the immense arches that are hewed out of its side, which have a span of over a quarter of a mile, and a height of about one thousand seven hundred feet; and which, with the Washington Tower, form the base of the great North Dome, represented in the engraving.

The Indian name of this arch-formed and dome-crowned mountain is To-coy-æ, derived from the prominence and depth (some fifty feet) of one of its projecting conchoidal fractures, having a resemblance to a poke bonnet-like shade to the Indian baby-basket, for protecting the occupant's eyes from the sun, and which is called "to-coy-æ." Owing to the curve of these wing-like arches, stretching as they do from a kind of lion-like head, near the top of Washington Tower—as the abutting angle of this mountain is called—a gentleman resident of Philadelphia suggested that "The Winged Lion" (one of the sculptures found by Layard in the ruined cities of the Euphrates Valley) would be a more expressive and suitable name for it than "Royal Arches."

There is a large cave among the talus lying here, that was once used as a store-room by Mr. Lamon, whenever his winters

Photo by C. Roach.
NORTH DOME, ROYAL ARCHES, AND WASHINGTON TOWER.
(North Dome, 3,700 feet above Valley.)

were spent outside the Valley. Near this there is also another talus-formed cave, that is a natural fortification, and which was used as such, by the Indians, when pursued by the avenging soldiers in 1851–52. A short turn out from the road, when returning from Mirror Lake, will afford the opportunity of seeing it.

When on the road towards Mirror Lake it may not be amiss to revert to the legend recorded on page 59, as it was here the exploit occurred that gave the name of "Yo Semite" to the tribe, and afterwards to the Valley itself. Riding over rocky hillocks, and among debris that has at some time fallen from the adjacent mountains, with a park-like array of trees on either hand, we first arrive at Little Lake; and, just beyond it, the bright bosom of the enchantingly beautiful Mirror Lake comes into full view.

At first its size is slightly disappointing, but that is soon lost sight of and forgotten in admiration of its transcendent loveliness. There is not a spot on earth, yet seen by man, that so charmingly blends majesty with beauty. And as soon as the beatified first impression somewhat subsides, and we can analyze its marvelous surroundings more in detail, the stronger becomes the conviction of its unequaled charms.

In full front of us, bearing a little to the left, perhaps, stands Mount Watkins, a second El Capitan (yet loftier), that exceeds four thousand feet in height above the bosom of the lake; then comes the deep gorge through which the waters of Lake Ten-ie-ya, (some twelve miles easterly), leap from crag to pool, then gurgle among huge blocks of granite, until they reach Mirror Lake, there to become the medium of so much satisfying splendor; on the right of this stands glorious Cloud's Rest, nearly six thousand feet above the lake; and directly southeast of us towers up nearly five thousand feet the over-shadowing and lofty wall of grand "Tis-sa-ack" (Half Dome), so called in affectionate veneration for the Indian's guardian angel of the Valley, bearing that name, as will become more apparent when the accompanying legend is read.

Almost one-half of this immense mass, either from some convulsion of nature, or

"Time's effacing fingers,"

has fallen over, by which, most probably, the dam for the lake was first formed. Yet proudly, aye, defiantly erect, it still holds its noble head, and it is not only the highest of all those standing more immediately around, but is one of the greatest attractions of the Valley. Moreover, in this are centered many agreeable associations to the Indian mind, as this was once the traditionary home of the

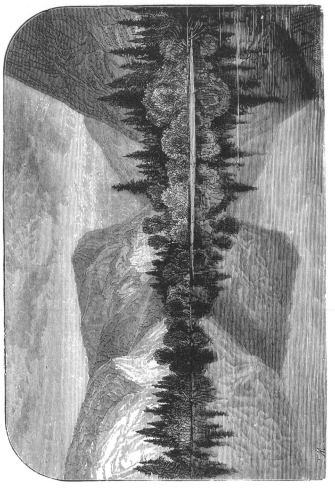

KE-KO-TOO-YEM (Sleeping Water), OR MIRROR LAKE.

angel-like and beautiful *Tis-sa-ack*, after whom her devoted Indian worshipers named this gloriously majestic mountain. While we sit in the shade of these fine old trees, and look upon all the objects around us, mirrored in the unruffled waters of the lake, let us relate the following interesting legend of Tu-tock-ah-nu-lah, after whom the vast perpendicular and massive projecting rock at the lower end of the valley was named, and with which is closely interwoven the history of Tis-sa-ack.

This legend was related in an Eastern journal, by a gentleman once visiting here, who signs himself "Iota," and who received it from the lips of an old Indian; the relation of which, although several points of interest are omitted, will, nevertheless, prove very entertaining:—

THE LEGEND OF TU-TOCK-AH-NU-LAH AND TIS-SA-ACK.

"It was in the unremembered past that the children of the sun first dwelt in Yo Semite. Then all was happiness; for Tu-tock-ah-nu-lah sat on high in his rocky home, and cared for the people whom he loved. Leaping over the upper plains, he herded the wild deer, that the people might choose the fattest for the feast. He roused the bear from his cavern in the mountain, that the brave might hunt. From his lofty rock he prayed to the Great Spirit, and brought the soft rain upon the corn in the valley. The smoke of his pipe curled into the air, and the golden sun breathed warmly through its blue haze, and ripened the crops, that the women might gather them in. When he laughed, the face of the winding river was rippled with smiles; when he sighed, the wind swept sadly through the sighing pines; if he spoke, the sound was like the deep voice of the cataract; and when he smote the far-striding bear, his whoop of triumph rang from crag to gorge— echoed from mountain to mountain. His form was straight like the arrow, and elastic like the bow. His foot was swifter than the red deer, and his eye was strong and bright like the rising sun.

"But one morning, as he roamed, a bright vision came before him, and then the soft colors of the West were in his lustrous eye. A maiden sat upon the southern granite dome that lifts its gray head among the highest peaks. She was not like the dark maidens of the tribe below, for the yellow hair rolled over her dazzling form, as golden waters over silver rocks; her brow beamed with the pale beauty of the moonlight, and her blue eyes were as the far-off hills before the sun goes down. Her little feet shone like the snow-tufts on the wintry pines, and its arch was like the spring of a bow. Two cloud-like wings wavered upon her dimpled shoulders, and her voice was as the sweet, sad tone of the night-bird of the woods.

" 'Tu-tock-ah-nu-lah,' she softly whispered; then, gliding up the rocky dome, she vanished over its rounded tops. Keen was the eye, quick was the ear, swift was the foot of the noble youth as he sped up the rugged path in pursuit; but the soft down from her snowy wings was wafted into his eyes, and he saw her no more.

"Every morning now did the enamored Tu-tock-ah-nu-lah leap the stony barriers, and wander over the mountains, to meet the lovely Tis-sa-ack. Every day he laid sweet acorns and wild flowers upon her dome. His ear caught her footstep, though it was light as the falling leaf; his eye gazed upon her beautiful form, and into her gentle eyes; but never did he speak before her, and never again did her sweet-toned voice fall upon his ear. Thus did he love the fair maid, and so strong was his thought of her that he forgot the crops of Yo Semite, and they, without rain, wanting his tender care, quickly drooped their heads, and shrunk. The wind whistled mournfully through the wild corn, the wild bees stored no more honey in the hollow tree, for the flowers had lost their freshness, and the green leaves became brown. Tu-tock-ah-nu-lah saw none of this, for his eyes were dazzled by the shining wings of the maiden. But Tis-sa-ack looked with sorrowing eyes over the neglected Valley, when early in the morning she stood upon the gray dome of the mountain; so, kneeling on the smooth, hard rock, the maiden besought the Great Spirit to bring again the bright flowers and delicate grasses, green trees, and nodding acorns.

Then, with an awful sound, the dome of granite opened beneath her feet, and the mountain was riven asunder, while the melting snow from the Sierras gushed through the wonderful gorge. Quickly they formed a lake between the perpendicular walls of the cleft mountain, and sent a sweet murmuring river through the Valley. All then was changed. The birds dashed their little bodies into the pretty pools among the grasses, and, fluttering out again, sang for delight; the moisture crept silently through the parched soil; the flowers sent up a fragrant incense of thanks; the corn gracefully raised its drooping head; and the sap, with velvet footfall, ran up into the trees, giving life and energy to all. But the maid, for whom the Valley had suffered, and through whom it had again been clothed with beauty, had disappeared as strangely as she came. Yet, that all might hold her memory in their hearts, she left the quiet lake, the winding river, and *yonder half dome*, which still bears her name *Tis-sa-ack*. It is 5,000 feet above the placid lake that mirrors its imposing presence, and every evening it catches the last rosy rays that are reflected from the snowy peaks above. As she flew away, small downy feathers were wafted from her wings, and where they fell—on the margin of the lake, and over the meadows beyond—you now see thousands of little white violets, which, if lovingly plucked and kissed, will bring happy thoughts and pleasant dreams to their possessor, wheresoever they are carried.

"When Tu-tock-ah-nu-lah knew that she was gone, he left his rocky castle, and wandered away in search of his lost love. But that the Yo Semites might never forget him, with the hunting-knife in his bold hand, he carved the bold outlines of his noble head upon the rock that bears his name; and there they still remain 2,000 feet above, guarding the entrance to the Valley which had received his tender care. After many years of far-off journeyings, without finding his beloved Tis-sa-ack, he returned to his disconsolate home, and near where Po-ho-no spreads her vapory veil, his majestic bust stands prominently out above the encircling walls of his once happy habitation."

Whole days could be enjoyably spent here, reading, musing, fishing, and rowing on the lake; and a drive to it with a pleasant party on a moonlight night, becomes a delightful entertainment. On one occasion the Hon. Mrs. Yelverton,with the gifted California writer, Mrs. Lawrence (better known by the *nom de plume* of "Red Ridinghood," and who has done so much by her rich and varied description to bespeak rapt attention to the Valley), and nine others, spent a gloriously memorable evening here. Mrs. Yelverton very kindly favored us with Tennyson's appropriate and inspiriting "Bugle Song:"—

> The splendor falls on castle walls,
>   And snowy summits old in story;
> The long light shakes across the lakes,
>   And the wild cataract leaps in glory.
> Blow, bugle, blow; set the wild echoes flying;
> Blow, bugle; answer, echoes, dying, dying, dying.

Pausing a little longer between the higher notes than the music provides for, *nine distinct echoes* could be heard repeating its delicious strains. In the early morning, when every sound is hushed, and before the breeze disturbs its quiet, the echoes will be found excellent; but in the evening, when the haze lingers on the mountain-tops, and possibly prevents the sound from passing far upward, the effect is strongest and best.

Speaking of echoes, as story-tellers would say, this reminds me of Mr. J. H. Lawrence's graphic description of an echo, when making his first trip to Yo Semite in 1855,* and Indians were supposed to be uninvitingly near:—

"Bang!" went the rifle, and a thousand echoes responded. "Great Scott!" exclaimed Hugh. "Just listen to it. Will it ever quit? Jee-whillikins! Who ever heard a gun crack like that? It seemed to stop for a while, but it's going yet—broke out in a new place."

"Well, now, I'm happy and content," responded Jim; "for if there are any Indians within ten miles of us, they are going to get up and dust. No little squad of Piutes, Diggers, or Monos, are going to stop within hearing of a whole army. They'll think there's about five hundred of us—won't they, Hugh?"

* See page 93.

"Yes a *thousand,* easy enough. Did you ever hear the like of those echoes? They rattled away along the crest of the mountain, jumping in and out of the ravines, butting against the tops of the tall sugar pines, till they got tangled up and lost in a big cañon somewhere away yonder, where they seemed to die out, muttering and grumbling; till directly they gathered themselves together again, and came rolling out big as pounds of wool."

If we have been so injudicious as to leave the hotel or camp ground before breakfast, or neglected a precautionary provision for our mid day repast, an admonishing voice from the organs of digestion will probably hasten our premature departure; otherwise we might be induced to tarry longer to examine the supposed existence of refractory rays of light, which are said to transvert the ordinary image of trees mirrored, and to place them upright in the mirror as in nature; or examine, in detail, the many objects that are represented on the mountain walls, such as the clothesline, fish, heads of men and forms of women, elephants, etc., discovered by persons with keen eyesight, and strong imaginations.

When leaving Mirror Lake, immediately after our emergence from the rocky talus over which we have been riding, should we look southward, and up the cañon to the left of Glacier Point, we would see the Too-lool-a-we-ack, or Glacier Cañon Fall, leaping down over the cliff. Before leaving this part of the Valley let me call your attention to

A FINE CHALYBEATE SPRING

That bubbles up, on the margin of Ten-ie-ya Creek. I once visited this spring in company with the eminent English chemist, Dr. F. R. Lees, of Leeds, and he pronounced it the finest and most valuable chalybeate spring he had ever seen. A carriage can go within a few yards of it.

Just below the chalybeate spring we take the Tis-sa-ack Avenue Road, a delightfully picturesque stretch, crossing the dark shady waters of Ten-ie-ya Creek on a strong bridge; and on the right hand, a few steps below it, can be seen the largest tree in the Valley, being twenty-eight feet in circumference at the ground. It is a red or Douglas spruce, *Abies Douglasii.* A couple of hundred yards from this, on our right, is the famous Lamon Orchard and cabin, where Mr. Lamon spent his two winters entirely alone, as related on pages 135 and 138. On the south eastern edge of the Lamon Orchard, lying between Ten-ie-ya Creek and the main Merced River,

WE PASS OVER AN OLD MORAINE.

This seems to have been deposited here by the combined action of two glaciers; one moving down Ten-ie-ya Creek, and the other by the main river, joined in the Valley by another from Glacier Cañon. Glimpses of the sparkling stream, fringed with dogwoods, alders, oaks, and balm of gileads, with here and there a noble pine; scattered masses of granite, huge bowlders, and rocky spurs, over which our road passes; these, with Glacier Cañon and Glacier Point, unite to make the Tis-sa-ack Avenue drive one of the most enjoyable of them all. Presently we find ourselves on Tis-sa-ack Bridge, which here spans the Merced River; and, looking northerly, obtain one of the finest of all views of the North Dome, which, from this standpoint, is shaped like a huge Prussian military hat; and the leaping cascades above the bridge, overarched by alders, are both beautiful and wildly picturesque.

Spinning down the Valley from the bridge, seemingly directly underneath the Glacier Point Wall, we cross several large and deliciously cold springs that apparently boil out from beneath it; and which are to be pressed into service for supplying the new hotel with a most liberal abundance of excellent water (and yet leave plenty for others), and soon thereafter arrive at

THE NEW HOTEL.

To becomingly provide for the growing wants of the traveling public in accordance with the progressive spirit of the age, a new and commodious hotel was resolved upon at Yo Semite, and the sum of $40,000 was appropriated by the Legislature of 1885, for its construction. The Board of Commissioners immediately advertised for suitable plans, and from among those submitted, selected the one they deemed most appropriate. In addition to its architectural picturesqueness it has seventy-four good-sized bedrooms, dining and sitting rooms, billiard hall, and bar room, hot and cold baths, office, and other convenient apartments, in addition to capacious verandas on two stories. It is to be first-class in all its arrangements and appointments.[1]

DOINGS OF THE "CYCLONE."

About a quarter of a mile below the new hotel, a so-called "cyclone" swooped down from a point apparently west of the Glacier Wall on March 13, 1881, and cut a swath of forest desolation over three hundred yards in breadth; snapping off pine trees exceeding five feet in diameter, as though they were mere pipe stems; uprooting others, twisting and breaking off the tops and branches of sturdy oaks, as though enviously angry at the umbrageous quiet they were enjoying; and strewed the whole plateau with tree wrecks. One hundred cords of fire-wood, besides an abundance of good logs adapted to saw-mill purposes, were scattered around.

Now I cannot accept the "cyclone" theory, as its first efforts were expended near an almost vertical bluff, where there was no room for such a force to concentrate, and all the havoc made was in a direction at right angles with the bluff. My theory, therefore, is this (and I freely concede the privilege of accepting or declining it): On the 7th of March, a fall of snow came, that measured fourteen inches; on the 8th, fifteen inches; on the 9th, fourteen and a half inches; on the 10th, twelve inches; on the 11th, sixteen inches; on the 12th, thirteen inches; all of this lay on the shelving side of the mountain, back of the wind swath. On the 13th of March, after making an additional deposit of the feathery element of some ten inches, a steady and heavy rain set in; which, running down the shelving wall, severed the clinging connection between it and the snow; when, having no support, its natural weight, infiltrated by the falling rain, caused the entire mass to suddenly give way, and as suddenly to displace the air, thus causing the devastation stated.

---

1. The Stoneman House, named for George Stoneman, governor of California from 1883 to 1887. It was a bulky, four-story structure, not only unattractive but of faulty design. It was destroyed by fire in 1896.

The lofty and bold surroundings on every hand may well charm us with their majesty and beauty, as we drive along; while the Yo Semite Fall in front of us all the way down, provides an everchanging and acceptable variety to this scenic feast. About a quarter of a mile before reaching Barnard's, as part of our course is upon the bank of the Merced River, we can see the trout disporting themselves in its transparent waters; and just beyond that, on our left, is the little school-house—and then, the hotels.

AFTERNOON RIDE DOWN THE VALLEY.

After a substantial lunch—called by many English visitors "tiffin"—made palatable by that best of all sauces, a good appetite, as our carriage is possibly waiting, let us make an excursion down the Valley and gaze upon some of its matchless wonders. On this pilgrimage it is usual to recross the upper iron bridge, again review many of the scenes witnessed on our way to Mirror Lake, pass the Yo Semite Fall, and, directly in front of us, stands Eagle Peak, three thousand eight hundred and eighteen feet above the valley. As we, at a future time, are to climb to its exalted summit, we will, if you please, only glance at its sky-piercing pinnacle, and pass down Pine Avenue to

ROCKY POINT.

This is just under the lower shoulder of the "Three Brothers," and is formed by large blocks of rocky talus that once peeled from its side. By the excellence of the road made over this difficult spot can now be seen how these huge masses had to yield to blasting powder, human will and muscle, pulley blocks, and mule power, for such results to be accomplished. From one part of the road here a magnificent view is obtained of the entire eastern end of the Valley. Soon after crossing Rocky Point—a reference to the tables will show the distances traveled—we arrive at and examine the Indian Camp and its inmates; but, as the manners and customs of these really interesting people will be given in a separate chapter, further present description will be unnecessary.

Photo by Geo. Fiske

TEN-IE-YA CAÑON, AND SURROUNDING MOUNTAINS.
From Glacier Point
(See page 469.)
Fiske #358. Facing page 408 in editions two, three, and four.

Photo by Charles L. Weed   Courtesy, The Bancroft Library

THE THREE BROTHERS

This half of a stereo view, made in June 1859, is the model for the engraving
on the opposite page. The engraving possibly was based on a wide-format
photo taken at the same time.

When about a mile below the Indian Camp, by looking back in a north easterly direction, we have an excellent view of

THE THREE BROTHERS.

By reference to page 67, it will be seen that this was so called from three brothers, sons of the old Indian Chief Ten-ie-ya, who were acting as Indian scouts during the Indian campaign of 1851, and were captured here. The Indian name is Pom-pom-pa-sa, which signifies "the three mountains playing leap-frog," and which becomes suggestive of the Indians' indulgence in that

Photo by C. L. Weed.

THE THREE BROTHERS (Highest 3,818 feet above Valley).

boyish pastime. But soon after passing these we find ourselves in the awe-inspiring and over shadowing presence of

GRAND OLD EL CAPITAN—TU-TOCK-AH-NU-LAH.*

But what finite mind can ever comprehend the marvelous massiveness of this monarch of mountains—a mighty fabric of granite towering up three thousand three hundred feet in the zenith? or who conceive the amplitude, or magnitude, of three thousand three hundred feet of vertical rock cleavage? Those who have seen the Palace Hotel in San Francisco will remember how that structure overtops all contiguous buildings; yet, that immense caravansary is but one hundred and ten feet from the sidewalk to the cornice; therefore, it would require just thirty Palace Hotels, on top of each other, to reach the edge of El Capitan, above the meadow in front of it. Then, supposing this mountain could be laid along Montgomery Street, San Francisco, it would extend from Post Street, at the corner of Market, to Broadway, over ten blocks, including the cross streets. Trinity Church steeple, New York, is two hundred and eighty-four feet high; therefore it would require eleven and a half of these to attain such an altitude. The statue on the dome of the Capitol at Washington, D. C., being three hundred and seven feet above the base of that structure, would take ten and three-quarters of that imposing building, to enable the lips of the Goddess of Liberty, on the top of it, to kiss the brow of Tu-tock-ah-nu-lah. St. Paul's Cathedral, at London, including the dome, is three hundred and sixty-five feet above the church-yard, so that over nine of those would be required to attain an equal elevation. St. Peter's, at Rome, four hundred and five feet high, would need to be over eight times its height, before the shoulder of its cross could touch that of El Capitan. And, allowing the possibility of its falling over,

* "Tu-tock-ah-nu-lah" was to the Indians of antiquity a semi-diety and chief in whose person was centered the double responsibility of head purveyor of creature comforts for the Ah-wah-nee-chees upon earth, and the superintendence of their enjoyments in the hunting grounds of their Indian heaven. "El Capitan" is Spanish for *The Captain*, a name given to this bold jutting mountain by the Mission Indians, and which was probably derived from their Spanish instructors, the priests.

into, and across the Valley, its grand old head would lie on the bosom of the opposite cliff! while forming a dam that would convert the whole upper end of the Valley into a lake exceeding half a mile in depth. Who, then, can fully comprehend the stupendous magnitude of incomparable El Capitan?

It has two immense faces exceeding half a mile in breadth; one to the south (which is said to overhang more than one hundred feet, a short distance east of the abutting angle), upon which Tu-tock-ah-nu-lah, according to the legend,* "carved the outlines of his noble head," and whose portrait attracts the attention of every curious passer-by; and the other face is on the west (which also overhangs) upon the top of which is the only place where a human foot can safely approach the edge, and from that standpoint look into an abyss exceeding three thousand five hundred feet in depth. Well might the Rev. Thomas Starr King, while reverentially gazing at this marvelous cliff, with deep emotion exclaim, "A more majestic object than this rock I never expect to see upon this planet!"

Then it should be remembered that the views obtained of it are generally from the road about half a mile away; but to *feel* the unutterable majesty of its sublime presence, the *debris* should be climbed, and one's back placed against its overhanging wall. The small proportionate amount of *debris* lying at its base, is cause for thoughtful musing as to the why and wherefore; and probably keeps our thoughts ruminatingly busy while reluctantly turning our faces away from it.

Emerging into the green meadow just beyond, the "Cathedral Group" of mountains strikingly confronts us; and possibly invites a comparison between those before and that we have just lingeringly left behind. The excellence of the road, and the scenes still awaiting us, both stimulate and invite to an increase in the speed of our horses; and in a few minutes we find ourselves on a straight and elevated roadway, beneath which numerous culverts provide for the unobstructed exit of the glinting waters of

* Page 388.

numerous branches of a pebbly and bowlder-strewn stream, that has just made an unbroken leap of over two thousand feet, and which is known as

THE RIBBON FALL.

The Indians call this Lung-oo-too-koo-yah, or the graceful and slender one; while a lady, whose name shall be nameless, once christened it "Virgin's Tears;" but, when a matter-of-fact person made inquiry for any legitimate reason why a virgin should weep, or, weeping, cause such floods of tears to flow, he was thought to possess as limited an amount of idealism as Bob Cratchet, who, according to Dickens, "tried to warm himself at the candle; in which effort, not being a man of strong imagination, he failed;" and when the same individual hazarded the casual remark that "his acquaintance was exceedingly limited with those of the masculine gender who would be likely to fall hopelessly in love with any virgin that wept like that," his organ of ideality was considered to be equivalent to the size of a mathematical point, which, paradoxically considered, has neither breadth nor length, height nor depth, except that which is imaginary!

Looking up towards the rim of the mountain, a white stream can be seen shooting out, at an altitude of three thousand three hundred and fifty feet above the road; which, in addition to its great height, being over a mile distant, appears to the eye to be descending very leisurely and with gentle grace, the two thousand one hundred feet of its vertical fall into the basin beneath it; but, when standing near, and almost underneath it, the rapidity of its descent is remarkable. The exceeding beauty of its lace-like and gauzy drapery is simply enchanting in the early spring. Nearly perpendicular, tower-like walls, of two thousand three hundred and fifty feet, frame a recess some three hundred feet deep from the general face of the mountain; and which, beyond question, has been cut out by the stream that forms this lofty water-fall; assisted, of course, by other disintegrating elements. The gneiss which here composes the northern wall of the Valley, being very friable, its constant crumblings have created a deposit of talus at their base over thirteen hundred feet in height, thus tending to confirm the probability that Yo Semite was formed by erosive rather than by volcanic agencies.

Near the western terminus of the straight stretch of carriage road across the Ribbon Fall streams, can even now be distinctly seen

THE REMAINS OF AN OLD TERMINAL MORAINE

That at one time extended entirely across the Valley, and formed an immense dam, by which the whole of the upper end of the Valley was converted into a lake—possibly the most remarkable one that ever existed upon earth. The height of this moraine-built dam, when the glaciers carried it there, in the fifty thousands or hundreds of thousand years ago, more or less, can only be conjectured; but now its crest is only about fifty feet above the present level of the meadow. During some great flood this lake must have overflowed, where the Merced River now runs; and, tearing away a portion of the moraine, cut the present channel of the river; as the rapids down which it so impetuously rushes are strewn with glacier-rounded bowlders. Standing upon the lower iron bridge—the floor of which, according to the Wheeler U. S. Survey, is only nine feet lower than that of the upper iron bridge, near Barnard's—these can readily be noted, and both of the river-cut ends of the moraine be seen.

As additional inductive data, suggestive of the upper end of the Valley having once been a lake, may be mentioned that, when the new piece of road was built near the blacksmith's shop, and the deep hollow there had to be filled up, the material was taken from the adjacent bank; where, underneath large blocks of granite, that had peeled off from the mountain's side, was an immense deposit of *lake sand*, not less than eighteen feet in thickness or depth above the road.

After the cutting away of a portion of the moraine, as above mentioned, the whole of the waters of the lake must have drained off, and left the surface of the Valley substantially as it now is; of course minus the wonderful plant life that now adorns it.

When the low back of the moraine is crossed, on our right hand we pass the junction of the Milton and Big Oak Flat road with that of the grand drive around the Valley. And but a short distance beyond this, on the rocky banks of the river, there is a fine view of a series of bounding cascades, that extend, apparently, up to the bluffs at the farther end, their diamond-tipped waves curling around moss-covered bowlders; and all overarched by lofty trees. Beyond this a glimpse is obtained of the ever-graceful Bridal Veil Fall. But on we drive, and near a bright green meadow, margined by alders, and liberally adorned with wild flowers that delight in moisture, we come to

THE BLACK SPRINGS.

These take their name from the color of the rich alluvial through which the delightfully refreshing waters of two full-flowing springs hurry down a deep-cut gully that crosses the road. This, in appearance, is only one spring, while in reality it is formed of two, that boil out from beneath a large flat rock about a hundred yards distant, on sides opposite to each other; one spring being chalybeate, and the other pure water. Here man (including the ladies) and beast find refreshing drink, and generally pause to take it. Turning to the left, just below this, at a bend in the road, we find the magnificent

VALLEY VIEW FROM "ENCHANTMENT POINT"—TOO-NU-YAH.[1]

Standing on the western margin of this beautiful stream, looking eastward, with the rushing, gurgling current in the immediate foreground, there opens up before us one of the most charmingly impressive scenes that human eyes can look upon. On the extreme left is the Ribbon Fall, with its broken yet massive wall; next adjoining comes glorious old El Capitan; in the far-away distance are Cloud's Rest and the Half Dome; then, The Sentinel, and Sentinel Dome; the Three Graces, flanked by the darkly scowling mountain over which leaps the bright-faced Bridal Veil Fall; the whole forming a captivating combination of majesty and

1. This is now named Valley View—looking east up the valley from the west side of Bridalveil Meadow.

loveliness. Turning away from this delighting spectacle the Pohono Bridge is soon passed, and we enter upon the

WILDLY PICTURESQUE ROAD TO THE CASCADE FALLS.

This is a portion of the Coulterville Turnpike, and is constructed on the margin of the cliff-walled and bowlder-strewn cañon of the Merced River, where it makes its hurried exit from the Valley. The many attractive forms of its bounding waters, as they dash, and eddy, and surge, and swirl among and over huge blocks of rock, with lofty and frowning bluffs on either side, whose faces are fringed with trees and shrubs, and beautified by numerous rivulets, that come leaping down from ridge to ledge, or trickling through the furrows, and among the wrinkles of their weather-aged yet open countenances. And at almost every stretch and turning of this live oak arched road, are wild flowers and shrubs in endless forms, combined with such variety of coloring as to make constant and inspiriting additions to our pleasurable ride. But the climax of all these charming scenes comes when we can catch the first sight of

THE CASCADE FALLS.

These are seen bounding over and adown the mighty crags, driving out eddies of sun-lighted spray, that wave and toss their vapory veils upon the rocks and trees with such graceful abandon that the eye never wearies in watching their aerial frolics. And it is not a little singular that these cascades, which are formed from two streams, although having their sources in directly opposite directions, join forces at the verge of the cliff, and make the leap together. From the road to the top of Cascade Falls the altitude is seven hundred feet.

In order to enjoy this visit thoroughly the larger portion of the day should be devoted to it, fortified by a good lunch, and fishing tackle; and, best of all, genial and appreciative companions. At the farther end of the flat, not very far from Vulcan's Workshop, there is a shady grove of California nutmegs, and other trees, that make this a pleasant picnic ground.

Returning we watch the silver-crested curls of the foaming river; note its dark green pools, and curving eddies, and listen to the deep pæan of its triumphal song, as it rushes on so fearlessly, I had almost said recklessly, down a cataract of two miles, wherein is a descent, vertically, of five hundred and fifty feet. As the ascent by the road from Cascade Falls to the floor of the Valley is somewhat of a tax upon the breath and strength of the horses, progress up it is naturally slower than when going down, and gives time and opportunity for noticing many points that were then overlooked. This is really no small advantage. We soon, however, find ourselves on

THE POHONO BRIDGE.

A casual glance at this substantial structure will present an example of the strength, solidity, and permanence with which the Board of Commissioners are making the necessary improvements about the Valley. Looking down upon the swiftly surging current below the bridge, or the placid stretch of dark green water above it, or at its matchless surroundings, one can scarcely refrain from exclaiming, "What a glorious picture gallery. Verily!"

THE POHONO AVENUE DRIVE.

The densely massed shadows of this tree-arched avenue, which we enter when leaving the bridge, become as refreshing as the blossoming dogwoods, which stand on either side, are exhilarating; and the many-voiced, plant-garnished Moss Springs, and Fern Springs, gushing out at our side, temptingly invite us to drink of their transparent and ice-tempered waters. Still tasting them retrospectively, we emerge from an umbrageous forest of evergreens upon the bright, grassy Bridal Veil Meadow, whence an apparently new combination of scenic effects is everywhere visible. Here, too, looking southwestwardly, we can see the "Inspiration Point" of early days, when the trail from Clark's neared the very edge of the precipice, and the first sight of glorious Yo Semite was obtained. Hence, also, can be seen "Mount Beatitude," and the sublime "Standpoint of Silence," a spot first

Bridal Veil Fall—900 ft.

The primitive methods of the day were not able to deal with
such a difficult photo. See the 1886 result on page 404.
Fiske #585

Photo by Charles L. Weed   Courtesy, The Bancroft Library

DISTANT VIEW OF THE "POHONO," OR BRIDAL VEIL FALL

The engraving on the facing page was made

from this photograph, taken in June 1859.

brought to the notice of visitors by Mr. C. D. Robinson, the artist. After crossing another terminal, and passing an additional lateral moraine, we come into full view of

THE POHONO, OR BRIDAL VEIL FALL.

It is impossible to portray the feeling of awe, wonder, and admiration—almost amounting to adoration—that thrills our very souls as we look upon this enchanting scene. The gracefully undulating and wavy sheets of spray, that fall in gauze-like and ethereal folds; now expanding, now contracting; now glittering in the sunlight, like a veil of diamonds; now changing into one vast

Photo by C. L. Weed.

DISTANT VIEW OF THE "POHONO," OR BRIDAL VEIL FALL.

Instantaneous Photo by Geo. Fiske.   Heliotype Co., Boston.

THE PO-HO-NO, OR BRIDAL VEIL FALL (900 feet high).

and many-colored cloud, that throws its misty drapery over the falling torrent, as if in very modesty, to veil its unspeakable beauty from our too eagerly admiring sight.

In order to see this to the best advantage, the eye should take in only the foot of the fall at first, then a short section upward, then higher, until, by degrees, the top is reached. In this way the majesty of the water-fall is more fully realized and appreciated.

The stream itself—about forty feet in width—resembles an avalanche of watery rockets, that shoots out over the precipice above you, at the height of nearly nine hundred feet, and then leaps down, in one unbroken chain, to the immense bowlder-formed caldron beneath, where it surges and boils in its angry fury; throwing up large volumes of spray, over which the sun builds two or more magnificent rainbows with which to arch the abyss.

INDIAN DREAD OF PO-HO-NO.

"Pohono," from whom the stream and water-fall received their musical Indian name, is, according to their traditions and legends, an evil spirit, whose breath becomes a blighting and fatal wind; and who, in consequence, is, in their apprehension, as much to be dreaded and shunned as the simooms of an African desert by an Arab. On this account, should necessity require them to pass by it, they do so with a reluctance that fills them with actual distress; and they will, if unseen by the whites, hurry past it at the top of their speed. To point at this water-fall contemptuously when traveling in the Valley, to their minds is certain death. No inducement could be offered sufficiently large to tempt them to sleep near it. In imagination they can hear the voices of those who have passed into the spirit world, through Pohono's destroying breath, warning them ever to shun him as the worst of all enemies.

CURIOUS PHENOMENA.

Nor is this so much to be wondered at when for a moment we pause to think that their untutored minds have never been taught, reasoningly, to look from effect to cause. They, therefore, see all natural phenomena through the delusive eyes of superstition only. In this connection an illustrative and explanatory fact should here be given: I have passed this fall at almost all hours of the night, and at nearly every season of the year, and for many years; and there has not been a dozen occasions in all that time that I have not experienced a peculiar and strong wind blowing, within a given radius of about half a mile. When without that radius scarcely a breath of wind was noticeable; returning into it, the same wind was bending and swaying the shrubs and trees as before. This has been many times repeated on the same evening, and always with the same results. And it is more than probable, that, from this simple, natural phenomenon, the Indian's imagination has created "Pohono," and invested him with a personality whose every attribute is clothed with angry enmity to the Indian race.

A PECULIAR AND SLIPPERY MOSS.

On the top of the Pohono Fall, moreover, there is a short and densely textured moss, not more than half an inch in height or thickness, which is as soft to the tread as a Turkey carpet; and which, when dry, will enable any one to go in perfect safety to the very brink of the precipice; but, if wet, it becomes as slippery, and as difficult to stand upon, as ice that is slanting, so that no one need expect to preserve his equilibrium on that wet moss. This, to the Indian apprehension, has been placed there by Pohono for the purpose of tempting and entrapping the thoughtless and unwary; and, as tradition has it, with more or less success.

PO-HO-NO AS A MISCHIEVOUS GHOST.

Some Indian women that were out gathering seeds, were led by curiosity to go to the edge of the fall to look over, when it is asserted that the shadowy and ghost-like form of Pohono was seen to throw one of the Indian women down; and the force of the current striking her swept her helplessly into the abyss below. Seeing this the other women hastened to the Indian camp as rapidly as possible and related the fearful story with terrible effect. In the hopeful expectation of affording relief to the unfortunate one, as courage rose in proportion to the numbers volunteering, every brave in camp was induced to sally out to search for the hapless one, determined to rescue her from the weird-like clutches of Pohono, at any risk. But, although diligent search was made for her everywhere, the missing victim was never seen afterwards; and it was, and is still, believed that Pohono spirited her away bodily to some unknown pandemonium; and is, moreover, constantly seeking after others for a like purpose. Several Indians of both sexes having lost their lives here, they believe that this stream is bewitched by Pohono; and, consequently, to be both dreaded and shunned at all times.

SOURCES OF THE BRIDAL VEIL FALL.

The creek which forms this graceful and beautiful fall derives its principal source from some large springs which flow into a crescent-shaped and rock-bound lake about thirteen miles distant;[1] and although this stream is never entirely dry, it becomes very low sometimes near the end of summer. In winter the icicles that feather both sides of the fall are very attractive, and the masses of ice that form here, in which there are grotto-like caves roofed with icicles, are resplendently dazzling.

The bright rainbows which are built by the setting sun on the tops of the eddying mists that roll out from the seething caldron at the base of the Pohono Fall, at all seasons of the year, are the most beautifully brilliant between four o'clock and half past five in the afternoon; therefore, the many tempting sights elsewhere should be made somewhat subordinate to this, if it is deemed desirable that this should be seen to the best advantage. At other times it is simply an enchantingly charming and graceful water-fall; but, when lighted up by brilliant rainbows, a halo of glory seems to enshrine it, that makes it a delightful memory forever. Please, therefore, to remember that although the Bridal Veil Fall "can be seen" at other times (in accordance with the established custom of society belles!) it "receives" only at the time mentioned.

1. Ostrander Lake, probably named in the 1890s by Lt. N. F. McClure. The name was borrowed from Ostrander Rocks, which were named by the Whitney Survey for Harvey J. Ostrander, a sheepman of the early 1860s.

TU-TOCK-AH-NU-LAH'S CITADEL.

The vertical and, at some points, overhanging mountains on either side of the Pohono, possess almost as much interest as the fall itself, and add much to the grandeur and magnificence of the whole scene. A tower-shaped and leaning rock, about three thousand feet in height, standing at the southwest side of the fall, sometimes called the "Leaning Tower," nearly opposite "Tutock-ah-nu-lah," has on its top a number of projecting rocks that very much resemble cannon. In order to assist in perpetuating the beautiful legend before given concerning that Indian semideity, we once took the liberty of christening this "Tu-tock-ahnu-lah's Citadel."

THE "WAITING AND WATCHING" CHIEF.

South of Tu-tock-ah-nu-lah's Citadel, or the Leaning Tower, stands a lofty point of exceeding prominence, having the form and resemblance of a finely proportioned human head. This, the Indian traditions assert, is Tu-tock-ah-nu-lah waiting in hopeful faith and patience for the return of the long lost and deeply mourned Tis-sa-ack, who is still expected to return and bless the heart and wigwam of its semi-deity and greatest chief, Tu-tockah-nu-lah, with her enrapturing presence.

The immense deposits of talus lying here, nearly a quarter of a mile wide, are deeply cut into and across by three main streams, through which the whole of the water from the Bridal Veil Fall impetuously rushes, and forming other sources of attraction, can be pleasantly witnessed and enjoyed from the three substantial bridges that span those streams.

After rounding the point easterly of the Bridal Veil Fall, although both the Ribbon Fall and El Capitan are immediately in front of us, we must not allow their attractive presence to divert our attention altogether from a portion of another moraine, that is lying directly on our right; or, to omit noticing the rapids that are bounding in such frolicsome glee over and among the glacialrounded bowlders that were washed from the terminal moraine before mentioned, as these continue to the El Capitan iron bridge, and over these rapids trees have constructed an avenue of great loveliness.

VIEW FROM THE EL CAPITAN BRIDGE.

Passing down the Valley on its northern side, and up on its southern, may, inadvertently, lead us to overlook the view from the lower iron, or El Capitan bridge. This would be an undesirable oversight, inasmuch as, in addition to the river ends of the terminal moraine, which it is thought once converted the upper end of the Valley into a lake, and which are so plainly visible here, a magnificent view is presented when looking eastwardly not only of the Merced River in the foreground, but of Cloud's Rest, ten miles away, in the far-off distance. This name of "Cloud's Rest" is derived from the interesting fact that clouds are frequently resting upon this mountain when there is not another cloud visible anywhere else upon the whole vaulted firmament. Looking west, another view of the rapids, and of the tree-vista inclosing them, can be obtained. After crossing the bridge and returning to the southern side, up which we are supposed to be traveling, we come to the

CATHEDRAL SPIRES,

Two very noticeable and remarkable formations; towering up as they do on our right, alone, and unsupported by any contiguous mountain for over seven hundred feet above their base, like two immense cathedral spires, suggested the appropriate name. The Indians call them Poo-see-nah Chuck-ka, on account of their resemblance to the acorn store baskets of that people. According to the Wheeler U. S. Survey the most southerly one is two thousand six hundred and seventy-eight feet above the road; and that northerly two thousand five hundred and seventy-nine feet.

On one occasion (October 6, 1877), the writer, with Mr. S. C. Walker, the photographer, accompanied by two Indians as packers, carried photographic apparatus, and worked our way up the rock-strewn gorge lying at the base of these spires, to the sag or

Photo by Geo. Fiske.   Heliotype Eng. Co., Boston.

MERCED RIVER VIEW FROM EL CAPITAN BRIDGE.

CLOUDS' REST. FROM EL CAPITAN BRIDGE

The retouched halftone/engraving on the opposite page
could convey little of what is in this subtle photograph.

Fiske #310

Mirror View of Sentinel Rock. 3270 ft.

See the heavily retouched halftone/engraving on page 415.

Fiske #317

hollow between the two highest of the "Three Graces," for its view. And it *was* a view, *par excellence.* The deep-cut, darkly frowning, and almost vertically-walled gorge up which we climbed was full of large and lofty sugar pines, firs, cedars, and spruces that were growing among huge blocks of granite that had at some time peeled off the sides of the gorge, and, being scattered everywhere, made the climb anything but easy. But, when once there, I believe it no exaggeration, or dreamy hyperbole, not only to assert but to affirm, that from what scenes I have personally witnessed in many lands, and from other individuals have heard, as well as from the illustrations and descriptions that have been published, I am convinced that this is probably

ONE OF THE MOST SUBLIMELY IMPRESSIVE VIEWS ON EARTH.

I am aware that this saying much. I am also aware that to those who do not know me it will be received with many grains of qualifying allowance; but, I nevertheless present it as the conviction of my unprejudiced judgment to be an actual, positive, and undeniable fact, and one to be verified the moment the Board of Commissioners shall have made the ascent possible by a good trail. To describe such a scene, therefore, would be simply impossible, so I will merely outline the principal points seen from thence. And, first to be mentioned, are the Cathedral Spires themselves, which are not only to be seen with their rocky needles standing boldly out from and above the mountain of which they form a part, but their entire masonry is visible from apex to base, a height of seventeen hundred feet; and which is apparently as true as though built by a plummet board, adjusted to an angle of say eighty-five degrees, or only five degrees from the perpendicular. While, on the other side is a perfect wall, standing at almost as steep an angle as the spires, and yet reaching to the foreground of the picture.

Deep down the narrow, tree-darkened hollow that is bounded by these walls, and over the tops of the trees, two thousand nine hundred feet below lies the Valley, the sheen of its serpentine river sparkling glintingly among the trees, with its meadows and pools, and gardens, and buildings there before one. All the northern rim of the Valley, with the Yo Semite Fall, North Dome, Royal Arches, Washington Tower, Mirror Lake, Mt. Watkins, and the whole distance up Ten-ie-ya Cañon, and the trail to Glacier Point, lie directly visible on our left; while over the shoulder whence spring the "Spires," Cloud's Rest, The Sentinel, Sentinel Dome, Profile, or Fissure, Mountain, can be seen; and in the far-off distance stands Ten-ie-ya, Monastery, Cathedral, Echo, Temple, Unicorn, and other peaks, stretching to the very crest of the Sierra Nevada Mountains. To those who can imagine what a picture could be when filled in by vertical precipices, and jutting or overhanging cliffs; the distance draped with ethereal haze; and the whole heightened by the magical effects of light and shade, it would seem almost impossible that such a scene could be overdrawn; or the statement questioned that this is one of the most sublimely impressive views on earth.

Returning in imagination to the Valley again, and still advancing up its southern side, we can see other wild and weird-like peaks and rents in the mountain's face, and among the niches of every cliff, so that it is not this or that particular rock, or chasm only, that attracts so much, but the infinite and ever-changing variety of all. Among these, however, one point stands out somewhat prominently, known as

PROFILE, OR FISSURE, MOUNTAIN.

The first appellation comes from the many faces that can be distinctly traced upon its northeastern edge at almost any hour of the day, but the afternoon's light streaming in between the points defines them strongest. It is in this crag, moreover, that the fissure (described on page 344) cuts so deep a crevice. The crown of this bluff is nearly three hundred feet higher than any of its illustrious compeers in this immediate vicinity, and its vertical depth greater than all, if we except El Capitan. The view from it, therefore, is very fine. A little northerly of this is a light-colored spot, whence, in 1857, a chip fell, the *debris* from which was said to cover over thirty acres. But as we keep advancing there is one strikingly prominent mountain before us, and one that seems to have been in front of us for miles. It is "The Sentinel," and near to it the Sentinel Cascades, and as they are in such close proximity we will, if you please, take a brief glance at both

THE SENTINEL, AND SENTINEL CASCADES.

Although the former has been the most conspicuous for some

Drawn by Thos. Moran.

THE SENTINEL (3,069 feet above the Valley.

time, let us look first at the two leaping cascades, as they shoot down from the ragged-edged crest, three thousand four hundred feet above us. When these are fullest, their picturesque effect is simply marvelous; and when their volume is less, the foaming whiteness is merely changed to diamond brightness, and they are always beautiful.

The "Sentinel" is the great central landmark of the Valley; and, whether draped in belts of cloud, or gilded by a golden sunset, its isolated prominence is ever imposingly magnificent. Looking at it from the objective point whence Mr. Moran's sketch was taken, or Mr. Fiske's photograph, its front resembles an obelisk, or the tower of some vast cathedral, of which it forms a part. Its face is almost vertical for nearly two thousand feet. It is said that the Indians once used this not only as a watch-tower, but as a signal station, on all important occasions. They call it Loya.

Now although the climb to its summit is both difficult and dangerous, one lady—and one only (Mrs. Geo. B. Bayley, of Oakland, California)—has undertaken the task, and with her husband, has stood upon its highest point; and there placed a white flag, that remained until it had been waved into shreds.

Soon we cross the streams that have formed the Sentinel Cascades; stop at, or pass, Leidig's Hotel, Fiske's photographic gallery, Yo Semite chapel, Galen Clark's residence, Cook's bath house, Coffman & Kenney's livery stable, Cook's Hotel, and Mr. Thomas Hill's studio—with the Yo Semite Falls and Eagle Peak nearly all the time in sight. Between Cook's and Barnard's hotels there is a stretch of tree-arched road, bordered on the right by a frowning bluff, upon the side and shoulder of which are unmistakable evidences of the attrition caused by the passage down of the old-time glaciers, that once filled this Valley with ice. Beyond this we arrive at the store, Mrs. Glynn's, the butcher's and blacksmith's shops, Mrs. Fagersteen's photographic rooms, Sinning's cabinet shop, the Guardian's office, Mr. C. D. Robinson's studio, and then Barnard's, a mile beyond which is the new hotel.

Photo by Geo. Fiske.   Heliotype Engraving Co., Boston.

THE SENTINEL CASTING REFLECTIONS.

CHAPTER XXIV.

MANNERS AND CUSTOMS OF THE INDIANS.

I would not enter on my list of friends
(Though graced with polish'd manners and fine sense,
Yet wanting sensibility) the man
Who needlessly sets foot upon a worm.
—Cowper's *Task, Bk. VI.*

To tell men that they cannot help themselves is to fling them into reckless-
ness and despair.
—Froud's *Short Studies on Great Subjects.*

Be noble! and the nobleness that lies
In other men, sleeping, but never dead,
Will rise in majesty to meet thine own.
—Lowell's *Sonnet, IV.*

Shortly after taking up our permanent residence in Yo Semite an Indian presented himself one morning, when the following
colloquy ensued:—

"You li-kee Indian man wor-kee?" "Are you a good worker?"
"You no li-kee me, you no kee-pee me, sab-be (understand)?"
"Well! that seems fair enough. How much-e you want, you work-
e one day?" "One dol-lar I tink wa-no (good)." "All right. What's
your name?" "Tom." "Well, Tom, you come work-e to-morrow
morning; sa-be, 'to-morrow' morning?" "Seh (*Si*, in Spanish), me
sa-be." "Seven o'clock?" "Seh, me sab-be." "You better come
before seven, Tom, then you get-tee good breakfast; Indian man
work-e better, he eat-ee good breakfast."

At this latter proposition Tom's somewhat somber face
lighted up with a glow of child-like pleasure; and, when the following morning came, he was on hand both for his meal and labor
also. Finding him to be the most faithful Indian worker that I had

(416)

ever seen—for, as a rule, Indians do not take kindly to steady labor—after some ten or twelve days, as we were becoming short of desirable articles for the household, and our packer was unwell, questions were put and answered thus: "Tom, you sa-be packing?" "Po-co" (little). "You sa-be Big Oak Flat, Tom?" "Seh. Me sab-be Big Oak Flat." "You li-kee go Big Oak Flat, get-tee some sugar, some flour, and such things?" "You li-kee me go, I go." "All right, Tom, you get-tee five horses—sa-be 'five'" (counting the number on my fingers). "Seh. Me sab-be." "Four you pack, one you ride, sa-be?" "Seh. Me sab-be."

Promptly at seven o'clock Tom was on hand, with the horses; when I handed him a letter, and explained to him that that paper would tell the store-keeper at the settlements the kind and quantity of articles wanted, and which would be handed to him for packing nicely, and bringing safely to us. Then, laying five $20 pieces, one by one, upon the palm of his hand, I said to him, "Tom, you ta-kee these five $20 pieces to Mr. Murphy, storekeeper, at Big Oak Flat (as Mr. Murphy no sa-be me), and they will pay for what he give you to bring us." "Seh. Me sab-be." Tom's eyes sought mine with bewildering yet gratified astonishment (while they filled with tears); as though apparently questioning the possibility that I could trust him, an Indian, with five horses, and as many $20 pieces. He seemed to have suddenly grown several inches taller, and more erect than I had ever seen him; as with an open and manly look he slowly responded, "Wa-no. Me go. Me ta-kee money. Me pack-ee sugar—flour, here."

When Tom returned with everything perfectly straight, and in good order, he was evidently as proud and delighted as a Newfoundland (or any other) dog could have been with two tails. His face had a smile all over it—an uncommon sight in an Indian. From that time Tom was not only my friend, but a friend to every member of the family; and he took as much interest in everything as though it was his own. The confidence reposed in him had completely conquered the *Indian*, by making him to feel that he was *a man*.

A few weeks after this he wanted to pay a visit to his people, whose camp was some forty miles below; and, as he said, "eat-ee some acorn blead (*bread*, as they seldom sound the r) and go hab fandango" (Indian dance). It may be cause for wonder that the best of good food, when provided and cooked by white people, is only satisfactory for a time, to the Indian; he longs (not for "the flesh-pots of Egypt," perhaps, but) for "acorn blead." It is an apparent physical necessity to him.

HOW TOM'S LIFE WAS ONCE SAVED.

Upon Tom's return an almost uncontrollable excitement seemed to quiver through his whole frame, while the perspiration exuded from his hair, and rolled down his somber face in streams. Breathlessly sinking upon a chair, a wild, agonizing frenzy, distorting every muscle of his features; while gleams of fire seemingly shot from both his eyes, as soon as his lungs could perform their office, and his tongue and voice could find utterance, he gasped out, "Oh! Mr. H., Mr. H., Indian men come kill-ee me." "Hullo! Tom, what on earth have you been doing, that Indians should want to kill you?" Gathering breath and effort gradually, yet simultaneously, he exclaimed, "Oh! Indian man say I kill-ee one Indian; I no kill-ee Indian man, Indian man kill-ee Big Meadows—I no go Big Meadows, I go Bull Creek. They tink I kill-ee him, though, and Indian men—five (counting on his fingers)—come kill-ee me." "Are you sure, Tom, you no kill-ee Indian man?" "I sure I no kill-ee Indian. How I kill-ee Indian man Big Meadows—I no go Big Meadows?? I *sure* I no kill-ee him. You hi-de me somewhere?" "You sure you no kill-ee Indian man, Tom, eh?" "I *sure* I no kill-ee him." "All right, Tom, then I hide you somewhere."

This had been successfully accomplished but about twenty minutes when up came the five Indians mentioned by Tom, "armed to the teeth," as the saying is, sweating and almost out of breath; when one of them inquired, in pretty good English, "Have you seen Indian Tom?" "Oh! yes, Tom was here about half an hour ago. Is there anything the matter?" "Yes, Tom killed an Indian at Big Meadows." "Yes? Why, Tom told me he did not kill the Indian at Big Meadows; he said that some Indians thought so, but that he was not at the Big Meadows—he went only to Bull Creek." "Yes. Tom killed an Indian man at Big Meadows; and if we find Tom we shall kill him. That is Indian fashion." "But, Tom told me that he did not go to the Big Meadows, and did not kill the Indian there; and if you go kill Tom, and Tom did not kill the Indian, as you say, then the Sheriff of Mariposa will take you to jail, and by and by they will hang you, as they ought to do, if you kill an innocent man. You Indian men too fast, and too hot. You cool down a little. Then, when you find the man who did kill the Indian, have him taken to Mariposa; and if found guilty they will hang him and save you all the trouble. You take my advice, and don't kill any man, especially when he may be entirely innocent of the crime with which you charge him."

Although they took reluctant departure for the present, they evidently thought that Tom was not far away; as they were frequently seen near, and upon the lookout. In about three days after their first appearance they absented themselves, and nothing more was seen of any Indian for over a week; when two Indian women came to me and asked if Indian Tom had been there. I replied that he had—about a week ago. "So," I suggested, as though questioning the truth of Tom's relation, "so Tom killed an Indian at Big Meadows, eh?" "No, no, no; Tom no kill-lee Indian Big Meadows. Two Indian men see Sam Wells kill-lee Indian at Big Meadows—Tom no kill-lee him." "Then if I see Tom I am to tell him that, eh?" "Yes, yes, I Tom's wife." "Oh! that is the way the land lies is it? All right, if I see Tom I tell-lee him."

Tom was soon seen, and the case stated, when he wished me to invite them over. Asking them if they were not hungry (and it was a rare sight to see an Indian that was not), and receiving an affirmative answer, they were soon eating where Tom could catch sight of them without being seen; and in a few minutes afterwards they were all walking happily together in the bright sunshine as fearlessly free and as happy as children.

When the would-be-avenging Indians made their reappearance a few days subsequent to this *denouement*, they acknowledged, though somewhat reluctantly, that Tom was proven to be entirely innocent of the crime; as two other Indians had seen the murder committed by another man, whose resemblance to Tom had caused the mistaken identity, that would have cost the innocent man his life, had they found him at the time of their impetuous search.

HIS GRATEFUL RETURN THEREFOR.

This thrilling incident very naturally made Tom's heart warm kindly and strongly towards the one who had afforded him such timely succor in the hour of his extreme need; and there can be but little doubt that his unwearying devotion and faithful services thereafter, in the best interests of all our family, were cause of many mysterious questionings among those to whom the secret was unrevealed. The assertion, therefore, that gratitude is an absent guest to every Indian's heart, is not true. This heavenly quality welled up, bounteously, not grudgingly, in Tom's heart, and

Photo by G. Fagersteen.
INDIAN TOM.

Photo by Gustave Fagersteen   NPS, Yosemite Collections

Indian Tom

The original from which the engraving on the opposite page was made.

Photo by Geo. Fiske   NPS, Yosemite Collections

Caches for drying acorns
Facing page 424 in edition one.
Fiske #422

flowed perennially in kindly actions; and that, too, while unsealing the fountain of his lips. Tom had succeeded in conquering the natural reticence of his race; and it is to this that I am so largely indebted for many interesting facts concerning it, that are embraced in this chapter. I therefore, with pleasure introduce

INDIAN TOM.

Owing to his many years of faithful service in our family, all of the other Indians (there being many "Tom's") called him "Tom Hutchings!" and as he so calls himself he evidently cannot be ashamed of it. Tom does not claim to be a full Yo Semite Indian; inasmuch as, although his mother belonged to that tribe, his father was a Mono (Pah-uta). After this, I trust not uninteresting, introduction, please allow me to present a few facts concerning

THE MANNERS AND CUSTOMS OF THE INDIANS.

The Indian Camp, and its People—Probable Numbers—Physical Characteristics—Acorns their Staple Breadstuff, How Prepared and Cooked—Kitchavi—Pine Nuts—Esculent Plants—Grass and Other Seeds—Wild Fruits—Fish—Game—Miscellaneous Edibles.

> I have learned
> To look on Nature, hearing oftentimes
> The still, sad music of humanity;
> Not harsh nor grating, though of ample power
> To chasten and subdue.   —WORDSWORTH.

One of the many attractive features of Yo Semite is the Indian camp, and its interesting people—the original owners and first settlers. Deplorable as the fact may be, however, there are less than twenty living of a tribe that, in 1851, numbered nearly five hundred.* The remnant being representative of the principal customs, occupations, manner of living, habits of thought, traditions, legends, and systems of belief, not only of their own people and the surrounding tribes, but of the California Indians generally, a visit to their village, and a sight of its

---

* The causes of this astonishing decrease are mainly given on pages 77, 78.

inhabitants, will be the more inviting and instructive. Before presenting ourselves at

THE INDIAN CAMP,

As we would not willingly do them even an unintentional injustice, let us not forget that they have always been nomadic, and have continuously camped out; that any appearance suggestive of untidiness is to be attributed more to circumstances than to mental antagonism to a higher social standard. They have no neatly furnished private apartments to which they can retire, and cultivate the attractive mysteries of the toilet. Like people of good common sense they accept their position, and make the best of it. Even among our friends, those who have sought the exhilarating elixir of mountain air, or rambled far from human habitations in pathless forests, to luxuriate upon the sublime or beautiful, know how difficult it is, at such a time, to keep comfortably clean. It was an abstruse problem to Mark Twain, you remember, who had passed through sundry such experiences, to solve the possibility of the Israelites keeping half-way clean while "camping out" forty years in the "Wilderness!" And the Indians have probably discovered, that necessity has compelled this for more than as many generations. With these preliminary suggestions, let us now seek their picturesque habitations.

Their principal location is just below the old, or "Folsom" Bridge, on the north side of the Valley, about half a mile westerly of Leidig's Hotel. The usual and most enjoyable manner and time of visiting them is during the afternoon drive, described elsewhere. Just before reaching their encampment, some singular structures, built upon posts, arrest our attention. These are

THE ACORN STORE BASKETS,

The platforms of which are about four feet from the ground. They are generally twelve feet in height, and three and a half feet in diameter. The sides are formed of bushes, interlaced and covered with pine boughs, inverted; the needles of which prevent squirrels from climbing up, yet conduct the rain down, and

INDIAN WOMAN GATHERING ACORNS.

to the outside of the basket. The top is roofed by pieces of pine bark, cloth, or other material, securely fastened to the sides. The center of these rude contrivances being hollow, acorns are safely stored therein. These are called by the Indians *poo-see-na chuck-ka.*

ACORNS FORM THE STAPLE FOOD FOR INDIANS,

Not only in and around Yo Semite, but through all the mountain districts of the State. Nor is this peculiarity confined to those dwelling west of the great chain of the Sierras, inasmuch as those upon the eastern slope embrace the opportunity of sup-plementing any lack of piñons, or pine nuts *(Pinus monophylla)*, which constitute their principal article of diet there, for acorns; oaks being almost unknown on that side of the mountains. It is a fortunate or providential coincidence, too, that whenever the piñon crop fails on the eastern slope, acorns are generally abundant on the western, and *vice versa*. It is not an unusual sight at Yo Semite for a single file—and all travel single file—of Mono Indians (a branch of the Pah-utas, commonly called Pi-utes), numbering from twenty to fifty, of almost all ages, and of both sexes, to pass along the Valley. They come for acorns, mainly. Nor do they come empty-handed, as the conical baskets, and discolored sacks, at the backs of their females, abundantly prove; for they are loaded down with piñons, Kit-chavi, and other articles, as presents, or for exchange. About the Kit-chavi there is more to be said hereafter.

The little group of huts, constructed of cedar bark set on end, being the Indian camp, let us advance towards it somewhat reservedly, as a rude intruder is never welcome; and it requires quite an effort on their part to conquer their unpretentious diffidence and natural modesty. Remember this. After the quiet smile of welcome is given, a glance around will reveal to us that the women are all busy and fully occupied. Like many other housekeepers, their work seems never done. This one is skillfully plying her nimble fingers upon a water-tight basket; that, in deftly arranging the frame-work of one of another kind; as these people still rely entirely upon themselves for all such articles, notwithstanding the manifold contrivances brought within their reach by civilization. The woman at our left has evidently caught up the spirit of her more favored sisters, and is adroitly arranging the parts of a bright calico dress (nearly all Indians revel in bright colors); that, in repairing or turning one. Old habits are steadily, yet noticeably, passing away, and new—may we not devoutly hope better—ones are taking their places. That female with a shallow basket at her side, half filled with acorns, is dexterously preparing them for to-morrow's meal, by speedily setting each particular acorn on end, and with a light tap from a small pebble separating the husk from the kernel. Thus freed and cleaned, they are next spread upon a rock to dry. As these are to be fittingly prepared for human food, it may not be uninteresting to trace the different processes by which this is successfully accomplished.

First, then,

THE GRINDING.

The morning meal being satisfactorily disposed of, nearly

every available female in camp, each carrying her load, trudges off to an adjacent rock that is capacious, smooth, as nearly horizontal in position as possible, and in which sundry mortar-like holes are worn. This being protected from the scorching sun—and human eyes—by bushes, or young pine trees, each worker takes her seat near the mortar; then, armed with a rock-pestle, weighing from six to ten pounds, the toilsome labor of grinding acorns into meal commences, by pounding them. This process is necessarily very slow. By this primitive method grass and other seeds are also ground into flour or meal.

INDIAN WOMAN CARRYING ACORNS.

When the acorns thus pulverized are about the fineness of ordinary corn meal, as the acorn flour needs to be relieved of its bitter tannin to prevent constipation, it is carried to the nearest stream where there is an abundance of clean white sand, in which a hollow is scooped, about three feet in width, by six inches in depth, and which is patted evenly and compactly down, preparatory to a continuation of the intended process. Meanwhile other Indians have been building a fire, and almost covering it with roundish rocks from four to six inches in diameter. These are made nearly white

with heat. Water-
tight baskets, half
filled with water, are
then brought, into
which a suitable
quantity of the acorn
meal is well stirred.
The hot rocks are
then dropped in, and
moved around, until
the whole mass is
made, and kept, sim-
mering (without al-
lowing it to boil) for
nearly half an hour,
when it is all dipped
out, and carefully
poured into the shal-

INDIAN WOMAN GRINDING ACORNS AND SEEDS.

low sand-bowl, if it may be so called; to which hot water is constantly added, for the purpose of infiltrating the meal; and by percolation
removing the tannin therein contained, into the sand beneath. This
process is repeated until every perceptible vestige of discoloration
by the tannin is removed.

INDIANS PREPARING AND COOKING THEIR ACORN BREAD.

The meal thus divested of its bitter principle and deleterious
qualities, is ready for removal from its sand-basin to a basket. To
accomplish this, free of sand, requires very careful manipulation;
but, after removing all the soft, pulpy material possible, by
cautious handling, without including a grain of sand, the
remainder is stirred rapidly around in a conical basket, half
filled with water; when the meal settles on the sides of the basket, and the sand down into the inverted cone at the bottom. In
this way the whole is secured with but trifling waste of material.

It is now ready to be made into bread, or, rather, mush.

INDIANS PREPARING AND COOKING THEIR ACORN BREAD.

Water-tight baskets, containing the requisite quantity of clear water, are again pressed into service, and hot rocks added as before, until it is made to boil, this time. When the meal is sufficiently cooked, it is allowed to cool enough to handle, and is then served up by setting it down upon the ground; around which every expected participant begins to assemble in anticipation of the feast provided. Before commencing to eat, on all great occasions at least, the mush is first sprinkled over with *Kit-chavi.* As this is one of the mysteries of Indian cuisine, it is not to be expected that every one is familiar with its nature; a little explanation, therefore, of what this condiment consists, may make the matter somewhat plainer.

KIT-CHAVI.

On the western borders of Mono Lake (whence many of the Indian visitors of Yo Semite come), there is an extensive stretch of foam forms every summer; and soon thereafter it is covered with swarms of flies; which, when they rise *en masse,* literally darken the air; these, "fly-blow" the foam; and, later in the season, make it alive with larvæ and pupæ from one end to the other. At such times every available native, young and old, and of both sexes, repairs to Mono Lake with baskets of all kinds and sizes, old coal-oil cans, and such articles; and, collecting this foam with its living tenants, repair to the nearest fresh water stream (Mono Lake water being impregnated with strong alkalies), and there wash away the foam, while retaining all the larvæ and pupæ. This is spread upon flat rocks to dry; and when cured, is called "Kit-chavi," and thenceforward forms one of the luxuries of Indian food, and becomes their substitute for fresh butter!

Before participating therefore in the festivities of a morning or evening meal, this appetizing addition is made to their acorn mush-bread; when all sit, or kneel, around the unctuous viands, and with his or her two front fingers, converted for the time being into a spoon, help themselves to this unique repast, all eating from the same basket.

Wild greens, clover, gnats, grubs, and mushrooms; grass, weed, and other seeds, next to acorns, are their staples for food purposes, and the best they can command for winter consumption. To obtain these the women and children beat them into broad-topped baskets; and, after taking them to camp, clean, dry, and store them like acorns.

Bulbous grass roots, eaten raw, are a favorite food; from the digging of which, so frequently seen in early days, sprung the despised term "Digger Indians," now so generally, and so unworthily in use to designate the lowest class of mountain Indians throughout the State. All kinds of wild fruits, excepting the wild coffee, *Rhamnus Californica*, are partaken of with avidity. The young shoots of the *Hosackea* vetch, used as greens, are considered the finest of all native vegetables.

GRASSHOPPERS A GREAT FOOD LUXURY.

These are eaten as meat and cooked in various ways. Sometimes they are caught, threaded on a string, and hung over a fire until they are slightly roasted, then eaten from the string. At others the grass is set on fire, which both disables and cooks them; when they are picked up and eaten, or stored for future use.

The most effectual method for securing grasshoppers, when they are abundant, is to dig a hole sufficiently deep to prevent their jumping out; then to form a circle of Indians, both old and

INDIANS CATCHING GRASSHOPPERS FOR FOOD.

young, with a bush in each hand, and commence driving them towards it until they fall in, and are there caught. They are thence gathered into a sack, and saturated with salt water; after which a trench is dug, in which a good fire is built, and when it is sufficiently heated, the ashes are cleaned out, a little grass put upon the bottom, when the grasshoppers are put in, and covered with hot rocks and earth until they are sufficiently cooked. They are then eaten in the same manner as we eat shrimps; or are put away to mix with acorn or seed mush, when they are ground into a kind of paste. Deer, bear, rabbits, rats, squirrels, gophers, and almost every other animal, excepting the polecat; with birds of every kind, and fish, are necessarily made subservient to their physical wants.

When the larger game is hunted, a large district is surrounded by every available Indian, and experts with the bow and arrow are stationed at a given point; when, by fire and noise, the affrighted animals are driven towards that spot, where they are killed. These general hunts take place in the fall of the year, when everything being dry is easily ignited, and when a winter supply of meat is needed. It is to this system of procuring game that so many forest trees have been burned in past years; but the sheepherder's vandal hands, mainly, are perpetuating this infamously wanton practice at the present time. Hunting, however, is too active an employment to square with their ideas of ease and comfort; so that to comport with these, and yet secure their game, they drive it into swampy places, where they mire down and are then caught and killed.

INDIAN FANDANGOS.

To the casual observer, a fandango, or Indian ball, is a wild, careless, free-and-easy dancing and feasting party, and nothing more. To the Indians it is a friendly gathering together of the remnants of their race, for the purpose of cementing and perpetuating the bonds of family and tribal union more closely; and at the same time to orally transmit to posterity the noble deeds and valorous actions of their ancestors.

Any particular tribe wishing to give a fandango sends messengers to all the chiefs of the surrounding tribes, to whom they wish to give the invitation; accompanied by a bundle of reeds or sticks, which indicates the number of days before it takes place; but sometimes notches are cut in a twig, or knots are tied in a string, for that purpose.

Extensive preparations are immediately entered upon for a grand feast, and everything within the limit of Indian purveyance is pressed into service; nor is it to be supposed that those giving the invitation are the only contributors, by any means; inasmuch as every attendant takes something to make up the general variety; and to add to that valuable quality in an Indian's estimation—quantity. At such times, too, presents of blankets and other valuables are brought and exchanged.

At these festive seasons, both males and females dress themselves according to their most extravagant notions of paint and feathers. Several weeks are frequently consumed in making headdresses, and other ornaments, of shells, beads, top-knots of quails, and the heads and wings of red-headed woodpeckers. When the great day of the feast arrives, groups of Indians may be seen wending their hilarious way to the festive scene; and as many have to travel fifteen or twenty miles, the whole first day is consumed in assembling together, and gossiping over family matters. In the evening, when all are assembled, the "band" (which consists of about a dozen men, with reed whistles, and wooden castanets, with which they beat the time) begins a monotonous *few-few* with their whistles; while the dancers follow their leader with the castanets, and with them keep time with a perpetual *hi-yah*, *hi-yah*, until they are out of breath, when they take their seats for a rest, and listen to their orator for the occasion.

These fandangos are generally kept up for a number of days; and, as frequently happens at others much more fashionable, it is at such times that many an Indian youth and maiden fall irretrievably in love, and seek to unite their hands and fortunes in wedlock. When this is understood, and the union receives the approbation of their parents and friends, both are allowed a personal inspection of each other in private; and if this proves satisfactory, the fortunate lover gathers together all his worldly wealth, and repairs with it to his expected future father-in-law. The old man generally appears surprised, hesitates, inspects the candidate for his daughter's hand from head to foot, then the

INDIAN MARRIAGE CEREMONY.

amount of earthly goods the lover has brought him, as an
equivalent for his daughter's hand and heart. After some eloquent
pleading, the old man's thoughtful face generally relaxes into a
smile, and as soon as he has accepted the presents, the ceremony
is ended, and thenceforward they are considered man and wife.

Strange as it may seem, the Indian men will not infrequently gamble away their wives, as they do other kinds of property, (for they are inveterate gamblers); and they are far too apt to consider the wife but little better than a chattel for barter and sale. Quite often a given number of Indian men agree to fight for a certain number of Indian women, on which occasion each party puts up equally. As soon as either side is victorious, the women, who have been awaiting this "hazard of the die" as interested spectators, arise, and without hesitancy, or question, accompany the victors; and are apparently contented with the result. To obtain women was frequently the only cause for war among them. And when any particular tribe ran short of squaws, it unceremoniously stole some from an adjoining tribe; which, on the very earliest favorable occasion, returned the doubtful compliment, and sometimes with considerable interest. Polygamy is quite common, some of the chiefs having from three to seven wives, the number being limited only, (as among the Mormons), by their ability to support them.

INDIAN DOCTORS.

This profession is very popular among the Indians, and although their knowledge of medical science, even in its rudest and most primitive form, is much more limited than with the tribes east of the Rocky Mountains, they sometimes perform a few simple cures, and on this account are looked up to with considerable respect. The Indians have got great confidence in their "medicine men," and believe them endowed with the power of insuring health, or of causing sickness, or even death; but if they think that the doctors have used this power arbitrarily, or unworthily, they are unceremoniously put to death. Their methods for relieving pain and curing disease are as unique as they would be amusing to a skillful practitioner. They have, however, learned a little of the sophistry and finesse of the profession, and use it with considerable skill. As illustrative of this, as they generally scarify, to suck away all pain, they will sometimes put small stones, or bits of stick, or wild coffee berries, into their mouth, and produce these to the patient to induce him to believe that this or that has been the cause of all his pain; and as he has been successful in removing the cause, the pain will naturally cease!

THEIR RELIGIOUS BELIEFS.

They all believe in a good spirit, and also in a very evil spirit. The good spirit, according to their apprehension, is always good; and, therefore, ever to be loved and trusted, without fear or dread; that, consequently, there is no use in giving themselves any trouble about him. But not so with the evil spirit, as in his nature are concentrated all the bad qualities of twenty Pohono's condensed into one; and, therefore, he is the one that needs watching, and conciliating if possible.

They also believe in a pleasant camping ground after death, one that is most bountifully supplied with every comfort, and where they will again meet all their relatives and friends, and live with them in ease and plenty forever. This camping ground is presided over by the good spirit, a semi-deity or chief of great power and kindness, and who is ever making them supremely happy. They also believe that the evil spirit is doing everything that he can to make them miserable, and keep them away from this happy camping ground; that, therefore, their principal religious duties consist in avoiding, circumventing, or placating him.

They believe that the heart is the immortal part, and that if the body is buried the evil one stands perpetual guard over the grave, and will eventually secure the heart as his wished-for prisoner and prize. With the view of defeating this wicked purpose, they invariably burned the bodies of their dead (a practice that has been largely discontinued in later years, and the example of the whites followed, in burying them), thinking by noises and grotesque motions, accompanied by expressions of poignant sorrow, to attract the attention of the evil one while the body is burning, and thus give the heart the opportunity of slipping away unobserved. Hence their custom of cremation.

When an Indian is known to be near his departure to the spirit land—as they are all in a certain sense more or less spiritualists—his head is generally pillowed in the lap of his wife, or dearest friend; when, all standing around commence a low, mournful chant upon the virtues of the dying; and with this soothing lullaby falling upon his ears, he passes to the deep sleep of death. As soon as his heart has ceased to beat, the sad news is carried by runners to all his relatives, both far and near; and the low chant is changed to loud and frantic wailings; accompanied by violent beatings of the chest with their clenched fists; while with tearful eyes directed upwards, they apostrophize the spirit of the departed one in their own behalf.

It is a singular fact that although some Indians now bury their dead, and others burn them, in either case the same preparations are made for final disposition, which are as follows: A blanket is spread upon the ground, and the corpse laid thereon,

PREPARING THE BODY FOR CREMATION.

when a brother, or other near relative, carefully, but firmly, folds the knees up towards the chin, places the arms down over them, and then binds the body and limbs together as tightly as it is possible so to do. All this time the wild howling and wailing continues until the body is ready; then, for about twenty minutes, or half an hour, the mourning ceases; and not a sound is allowed to intrude upon the stillness and rude solemnity of the scene. At a given signal all rise simultaneously; the women to renew their wailings, and the men to build the funeral pyre, or to prepare the grave.

When the fuel, composed mainly of pitch pine and oak, is about two feet high, every sound again ceases; and, amid a death-like stillness, the men place the body upon the pyre. This accomplished, additional wood is piled upon and around it, until all except the face is completely covered up. Then, slowly and solemnly, the nearest and oldest relative advances, with torch in hand, and with deep yet suppressed emotion sets the wood on fire.

INDIANS BURNING THEIR DEAD.

The moment the first cloud of smoke eddies up into the air, the discordant howling of the women becomes deafening, and almost appalling; while the men, for the most part, look on with sullen and unbroken silence.

Those who are nearest and dearest to the fire-consuming dead, with long sticks in their hands, dance frantically around; and occasionally stir up the fire, or turn the burning body over, to insure its more speedy consumption by the devouring element; hoping by these united movements to attract the evil one's attention, and give the heart the opportunity of eluding his watchful glances, and of escaping unseen to the happy camping ground.

After the body is nearly consumed, the blackened remains are taken from the fire, rolled up in one of their best blankets, or cloths, and allowed to cool a little; when his wives, or those nearest and dearest, segregate the unconsumed portions, and wrap every piece separately in strings of beads, or other ornaments; they then place them carefully in a basket that has been most beautifully worked for the occasion, with any other valuables possessed by the departed one, and the fire being rebuilt, the basket and its contents are placed upon it; with blankets, cloths, dresses, bows and arrows, and every other article that has been touched by the deceased, and all are then committed to the flames. When these are burned, every unconsumed log is carefully scraped, the ashes swept together, and the whole, with the exception of the portion always reserved for mourning, are then placed in another basket and carefully buried. All Indians, without exception, cast the personal property of the deceased, as well as presents of their own, into the grave; so that he may want nothing when he enters the camping ground, believed to be somewhere in the far distant West. The reserved ashes being mixed with pitch is spread over the faces of the female relatives as a badge of mourning; and which, although hideous to our sight, is sacred to theirs; and is allowed to remain until it wears off, which is generally about six months. Sometimes the old squaws renew their mourning from the cheeks to the ears. A married woman, when her husband dies, invariably cuts off her hair. Mr. Galen Clark, one of the oldest residents of Yo Semite, assured the writer that when in their deepest lamentations for their dead, they cry out, "Him-mah-lay-ah," "Him-mah-lay-ah," gesticulating westward.

CHAPTER XXV.

VERNAL AND NEVADA FALLS.

These are thy glorious works, Parent of good.
—Milton's *Paradise Lost, Bk. V, Line 153.*

The rustle of the leaves in summer's hush
　　When wandering breezes touch them, and the sigh
That filters through the forest, or the gush
　　That swells and sinks amid the branches high,—
'Tis all the music of the wind, and we
　　Let fancy float on this Æolian breath.
—M. G. Brainard's *Music.*

But on and up, where Nature's heart
Beats strong amid the hills.
—Richard Milnes.

As a rule it is desirable that the trips to Mirror Lake, and to the Vernal and Nevada Falls, should be taken conjointly; inasmuch as the two can be comfortably included on the same day. Besides this when we are at the Tis-sa-ack Bridge, after the Tis-sa-ack Avenue drive, we are two miles on our way to those falls. To avoid doubling the two miles of distance, between Barnard's and the Tis-sa-ack Bridge, while utilizing the stretch gained, as the remaining two and three-fifths miles to Snow's Hotel have to be taken on horseback, our *saddle animals should meet us at the bridge.*

TIMID PEOPLE HAVE NO CAUSE FOR FEAR.

As many persons who visit Yo Semite have never sat on a horse before, and many others have been entirely out of practice of later years, and in consequence are possibly a little nervous about it, it seems to me to be eminently proper that I should here invite their encouraging confidence in themselves, by stating that each horse is well trained, and knows where to set down every foot; so as to insure not only his own safety but that of the

(438)

precious burden he is bearing. Then, it should be borne in mind that, notwithstanding the many, many thousands who have ridden up and down these mountain trails, there has never been a serious accident upon any one of them, in the thirty-one years this Valley has been opened to the public. Think of this.

BY THE ANDERSON TRAIL TOWARDS VERNAL FALL.

Owing to the intersecting connection that has recently been made between the new Anderson trail up the northern bank of the main Merced River, and the Snow trail on the southern bank, at Register Rock, a new, and if possible, more picturesque ride than the former one along the base of Echo Wall, has been opened up. Therefore, instead of crossing to the southern end of Tis-sa-ack Bridge, we will, if you please, take the broad and well-graded Anderson trail at the northern end of the bridge. Maples, dogwoods, oaks, pines, and cedars edge in and arch over our path; and near Cold Spring—the only one on this route— grows a fine clump of tall and feathery *Woodwardia* ferns. By looking back a few yards beyond this the Valley has the semblance of a forest walled in; while over its distant boundary the Yo Semite Fall is leaping.

Passing just immediately along the foot of Grizzly Peak, where the horse-path has been hewn out of solid granite; or high supporting walls have been built upon it, to make a thoroughfare possible here, it can be readily seen how great were the difficulties to be surmounted.

The late George Anderson, who engineered and constructed it, and after whom it will probably be named, made a contract to complete it to Snow's Hotel for $1,500. This, however, was all expended before Grizzly Peak was passed. A similar amount was voted him for finishing it, but this was also found to be far from sufficient; he was then engaged to continue it, *ad libitum;* but, after some $5,000 had been expended upon it, and the granite wall along the north side of the Vernal Fall, over which the trail was to run for over eleven hundred feet, had scarcely been touched, further work upon it was for the present suspended. This broad and substantial trail, however, remains a monumental acknowledgment of Anderson's skill, pluck, indomitable will, and undiscourageable perseverance.

The trail (almost wide enough for a wagon road), presents sublimely delightful pictures of the rushing, boiling, surging river; and the finest of all views, of the Too-lool-a-we-ack, or Glacier Cañon, stretching the entire length of it to its four hundred feet water-fall, near the Horseshoe Grotto at its head. This cañon is called by Prof. J. D. Whitney the "Illilouette," a supposed Indian name; but I have never questioned a single Indian that knew anything whatever of such a word; while every one, without an exception, knows this cañon either by Too-lool-a-we-ack or Too-lool-we-ack; the meaning of which, as nearly as their ideas can be comprehended and interpreted, is the place beyond which was the great rendezvous of the Yo Semite Indians for hunting deer. However this may have been, the way up to it was certainly never through this cañon, if it always had surroundings as wildly impassable as the present ones.

VIEW FROM ANDERSON'S OLD BLACKSMITH SHOP.

Before crossing the Merced River, those who are good walkers and delight in grand scenes, should leave their horses at the junction of the trails, and make their way afoot to the top of the *debris* at the back of Anderson's old black smith shop; as thence magnificent views are obtained of both the Vernal and Nevada Falls, with all their varied mountainous surroundings. Before very long a good horse-path will probably be made to this point; and, possibly, to the foot of the Vernal Fall, on the north side of the river.

THE VERNAL FALL FROM REGISTER ROCK BRIDGE.

Those who have ever witnessed the glorious scene this fall presents from the Lady Franklin Rock, some two hundred yards above, can form an approximating idea of its impressive majesty from *this* fine standpoint. Dr. Wm. B. May, Secretary to the Board of Commissioners, thus reports this scene to the Board: "Standing upon the new bridge, with the Vernal Fall in the near upper view, and the wealth and war of rushing waters beneath one's feet, there is a presence of power and grandeur, hardly equaled in the Valley." The musical Merced, as it roars, and gurglingly rushes among and over huge bowlders, that here throng the channel of the river, possibly calls to memory that passage of holy writ: "And I heard as it were the voice of a great multitude, and as the voice of many waters, and as the voice of mighty thunderings, saying, Alleluia; for the Lord God omnipotent reigneth."

REGISTER ROCK.

This is an immense, overhanging, smooth-faced "chip" of rock about the size of an ordinary village church; upon which very many have, at various times and seasons, inscribed their names; not so much for expected immortality, perhaps, as to inform their friends, who may at some subsequent season see it, that they have been here. There is one entry upon a sloping side rock, that is perhaps worthy of notice, as it reads, "Camped here August 21, 1863. A. Bierstadt, Virgil Williams, E. W. Perry, Fitzhugh Ludlow." It was during this visit to the Valley that Mr. Bierstadt made the sketch from which his famous picture, "The Domes of the Yo Semite," was afterwards painted.

A VISIT TO THE LADY FRANKLIN ROCK.

This name was given in honor of the devoted wife of the great Arctic voyager, Sir John Franklin, who paid Yo Semite a visit in 1863. From this rock one of the best of all views is obtained of

THE VERNAL FALL.

The Indian name of this magnificent water-leap is "Pi-wy-ack," which, if it could be literally interpreted, would express a constant shower of scintillating crystals. Seen from below, it is an apparently vertical sheet of water, of sparkling brightness, and of almost snowy whiteness, leaping into a rock-strewn basin at its foot; whence vast billows of finely comminuted spray roll forth in surging waves, and out of which the most beautiful of rainbows are built, to span the angry chasm with a befitting halo of exalting glory. This fall, if possible, impresses one more than any other with the feeling of Infinite Power.

Its vertical height, by nearly every measurement, is three hundred and fifty feet; and its breadth on top, varying of course somewhat with the differing stages of water, is about eighty feet. The Wheeler U. S. Survey corps made the altitude of this fall three hundred and forty-three feet. Professor Whitney, State Geologist, thus speaks of it:—

> The first fall reached in ascending the cañon is the Vernal, a perpendicular sheet of water with a descent varying greatly with the season. Our measurements give all the way from 315 feet to 475 feet for the vertical height of the fall, between the months of June and October. The reason of these discrepancies seems to lie in the fact that the rock near the bottom is steeply inclined, so that a precise definition of the place where the perpendicular part ceases is very difficult amid the blinding spray and foam. As the body of water increases, the force of the fall is greater, and of course it is thrown farthest forward when the mass of water is greatest. Probably it is near the truth to call the height of the fall, at the average stage of the water in June or July, 400 feet. The rock behind this fall is a perfectly square-cut mass of granite, extending across the cañon, etc.

Now, inasmuch as, according to Professor Whitney's admission, it is a "perpendicular sheet of water," and "the rock behind this fall is a perfectly square-cut mass of granite extending across the cañon," I must confess my inability to see that there could, by any possibility, be a difference, at any time, of more than a foot or two at most; as, when the water was highest on the top, the same result would be noticeable in the pool at the bottom; thus precluding the probability of a difference of one hundred and sixty feet in a "perpendicular" fall of three hundred and fifty feet. Had the steep inclination spoken of been applied to the Nevada Fall wall, it would have been perfectly correct, but it is not in the least degree when speaking of the Vernal.

THROUGH THE SPRAY TO THE "LADDERS."

Many attempt this when the fall is fullest; but, novel as the experience may be, the proceeding, in my judgment, is not among the wisest to the average visitor. Over two hundred feet of altitude has to be attained through blinding spray; which not only closes the eyes, but takes away the breath needed for the climb. It is far better to come down through this, and have it helpfully at our backs, than defiantly and drenchingly in our faces. But, should it be attempted, one is soon enveloped in a heavy sheet of spray, that is driven down in such gusty force as to resemble a heavy beating storm of comminuted rain. It is true that to an athletic climber, with good lungs, it is not only possible, but enjoyable; and, moreover, is very soon accomplished. Ladies, however, attempting this will need suitably short dresses; or they will not only be inconvenienced at every step, but incur the danger of falling; and, possibly, of rolling down into the angry current below.

RIDE UP THE TRAIL.

Prudence, therefore, suggesting that this should be deferred until our return, let us retrace our steps to the horses at Register Rock; that, by this time, are sufficiently rested to carry us safely up the zigzagging trail to the top of the hill, some eight hundred feet above us. At almost every turning in the trail its sinuosities enable us to look upon the members of our party, and exchange with them a greeting look, a kindly word, or snatches of a favorite song. Our progress upward is necessarily slow, as the animals need to pause for breath, if not for strength; but trees and tree shadows, mossy rocks, and towering cliffs bespeak admiring thoughts for every moment. When about two-thirds of the climb has been overcome, from a corner of the trail, looking back, the top of Yo Semite Fall comes into view. But presently we find ourselves crossing the highest point on the way to Snow's, and before us opens a scene never to be forgotten. It is the Cap of Liberty, and Nevada Fall.

Of these two there seems to be a difficulty in determining

Photo by Geo. Fiske.

CAP OF LIBERTY AND NEVADA FALL.

Cap of Liberty 3100 ft. & Nevada Fall

The photograph from which the halftone/engraving on the
opposite page was taken. The buildings of Snow's Hotel
(La Casa Nevada) are on the flat just to the left of center.

Fiske #347

ZIGZAGS TO TOP OF NEVADA FALL

(See page 463)

Original caption: Stairway on Clouds' Rest Trail.

Fiske #441. Facing page 462 in edition three, and page 463 in edition four.

which is the most attractive; but, taken together as here presented, the scenic combination is marvelously imposing. Let us, however, separate them, momentarily, for consideration, notwithstanding "they are but parts of one stupendous whole."

THE CAP OF LIBERTY, HOW AND WHEN SO NAMED.

Owing to the exalted and striking individuality of this boldly singular mountain (some most excellent judges pronouncing it only secondary to El Capitan), it had many godfathers in early days; who christened it Mt. Frances, Gwin's Peak, Bellows' Butte, Mt. Broderick, and others; but, when Governor Stanford (now U. S. Senator) was in front of it with his party in 1865, and inquired its name, the above list of appellatives was enumerated, and the Governor invited to take his choice of candidates. A puzzled smile lighted up his face and played about his eyes, as he responded, "Mr. H., I cannot say that I like either of those names very much *for that magnificent mountain;* don't you think a more appropriate one could be given?" Producing an old-fashioned half dollar with the ideal Cap of Liberty well defined upon it, the writer suggested the close resemblance in form of the mountain before us with the embossed cap on the coin; when the governor exclaimed, "Why! Mr. H., that would make a most excellent and appropriate name for that mountain. Let us so call it." *Thenceforward it was so called;* and as every one preferentially respects this name, all others have been quietly renunciated.

THE SUMMIT OF THE CAP OF LIBERTY.

Its altitude above Snow's Hotel, by my aneroid barometer, is one thousand eight hundred feet. The singularity of its form and majesty of presence must impress every beholder. For many years it was pronounced inaccessible, but a few enthusiastic spirits found their way to the top. Apparently such an isolated mass of granite could scarcely find foot-hold for a few bushes, that strugglingly eked out a half-starved existence; but, strange as it may seem, when once upon its crown, quite a number of goodly sized trees and shrubs are found; among which are nine juniper trees, *Juniperus Occidentalis* two of which are *over ten feet in diameter*, and must be some fifteen hundred years old. The moss on these is the most beautiful when in blossom, of any that I ever saw. There are also several Douglas spruce trees, *Psudotsuga Douglasii;* and the dwarf shrub oak, *Quercus dumosa*, manzanita, and others; besides flowers, flowering shrubs, and ferns.

But a view from the top of the Cap of Liberty repays for all the fatigue attending the scrambling climb to reach it. Deep down in the Little Yo Semite Valley (the entire length of which is visible), meanders the Merced River. Tall pines and firs, everywhere abundant, appear like toy trees about the right size for walking-canes. But, let us take courage, and walk out to the edge of the Cap; as, at the southeastern corner, there is a large glacier-left bowlder which offers clinging support for our fingers, while steadying our nerves, so that we can look down into the abyss between us and the Nevada Fall; noting the form and graceful sweep of its waters and the dazzling whiteness of its sheeny foam. Echo Wall, Glacier Point, Sentinel Dome, the top of El Capitan, Eagle Peak, Yo Semite Fall, Grizzly Peak, omnipresent Half Dome, Cloud's Rest, and Mount Starr King, with numerous points and ridges, are all in full sight.

SIDE VIEW OF THE VERNAL FALL.

Returning, in thought, to the point whence our first glimpse of these wonders was obtained, we follow the sinuosities of the trail nearly to the brink of the chasm, into which we can see the Vernal Fall leaping. When nearest, it would be well here to dismount; and, carefully picking our way down within a few feet of the edge (where a safe and convenient opening between blocks of rock enables us to sit comfortably), by leaning over a little, we can watch the water-fall leaping from its verge on the top to the pool at the bottom. This charming view is too often passed by without being noticed and enjoyed.

Before bestowing more than a passing glance on the multitudinous objects of uncommon interest in this vicinity, if they are to be enjoyed, thoroughly and in detail, it would be well to repair directly to Snow's, for rest and refreshment.

SNOW'S "CASA NEVADA."

This hospice is situated about midway between the top of the Vernal, and foot of the Nevada Falls.[1] It has become deservedly famous all over the world, not only for its excellent lunches and general good cheer, but from the quiet, unassuming attentions of mine host, and the piquant pleasantries of Mrs. Snow. I do not think that another pair, anywhere, could be found that would more fittingly fill this position. And, although they do not know whether the number to lunch will be five or fifty-five, they almost always seem to have an abundance of everything relishable. On one occasion—and this will illustrate Mrs. Snow's natural readiness with an answer—a lady, seeing so great a variety upon the table, with eager interest inquired, "Why! Mrs. Snow, where on earth do you get all these things?" "Oh! we raise them!" "Why! where can you possibly do so, as I see nothing but rocks around here?" "Oh! madam, we *raise them*—on the backs of mules!"

From the porches of the Casa Nevada, and its comfortable "cottage," the glorious Nevada Fall, where the whole Merced River makes a leap of over six hundred feet, a magnificent view is obtained. The roar of this fall, and the billowy mists that in early spring roll out such eddying and gusty masses of spray, arched by rainbows on every sun-lighted afternoon, will captivate and charm our every emotion. The best view, probably, of this sublime spectacle is from the foot-bridge, over the hurrying and wave-surging river. There a scene is presented that fills the soul to overflowing with reverential and impressive awe; as, with uncovered head, the self-prompted mental question is in silence asked, "Is not this the very footstool of his throne?"

"The Nevada Fall is," says Prof. J. D. Whitney, "in every respect, one of the grandest water-falls in the world; whether

---

1. The Snows ran their three-building hostelry from 1870 to 1891. The buildings burned in 1897.

we consider its vertical height, the purity and volume of the river which forms it, or the stupendous scenery by which it is environed." This is an opinion that I have frequently heard expressed by travelers from many lands. When in front of it, and looking upward, it can readily be seen that this fall differs in form with either of the others; for, although it shoots over the precipice in a curve, it soon strikes the smooth surface of the mountain, and spreads out into a sheet of marvelously snowy whiteness, and of burnished brightness, widening as it descends, until it sometimes exceeds one hundred feet in breadth, at the pool into which it is leaping. The height of this fall is given at six hundred and five feet by the Wheeler U. S. Survey corps.

This point being as near as visitors generally go—although many enthusiastic climbers and appreciative lovers of the beautiful seek the wonderful view from its top—we will, for the present, if you please, ask the guide to take our horses down to Register Rock, while we say good-by to our genial host and his wife, and then seek the wondrous scenes below, afoot.

ELEVEN FEET OF SNOW.

A gentleman who, from modesty, desires that his name may be kept a secret, once took an unfair advantage of a confiding visitor, by informing him that there were nearly eleven feet of snow visible here throughout the hottest days of summer. "Is it possible? Oh! how much I should like to see it." "Please allow me, then, to introduce you to Mr. and Mrs. Snow—the former being five feet nine inches, and the latter making up the remainder!"

Soon after leaving "Snow's," we find ourselves upon the bridge that here spans the river. Listening to the roar of the fall above, we naturally turn our faces towards it, and then look down into the apparently insignificant stream beneath us, and think, can this be the whole of the main Merced River? It scarcely seems possible, but so it is. Its narrow, rock-bound, and deep, trough-like channel confines it to a width seldom exceeding ten

Photo by Geo. Fiske   NPS, Yosemite Collections

THE LADDERS BELOW VERNAL FALL. 80 ft.
See the retouched early halftone on page 452.
Fiske #234

Photo by Charles L. Weed   Peter E. Palmquist

THE RAPIDS

The engraving on the opposite page was taken from Weed's Stereo #12,
made in June 1859. The Silver Apron is the name for the stream at the
lower left in the engraving. The name "Diamond Cascade,"—the rapids—
which was applied to the Merced River below the Nevada Fall bridge,
has never been on maps.

feet. While it is swashing and rushing on, let us turn our gaze to the opposite side, and look down on

THE DIAMOND CASCADE.

We now readily appreciate the apposite character of its name; for, down, down, the whole river is leaping, as if in very wantonness and exultation at the liberty it has gained; and, being seized with an uncontrollable fit of frolicking, is tossing up diamonds (of the purest water) with a prodigality and apparent improvidence that would shock the sensitive acquisitiveness of "My Uncle," if he could see it. By the demureness of its demeanor, however, below, as it "pursues the even tenor of its way," it would seem to be laughing in its sleeve, and saying, "You see, I was only in fun—don't mind me!" Around a jutting point of rock, we find ourselves at the Silver Apron.

SILVER APRON, AND DIAMOND CASCADE, FROM BELOW.

When standing near the edge of the impetuous current, and looking up towards the Diamond Cascade Bridge we have so recently crossed, the whole river seems to be attempting, in the most reckless manner, to throw its separated and scintillating drops and masses into our faces; but, unmindful of, or excusing this, we cannot resist the temptation of watching the sportive and sprightly fearlessness of its dashing abandon; or the astonishingly brilliant beauty of this sparkling outlet from the Diamond Cascade.

Directly in front of us, and down at our left, the whole river is scurrying over smooth, bare granite, at the rate of a fast express train on the best of railroads. Pieces of wood or bark tossed upon its silvery bosom tell instantly of its marvelous speed.

TAKING A "BAWTH."

An English gentleman who was making his temporary residence at Snow's Hotel, amazed its inmates one morning by appearing on the scene with his face badly cut, and his hands bleeding. With astonished surprise at such a sight Mr. Snow innocently inquired:—

"What on earth, man, have you been doing to yourself, to get into such a plight as that?"

Looking steadfastly at the questioner, while wiping the red stains away with as much easy deliberation as though a little dust had fallen upon his face, and needed removal, he hesitatingly made answer:—

"Th-the-there is, you k-know, a s-smooth k-kind of place in the-the river, j-just b-be-low the-the lit-tle bridge, you know, w-where the-the wa-water p-passes s-somewhat r-rapidly over the-the-rock, you know."

"Oh! yes," replied Mr. Snow, "I remember; that is what we call the 'Silver Apron.' Well?"

"W-well, w-when I g-gazed up-upon it, I-I-th-thought it-it w-would be a-a-de-lightful p-place to t-t-take a-a b-bawth, you k-know."

"Why, sir," responded the landlord of the 'Casa Nevada,' aghast, and interruptingly, "why, the whole Merced River shoots over there, at the rate of about sixty miles an hour—faster than a locomotive goes upon a railroad!"

"Is-is i-it p-possible? W-we-well, I h-had n-no s-sooner d-dis-robed m-my-s-self, and s-set m-my f-foot in-into th-the h-hurrying c-c-current, y-you k-know, t-than i-it k-knocked m-me off m-my p-ins, you know! an-and s-swept me d-down s-so s-swiftly th-that it q-quite t-took my b-breath a-away f-for a f-few m-moments, you k-know; s-sometimes i-it r-rolled me o-over and o-over, a-and a-at o-other t-times s-shot me d-down en-endwise, y-you k-know; a-and fi-finally b-brought m-me up-in a s-sort of pool, y-you know!"

"The Emerald Pool," suggested Mr. Snow.

"And, b-by G-George, if I h-had no-not b-been an ex-excel-lent swim-swimmer, I s-should cer-certainly h-have l-lost my life, you know! A-and, it is n-not my h-hands a-and m-my f-face o-only-i-it is a-all o-over m-me-like that, you know!"

Opinions are sometimes hastily formed, and are not always supported by the best of good reasons; and it may be so in this case, but the supposition most generally prevails, that, when this gentleman wishes to take another "bawth," he will not seek to do so at the "Silver Apron."

THE EMERALD POOL.

This is a beautiful lake, or pool, whose waters are, as its name signifies, "emerald." The river's current, driving with great force into its upper margin, causes a constant succession of waves to disturb its surface, especially during the spring flow. Its moun-tainous surroundings, trees, and bowlders, add much to the pic-turesqueness of its character. Descending towards

THE TOP OF THE VERNAL FALL,

Little patches of glacier-polished rock surface are still distinctly visible, the striations of which indicate the exact course the great ice-field must have once taken. Approaching the edge of

Photo by Geo. Fiske.

THE LADDERS—IN WINTER.

the fall, almost before we have glanced at its diamond-fringed lip, we walk up to, and lean upon, a natural balustrade of granite, that seems to have been constructed there for the especial benefit of weak-nerved people; so that the most timid can look over it into the entrancing abyss beneath. After this experience many have sufficient nerve to stand on the edge near the side of the fall, especially if some less nervous person should take them by the hand, and thence looking down the entire front of its diamond-lighted, rocket-formed surface, follow it with the eye to the pool beneath. Sometimes bright rainbows are arching the spray at its foot, and which, extending from bank to bank, completely bridge the billowy mist and angry foam below. But, turning away from these delightful sights, let us seek the "Ladders," so called from the original, but which have been transformed into substantial steps (to which the old term "ladders" still clings), by which we can descend to Fern Grotto, on our way to the foot of the Vernal Fall Wall.

FERN GROTTO.

Here a portion of the mountain has been removed, and left a large cave or grotto, in the interstices of which numerous ferns, the *Adiantum pedatum,* mainly, one of the maiden hair species, formerly grew in abundance; but constant plucking of the leaves, and removal of the roots, have shorn it of its fern-like character, where they could be reached without danger. A glance at the accompanying engraving will enable the visitor, measurably, to conceive the superb, fairy-like creations of the enchanter's wand to be found here in winter. Hours might be pleasantly spent at this spot, but we must hurry through the spray to our horses; and while some are returning to the hotel, let us retrace our steps, at least in imagination, as some more enthusiastic natures yearn to see what there is of interest above and beyond this; and which necessarily forms the substance of the ensuing chapter.

CHAPTER XXVI.

GRIZZLY PEAK, HALF DOME, AND CLOUD'S REST

> The broad blue mountains lift their brows
> Barely to bathe them in the blaze.
> >   —HARRIET PRESCOTT SPOFFORD'S *Daybreak.*

> He prov'd the best man i' the field; and for his meed
> Was brow-bound with the oak.
> >   —SHAKESPEAR'S *Coriolanus, Act II, Sc. 2.*

> Round its breast the rolling clouds are spread,
> Eternal sunshine settles on his head.
> >   —GOLDSMITH'S *Deserted Village.*

When standing on the bare granite in front of Snow's Hotel, with the Nevada Fall and Cap of Liberty at our backs, not only are the Silver Apron, Emerald Pool, and Glacier Point (including McCauley's House) distinctly visible before us; but, looking northwestwardly, there towers up the bold, rugged point of a mountain, and one that has also attracted considerable attention from us when in the Valley, that, at its base, is skirted by the Anderson Trail, and which is known as

GRIZZLY PEAK.

Seen from this standpoint it resembles an immense Moorish head, with a long, prominent nose, formed of one large slab of rock set edgewise, with dwarf trees for eyebrows. This, and the Cathedral Spires, are the only points upon which I have never set foot. Mr. Chas. A. Bailey climbed this a year ago, and has kindly sent me the following account of his difficult feat:—

Stimulated by the assertion that Grizzly Peak had never been ascended by any white man, I determined to attempt it. Leaving Snow's with a stout staff and a good lunch, I crept up a narrow and steep ravine, flanked by the great Half Dome, to a narrow connecting neck between

(454)

the latter and the object of my ambitious climb. This was attended by many a rough scramble, as its nearly vertical sides loomed up like a church steeple. Crossing the neck to its southerly side, there was but one spot that was possibly accessible, and this was made so only by the aid of friendly bushes that grew in the interstices of the rock. An unbroken precipice extended from the edge of the peak to the Valley on one side, but which developed a slab-cleavage of granite on the other, the edge of which, although sharp, was rapidly disintegrating; but this I mounted, and, by striding, clasping, hitching, and crawling along it, reached its farther and upper end in safety.

Further on the ascent had to be made by climbing up a narrow fissure, by pressing my knees and elbows against its sides, until either finger or foothold could be obtained. This passed, a steeply slanting rock was crossed by moving over it with a crawling kind of motion, where friction and the force of gravitation were my principal helpers, to keep me from sliding over the cliff. As a safeguard, however, I kept my eye on some projecting slabs below, for which I intended to spring, should I unavoidably slide from my position. Fortunately I eventually reached the top, some two thousand five hundred feet above the Valley, in safety.

The glories of these crags seem to be immeasurably heightened and deepened, and the uplifting peaks made grander and loftier, when their summits are attained by a hard and perilous climb; and the view from Grizzly Peak was so unlike that I had obtained elsewhere, that the very novelty charmed and repaid me. Resting, as it apparently does, in the shadow of the great Half Dome; on the edge, and almost projecting over the Merced River, its position is commandingly impressive. Glacier Point, though seemingly near, with a much greater altitude, has a wonderfully imposing presence from this standpoint. Looking east and south, Mt. Broderick (the peak next westerly from the Cap of Liberty), Mt. Clark, and Mt. Starr King, stand grandly out above their lesser mountain brethren. From here, too, a bird's-eye view is obtained of Snow's, which, with its surrounding trees, and the Emerald Pool, looks like a place of enchantment. Perhaps the finest single view of all these is the Too-lool-a-we-ack, or Glacier Cañon, which can be seen for its entire length; with its narrow mountain-walled channel, its numberless bowlders, its dashing and foaming torrent, and its distant water-fall of some four hundred feet at the end. I fondly hoped to get a view of the upper falls; this, however, was intercepted by a jutting spur. But for this I could have seen the four great water-falls of the Valley from a single standpoint—the Vernal, Nevada, Too-lool-a-we-ack, and Yo Semite—a spectacle that would have been unparalleled. The first ascent of Grizzly Peak accomplished, I left my card, and water bottle, as mementos of my visit.

THE HALF DOME.

Until the fall of 1875 the storm-beaten summit of this magnificent landmark was a *terra incognita*, as it had never been trodden by human feet. In the summer of 1869 three of us set out for the purpose of climbing it, taking the "Indian escape trail" north of Grizzly Peak. There was absolutely no trail whatsoever, as we had to walk on narrow ledges, and hold on with our feet as well as hands, trusting our lives to bushes and jutting points of rock.

AN "INDIAN ESCAPE TRAIL."

In some places where the ledges of rock were high, their tops had to be reached by long broken branches of trees, which the Indians used to climb; and, after they were up, cut off the possibility of pursuit from enemies, by pulling up these primitive ladders after them. Not a drop of water could we find. A snow bank increased rather than diminished our terrible thirst. Finally, after many hair-breadth escapes, and not a little fatigue, we reached the top of the lower dome, or eastern shoulder, and were then within four hundred and sixty feet, vertically, of realizing our ambitious hopes. To our dismay, as well as disappointment, we found a great smooth mountain before us, standing at an angle of about 40°, its surface overlaid and overlapped, so to speak, with vast circular granite shingles, about eighteen inches in thickness. There was not a place to set a secure foot upon, or a point that we could clutch with our fingers. The very first sight put every hope to flight of reaching its exalted summit by the means at our command; and, deeming it a simple impossibility, "we surrendered at discretion," and returned without the realization of our ambitious hopes.

ASCENDING THE LOWER DOME.

Seven years after this an athletic youth informed the writer that he was "going to climb to the top of the Half Dome." I quietly suggested that such a feat was among the doubtful things of this life. He was willing to bet any amount that *he* could accomplish it. I informed him that I was not a betting man,—had never made a bet in my life, and was too old to begin now,—but, if he would put a flag upon the only visible pine tree standing there, I would make him a present of twenty dollars, and treat him and his friends to the best champagne dinner that could be provided in Yo Semite. Three days after this he walked past without deigning to stop, or even to look at us,—and there was no flag floating from the top of the Half Dome either!

This honor was reserved for a brave young Scotchman, a native of Montrose, named George G. Anderson, who, by dint of pluck, skill, unswerving perseverance, and personal daring, climbed to its summit; and was the first that ever successfully scaled it. This was accomplished at 3 o'clock P. M. of October 12, 1875.

The knowledge that the feat of climbing this grand mountain had on several occasions been attempted, but never with success, begat in him an irrepressible determination to succeed in such an enterprise. Imbued with this incentive, he made his way to its base; and, looking up its smooth and steeply inclined surface, at once set about the difficult exploit. Finding that he could not keep from sliding with his boots on, he tried it in his stocking feet; but as this did not secure a triumph, he tried it barefooted, and still was unsuccessful. Then he tied sacking upon his feet and legs, but as these did not secure the desired object, he covered it with pitch, obtained from pine trees near; and although this enabled him to adhere firmly to the smooth granite, and effectually prevented him from slipping, a new difficulty presented itself in the great effort required to unstick himself; and which came near proving fatal several times.

Mortified by the failure of all his plans hitherto, yet in no way discouraged, he procured drills and a hammer, with some iron eye-bolts, and drilled a hole in the solid rock; into this he drove a wooden pin, and then an eye-bolt; and after fastening a rope to the bolt, pulled himself up until he could stand upon it; and thence continued that process until he had finally gained the top—a distance of nine hundred and seventy-five feet! All honor, then, to the intrepid and skillful mountaineer, Geo. G. Anderson, who, defying and overcoming all obstacles, and at the peril of his life, accomplished that in which all others had signally failed; and thus became the first to plant his foot upon the exalted crown of the great Half Dome.

His next efforts were directed towards placing and securely fastening a good soft rope to the eye-bolts, so that others could climb up and enjoy the inimitable view, and one that has not its counterpart on earth. Four English gentlemen, then sojourning in the Valley, learning of Mr. Anderson's feat, were induced to follow his intrepid example. A day or two afterwards, Miss S. L. Dutcher,[1] of San Francisco, with the courage of a heroine, accomplished it; and was the first lady that ever stood upon it.

1. Sarah L. ("Sally") Dutcher was born in Australia in 1847 to English parents. As early as 1868 she went to work for the photographer Carleton E. Watkins in his Yo-Semite Gallery in San Francisco. She was employed by Watkins until at least 1878, and was with him in Yosemite in the summer and fall of 1875 on a photographing expedition, and thus was there at just the right time to become the first woman to climb Half Dome. She was tall, and was characterized as being "self-assured, aggressive, and widely admired by men, if not by women." (Palmquist)

In July, 1876, Miss L. E. Pershing, of Pittsburgh, Pa., the writer, and three others found their way there. In October following, six persons, among them a lady in her sixty-fifth year, and a young girl, thirteen years of age (a daughter of the writer), and two other ladies, climbed it with but little difficulty, after Anderson had provided the way. Since then very many others have daringly pulled themselves up; and enjoyed the exceptionally impressive view obtained thence.

The summit of this glorious mountain contains over ten acres, where persons can securely walk, or even drive a carriage, could such be transported thither. There are seven pine trees upon it, of the following species: *Pinus Jeffreyi, P. monticola,* and *P. contorta;* besides numerous shrubs, grasses and flowers. A "chip-monk," some lizards, and grasshoppers, have taken up their isolated preëmption claims there. Two sheep, supposed to have been frightened by bears, once scrambled up there; to which Mr. Anderson daily carried water, until they were eventually lost sight of. Their bones were afterwards discovered side by side, in a sheltered hollow.

The commanding position of the Half (or South) Dome at the head of the Valley, with a vertical altitude above it of nearly five thousand feet, two-thirds of which is absolutely in the zenith, makes the vies from its culminating crest inexpressibly sublime. There is not only the awe-inspiring depth into which one can look, where everything is dwarfed into utter insignificance, but the comprehensive panorama of great mountains everywhere encompassing us. As Yo Semite, confessedly, has not its emulative counterpart on earth, so is this view the culminating crown of scenic grandeur, that is utterly without a rival upon earth.

When sitting upon its edge our feet swing over a vortex of five thousand feet; and if we can imagine forty-five San Francisco Palace Hotels placed on top of each other, and ourselves seated upon the cornice of the upper one, surrounded by mountain peaks, deep gorges, beautiful lakes, and vast stretches of forest, with here and there bright pastures, some realizing sense of the preëminently glorious scene may partially be conceived.

THE HALF OR SOUTH DOME—TIS-SA-ACK.

A precipice of 5,000 Feet, with Geo. Anderson Standing on it.

(See page 460.)

Note how much retouching has been done to lighten up the valley floor
and the cliff at the left. This photo followed page 458 in all editions.

The Half or South Dome—Tis-sa-ack

A very close companion to the photo-typo on the opposite page.
Anderson has shifted his position slightly.

ANDERSON ON PRECIPICE OF HALF-DOME—5,000 FEET.
(Looking East up Ten-ie-ya Cañon.)

Photo by S. C. Walker   Peter E. Palmquist

ANDERSON ON HALF DOME—LOOKING EAST
(Editor's caption)

This half of a stereo is attributed to Walker and Fagersteen, or perhaps
to M. M. Hazeltine. It is not always possible to determine who is the
photographer and who is the publisher. But it seems obvious that
Mrs. Brodt's pen sketch was made from this photograph. And Walker
is on record as having taken photographs of exactly this sort in the
summer of 1877. See page 460.

Such a position, to those whose nerves had not been disciplined, might be trying in the extreme, if not impossible; but to those whose daily life brings them in constant and familiar contact with such, there is no perceptible nervousness whatsoever; therefore there is no particular merit in it. In 1877 Mr. Anderson, after assisting Mr. S. C. Walker, the photographer, and the writer, to pack up all the photographic apparatus necessary for taking views from its summit, deliberately placed upon a large flat rock, projectingly, on the margin of the precipice, and stood upright upon it while the photograph was taken; one of his feet being over, and beyond the edge eleven inches, as presented in the accompanying view, taken at that time. Although unsteadied and unsupported, not a nerve or muscle quivered.

About seventy feet from the face of the Half Dome wall, there is a narrow and nearly vertical fissure, several hundred feet in depth judging from the time stones dropped in were traveling to the bottom. This becomes suggestive that ere very long a new fracture may here take place.

A THRILLING ADVENTURE.

During the severe winter of 1883–84 the ice and snow sliding down the smooth back of the great Half Dome, carried with it over four hundred feet of the rope Anderson had put up with so much care and risk, and several of the iron eye-bolts with it. This deprived every enthusiastic climber of the pleasure of ascending to its wondrous summit, and of obtaining the unequalled view from that glorious standpoint. No one seemed imbued with sufficient ambitious courage to replace it—Anderson having passed away to his rest.

But, just after sunset, one evening of the ensuing summer, every resident of the Valley, familiar with the fact of the rope's removal, was startled by the sight of a blazing fire upon its utmost crest; and all kinds of suppositious theories were indulged in concerning such phenomena. No one knew of any one contemplating so hazardous a venture. What could it mean?

Eventually it transpired that two young gentlemen, who were summering in the Sierras, hunting, fishing, reading, and sketching, had been missed some days from their camping-ground in the Valley; and, therefore, there was the possibility that these might have unknowingly attempted to ascend it, and succeeded. But that possibility shared the companionship of another, which filled every mind with consternation; that they were up there, and could not come down; that the fire seen was at once a signal of distress as well as of success, and a call for help.

Before daylight the following morning, therefore, four of us, well supplied with ropes, extra bolts, and other essentials, were upon the way for their deliverance. At Snow's, however, we met the daring adventurers; and found that, although they had made the perilous climb up, they had also accomplished the descent in perfect safety. These twin heroes were Mr. Alden Sampson, of New York City, and Mr. A. P. Proctor, of Colorado.

Grateful for the intended, though unneeded deliverance, these young gentlemen very thoughtfully presented themselves at the cabin, to tender their thanks, and express their acknowledgments of the good services premeditated; when Mr. Sampson kindly favored me with the following recitative of their danger-defying exploit:—

Our challenge, if I may so call it, to make the ascent, came with the first inspiring sight of the Valley and of the Half Dome beyond. We were traveling in the saddle, with pack-animals, camping whenever the outlook was finest, or when we could find grazing or a night's feed at some ranch for our stock. From Wawona, we had come in by the Glacier Point trail, and had pitched camp for the night at Glacier Point. Here we had the good fortune to meet Mr. Galen Clark, one of the pioneers of the Valley, and in answer to our inquiries as to the view from the Half Dome, which was the most prominent feature of the landscape, were told that there had formerly been a rope to the summit, put up by Anderson, but that it was down, and would probably so remain until some venturesome member of the English Alpine Club should come along and have the goodness to replace it. This aspect of the matter, I must own, galled our pride; and the more we thought it over the less we liked this solution of the difficulty. Should we, forsooth, wait for foreign sinew to scale for us a peak of the American Sierras? Not if it lay in our power to prevent so humiliating a favor! But we did not by any means decide then that we would make the ascent; when we had at last made up our minds to do so, we quietly reconnoitered the place, and made all necessary preparations in entire secrecy, so that no one should have the satisfaction of laughing at us if we failed. Then taking two hundred feet of picket rope, a handful of lunch, and a lemon apiece, in the early morning we rode from our camp in the Little Yo Semite to the base of the dome.

Fortunately, in making this ascent, my companion and myself supplemented one another's work. He would throw the reata like a native Californian, so that when a pin was not thirty feet off, he would be sure to "rope it" the first cast. The end of the reata once fast, one of us would pull himself up by it, then stand upon the pin, ready to take up and make fast the old rope, when the other had tied the lower end of the reata to it. But after a while we came to a clean stretch of a hundred feet, where every pin had been carried away; yet, at this point a difficult corner of the ledge had to be turned. My companion, being barefooted, found that he could not cling to the surface as well as I could, with hob nails under my feet, so I had the pleasure of attempting this all to myself. The sensation was glorious. I did not stake my life upon it, for I was sure I could make it. If I had slipped in the least I should have had a nasty fall of several hundred feet. To be sure, I was playing out a rope behind me attached to my waist, but supposing I had fallen, with all this slack below me, my weight would have snapped it, or the rope would have cut me in two. The difficult part here was that a point had to be rounded on naked granite, that was both steep and slippery; not the coarse, rough variety that one sometimes sees, but polished by beating Sierra storms, and the snow-slides of innumerable winters. In the hardest place of all, a little bunch of dwarf *Spirea*, six or eight inches high, which was growing in a crevice, gave me friendly assistance. What it lived on up there I cannot imagine, as it grew in such a narrow crack of the ledge. However, its roots had a tenacious hold; and a piece of partially rotten bale rope afforded me a pull of ten or twelve pounds, quite enough to steady one at the most dangerous moment.

My companion exercised great skill and patience in making throws with the reata, often having to sit on the edge of a seemingly perpendicular precipice, morally supported, to be sure, by a rope from his waist, attached to the pin below him, but for actual physical support relying solely upon his foothold on the iron eyebolt under his feet. I dare say that his experience in one thing was similar to my own,—the feeling that when he clung to the face of the rock it was seemingly trying to push him off from it. We succeeded in putting up about half the rope the first day, and spent the night at our camp below. In the afternoon of the second day we came to a long, smooth stretch, without eyebolts or anything to offer assistance, not as steep as we had encountered, but very slippery. After many unsuccessful attempts to lasso the first pin a hundred feet away, with such precarious foothold as we had, nearly two precious hours were consumed, and the task was apparently hopeless, which would have given us another rather dangerous climb without any assistance whatever to rely upon; at last by a fortunate cast the reata caught the distant pin firmly, and as we made it taut, we could not repress a shout of joyful exultation, for the enemy was now conquered and the remainder of the ascent could be made with ease. We were soon upon the summit, signaling those that we thought might possibly be watching us from below.

CLOUD'S REST.

As intimated elsewhere, there is a singular appropriateness in the name of this grand mountain crest, inasmuch as there is frequently a cloud lingering there when there is not another visible in the firmament. Seen from the Valley it is always a point of attractive interest especially when wreathed in storm. It is about one thousand feet higher than the Half Dome; its height being six thousand feet above the Valley.

From its cloud-crested top one vast panorama of the High Sierra, embracing an area over fifty miles in length, is opened at our feet. Nestling valleys, pine-margined lakes, bleak mountain peaks, lonely and desolate, and deep gorges half filled with snow, are on every hand. To the eastward, above the timber line, (here about 10,800 feet high), stands boldly out Mt. Hoffmann, 10,872 feet above sea level; Mt. Tuolumne, 11,000 feet; Mt. Gibbs, 13,090 feet; Mt. Dana, 13,270 feet; Mt. Lyell, 13,220 feet; Echo Peak, 11,231 feet; Temple Peak, 11,250 feet; Cathedral Peak, 11,200 feet; Mt. Clark (formerly known as Gothic Peak, the Obelisk, etc.), 11,295 feet; Mt. Starr King, 9,105 feet, with numerous others that are as yet nameless; while the point upon which we are supposed to be standing (Cloud's Rest) is 9,855 feet.

Turning our eyes westward, we look down upon the crown of the Half Dome, and the great Valley below. But who can paint the haze-clothed heights, and depths, of the wonderful scenes before us? Almost at our feet, 6,000 feet beneath us, sleeps Mirror Lake; yonder, the North Dome, the Yo Semite Fall, Eagle Peak, El Capitan, Sentinel Dome, Glacier Point, and many others that margin the glorious Yo Semite. Verily this view must be seen to be even partially realized.

The way to these wondrous scenes is past the base of the Cap of Liberty, up a somewhat steep ascent; at the right of which a splendid side view of the Nevada Fall is obtained. At the top of the "zigzags" the horses should be tied, and a tramp taken of about two hundred yards to

THE UPPER LIP OF THE NEVADA FALL.

Here the Merced River, for some distance, forms a series of rapids, near the edge of which are numerous patches of bare, glacier-polished granite. Leaving these on our left, we seek the edge of the cliff, over which the Nevada is making its marvelous leap. On the way we see a singular botanical freak of nature, known as

THE UMBRELLA TREE.

It is a Douglas spruce, *Pseudo tsuga Douglasii.* Just beyond this we can stand on the edge of the precipice; but, as it is flat, nearly all lie down to take a soul-filling glimpse of the awe-inspiring majesty and glory beneath. The fall, almost directly after it daringly leaps its rocky rim, strikes the inclining wall, and apparently forms into a wavy mass of curtain-like folds, composed from top to bottom of diamond lace; now draping this side, then lifted, as by fairy hands, to the other. The base, as though it would make the whole scene a miniature heaven, and through it lead men to the outer footstool of the Almighty throne, is spanned with gorgeous rainbows; while the beautiful river hurries on, and the grand mountains around stand sentinel forever.

About a mile beyond we enter the Little Yo Semite Valley, at the head of which, some three miles distant, is a sugar-loaf-shaped mountain, and a cascade one hundred and fifty feet in length, down which the Merced River rushes at an angle of about 20°. Just beyond this a bold bluff, a thousand feet in height above the river, juts across the entire upper end, the top of which is highly polished by glaciers; and around it every hollow is filled with the detritus of old moraines.

The picturesque Little Yo Semite left behind, with its glacier-polished mountains around it, our course hence, to both Half Dome and Cloud's Rest, is, for the most part, over old moraines, where bowlders from every conceivable texture of granite, totally unlike that which forms the base here, are strewn on every hand. Those who have entertained a doubt about ancient glaciers having once covered the whole broad field of the Sierras, can here find evidence beyond question to dispel it.

As we journey upward and onward, new mountain peaks and spurs and ranges come into view; while flowers of every hue bloom at our side. The one most conspicuous of all, however, is

THE SNOW PLANT OF THE SIERRAS *(Sarcodes sanguinea)*.

This blood-red and strikingly attractive flower is to be seen upon every route to the Big Trees and Yo Semite Valley, as upon nearly every trail or by-path in or around them, at an elevation above sea level, ranging from four to eight thousand feet; its brilliant, semi-translucent stem, and bells, and leaves that intertwine among the bells, being all blood-red, their constituents seemingly of partially crystallized sugar, make it the most conspicuously beautiful flower born of the Sierras.

From the common name it bears might come the impression

that its birthplace is among the Sierran snows, but this is not the case; for, although its growth and early development is beneath deep banks of snow, it seldom shows its blood-red crown until some days after the snow has melted away.

Many eminent botanists consider this a parasitic plant, some affirming that it grows only upon a cedar root *(Libocedrus decurrens)* in a certain stage of decay; but these deductions may have been made from the close resemblance in outline of the *Sarcodes sanguinea* with the *Boschniakia strobilacea,* which is positively a parasitic flower, that prefers the manzanita as its host. I have, however, seen this floral gem flourishing over a thousand feet above the habitat of cedars; and, after carefully digging up over twenty specimens, could find no indication whatever of their parasitic character.

The height of its panicled blossom above ground is from seven to sixteen inches, with a diameter of from two to four inches; its bulb-root extending as far down into the earth as the flower is above it. When digging up specimens, therefore, this fact should be remembered; as to break them off—and they are exceedingly brittle—is to spoil them.

THE SNOW PLANT OF THE SIERRAS.

On those eternal peaks where winter reigns,
 And cold and frost their icy splendors shed,
Like drops of blood on pallid banks of snow,
 This hyacinthine blossom lifts its head,

A pyramid of tiny tongues of flame
 Darting from out the rifts of dazzling white—
A strange, bright phantom, born of ice and fire,
 Flushing pale wastes with gleams of crimson light.

'Tis said that when a holy man of old,
 Bearing the cross, on sacred mission bent,
Beheld upon the mountain's snowy crest
 This blood-red flower—his pious fancy lent

A charm miraculous, and, kneeling there
 In adoration, on the mountain-side,
With heavenward gaze and hands upraised in prayer,
 "*Sangre de Cristo*"—blood of Christ—he cried!

—SARAH J. PETTINOS.

CHAPTER XXVII.

GLACIER POINT, AND ITS GALAXY OF GLORIES.

Acuse not Nature, she hath done her part;
Do thou but thine.
—MILTON'S *Paradise Lost, Bk. VIII, Line 561.*

The pleasantest things in the world are pleasant thoughts, and the great art of life is to have as many of them as possible.
—BOVEE'S *Summaries of Thought.*

Beauty was lent to nature as the type
Of Heaven's unspeakable and holy joy,
Where all perfection makes the sum of bliss.
—S. J. HALE.

Supposing that we are not over-fatigued, and that the champagne atmosphere we are drinking daily is becoming to us the fabled fountain of perpetual youth, let us attempt the ascent of the Glacier Point Trail, to Glacier Point and Sentinel Dome, and look upon the imperishable grandeur there portrayed.

Seeking the entrance to the horse-path at the back of the little chapel, we commence the ascent. Formerly, the glorious scenes we are about to witness were denied to the many on account of the difficulty, danger, and fatigue attending the climb; as it had to be made on foot, and up a trailless mountain-side, where rocky points had to be carefully surmounted, and dense masses of shrubbery defiantly overcome. Still, with all the numerous obstacles impeding the journey, it was occasionally accomplished. Now, however, through the enterprise and perseverance of Mr. James McCauley, a wide, safe, easy graded, and remarkably picturesque trail, zigzags the mountain from base to summit.

At almost every turning new and enchantingly picturesque scenes are revealed between, or over, the tops of trees and shrubs that margin our way, until we arrive at

(467)

UNION POINT.

And an elevation of two thousand three hundred and thirty-five feet above the Valley. Here let us dismount, and while our horses are resting and breathing, enjoy the wonderful sight. It will be seen that now we are on an elevated flat or table, formed by nature, on the edge of the mountain from whence the whole panorama of the lower end and middle of the Yo Semite is visible. The Sentinel, Cathedral Spires, El Capitan, Eagle Point, Yo Semite Falls, and other points of interest, with all the serpentine windings of the Merced River, are strikingly seen.

THE AGASSIZ COLUMN.

Near the trail at Union Point there is a rock standing on end, like a huge ten-pin, some thirty feet in height, and ten in thickness. It looks as though a good strong breeze would blow it over, but which has thus far successfully withstood all storms and earthquakes. It is known as the Agassiz Column. From Union Point we make a detour to the eastward, on a foot-trail, to

MORAN POINT,

Whence the whole upper end of the Valley, with all its sublime scenes, can be witnessed to excellent advantage. The great Half Dome, Cloud's Rest, North Dome, Mirror Lake, the Ten-ie-ya Cañon, and many other views, are here before us. Remounting our now rested steeds, we steadily climb, filled with admiring wonder at every step as we advance, until, at last, we are at

THE GLACIER POINT HOUSE.[1]

Here let me introduce you to its proprietor, Mr. James Mc-Cauley, a stalwart son of Erin, whose every feature bespeaks progressive energy and irrepressible determination. It is to him, and to those qualities, that we are indebted for the Glacier Point Trail. He was its architect and builder; and its proprietor until it was purchased by the State.[2] Mr. McCauley is the fortunate possessor of an excellent wife, and two healthy sons, twins, and the first ever born of white parents in Yo Semite. Mrs. McCauley,

---

1. Both this building, generally known as the "Mountain House," which opened in 1875, and the Glacier Point Hotel, built in 1917, were destroyed by fire in 1969.

2. The Four-Mile Trail. McCauley put up the money for the trail, which was surveyed and built by John Conway.

among other good qualities, is an excellent cook; and prepares for guests as nice, clean, and relishable a meal as could be obtained at any first-class city hotel. Try it. But, while lunch is preparing, let us seek

THE VIEW FROM THE HOTEL PORCH.

The broad sweep of the great chain of the High Sierra is directly before us; and, apparently, so boldly near that one feels he could hold converse with any adventurous climber that might be seen upon either of their crests. A glance at the accompanying engraving will give but a faint impression only of the glorious scene. Once looked upon, the memory of its sublime impressiveness will remain an exalted mystery forever. Leaving this, therefore, for a frequently recurring feast, let us repair to

GLACIER POINT.

Here we are on the edge of an abyss three thousand two hundred and fifty-seven feet deep, with all its wondrous environments on every hand. As Derrick Dodd expresses it in his "Summer Saunterings:" "It is something to stop the beatings of a chamois' heart to lean over the iron railing, set between two verge-toppling bowlders on the peak's brink, and glance down into the bottomless, awful gulf below. It causes spiders of ice to crawl down one's spine." Large trees, two hundred feet high, are dwarfed to utter insignificance. The little checker-board-like spot first attracting notice, possibly, is Lamon's apple orchard of four acres, and which contains over five hundred trees, set regularly twenty feet apart. The other cultivated point, formed by the junction of Ten-ie-ya Creek with the Merced River, is Lamon's other orchard. The bright speck which throws out its silvery sheen in that deep, tree-dotted cañon is Mirror Lake, and although the great sweep of the northern rim of the Valley is before us, with its multitudinous crags and rents, the Half Dome, as omnipresent as ever, overshadows and eclipses every lesser object.

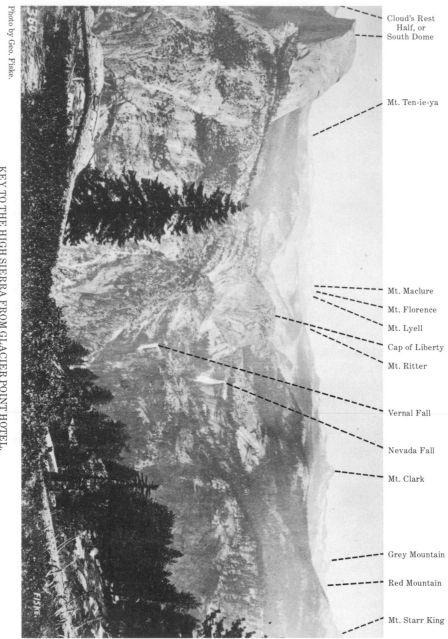

Photo by Geo. Fiske.

KEY TO THE HIGH SIERRA FROM GLACIER POINT HOTEL.

Cloud's Rest
Half, or
South Dome

Mt. Ten-ie-ya

Mt. Maclure

Mt. Florence

Mt. Lyell

Cap of Liberty

Mt. Ritter

Vernal Fall

Nevada Fall

Mt. Clark

Grey Mountain

Red Mountain

Mt. Starr King

DERRICK DODD'S TOUGH STORY.

As a part of the usual programme, we experimented as to the time taken by different objects in reaching the bottom of the cliff. An ordinary stone tossed over remained in sight an incredibly long time, but finally vanished somewhere about the middle distance. A handkerchief with a stone tied in the corner, was visible perhaps a thousand feet deeper; but even an empty box, watched by a field-glass, could not be traced to its concussion with the Valley floor. Finally, the landlord appeared on the scene, carrying an antique hen under his arm. This, in spite of the terrified ejaculations and entreaties of the ladies, he deliberately threw over the cliff's edge. A rooster might have gone thus to his doom in stoic silence, but the sex of this unfortunate bird asserted itself the moment it started on its awful journey into space. With an ear-piercing cackle, that gradually grew fainter as it fell, the poor creature shot downward; now beating the air with ineffectual wings, and now frantically clawing at the very wind, that slanted her first this way and then that; thus the hapless fowl shot down, down, until it became a mere fluff of feathers no larger than a quail. Then it dwindled to a wren's size, disappeared, then again dotted the sight a moment as a pin's point, and then—it was gone!

After drawing a long breath all round, the women folks pitched into the hen's owner with redoubled zest. But the genial McCauley shook his head knowingly, and replied:—

"Don't be alarmed about that chicken, ladies. She's used to it. She goes over that cliff every day during the season."

And, sure enough, on our road back we met the old hen about half up the trail, calmly picking her way home!! (?)

D. D., you are a trump. Mark Twain could not beat that story—except, perhaps, the one about a mean man in "Roughing It," where the boss deducted ten minutes from a miner's time, after being tossed up by a premature blast, for being absent in the air that long from work!

Our enjoyable midday repast being over, let us now ride to the summit of

SENTINEL DOME.

This is four thousand one hundred and sixty feet above the meadows of Yo Semite. It is a striking landmark, and as its crown is almost as clear of trees as though a tornado had swept

ruthlessly across it, the view in every direction is entirely unobstructed. The vast amphitheater of the Sierras is before us. Did
time permit us we might profitably tarry here for hours, or even
days as new beauties would be opening, and strange forms made
manifest on every side and at every moment. But the rapidly
declining sun admonishes us not to linger too long, if it is our fixed
purpose to return to the Valley in time for the evening meal.

If our spirit of enjoyment could be consulted, and the rich
scenic feast could be prolonged, we should tarry here until sunset, as the effects from this lofty eminence are not only magical
and majestic, but are simply glorious; then, after spending the
night at Glacier Point, watch the streaming tails of mighty com-
ets, that come at day-dawn to herald approaching morn from
among the snow-clad peaks and forest heights of the Sierras.

Then, after an appetizing breakfast, we can visit the "Fissures," some three miles distant, and then make an early return
to the Valley; or, journey upon its southern rim through primeval forests, across grassy meadows, and adown flower-covered
slopes, to Inspiration Point, Mt. Beatitude, and the Standpoint
of Silence; thence to the Valley by the Wawona Road, and live
over again its marvelous scenes. This, believe me, is a glorious
jaunt. But, if it is preferred, we

CAN RE-ENTER THE YO SEMITE VALLEY VIA SNOW'S.

The views upon either of the routes suggested are so utterly
unlike any others, here or elsewhere, that their very novelty
doubles the charm of looking upon them. Take, for instance, the
view of the Half Dome from the Snow trail. It is so unlike any
other of this marvelous mountain that it might be most readily
adjudged a different one. From this standpoint it is a sugar-loaf in
granite, as no portion of its vertical cleavage is anywhere visible.

Then, presently, we come to the yawning gulf of the Too-lool-
a-we-ack Cañon beneath us, with its four hundred feet water-fall;
and follow the wave-tossed cataract it is forming, with our eye,
down the entire length of the gorge. Soon thereafter we are

Photo. by Geo. Fiske.   Photo-Typo by Britton & Rey, S. F.

The Agassiz Column.

(See page 468.)

Fiske #352. Opposite page 468 in editions three and four.

Photo by Charles L. Weed   Peter E. Palmquist

The back of Half Dome from Illilouette Canyon
The engraving on the opposite page was made from
half of Weed's Stereo #29, taken in June 1859.
Published by E. & H. T. Anthony.

riding on top of Echo Wall, nearly three thousand feet above the mighty chasm of the Merced River; and then thread our way among the troughs, or across the ridges of bowlder-built moraines which form the lower base of

MT. STARR KING.

Did time and opportunity permit, we might climb to its shoulder, and thence obtain that magnificent view; but could not go beyond this with-

THE SOUTH DOME AS SEEN FROM TOO-LOOL-A-WE-ACK, OR GLACIER CAÑON.

out jeoparding life and limb. Less than a dozen persons have been able to ascend it. The first to do so was Mr. Geo. B. Bayley and Mr. E. S. Schuyler; followed by Geo. Anderson and the writer, a few days afterwards, who, having attached ropes over difficult places, enabled Mrs. A. L. Hutchings and our daughter Florence to ascend it, who were the first and only ladies, at this writing, that have accomplished the difficult task. Its crest is five thousand one hundred and seventy-one feet above Yo Semite Valley, and nine thousand one hundred and five feet above sea level.

Soon the Nevada Falls, Cap of Liberty, Half Dome, and other

Photo by C. L. Weed.
THE TOO-LOOL-A-WE-ACK, OR GLACIER CAÑON FALL (400 feet high).

familiar points, come into review, and not long afterwards we are at Snow's, and on the great trail thoroughfare to the Valley.

Before taking our farewell of Glacier Point, it should be remarked that the Yo Semite Stage and Turnpike Company has constructed an excellent and highly picturesque carriage road, from the Wawona Turnpike at Chinquapin Flat to Glacier Point; thus affording the opportunity of looking upon its wondrous sights, to those who could not make the ascent on horseback. Many visitors ride up the Glacier Point Trail and take the western-bound stage thence; but, where it is preferred, visitors can go direct from Chinquapin Flat, by coach, to Glacier Point, and thence down the trail to Yo Semite—a severe experience to those unaccustomed to the saddle.

Illilouette Fall

The engraving on the opposite page was made from
this photograph, taken in June 1859.

Photo. by Geo. Fiske.

Photo-Typo by Britton & Rey, S. F.

THE SIERRAS, FROM GLACIER POINT HOTEL PORCH.
Possibly Fiske #359. It is almost the same as #360, on page 470.
These two photos faced each other in all editions.

CHAPTER XXVIII.

THE UPPER YO SEMITE, EAGLE PEAK, LAKE TEN-IE-YA, AND HIGH SIERRA.

> I love to wander through the woodlands hoary
> In the soft light of an autumnal day,
> When summer gathers up her robes of glory,
> And like a dream of beauty glides away.
> —Sarah Helen Whitman.

> I hear the muffled tramp of years
> Come stealing up the slope of Time;
> They bear a train of smiles and tears,
> Of burning hopes and dreams sublime.
> —James G. Clarke.

> Hills peep o'er hills, and Alps on Alps arise.
> —Pope's *Essay on Criticism*.

When undertaking the delightful jaunt now proposed, we repair to the north side of the Valley, and enter upon the Eagle Peak Trail. This was engineered and constructed by Mr. John Conway and sons, who performed a very valuable service to the public by opening up very many of the magnificent scenes we are about to witness, and that were before sealed from human vision; but for which, I regret to say, no adequate compensation was returned them.

As we zigzag our way up it by an easy grade, stunted live-oaks offer grateful shade, and manzanita and wild lilac bushes border it on either side. Trees, buildings, gardens, cattle, and horses grow gradually more diminutive; while surrounding granite walls tower up bolder and higher. In peaceful repose sleeps the Valley, its carpet of green cut up, perhaps, by pools of shining water, and the serpentine course of the river resembles a huge silver ribbon. At an elevation of 1,154 feet we rest at

(475)

COLUMBIA ROCK,

And thence look down upon the enchanting panorama that lies before us. Everything visible below has become dwarfed; while in the far-away distance above and beyond us, mountain peaks are constantly revealing themselves impressively, one after the other. Remounting, we ascend a little, then ride along a broad ledge of granite that, from the Valley, appears to be far too narrow for a horse and its rider to travel upon in safety; but, finding ourselves mistaken, we presently arrive at

TRANSPORT POINT.[1]

Here the horses are again left upon the trail, while we foot our way to the edge of the overhanging wall, that, from below looked so formidable a precipice. From this standpoint, not only can the entire length of the lower Yo Semite Fall be seen; but the interjacent depths and irregularities of the intervening cañon between the top of the lower, and foot of the upper fall; while in front of us the entire Upper Yo Semite Fall is in full view. Charmingly attractive as this scene may be, we naturally wish to seek a closer communion with its glories, and cannot rest until we are almost

BENEATH THE UPPER YO SEMITE FALL.

Speechless with reverential awe, we have reached the wonderful goal. But, alas! who can describe it? who fittingly tell of its wonderful beauties, or describe its manifold glories, and majestic presence? It is impossible. We look upward, and we see an avalanche of water about to bury us up, or sweep us into the abyss beneath. By degrees we take courage; and, climbing the watery mass with our eye, discern its remarkable changes and forms. Now it would seem that numerous bands of fun-loving fairies have set out for a frolic; and, assuming the shape of watery rockets, have entered the fall; and, after making the leap, are now playing "hide-and-seek" with each other among its watery folds; now chasing, now catching; then, with retreating surprises, disappearing from view, and re-forming, or changing, shoot again into

---

1. This name is not on maps. It's the point where the trail changes direction from northeast to north. John Conway used the name "Valley View Point" for the same place.

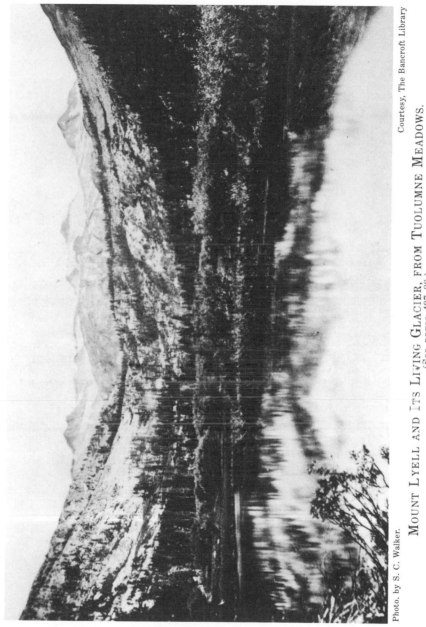

Photo. by S. C. Walker.

Courtesy, The Bancroft Library

MOUNT LYELL AND ITS LIVING GLACIER, FROM TUOLUMNE MEADOWS.
(See pages 487–88.)
Made from a Britton & Rey photo-typo.
Facing page 487 in all editions.

Photo by Carleton E. Watkins   NPS, Yosemite Collections

Under the Upper Yo Semite Fall

The photo from which the engraving on the opposite page was made.
The seated figure is Charley Staples, Watkins' assistant, packer, and cook.
Also in view are his tripod, and his dark tent—at the left.

Watkins' Pacific Coast Stereo #72

sight. While the wind, as if shocked at such playful irreverence, takes hold of the white diamond mass, and lifts it aside like a curtain; when each rocket-formed fairy, leaping down from its folds, first fringes its edge, then disappears from our sight, and is lost among rainbows and clouds.

The first great vertical leap of this fall being fifteen hundred feet, makes it scarcely less impressive than El Capitan, when standing against the wall at its foot. Just at the back of, and immediately beneath it, there is a cave some forty feet in depth. As the fall itself veils the entrance to this cave, it can only be entered when the stream is low; or, as not infrequently happens, when the wind has sufficient force to lift the entire fall to one side. On one of these occasions two venturesome young men, who had climbed to the foot of the cliff, seeing the entrance to the cave clear, ran into it; but they had scarcely entered when

Photo by C. E. Watkins.
CAVE AT THE BASE OF THE UPPER YO SEMITE FALL.

the fall, returning to its normal position, filled the aperture with dense and comminuted spray, which made it next to impossible to breathe, while effectually cutting off their retreat. In this nearly fatal dilemma they were helpless; but, fortunately, the wind again swept its folds to one side, and they lost no time in effecting their perilous escape. When relating their hazardous feat, they both made voluntary confession never to be caught at so foolish and so dangerous an experiment again!

Leaving this interesting and truly captivating spot, we continue our crinkled way up the *debris* lying at the base of Eagle Tower wall (vertical for 1,600 feet), passing flowers and flowering shrubs, to enter into the refreshing shade of a grove of yellow pines, *Pinus Jeffreyi*, and soon thereafter find ourselves at the

TOP OF YO SEMITE FALL.

The current of this stream is very irregular. For nearly half a mile it has a speed of about eight knots an hour; then, for about two hundred yards from the lip of the mountain, it leaps over a broken series of ledges into eddying pools, from which it swirls, and swashes, and jumps, until it makes its final bound over the precipice, and is lost to view. For about ten yards back of the edge, the gray granite is so smooth that, lying down upon it, clingingly, when the stream is absent, it would be impossible to prevent sliding over the brink, but for a narrow crack in the rock where there is finger-hold. This enables us to cling sufficiently, until we can work our way out to a flattish, basin-like hollow, in safety; whence one can creep out to the margin of the abyss, and look down into it. My measurement here, by aneroid barometer, made its height above the Valley two thousand six hundred and forty feet. Its breadth at the lip is thirty-four feet; and, twenty feet above it, seventy feet. One position on a projecting ledge enables the eye to follow this water-fall from top to base, and watch the ever-changing colors of its rainbow hues the entire distance.

From this point it is a most delightful forest ride to Eagle

Meadows, their grassy glades, and pools covered with bright yellow water-lilies, *Nuphar polysepalum*, and thence to

EAGLE PEAK.

This was so named from its being such a favorite resort of this famous bird of prey. I once saw seven eagles here, at play; they would skim out upon the air, one following the other, and then swoop perpendicularly down for a thousand or more feet, and thence sail out again horizontally upon the air with such graceful nonchalance that one almost envied them their apparent gratification.

The altitude of this rugged cliff above the Valley is three thousand eight hundred and eighteen feet, three hundred and thirty feet lower than the Sentinel Dome on the other side; but, owing to the great vertical depth of the gulf immediately beneath it, as well as the comprehensive panorama from and around about it, not only is the entire upper end of the Valley, with its wild depths and cañon defiles, visible therefrom, but the whole sweep of the distant Sierras, as far as the eye can reach.

I once had the pleasure of conducting the Rev. J. P. Newman, D. D., and Rev. —— Sunderland, D. D. (each, then, of Washington, D. C.), to its wondrous summit; when, after a long, and evidently constrained silence, the former suddenly ejaculated, "Glory! Hal-le-lu-jah—Glory! Hal-le-lu-jah!" (the doctor was a Methodist, you know) then, turning around, the tears literally streaming down his cheeks, he thus expressed himself: "Well, Mr. H, if I had crossed the continent of America on purpose to look upon *this one view*, I should have returned home, sir, perfectly satisfied."

Eleven of us (six ladies and five gentlemen), after a most delightful camping sojourn of three months in the High Sierra, concluded that to revisit this spot would be a befitting *finale* to our summer's pilgrimage. Accordingly some eight additional days were spent upon the grassy meadows below, and in making daily ascents to the culminating crest of Eagle Peak. It is a view that seems never to weary, or to become common-place. Gathering storm-clouds admonishing an early departure we gave reluctant consent; to find, that, within twenty-four hours after breaking up camp, three feet of snow had covered the ground.

LAKE TEN-IE-YA.

As Eagle Peak Trail is the one necessarily traveled from the great Valley to Lake Ten-ie-ya, and as we have supposedly reached the top of the mountain, and are thus far on our way; let us continue our journey up or down forest-clothed ravines, amid and over low ridges, and across the heads of green meadows, with here and there an occasional glimpse of distant mountain peaks, until we reach Porcupine Flat; thence to travel upon the Great Sierra Mining Company's Turnpike road all the way to the beautiful lake. It should here be stated that by this thoroughfare travelers can now drive not only among the tops of the Sierras, but over their summit, by leaving the Big Oak Flat road near Crocker's.

Following the dancing and sparkling waters of Snow Creek, which have their source in the snow-banks of Mt. Hoffmann, there can, on every hand, be witnessed the unmistakable evidences of glacial action, in the moraines, and highly polished and deeply striated granite that can everywhere be seen; not in mere patches only, but many miles in extent. On every peak, mountain shoulder and bare ledge, where disintegration has not removed the writing, the record is so plain that "he who runs may read." This is most strikingly manifest from the Hoffmann Ridge down to Lake Ten-ie-ya. The entire slope, some three miles long, is glacier-polished, and before the road was built the utmost care was needed, in passing down the trail, to prevent horses from falling. The glistening surfaces attract almost as much attention, for the time being, as the scenery.

Refulgent, however, with sheen, the bright bosom of

BEAUTIFUL LAKE TEN-IE-YA

Can be seen glinting between the trees, and erelong we are treading upon its pine-bordered shores. Oh! how charming the landscape. Mountains from one thousand to two thousand five hundred feet in height bound it on the east and on the south. At the head of the lake they are more or less dome-shaped, glacier-rounded, and polished; on the south, Ten-ie-ya Peak towers boldly up, and throws distinctly and repeatedly back the echoes of our voice. But for persuasive remonstrances from our organs of digestion, we could almost believe that we were in Fairy Land. These humanizing appeals, however, are not to be repressed, and, as a sequence, we find ourselves crossing the hospitable threshold of

MURPHY'S CABIN.

The name of its builder and proprietor being John L. Murphy, let me without ceremony introduce him. Mr. Murphy is one of the old-time residents, and was, formerly, one of the most obliging and reliable of the guides of Yo Semite. If you will read H. H.'s "Bits of Travel,"[1] you will find a correctly drawn and full length pen-portrait of him. Wiry with exercise, grizzled by exposure, and healthy from breathing pure mountain air, he is a little Hercules in strength and endurance. Then there are but few, if any, more kindly-hearted, genial, and thoughtfully careful of your comfort than he. Be sure of one thing, the moment you feel the grip of his manly hand, and have one look into his honest face, you will feel thoroughly at home with him; in entire confidence, therefore, we may share his kindly care.

This charming mountain-locked lake is about one and three-quarters miles in length by three-quarters of a mile in width; and although very deep on its southern side is quite shallow on its northern, so that before the new road was built, the course of the trail eastward was, for half a mile, directly through it, to avoid the mountainous defile north of its encompassing bluffs.

A "WHAT IS IT."

There is a most curious phenomenon observable here, nearly every still morning during summer, that deservedly attracts attention. It is a peculiar sound, something between a whistle and a

1. Helen Hunt Jackson, *Bits of Travel at Home.*

hiss, that shoots through the air with startling velocity, apparently about a mile above the surface of the water. Its course is generally from south and west to north and east; although it seemingly travels, at times, in all conceivable directions, and with a velocity much greater than a screeching shell in battle. Now the question arises, "What is the cause of all this?" Can it be from the rapid passage of currents of electricity through the air, or the rush of air through some upper stratum? Will someone who knows kindly answer the question, "What is it?"

The mountains around the lake—Ten-ie-ya Peak, Ten-ie-ya Dome, and Murphy's Dome, standing out most prominently—are very irregular in their form and cleavage, but yet are unspeakable picturesque.[1] This, with the quaint ruggedness of the *Pinus contorta* trees which grow upon its margin; the glacier polish and striæ upon nearly all of its surrounding granite; the balmy healthiness of its summer air (as meat never spoils, on the hottest of days), its altitude above sea level being seven thousand nine hundred and seventy feet, the purity of its waters, and its central position for climbing every grand peak around it, should make Lake Ten-ie-ya one of the most delightful summer resorts in the world; especially when its waters are well stocked with fish, and the sheep-herder no longer pastures his sheep near, which drive away all the game that would naturally seek these great solitudes. Attractive as this wildly romantic spot may be, we must leave it and its genial hermit, for a time at least, to visit, in spirit, some of

THE GLORIOUS SCENES IN THE HIGH SIERRA.

From Yo Semite to the summit of the Sierra Nevada there abounds more grand scenery than can be found in any other portion of the State.
—Prof. W. H. Brewer.

The marvelous scenic and natural phenomena of the High Sierra was as a closed volume to nearly all except the irrepressible prospector and vandalistic sheep-herder, until its wondrous pages were opened to the public by the California State Geological Survey, under Prof. J. D. Whitney. Although nature here

1. Murphy's Dome is the present Pywiack Dome; Murphy's name appears only on Murphy Creek. Ten-ie-ya Dome probably is the unnamed dome on the north side of the lake.

builds her prodigious reserves of snow, storms hold unchecked carnival, and the chemistry of trituration is silently manipulating its manifold forces, and eliminating scenes of grandeur that charm both eye and soul, human eyes and thoughts could not before look in upon her astonishing laboratory. Now, however, the glorious book is wide open, and its inviting leaves can be turned by every mind. Being a vast and interesting volume of itself, I can

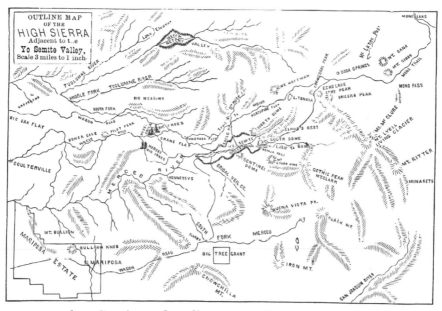

now only epitomize and outline some of its principal attractions, that are as wild and wonderful in their way as the Yo Semite itself, while being utterly unlike it. The one nearest, and whose bold prominence we have noticed from all the high points more immediately around the Valley, is

MOUNT HOFFMANN.

The summit of this mountain is ten thousand eight hundred and seventy-two feet above sea level, and the view from it commandingly fine. Just beneath its northern wall is the horseshoe-shaped head of Yo Semite Creek, with its numerous little glacier-scooped lakelets; and which, with deep snow banks, form the main source of Yo Semite Creek. Here that stream heads. About one hundred feet from its apex is

THE UPPER MARGIN OF THE TIMBER LINE,

Where stunted pines, *Pinus albicaulis*, form the only and highest occupant. Owing to the density of foliage and singular contour of these trees, caused mainly by exposure of situation and the depth of winter snows. one could, with care, walk on their tops, seldom over a dozen feet above the ground. As intimated elsewhere, the upper timber line of the Sierras in this latitude never exceeds eleven thousand feet; at Fishermen's Peak (unfairly called Mt. Whitney) it is twelve thousand two hundred and twenty, while at Mt. Shasta, it is only eight thousand feet. Beyond and above these the whole chain consists of bleak and storm-beaten peaks and crags; yet, though forest verdure is denied them, beautiful flowers bloom in sheltered hollows, to their very summits. How thoughtlessly do we sometimes allude to "the bleak and desolate mountains," forgetting that in these are treasured the subtle essences needed for the pabulum of plant, and other organic life, even to their coloring and fragrance.

Were we to lingeringly dwell on these, or upon the echoes thrown from peak to peak upon this crest, where "Every mountain now hath found a tongue," or in viewing the numberless rocky pinnacles and placid lakes in sight, I fear that other scenes and charms would remain unenjoyed; therefore, let us return to Lake Ten-ie-ya, with the impression that another glorious and soul-filling day has been most profitably spent.

Rafting on the lake, musing, sketching, day-dreaming, nor even pleasant chats with the kind old Hermit of Lake Ten-ie-ya, must detain us from taking the picturesque road along the margin of this captivating sheet of water; and, threading our way by the side of bold bluffs, along the tree-arched road, and across a low ridge into the

TUOLUMNE MEADOWS.

These afford such striking contrast to other sights witnessed that they somewhat calm the excited imagination by their sylvan peacefulness, and by gratified change prepare us for the sublime scenes that everywhere stand guard. Of course, we must visit

THE SODA SPRINGS.

There are several of these that flow bubblingly up in close proximity to each other, and offer us a deliciously refreshing drink of aerated soda water. Here, too, we may meet a hermit-artist named Lembert, who annually brings his Angora goats to feed upon the succulent pastures, whilst he makes sketches. Here we are eight thousand five hundred and fifty-eight feet above the sea. Leaving these we pass glacier-polished bluffs, cross entire ridges and valley stretches of moraine talus, and in about nine spirit-delighting miles, reach the camping ground of Mount Dana. Knowing that blankets and other creature comforts are essential for these extended trips, such things have naturally been provided, preparatory to spending a pleasant night here before attempting

THE ASCENT OF MOUNT DANA.

Our course to the summit of this lofty standpoint, after leaving camp, is on the back of an old moraine for some three miles, where Dana Cañon is entered. Here we leave the last tree behind and below us, and thenceforward find nothing but stunted willow bushes, which also are soon left behind, and at an elevation of eleven thousand seven hundred and fifty feet, we are on the saddle, or connecting neck, between Mt. Gibbs and Mt. Dana. Just over the ridge is a large bowlder which, when a rope is tied around it, makes a fast and sheltered point for tethering horses. The ascent thence is on foot, over fragmentary chips and blocks of metamorphic slate, of which this entire mountain is composed, in an endless variety of colors and shades. Once upon its glorious apex, we are thousand two hundred and twenty-seven feet above the level of the sea.

VIEW FROM THE SUMMIT OF MOUNT DANA.

The most expressive of language must utterly fail to describe this scene. The vast amphitheater of mountains, cañons, and lakes extending in every direction to the horizon is unutterably sublime and bewildering. North of east, down in a gulf of six thousand seven hundred and seventy-three feet, restfully sleeps Lake Mono, which, although eighteen by twenty-three miles across, is dwarfed into comparative insignificance; beyond this lie the vast deserts and green oases of the State of Nevada, with their inexhaustible mineral wealth. Trending northward, the irregular mountain-formed vertebræ of the great backbone of the Sierras, with Mts. Warren, Conness, and Castle Peak[1] stand up above yet among thousands of lesser ones; while southward, in stately prominence, soar Mts. Lyell, Ritter, and numberless others. Westward the penumbra of light and shade defines every lofty crag and peak that surrounds the wonderful Valley, with every bristling intermediate spire, and cone, and dome.

EVIDENCES OF ANCIENT GLACIERS UPON MT. DANA.

Along the western and southern slopes of Mt. Dana [says Prof. J. D. Whitney*] the traces of ancient glaciers are very distinct, up to a height of 12,000 feet. In the gap directly south of the summit a mass of ice must once have existed, having a thickness of at least 800 feet at as high an elevation as 10,500 feet. From all the gaps and valleys of the west side of the range, tributary glaciers came down, and all united in one grand mass lower in the valley, where the medial moraines which accumulated between them are perfectly distinguishable, and in places as regularly formed as any to be seen in the Alps at the present day.

It is, therefore, reasonably presumable that glaciers once covered the apex of Mt. Dana also, then probably much higher, to a depth "of at least eight hundred feet," which would give an aggregate approximate depth or thickness of glacial ice in Yo Semite Valley of *nearly two miles!*

* Yosemite Guide Book, page 103.

1. This probably is Dunderberg Peak, although it could also be Tower Peak. Duplication of and switching of names involved three peaks in the 1870s and 1880s: those two peaks, and Mount Warren. There is today no "Castle Peak" in the Sierra Nevada.

THE LIVING GLACIERS OF MT. DANA.

In the deep vertical chasm under the northern wall of Mt. Dana and near its crest, there is a vast deposit of ice that remains unmelted through all seasons of the year. Unlike that on Mt. Lyell, however, it is completely locked in by an encompassing mountain that precludes the possibility of motion, except normally, as the ice melts. This forms one of the main sources of the Tuolumne River. On the very summit of this bleak landmark grow bunches of bright purple flowers, the Jacob's Ladder of the High Sierra, *Polemonium confertum.*[1]

Leaving these enrapturing scenes and mysteries, let us wend our delighting way, over old moraines, and past the glacier-polished floor of the Lyell branch of the Tuolumne meadows, to their head, where there is an excellent camping ground, whence the hoary head of Mt. Lyell itself looms grandly up, six miles away. Here we are at an altitude of eight thousand nine hundred and fifty feet. Forest fires set by sheep-herders having denuded much of the lower portion of the ascent of its timber, we must not expect the refreshing shade formerly enjoyed from it. At this altitude, however, the heat is in no way oppressive, although we have on foot to make

THE ASCENT OF MT. LYELL.

Believe me, this is a glorious climb. The invigorating air seems to permeate every fiber and nerve, and to penetrate almost to the marrow of one's bones. Flowers, flowering shrubs, and ferns, with occasional groups of trees, continue with us to the limit of the timber line, and the former to the very summit, which is thirteen thousand two hundred and twenty feet above sea level.

THE LIVING GLACIER OF MT. LYELL.

About fifteen hundred feet below its culminating crest we reach the foot of the glacier, portions of which having broken off and fallen into a small deep lakelet, distinctly reveal the ethereal blue of the icy deposit. This fine glacier is about two miles in

1. Sky Pilot, *Polemonium eximium.*

length, having a direction southeasterly by northwesterly, by half a mile in width, with an estimated depth, or thickness, of from three hundred to five hundred feet. Deep down in the unseen profound of its blue crevasses, water can be heard singing and gurgling, from which emanate the streams that form the source of the main, or Lyell branch, of the Tuolumne River. By several experiments, such as the setting of stakes in line with the general trend of the glacier, it has been ascertained to move at the rate of from seven-eighths to one inch per day. A large portion of its surface is corrugated by a succession of ridges and furrows, from about twenty inches to two feet apart, and the same in depth; having a resemblance to a chopping sea whose waves had been suddenly frozen.

The upper edge of this living glacier is about one hundred and seventy feet below the rocky apex of Mt. Lyell, "which was found to be a sharp and inaccessible pinnacle of granite rising above a field of snow."* Members of the State Geological Survey Corps having considered it impossible to reach the summit of this lofty peak, the writer was astonished to learn from Mr. A. T. Tileston, of Boston, after his return to the Valley from a jaunt of health and pleasure in the High Sierra, that he had personally proven it to be possible by making the ascent. Incredible as it seemed at the time, three of us found Mr. Tileston's card upon it some ten days afterwards.

MT. LYELL THE MAIN SOURCE OF TWO RIVERS.

On the southern side of Mt. Lyell there is an almost vertical wall of granite some twelve hundred feet high, rising from a rock-rimmed basin, whose sheltered sides hoard vast banks of snow, which, melting, form the main water supply of the Merced River, flowing through the Yo Semite Valley. Thus Mt. Lyell becomes the source of two valuable streams, the Merced on the south, and the Tuolumne on the north and east.

Of course the view from this magnificent standpoint is

* Yosemite Guide Book, page 104.

exceptionally imposing. Not only are there lofty and isolated single peaks without number, but distinct groups of mountains, that form the sources of as many streams, or their tributaries; with broad lakes and deep cañons on every hand, extending as far as human vision can penetrate, but of which Mt. Lyell seems to be the center. Leveling across to Mt. Ritter (apparently only a stone's throw from us, although some five miles distant), we judged its altitude to exceed that of Mt. Lyell by about one hundred and thirty feet. The glaciers of Mt. Ritter, and the Minarets, originate and supply the waters of the San Joaquin River. While seated among the blocks of rock that lie on the edge of this glorious crag, a little "chipmunk" ran out from a crevice and began to chatter at us; but we assured him that we were in no way envious of his exalted choice, nor anxious to disturb his prior possessory right or preëmption claim.

Loose masses of rock, having become detached from its crest, have toppled down upon the glacier; which, in its almost imperceptible declivity, has silently borne them to the edge of the glacier basin, and there dropped them. These form an irregular wall some two hundred feet in height, among which the new-born stream creeps gurglingly, and thence issues forth. These visible glacial "dumps," as miners would call them, are suggestive of the way that many moraines are first formed.

Treeless slopes, pools, piles of disintegrated rock, broadening streams, and water-worn crevices, with abundant plant life, continue with us from the summit of Mt. Lyell down to the timber line (here some two thousand four hundred feet below), where the *Pinus albicaulis* becomes the only forest tenant for some distance; soon, however, to be left behind for the companionship of the *Pinus contorta, P. Jeffreyii, Abies Pattoniana,* and other trees, until we arrive at picturesque "Camp Mt. Lyell;" thence through God's most glorious picture gallery back *via* Cathedral Spires and Cathedral Lake, Echo Peak and Echo Lake, Temple Peak, Monastery Peak, Moraine Valley, Sunrise Ridge, Nevada and Vernal Falls, to Yo Semite.[1]

1. Some of these names do not presently exist. Temple Peak and Monastery Peak may possibly be early names for Columbia Finger and Matthes Crest; Moraine Valley for Long Meadow; and Sunrise Ridge for the route of the Muir Trail east of Sunrise Mountain.

CHAPTER XXIX.

THE SEASONS AT YO SEMITE VALLEY.

The spring, the summer,
The chilling autumn, angry winter, change
Their wonted liveries.
—SHAKESPEAR'S *Midsummer Night's Dream, Act II.*

Everything lives, flourishes, and decays; everything dies, but nothing is lost.
—GOOD'S *Book of Nature.*

Perhaps it may turn out a song,—
Perhaps turn out a sermon.
—BURNS' *Epistle to a Young Friend.*

Frequently and earnestly has the question been asked,

WHICH IS THE BEST TIME TO GO TO YO SEMITE?

To which I would make answer—not flippantly, or inconsiderate-ly—*That which best suits your own personal convenience.* The rest should be determined by individual taste and preference. When a warm, early spring first lifts the flood-gates of the snow-built reservoirs above, the water flows abundantly over the falls; but the deciduous trees are leafless, and the earth, unkissed by renewing sunshine for so many months, has put forth no grasses or flowers. Later, when the trees are budding and the blossoms are just peeping, there is a suggestive softness in the new birth developing. Later still the fragrant blossoms fill the air with redolence, and the birds with morning and evening songs. Still later, luscious fruits contribute their inviting treasures to the generous feast; while the deep rich music of the leaping water-falls rolls out its constant pæan of joy. And, still later, possibly there is less of the aqueous element, but ethereal haze drapes every crag and cañon, so that each mountain crest apparently penetrates farther and higher into the deep blue of

(490)

the vast firmament above. This of all others would seem to be the most befitting time for day-dreaming, reading, and renewing rest for both body and mind; and is, moreover, the one *par excellence* for the indulgencies of an angler's heaven.

But, still later, comes "Jack Frost," with his inimitable color brush, and tips all deciduous leaves with brightness; and so dyes and transforms the landscape that one impressively and conscientiously feels that this, above all others, is the best season to visit Yo Semite. Then, as though all nature was in fullest sympathy with such transcendent loveliness, every stretch of still water, in lake or river, doubles every wondrous charm by reflecting it upon its bosom, so that every bush or tree that may be struggling for life in the narrow crevices of the mountain walls around, are all most faithfully mirrored.

Then, the glorious fact should not be overlooked, that the marvelous mountain walls, and spires, and domes, are always there; and, being there, are, in themselves, an all-sufficient recompense without any supplementary accessories whatsoever. It will, therefore, and at once be seen that my statement is both correct and conclusive, that the best time to visit Yo Semite is "that which best suits your convenience," all others being merely a matter of taste.

There is, however, one season, apart from all others, when it is next to impossible, for the average traveler, at the present, to visit Yo Semite, and that is in the depth of winter. Therefore, as this cannot be conveniently witnessed, and as the writer, with his family, spent many there, as narrated on pages 141, 142, he feels that this work would be incomplete without a brief outline of

THE YO SEMITE VALLEY IN WINTER.

As intimated on pages 347, 348, snow begins to fall early in November, but this soon disappears before the delightfully balmy Indian summer which succeeds, and which continues with but little intermission, both days and nights gradually growing colder, until late in December, when a light fleecy film commences to

THE ADVENT OF WINTER AT YO SEMITE VALLEY.

(See page 493.)

Fiske #553. Heavily retouched on the face of El Capitan,
and to show a strong flow of water over Bridalveil Fall—
which is not true in winter.

Yosemite Valley after a Snow Storm.
Fiske #553. Opposite page 491 in editions three and four.

drift across the chasm from the south—the usual quarter for rain in California—which soon begins to intensify and deepen; then, large dark masses of cloud begin to gather beneath the lighter strata, with occasional stretches of sunlight sandwiched in between the different layers. At intervals those dark masses of cloud break into fragmentary patches, when a lambent sheen illumines all their edges with a golden glow; then the wind in fitful gusts commences to toss them into different shapes, seemingly in playful preparation for marshaling all these aerial forces into line, before making the final swoop upon the sleeping Valley. Nearly every rain or snow-storm in the Sierras is heralded in by a strong, squally wind; and the same phenomenon is generally observable when marching it out. Soon thereafter broad belts of cloud come sweeping down among the mountain peaks, "Like a wolf on the fold," probably just as night closes in; then how steadily does the rain or snow fall down!

THE GREAT FLOOD OF 1867.

On December 23, 1867, after a snow fall of about three feet, a heavy down-pour of rain set in, and incessantly continued for ten successive days; when every little hollow had its own particular water-fall, or cascade, throughout the entire circumference of the Valley; each rivulet became a foaming torrent, and every stream a thundering cataract. The whole meadow land of the Valley was covered by a surging and impetuous flood to an average depth of nine feet. Bridges were swept away, and everything floatable was carried off. And, supposing that the average spring flow of water over the Yo Semite Fall would be about six thousand gallons per second, as stated by Mr. H. T. Mills,* at this particular time it must have been at least twelve or fourteen times that amount, giving some eighty thousand gallons per second. Large trees, that were four to six feet in diameter, would shoot, endwise, over the lip of the upper Yo Semite; and, after making a surging swirl or two downwards,

* See page 376.

strike the unyielding granite and be shivered into fragments. At this time our family, consisting of two of the gentler sex, two young children, myself, and one man-servant, were the only residents of the Valley. The latter named, was dreadfully exercised over it, as he feared that the last day had come, and the world was about to be destroyed the second time by a flood! Immense quantities of talus were washed down upon the Valley during this storm,—more than at any time for scores, if not hundreds, of years, judging from the low talus ridges, and the timber growth upon them. After this rain-storm had ceased, a wind sprung up, and blew down over one hundred trees. In one spot of less than seven acres twenty-three large pines and cedars were piled, crosswise, upon each other.

Alas! at such a time, how fortunate the man or woman who has a cozy cabin, with an open fire-place; plenty of fire-wood, an abundance of provisions, books, agreeable companionship, and pleasant occupation. The beating of the storm upon the window panes, its heavy rain-drops on the roof, or the silent footfall of the fast deepening snow, with such surroundings, have no appalling terrors for him. But—to the benighted traveler, far from home and shelter, what? "God help him!" will be the spontaneous ejaculation of every earnest and feelingly humane heart.

Morning dawns, and the feathery crystals are still falling rapidly; the day rolls slowly on, and night again drops down her curtain, yet still it snows. Day follows day, and night succeeds night, for many days and nights, perhaps, without the least cessation of the storm. I have known eleven feet of snow to fall without the shortest intermission. But, finally it comes; and, while hostilities are suspended, let us take one lingering look upon our fairy-like surroundings on the outside. Believe me, the scene without seems like

A WORK OF ENCHANTMENT.

And we intuitively ask, "Is this, verily, the same spot of earth upon which we looked previous to the advent of the storm?"

THE NORWEGIAN SNOW-SHOE USED AT YO SEMITE IN WINTER.

Alas! how changed. Every twig is bent down, every branch laden, and every tree covered with the silvery garment.

Along every bough most delicately reposes a semi-translucent frosting of snow, with diamond settings between the forks of each and every twig or branch, which, when the sun shines upon them, or rather through them, lights them up with a frosted glory that seems more like the creations of some wonderful Magi, by ages of labor, than of crystallized water within a night or two. Then, to look upon and up the mountain walls that surround the marvelous Valley, and see every bench, and shelf, or jutting rock; every lofty peak, or noble dome; and every sheltering hollow filled with snow. Can artist or poet, painter or writer, do justice to such a scene? Alas! no.

Speechless with admiration, even while we are gazing upon

it, a new revelation dawns upon us, for everywhere around we near rushing, rattling, hissing, booming avalanches come shooting from the mountain-tops, adown precipitous hollows, and creating fresh sources of attraction; with new combinations of impressions, that must be alike diverting and satisfying to both artistic and poetic feeling. Then, before these sounds can have been repeated in echoes, and hurled from wall to wall, or from crag to peak, another avalanche makes the leap; and, like its predecessor, indicates the birth of a new water-fall, in some strange and unheard-of place.

THE YO SEMITE FALL IN WINTER.

On every frosty night immense masses of ice fringe both sides of every water-fall at Yo Semite; the upper Yo Semite most noticeably so. Icicles over a hundred and thirty feet in length, and from fifteen to twenty-five feet in diameter, are often seen; and which, when illuminated by morning sunlight, scintillate forth all the prismatic colors. These, however, resplendently brilliant and beautiful as they appear, have but a brief existence, inasmuch as the same sunlight that creates such gorgeous hues, melts away their frozen shackles, and drops them down, thunderingly, many tons in a minute; and before the echoes of one reverberating peal have died away others keep following in rapid succession, until every fragment of ice has peeled off and fallen.

This being repeated nearly every bright winter's morning, causes vast quantities of ice to accumulate at the base of the fall; to which constant additions are made of infinitesimal atoms of spray, that percolate filteringly among the broken icicles, and which, by freezing, cement them all so compactly together that an enormous cone of solid ice is built immediately beneath it, to which every snow-storm supplements its due proportion. The net results of this hibernal aggregation being to fill the entire basin at the base of the fall, some ten acres in extent, with consolidated ice; and which varies in depth or thickness from three hundred to five hundred and fifty feet, according to the season. In 1882, when

Photo by Geo. Fiske.   Engraved by J. M. Hay, S. F.

ICE CONE OF 550 FEET, BENEATH THE UPPER YO SEMITE FALL.

UPPER YOSEMITE FALL. 1600 ft, and ICE CONE 550 ft.
The photograph from which the engraving on the opposite page was made.
Fiske #218

the photograph was taken from which the accompanying engraving was made, it was at the maximum stated.

When the spring thaw in the mountains commences in real earnest, a vast sheet of water shoots over the top of the fall wall, down upon this cone of ice, in which it soon excavates a basin; and when this is cut out to a depth of from twenty to fifty feet, the entire fall leaps into it, and at once rebounds in billowy, volumes of cloud over a thousand feet; and, when the sunlight strikes this seething, eddying mass of comminuted spray thus rising, it lights it up with all the colors of the rainbow and presents one of the most gorgeous spectacles ever seen by human eyes.

The constantly recurring scenic revelations at Yo Semite lead us, in worshipful admiration as we say farewell, to breathe the beautiful words of Moore:—

> "The earth shall be my fragrant shrine!
> My temple, Lord! that arch of thine;
> My censer's breath, the mountain airs;
> And silent thoughts, my only prayers."

INDEX

Cover design by Larry Van Dyke
Front cover photograph by Peter Browning
Back cover engraving designed by Charles C. Nahl,
and engraved by Durbin Van Vleck, circa 1858
Text typeface: Century Expanded 10/12.5
Text paper: 60-lb. Glatfelter B–16, acid-free
Printing and binding: McNaughton & Gunn, Inc., Saline, Michigan

You can order additional copies of this book directly from the publisher:
Great West Books
P.O. Box 1028
Lafayette, CA 94549
(415) 283–3184

Hard cover: $44.95
Paperback: $29.95
California addresses please add 7.25% sales tax
        (Hard cover, $3.26; Paperback, $2.17)
Shipping and handling: $1.50 for one book; add 50¢ for each additional book.